FACE, SURFACE, INTERFACE: ONTOLOGY OF ODIA CULTURE

FACE, SURFACE, INTERFACE: ONTOLOGY OF ODIA CULTURE

Ramesh P. Panigrahi

BLACK EAGLE BOOKS
Dublin, USA | Bhubaneswar, India

 Black Eagle Books
USA address:
7464 Wisdom Lane
Dublin, OH 43016

India address:
E/312, Trident Galaxy, Kalinga Nagar,
Bhubaneswar-751003, Odisha, India

E-mail: info@blackeaglebooks.org
Website: www.blackeaglebooks.org

First International Edition Published by
Black Eagle Books, 2023

**FACE, SURFACE, INTERFACE: ONTOLOGY OF ODIA CULTURE
by Ramesh P. Panigrahi**

Copyright © Ramesh P. Panigrahi

All rights reserved. No part of this publication may be reproduced, stored in a retrieval system, or transmitted, in any form or by any means, electronic, mechanical, photocopying, recording or otherwise without the prior permission of the publisher.

Cover & Interior Design: Ezy's Publication

ISBN- 978-1-64560-418-1 (Paperback)
Library of Congress Control Number: 2023941803

Printed in the United States of America

Finally, this book is also dedicated to all those Odia children, who are born and nurtured outside Orissa, (also outside India). Perhaps, they may like to know one day about their mother/father land when they would grow up.

A page of dedication and gratitude

This book is dedicated to you Tiki; you have named it. I remember that lonely midday at Cuttack, when we went to eat some junk food at the Balijatra padia. That was the post-super cyclone month- December 1999. You suggested this title to me sharing some of my intentions for this self-financed project, which had just started.

Now this book is ready for dedication to Shruti and Richi. This is also dedicated to Gita and her husband and also to your younger cousin and her husband who stay abroad. These children born and brought up in US didn't get an opportunity to know about their father's home state.

CONTENTS

Pretext	13
Why should we show case Odia Culture?	21
Odissa : An appraisal	25

SECTION – I
Historical Silence : Notes on the unwritten Civilizations 33

Paleontological Odissa	35
Pre-historical Evidences	51
Evidences from the Paleolithic Age	52
Numismatic Evidences	53
Odia Culture in and around 1700 B.C	54
The Savaras and the Asuras	59
The Suktimati Civilization	61

SECTION – II
Our Multiple Cultural Faces 77

Kharvela and Jain Culture in Odissa	79
The Civilization of Kalinga	80
Kalinga and Odra : Multiple Interpretations	89
Trikalinga : The Notion of three Kalingas	96
Traces of the Culture of Kalinga	98
(between Jhanjavati and Rishikulya rivers)	
Kalinga in mythologies	115
Evidences from Archaeology : Odia Culture and history	115
Kalinga in Sanskrit Literature : The Land of the hill...	116
The Language of Trikalinga	119
Kalinga and its Culture	123
Hieuen Tsang's Records	125
Commercial Culture in Ancient Kalinga	127
(a) Water Routes	130
(b) The exportation of Odissi goods	141

Yuan Chwang's Report	144
Odishan Theories of Architecture: Silpa Sastra	147
Odisha's attitude to sex in medieval literature	148
The Mountain Culture: Mahendragiri	158
The Bonda Tribe: Hill top dwellers	162
Modern and post modern response to legends	163
The History of Odra Desha(present Koraput)	170
The language of primitive Odisha	173
Village System and Agriculture	175
Odia Tribal Culture	180
Mahakosala in History	190
(a) Mahakantara:A Brief Account of Kalahandi	194
The tribes of Mahakantar	195
Different systems of Belief	198
Cultural Osmosis: Vedic, Buddhist and Tribal cultures	200
Dasaratha Jataka: One more Version of the Ramayana	205
The Vratya Culture	213

SECTION-III
Religion, Education and Archetecture 215

The Spiritual life of Dongria Kondhs	217
Religion and Magic in Odia Vratya Culture	227
Mahabira and Buddha's influence on Odia Culture	228
The Impact of Jainism in Koraput	229
Jainism and the Jain Gurus: An Introduction	233
Buddhism in Odissan Culture	238
Oddiyana: The centre of Buddhist Religion	243
The Ramayana and Mahakosala	250
Koshala and Nagarjuna	252
Shakta culture in Mahakoshala	261
The Cult of Yoginies in Western Odisha	263
Mahakantara and the cult of Stambheswari	264
The tribal culture and Tantrism	266
Sun worship in primitive Odisha	268
The beginning of Education in Orissa	271
Ancient Disciplines of Education	273
Mathmatics, Astrology and Almanacs	282
Studies in Ayurvedic Medicine	287
Vocational Education in Ancient Odisha	299
Architecture	300

SECTION-IV
Searching for the Deep Roots: Odisha in the Micro-Histories 311

The History of Kantilo	313
The History of Ranapur	318
The History of Nayagarh	324
The History of Banki	324
The History of Buguda	329
A Thread of Continuity	333
Cultural Roots through micro history	339

SECTION-V
Folk Culture of Odisha 349

Folk Literature	351
Folk Music	352
Tribal Songs	353
Folk Dances	355
Folk Performing Arts	356
Folk Religion and Other Belief Systems	356
Folk Arts and Crafts	365
Folk Rituals	370
Folk Customs	377
Folk Festivals	381
Summer Festivals	394
Monsoon Festivals	471
Autumn Festivals	424
Winter Festivals	424
Spring Festivals	426
Tribal Festivals	428
Bibliography	432

PRE-TEXT

This initiatory book on Orissan Culture reminds me repeatedly how history has been politicized in India and how the Odissan perspective has been thoroughly marginalized. I begin to question the fundamental role the Indian historians assign to the concept of a state called *Orissa*. But my question reverbs back to me. However, I believe that there is a purpose/agenda in history and that it involves man's development through culture.

Culture is nature's way of nudging us to become independent of nature, liberating us from conditions that impair our freedom. Culture should aim at establishing institutions that leave individuals as free as possible to develop their moral goodness.

The cultural tradition of Orissa does not have a linear sequence of evolution. It does not run through epochs like a strand, which ties them together; rather the tradition emerges each time from the concealment of the destiny. The tradition of *being* that reemerges in the different interpretations of it, offered by various epochs of our cultural history, is thus, characterized by breaks and ruptures. The first section of this book would show no retrieval of an original beginning of our culture. It reveals a series of repetitions that have no distinct beginnings, one that can ground it and justify the hermeneutical search for determinate meaning.

Broadly speaking, therefore, I had almost no viable

option except organizing the material on Orissan culture from three different perspectives. First of it, as the title of the book states, this author is concerned with questions of ontology and epistemology; that is with issues oriented toward the very basis of "being" and "knowing". There is, in fact, a distinct theological flavor to much of this work in that it is deeply concerned with questions of ultimate meaning, existence and transcendent being.

To make things seem less esoteric, I have endeavored to deal with fields like sociology of knowledge, religion, theology, and modernization. I have also added conceptual apparatus capable of dealing with such micro-sociological problems as internalization of values, as well as more microscopic problems such as the cultural construction of institutions, ideologies and changing social patterns.

Secondly, this book has also been garnished heavily on the empirical material culled from the tribal groups. This author has visited the tribal areas, preoccupied basically with questions of social order. Drawing on a wide range of materials from the primitive groups, I was eager to formulate arguments about rituals, symbolic deviance, social boundaries and comparative cosmologies. Therefore, this work, at places, has become more descriptive and ethnographic than critical and theoretical. My field studies (also twice with Prof. Tatiana Oranskaia of Germany while she was working on Indian culture) have sort of impelled me to realize that knowledge about culture is a large undecipherable mosaic of enlightenment whose authenticity can only be recognized when the wide array of puzzle pieces are collaged together (which is metaphoric of researched information culled from history books, field studies knowledge from oral history etc) come in all shapes and sizes, some accurate and authentic while others may only contain the smallest bit of true information. Knowledge gathered from the oral and folk traditions are suspected in the hegemony of Indian historiography since we are biased by the colonial methods.

The oral tradition is by far the oldest form of

communication, and is vital to my pursuits.In a sense it is living and ongoing account of history. As a creative writer I believe that like life history will also grow and continue. The primary problem with the oral tradition is the possibility of intended manipulation and unconscious corruption of the accounts. Such factors do make the oral tradition at times unbelievable, but none the less, integral to such non-profit pursuits in the field of culture. I have used such knowledge with a risk and quite advertently, since our people have certainly lost much of their knowledge that has died with those of their generation. What is preserved here from oral history is just a figment, passed down to me by the old men who might have been dead by the time this book is published. People whom I met in Bhatipada village near Titilagarh and in Umarkote, Machhkund and Jeypore with regard to myths of creation,the reasons for the nakedness and clean-shaven heads of a 'remo' woman, and even about Ashoka's futile invasion and massacres. These accounts from the oral tradition look incredible, but vital to our study of the cultural mindset of the tribal people, whose oral traditions are not built-up fictions but real transmissions from their ancestors.

While showcasing the culture of a state that is an abode for 62 tribes, this author observes the Odia Metro dwellers as an emerging decadent majority, counterpositioned to treat everything about these primal inhabitants of the land as subaltern nuisances deserving the treatment of a marginalized lot. The tribes on the other hand, implore the metro-dwellers to treat them as human beings. They too are capable of singing and reminiscing of their dead ancestors in songs that are also applicable to their inflictors:in the city. We may quote a song from the poor Kondh fraternity:

    This we offer to you.
    We can,
    Because we are still alive;
    If not,
    How could we offer at all,
    And What?

We give a small baby fowl,
Take this and go away
Whichever way you came.
Go back and return.
Don't inflict pain on us after
your departure.

The loaded and frozen feelings of silence are inscribed in this song.. (This Kondh song of death is used here in a different context)

As an answer to the apathy of the people in power, the HO tribal sings: "Come back today and receive/our meager offering/ A piece of meat, a morsel of rice-beer/witness our rejoicings/Witness the ancient/the celebration and the joy".

This author does not believe that the state power has been able to bring any qualitative-transformation in these self-sufficient, half-clad non-state tribal cultures; non-state because eighty percent of the highlanders in Jolaput Machhkund, Keonjhar and the Soura countries of Ganjam do not participate in the voting rituals during the election seasons.

This book highlights the culture of these tribal groups with the holistic approach of anthropology that calls itself the study of humanity and has been accepted by this author as a discipline broad in scope and as one of the most generalizing of the disciplines. This has, perhaps, helped this author to study the psychopathological limits of our ability to adapt to a rapidly changing culture, and to explore systematically the interrelationships between symbolic, religious systems and a culture's adaptation to nature.

-II-

This book unintentionally negotiates a polemic space. Such a sub-national study raises urgent questions of what shape a culture-book like this should take in the twin context of economic globalization and weakening of the national culture. (Do we have one except in political advertisements?). The bureaucracy of our state withdraws from its regulating responsibilities to the national economy and consequently, shrinks the available space for civil action on culture. The national leaders would be diplomatic to allow only "neutral accounts" about the construction of an Odia identity because of political reasons. Out of the two categories of culture study namely (i) the sub-national, forming the "cultural right" and focussing on the survival of Orissa as a political entity, and the other, (ii) the 'transnational', forming the 'cultural left" and endeavoring to erase all boundaries between cultures - I have chosen the former. Thus, I contribute to the notion of cultural diversity or multiculturalism.

Our national leadership has failed in matters of ideological shaping of subjects. They are not aware that because of the fracturing of national culture, we have splintered into a multitude of marginal identities. Under the circumstances, one has nothing to do with the Rightist's nostalgia for cultural coherence and the Leftist's concern about a cultural practice that would succumb to the hegemony of the global market place. The country's (nation state's) existence as a unified entity is weakening either through globalization or, through the consequent erosion of its boundaries. In the case of Odissa, it is more acute. The culture of the northern Odissa is purely Bengali directed, the south imbibes the traits of Telugu and the west is linked to the culture of Madhya Pradesh or Chhatisgarh. Sareikala and Kharasuan estates have already merged into Bihar and their culture has thoroughly been hybridized.

I doubt whether we actually live in a post-national space in matters of culture. The Odias living in Manjusha (Mandasa, in Andhra Pradesh), cannot transform them selves into Telugus. Their sons, who have bought apartments in Berhampur and Bhubaneswar, do not, strangely, like to sell their native house in Andhra either. In the absence of the owner, one such house in Andhra has been turned into a house of judiciary decisions. Whenever there is a dispute, the villagers come to that forsaken Odia Panigrahi's house and sit on the verandah for a discussion. The dispute gets settled on the forsaken verandah automatically. Mr. Panigrahi, the owner was a judge once upon a time, and the villagers still believe that the house is auspicious for settlement of all disputes. The Oriyas, who belong to Parlakhemundi may feel that they live on some margin, fringe, or borderland, or, at least, at the periphery. But this author considers such borderlands as exclusive sites of this cultural-writing because of historical reasons. These are *interfaces* of culture.

If we add such borderlands beyond Jaleswar, Rairangpur or Narayanpatna, the fringe areas multiply and with that the cultural communities. Their voices and other cultural symbols promote "plural swarming" which no Hebermassian dialogue or communicative discourse could bring to a consensus. At the same time, the late-capitalist fantasy of a border-less world cannot entirely absorb the identity politics of these Odias.

There is a culture University in the state and its curriculum does not include such problems. An administrator, or, a superannuated academician, who officiates as its vice Chancellor, does not admit controversies. The corporatization of learning in the Humanities, the BJP-BJD-Congress-Communist controversies about the sanitization of Indian history, or the arguments of the smooth-cheeked professors for the aestheticization of multiculturalism would not help us in any way to provide a solution to the crises. The Odias suffer in matters of identity. The relationship between political subjectivity and cultural production is so strained and self-betraying in our state that Althursserian structuralism and Gramsci's version of hegemony as a mode of resistance against state cultural education also fail to provide this author with any answer. On the contrary, the hiatus between "culture" and "power" seems to have been broadened here.

This author does not like the marginalized and deterritorialized identities of the Odias to be redefined by the centre (here, it means the cultural capital, and it is Bhubaneswar). That would be another kind of new-fangled and politicalized subjugation if the center (Bhubaneswar) starts defining the cultural segments of the margins and prioritize them according to their whims and diplomatic capacities. A set of culture-politicians has been engaged by the government to write micro histories of different districts. I do not mind the occasional ego-hypes and small endeavors of the local historian politicians to highlight a point of glory, the birth of a historical hero or, so forth. But when the district of Khurda claims superiority over districts like Sonepur, Jajpur or Gajapati, a cultural imbalance is generated and the ethnoscape of the state is distorted in addition to creation of hegemony, a power-centre and its multiple margins.

This book, therefore, endeavors to share an interest in understanding how a culture, in order to define its boundaries, designates the others through a motif of abomination. The Bondas living on the hilltops around Jolaput may be curiosities for the anthropological museums at Bhubaneswar, or the subjects of the fictional world of Pratibha Ray's novel, *Adibhoomi*. But, they are living human beings also; and they are functioning with great self-esteem under the protective range of *Patakhanda Mahaprabhu* (the Bonda God). Any attempt, at the state capital, to represent them with distortion, may provoke animosities generating great violence. If the historians of our generation were willing to participate actively in the general intellectual and cultural life of our time, the worth of a particular culture of a particular region would not have to be defended in the timid and ambivalent ways that are now being recorded for the posterity.

The present author views such anomalies as cultural pathology and by such an approach, the tribal cultures have been identified as major culture types that do not suffer from such manipulative diseases. To record the views of Paul Bohannan in his book, *"Beyond Civilization,"* I would quote; "Obviously we stand on the threshold of post civilization. When we reach solution to todays' problems, the society and culture that we will have built for the purpose will be of a sort the world has never seen before. It may be more, or less, civilized than what we have, but it will not be civilization as we know it." Every care has been taken in this book to compare and diagnose the culture of Odissa with other cultures in the context of our terminal civilization.

Saussure, one of the acknowledged father figures, famous for inquiring into language and culture in our time, seems to have drawn from Durkheim, the notion that language, and by implication culture, is at once an entity in itself and a principle of classification. The title of this book in four chapters *"Face, Surface and Interface"* signifies entities as well as the taxonomy of our culture. You may read a literary deployment of language in the title, but it also helps us to classify our culture. Culture, like language, has an external side - what is visible on the face, tangible and heard - and an internal side, what may be dug, explored and is brought to the surface - some internal aspect which may be understood, but deposited in the unconscious as myths, totems or rituals. The 'interface" is a space claimed by other cultures, too.

Let us, for example, examine one of our most significant cultural signs - literature. The beginning of Oriya literature is demarcated by poems classified under the umbrella of *Charya geeti*, or songs of *Buddhist charya tantrik* mode. The historians of Bengali, Assames and Maithelee literatures also claim that "*Charya geeti*" is their beginning of literature. They try to investigate into the primitive mode of language deployed in *charya Geeti* and trace their linguistic origin to the vocabulary of *"Charya'*. In fact, none of these literatures/languages had invented their own alphabets around to the 7th century, when the first *charya* song was written and sung. These songs were composed orally and they are a part of orature. However, it is presumed that one particular mode of language was used in the eastern region for communication. If we admit Jaccques Lacan's poststructural reading of Freud, we would realise that language has been accorded the central role in defining and explaining the Freudian topology of unconscious motif and meanings. For Lacan, the unconscious is very literally structured like language and its effects are to be diciphered in those knots and slippages of sense, which everywhere punctuate the discourse of human desire. At this point, Sassure, Lacan, Derrida and even Roman Jakobson (who suggested that "metaphor" and "metonymy" were the two chief organizing principles of language) would be helpful in understanding some of the problems of our culture. Linguistic signs, as one would cull from *charya* songs, are mental in nature, but they are not, on that account, abstractions. They are cognitive realities. In the same manner, one can propose that human activity is not concrete while cultural meaning is an abstraction. Groups of cultural signs like temples, rock paintings and sites of ritual worship, even the baskets and handiwork and weaving designs are treated as cultural texts. Culture, like language, is also a system of signs expressing ideas.

The transition from orature to literature has not been properly narrativized by the historians of our literature. Nevertheless, orature was a part of our ancient culture (this reminds one of Rousseau's *State of Nature* and Derrida's book, *Of Grammatology*) and we can figure out the cultural mindset of the Odias from these recorded signs(I mean, the *Charya* literature) of literature after the invention of alphabets. But external signs only do not constitute a culture. Even in the 1876 edition of *Origin of species*, Darwin admits difficulties in his theory and suggests that researches in future might have to include the principle of innate purpose of account for variations. In our book, we found it useful to eliminate the "unfit", but we believed in the production of the "fit".

What we have found on the **face** are the cultural symbols, what we discovered and brought on to the **surface** and even those creations claimed by other cultural communities (**interfaces**) have been recorded as our cultural ontology.

Why should we showcase Odia Culture?

Our system of education ultimately reproduces racism and racists. But the entire world thinks in terms of racial reconciliation. It is being treated as a top priority for every one, of any race or of cultural background.

Odisha, known to other Indians as "Orissa" has, for no reasons, been marginalized in the books of history. Jawaharlal

Nehru, if he is a historian at all, has deliberately forgotten about Kharavela, who ruled over this state in 1st-2nd century B.C. This is more a politicalization of history than anything else. Most of the North Indian historians had little capacity for tolerance towards racial and ethnic minorities, mainly in the areas of dress, language, food, religious beliefs and other cultural manifestiastions.This lack of tolerance, or an attitudinal limitedness has dominated the mindset of the historian politicians and politician historians when they decided to overlook and bypass Odisha. Hatred for the Odias as the inhabitants of a Vratya country persists since the Aryan-Vedic hegemony and this author has encountered several cultural assaults during his life time.

The Odias, as victims of such xenophobia did hardly dare to assert them at the 'national level'. The notion of a centre is unintelligible to them. They accept the political term as something abstract and nonexistent for them. Most of our parliamentarians are unable to communicate assertively in fluent Hindi and English. So, they retreat themselves away from the rest of the country. The administrative officers do not prefer to interfere in matters that would not fetch them fiscal gains. The academicians who kept themselves busy mugging up class-room-lessons (the younger generation does not prefer to do that, though) found that "Culture"was something out side their academic caricullum which they should not mug up to evade disciplinary action. So, studies on Odia culture are left abandoned. A senior chef in a posh government-sponsored hotel at Bhubaneswar asked me: "What is an Odia recipe? There's no such speciality of food in Odissa!" This was when I ordered for special dishes for the chairman of the Central Board of film Certification, Mumbai, a very reputed film Director from Mumbai who was my guest as the Delegated Board Member of the Film Censor Board, Mumbai.

Multiculturalism has taken grip at this growing capital city and people believeing in such trends assume that truth is based on cultural epistemes. It is also argued that a cultural community's language dictates what ideas about God, human nature and morality are permissible.

We need not look at Europe and America for latest trends about reality since their ideas are rooted in Greek, Roman and Judeo-Christian heritages. The Odias see the world differently, and their vision is rooted in their *vratya* traditions.(The concept of 'soul' was nourished here, not in Vedic tradition) Multiculturalists of the state capital conclude that since multiple descriptions of reality exist, no single view can be true in any ultimate sense. Further more, since truth is a function of languages, and all languages are created by humans; all truth is logically created by humans.

"Truth", in Odisa, however, is not created by sentences. Our tribals do not define it through grammatological sentences. Finally, if all truth is created by human beings, how can the Odias tolerate damaging sentences and marginalizing words of the National historians who, appear to be liliputians in their mindsets? Cultural ideas, like human sacrifice or welfare system, are equally valid if they are useful for a given group of people. We should be aware that we are living in a universe that is blind to moral choices. We are the final judges of how we shall live.

In our tribal, Austric, Dravidian and other primitive belief systems we believe that the ontological flash of an "idea" is the mother-Goddess herself, the *Kundalini*. Thus, ideas do have consequences. These truths can be communicated cross-culturally in a sensitive way, regardless of the people-group involved.

Bhubaneswar, because of its availability of sprawling abandoned space all around, has been attracting thousands of immigrants annually. More of multi-national companies would come and settle here and in future, this city would become religiously, racially and linguistically more diverse. Odissa, then would be argued, would be a melting-pot society, and that regardless of an immigrants' origin given a generation or two, his family would be assimilated into odia culture.

But before that, the Odias must know who they are in a multi-cultural format of society. At the centre of this issue are the Odia individual's feelings of self-esteem. The multiculturalists argue that if a person's self-esteem is damaged, no learning and teaching would be possible in schools and colleges. Boys and girls who come to JNU and other universities out side the state know that they do not have an identity of their own.

The people of Utkala, in postcolonial times, have taken aggressive and violent steps to demolish the self esteem of the people of Kosala and Kalinga. If calling people Telengas, tribals, and mountain-dwellers makes them feel diminished in importance or some how less human, the Utkala people need to be empathetic and make changes in their use of language at least because of fiscal reasons. The Utkal people collect lots of money as revenue from the Kosala and Kalinga regions. So, such sensitivity should grow out of humility that should come when they utilize the lion's share of the state exchequer for their benefits. The cultures they ridicule in gossip centres of the capital city provide them the money for their survival and prosperity. In their words, language should be used to legitimize behaviour, a behaviour that should not be normally wrong; politically and economically, too.

This book, which endeavours to respect multi-cultural ideas, also contends that marginalized people need to be brought into the curriculum and the market place of ideas on academic campuses. No group should ever have to feel left out. Along with the groups, the minorities living at Malkangiri or Bhanjanagar, Rairangpur or Kantabanji, Baragarh, Rampur or Ullapgarh, and the women folk who live in a stifled state, should properly be voiced. The small children taught in the schools at Redhakhole, Gunupur or Khadial should not feel negative about their region and culture. If they feel so, Odisa cannot remain a collabortion of three different cultures – Kalinga, Udra and Kosala for all times to come. Symptoms of cultural hooliganism at the centre are already seen with consequent protests for disaffiliation at the margins.

Under the present day conflicting milieu of culture, paramount should be the belief that no truth transcends culture, that no idea or moral concept might be true for every cultural group or every human being.

Care is being taken to represent all the marginalized sections through their cultural heritages. My appeal for tolerance, when executed, would turn out in reality a thinly veiled pursuit of power.

Multiculturalists of the world occasionally refer to a concept for justice. It cannot be the foundation of their movement. This is for the simple reason that justice is not possible without truth. In order to claim that some one's actions or words are unjust, one must assume that a moral order really does exist, and moral laws imply that a lawgiver exists.

However, by declaring tolerance an *absolute*, multiculturalists are consistent with their view of reality. They see all human creatures as morally equal. But this can not be allowed to end up in a godless universe, a universe within the neutral zone of post-modern (a)- morality, secularism or logic of scientism. Despite all kinds of postmodern commodification of life and its global marketing, the Odias are deeply rooted in a culture where the gods and goddess are plenty and yet central to their systems of belief.

Once aware, the younger generation, would perhaps guard against further disintegration of Odia culture. But the outsiders must also know what Orissa is.

ODISSA: An Appraisal

The triangular piece of land identified as Orissa in the political map of India (extending from 17 49' N to 22 "34' N latitude and from 81 29 E to 87 29 E longitude) is only a colonial construction. Our colonial political activists failed to visualize in 1936 that the British Government splintered our cultural identity by tagging some of the Oriya linguistic zones with West Bengal, Bihar, Madhya Pradesh and Andhra

Pradesh. Partly because of our self-centered motifs that ended up in political failure to assert our language and culture, and partly because of the Imperial divisive principles, the Orissa of today is writhing under severe fiscal crises. Perhaps, it has also infected the moral morrows of the Odias.

The name "Orissa" is purely a colonial construction. It has undergone several phonetic transformations through the ages: *Oddiyana, Oda, Odra, Udra, Odivisa* (A Tibbetan playwright whom I met in Delhi in 2000 could pronounce only *Odivisa* and he did not know what Orissa is), *Odavadi, Udishia* and *Odisa*. Historically, this region was named differently - as Kalinga, Odra, Kosala, Moshala Kangoda, and Utkala. Its geographical territory varied, too, at different periods of history. The people of Utkala are trying to rename the state as Utkala ignoring Kosala and Kangoda, and if such a cultural political game is played, there will be severe regional disturbance. Orissa is never, and was never Utkala. It is a unification of Kangoda, Utkala and Kosala (a part of Maha kosala). People who clamour to rename Orissa as Utkal make ungrateful regional statements of euphoria. They are making political attempts to exert their dominance over Kosala and Kangoda.

Perhaps the mainstream historians of Orissa are not very much aware of the fact that there is a village in Koraput district called *Oda Badi Mandala* or *Odra Gada*. The place is situated 24 kms away from Padua, a small town located on the Andhra-Orissa border. The people of this area identify themselves as subjects of Odra dynasty. We do not know who actually they were since our main-stream history books do not make us informed about any such dynasty. The mainstream historian-politicians of Odra Desha have erased the identity of these kings from our history and during the colonial period, the three districts of that time which had Zilla schools, called themselves as Utkala.

Some other people also take pride in identifying themselves as *kshatriyas* belonging to *Chandravamsa dynasty*. If the contemporary historians do not equate them with the heirs of the Panduvamsi- Somavamsi rulers of 6th-8th century, they would be relegated to a farther antiquity and would be identified with the proto-Austroloid races who had settled in these remote parts of the undivided Koraput district.

These proto-Austroloid races had classified themselves later under different tribes like Gadaba, Bonda, Dora, Suka Dora and Konda Dora. Their habitats,clubbed together, was called *Udra-konda* or *Odabadi Mandala*. (Konda in tribal languages refers to a mountain-i.e.the Odras were highlanders, not the delta dwellers)

That is about the mountain regions of the-then Udra. But before we concentrate on that part, I would like to refer to Ptolemy's *The Geographike Huphegesis.It* refers to a territory on the Gangetic Gulf (G.H.vii.1.16-18). The inclusions within this area of inter alia Palaoura (located by S.Levi in the Ganjam district.Ref. to G.H.vii.1. 16 and Journal Asiatique 1925.vol. cciv pp.46-57 and *Indian Antiquary.1926. Vol. iv pp.94f*) and the mouth of the river Manada (Mahanadi) surely indicates that that the region concerned incorporated a part of coastal Orissa. Ptolemy also alludes to the inclusion of the mouths of the Ganges in the region in question. Thus, littoral Odissa and the deltaic portions of West Bengal and Bangladesh were within the limits of the territory on the Gangetic Gulf in the period of Ptolemy(2nd. century A.D. as referred to by B.N.Mukherjee in *The Kushanas and the Deccan*.P.128)The topographical position of that territory suggests the identification of the Gangetic Gulf with the Bay of Bengal.

It is interesting to note that the same territory is also referred to in a treatise called *Periplous tes Exo Thallasses*, compiled by Marcianus of Heraklea some times between C.A.D. 250 and 500(Ref. E.H.Bunbury.*A History of Ancient Geography*.rpt.1959.Vol.II. P.660) This source has hardly been utilized by the students of Indian history. According to it,"the entire (course of) sailing around (periplous) along that part of(the territory on) the Gangetic gulf from the point of departure(apheterion) up to the fifth mouth of the Ganges, called Antibole, is a distance of 5660 stadia." This apheterion is described by Marcianus as a place from which" all those navigating to Khryse leave."(Please refer to *Thalasses, Sec.39; C.Muller.Geographie Graeci Minores,Vol.1. P 536)*

The term 'Khryse' denoted different parts of South East Asia like:

Khrysenesos(Suvarna Dvipa), KhryseKhora(Suvarna bhumi), and KhryseKhersonesos. The first region included Sumatra, Java and some other areas of Indonesia. The second territory incorporated inter alia the deltaic country including Thaton and Pegu in Burma. The third area included at least parts Malaya peninsula. Thus, the name Khryse could have broadly meant some parts of South-East Asia. According to the evidence used by Marcianus, these parts (or at least some of them) were in contact with a place on the coast of the Gangetic gulf. The ships used to sail from this place for Khyrse.

The point of departure (apheterion) for ships bound for Khyrse" was located by Ptolemy in Maisolia, which according to him, was situated immediately below (i.e. to the south of) the territory on the Gangetic Gulf.(Ptolemy.VII.1.15). "The point of departure was located somewhere to the north of another locality of Maisolia called Koddoura (Ptolemy. Ibid), identifiable with modern Guduru near Masulipatanam (Ref.D.C.Sircar, *The Successors of the Satavahanas in the lower Deccan*. pp.33 and 42). On the other hand, Ptolemy's "point of departure" was immediately to the south of a town of the territory on the Gangetic gulf called Palloura, which was probably situated in a locality now included in the Ganjam district of Orissa."This information is gathered from an essay written by Mr. B.N. Mukherjee captioned "The Relevance of the Periplous Tes Exo Thalasses to the History of Orissa" published in *Journal of the Orissa Research Society (Vol-1.* October, 1981).

I have quoted extensively from Mr. Mukherjee's essay because that is what I gather about Orissa of the 2nd century A.D. This historical research pertaining to Ptolemy's record of Palur (Palloura) proves that the Udra country was not only a place of the highlanders, but also a prosperous land of mercantile ships. A large section of them might have settled in the mountains and hilly tracts, but the coastal people had sufficient exposure and they traded in khysre regions. But we must also know what happened in the forest areas.Among the forest areas, Koraput had the densest jungles.

Shri Jaladhara Swain, a poet and a historian of Koraput records in one of his vernacular essays that Udragada was the capital of this land of proto-Austroloid settlers. Since the main stream historians have not mentioned about this part of our origin, Sri Swain has collected evidences from *Puranas* and legends to reconstruct the *purakalpa* of the present Orissa. The contemporary historians of Orissa should make deeper studies on *Purakalpa* and its application into the formats of histriography, This comparatrive space would encourage new areas of investigation in the postcolonial historical studies.

At present, the state is bounded by West Bengal on the North East, Bihar on the North, Madhya Pradesh on the west, Andhra Pradesh on the South and the Bay of Bengal on the east side. This peculiar geographical location not only makes Orissa a pluricultural state and a miniature India, but at different points of time different states have claimed that Orissa is a "non entity". During the colonial period Bengalies claimed that Oriya is not a separate language, it is a byproduct of Bengali language.Some misinformed Malayali writer reinstated such a statement in 1999, a time when the backbone of Orissa was broken by the supercyclone.

Such instances of political-cultural underrating, of assertion and marginalization,is not new to human history. It has affected the Indian culture, too, long back, since the invasion of the Aryans.

The Aryans after defeating the local non-Aryans metaphorised the latter as *the Asuras* (demons) and *the Mlechhas* (Boors). In order to keep the vanquished under their feet for ever, they invented a category of caste called the Sudras. In the Eastern region (also in Orissa) they were called the *Vratyas*, i.e. the people who flouted the Aryan norms of life.The Odias have always flouted the social codes/moral-religious codes prescribed by the Aryans. Hence they are politically and fiscally neglected.

The contemporary power politics played with the casteist cards is nothing other than a legacy inherited from the Aryans. The stupendous proliferation of social codes and the compelling political strategies of grabbing cultural power, today, however, have rendered our indigenous culture studies more complicated.But the origin of the casteist politics owes its origin to the Aryans, who were outsiders to India. After their settlement in the delta of the Ganges, they began to treat the natives as the 'Others'.

According to another school of cultural anthropologists, the primitive inhabitants of India were also not the insiders. They place the Negrites as the first invaders, who came from Africa. Then the proto-Austroloids came from the Ancient Palestine and Syria. They are also called the Mediterranians. The Dravidians have come after them. The Aryans or the Indo-Europeans have stepped into India around 15th century B.C. and after them have come the Mongoloids. The Sanskrit texts have named the Austriks as *Nishada*s the Dravidians as *Dramil*, the Indo-Europeans as Aryans and the Mongoloids as *Kiratas*. One should never believe that ancient India belonged only to the Aryans.The Indo-Europeans (the Aryans) have dominated since they have composed the slokas of the Vedas at different places and by different writers and have compiled them together as the Vedas.

The findings of the Indus Valley Civilization discovered at Mahenjo-daro in Sind and at Harappa in the Western Punjab provide us with the earliest picture of India's past. Jawaharlal Nehru, a politician turned historian of North-India, writes in his book *The Discovery of India*, "The Indus Valley Civilization, as we find it, was highly developed and must have taken thousands of years to reach that stage. It was surprisingly enough, a predominantly secular civilization, and the religious element, though present did not dominate the scene. It was clearly also the precursor of later cultural periods in India." (Nehru: P 70)

But the Austriks/*Nishadas* (some others name them as *Agneyas* also) and the *Dravidas* had a combined civilization here through osmotic cultural appropriations. While discussing about the roots of Odissi culture we would take into consideration the cases of the Austriks or the *Nishadas* amongst whom the *Kolha, Munda, Bhumija, Bonda, Paraja, Santal, Ho, Sabara* and *Gadaba* tribes are still surviving here.

To state this with a more broad and generalized way, Orissa has been laying at a set of cultural interfaces and at different points of evolution, the structural elements of the interfaces changed positions. The Aryans seem to have appropriated all the essential ingredients of the Austrik and the Dravidian culture and dumped them out as *Anaryas* (non-Aryans: a derogatory term), *Sudras*, untouchables and so on.

However, it should be kept in mind that this story does not endeavour at all to re-organise the Orissan culture by appropriating a jargon from Edward Said ("reorientalization"). But it should also be mentioned here that the Aryans have appropriated all the devotional practices, icons of the gods and Goddesses, rituals of birth, death and marriages, food habits and festivals from the Austriks and the Dravidians. The word '*Puja*' (worship) is itself an Austrik word. Perhaps the Aryans had learnt the art of cultivation from the Austrik-Dravidian culture. The word '*Langala*' used in Oriya for 'plough' is an Austrik word. Although I don't remember the sources, I have read in a dissertation that there is a lingusitic affinity between the language of *Beluchistan* and the South Indian languages- (Mishra: Hindi dissertation)

The Orissan inhabitants of this prehistoric period were also undergoing an epochal transition to a new cultural order because of such interaction with different races and cultures that have migrated into this land. Out of this fusion grew the culture of Orissa. In the ages that followed, there came many other races: the Kannads, the Tamils, the Telengas, and the Bengalies. They came, asserted their own points of view and their differences and were later absorbed into this land of the *Vratyas*. Orissa seems to be a great and infinite absorbent like the Bay of Bengal, like its dust that lies on the grand road of Puri.

During this period of hybridization of culture, the Vedic Brahmins, however, never treated the tribals and the non-Aryans as aliens. There are evidences of *Pratiloma Vibaha* (marriage between a high caste girl and low-caste boy) held between the *sudras* and the *Brahmins*. As a consequence of these lopsided marriages, pure Brahmins were not available for *Yajna* and *Homa* rituals. In some states the pure Brahmins were to be imported from outside. Most of the *Brahmins* were imported from *Kanyakubja* to Orissa by the ancient kings (Padhi:25).

Orissa of those days was a confluence of three cultures and three political entities: (a) the culture of *Utkala* extending from Jajpur to Radha: Aryan culture (b) The culture of Kalinga, extending from Jajpur to Vishakhapatnam: Dravidian culture (c) the culture of *Kosala*, extending from Boudh to Bilaspur: Proto-Austroloid culture.

The name *Utkala* has been derived from *Uttara Kalinga* (North Kalinga) (also *Ut-Kalinga*). By the time Kali Dasa composed *Raghuvansam*, Utkala and Kalinga were two different countries. Kali Dasa mentions two names while describing the victories of Raghu: *Sa teerthva kapisam Sainyer baddha dvirada setuvih Utkala darpitapathah Kalingabhimukham Jajau*. The boundaries of *Utkala* extended upto the river *Kapisa* in the north (now called *Kamsei Nadi*) and river Baitarani in the south.

SECTION-1

HISTORICAL SILENCES: NOTES ON THE UNWRITTEN CIVILIZATION

Pale-ontological Odissa

Introduction:
Paleontology is the study of prehistoric life including the organisms' evolution and interaction with each other. It lies on the border between biology and geology, and shares with archaeology and thus, a border on the interface is difficult to define.

The Plestocene epoch had highly glaciated climates. The Holocene epoch (Modern climate) called alternatively as Mesolithic or Epi-paleolithic had identical groupings like Neolithic, Copper Age, Bronze Age and Iron Age. Traditionally, the Paleolithic (750,000-500,000 B.P.) until the end of the last Ice Age (About 8,500 years B.C).is divided into three overlapping periods: **Lower**

Paleolithic (C.2.6 million years), **Middle Paleolithic** (300,000-30,000 B.P.) and the **Upper Paleolithic Age**, spread between c.45000 to10, 000 B.P.

John Lubbock coined the word "Paleolithic". It derives from Greek *palaios* and *lithic* stone literally meaning Old Stone Age.

Due to a lack of written records fromthis time period, nearly all of our knowledge of Paleo human culture and way of life comes from archaeology and ethnographic comparison to modern hunter-gatherer culture such as the Kung San who lived similarly to their Paleolithic predecessors. It was a hunter-gatherer economy. At the end of the Paleolithic, specifically the Middle or Upper Paleolithic, the humans began to gather fire wood, materials for their tools, clothes and shelter.

The Mesolithic man grouped together in small societies also subsisted by gathering plants and by hunting or scavenging wild animals. The Paleolithic Age is distinguished by the first stone tools and covers roughly 99% of human technological history. It extends from the introduction of the stone tools by the hominids such as austral pithicenes living around 2.6 million years ago to the time of the introduction of agriculture and the end of plestocene Age aound 12000 B.P. Paleolithic is characterized by knapped stone tools and also with bone tools.

We do not have such geo-biologic records pertaining clearly to Odissa. We have traced our history from archaeological digs and numismatic configurations from 1000 B.C. This belongs to a much civilized period in which the Odias of the Bronze and Iron Age invented their coins and conducted commercial transactions with the then Naga-desa referencing probably to the present land of the Tamils. Such a configuration presupposes the essentials for the adequate understanding of our land's climactic changes, biodiversity and geochemical cycles.

-II-

It is an irony that Indian historiographers are still guided by colonial standards of time frame. William Jone's first documentation of Indian history and culture is centered on Alexander's conquest and this 18th century imperialist has played a political game of power both in his interpretation and manipulative datings. Although he was able to convert the *Kaliyugabda, Salibahana Sakabda* and *Saka Nrupabda* into Christian dates to certain extent, his colonial bias did not allow him to write about any thing that was pre-Alexanderian and pre-Christian. The world, in his narrow religious vision, did not exist before Christ. Indian historical accounts suffer from that western bias till today and the present- day historians are formatted according to that colonial bias

William Jones seems to be guided by the European mediaeval belief –system and he has written everything to the exclusion of the ancient Indian dynasties documented in the epics. This act of politico-religious subversion in historiography has resulted in grave misreading of the coins, rock edicts and copper plates especially with regard to periodization of culture that prevailed at different phases of history in India. German historians like Schwanbeck and Max Mueller have also failed to construct authentic standards of periodization with regard to the events and the watersheds of Indian history.

Records of Orissan histriographic datings suffer from similar colonial misconstructions. In this paper, endeavours are made to reconstruct the culture of Orissa through numismatic evidences, motif studies, rock arts and paintings, folk tales, legends and their semiotic interpretations. The interpretations are made obviously in an interdisciplinary mode and the conclusions taken are purely post- colonial in nature.

Historical configurations about prehistoric Orissa stay limited to the discovery of stone implements belonging to the early, middle and late stone -age cultures. Dr. G.C. Mahapatra observes that "the tools of this culture, taking shape in the secondary laterite pits and cemented coarse gravels of the river sections are generally made out of coarse grain quartzite pebbles."[1]

If these hand-axes, cleavers, scrapers, discoid and irregularly flaked bifaces were used by the primitive men, the historical focus for the pre-historical Orissa goes toward the tribal settlements. Dr. K.C. Panigrahi situates these primitive tribal men in the Northern Tribal Region lying between 21^0 $16'N-22^0.34'$ latitudes and $83^0E - 87^0.11'$ E longitudes. [2]

Dr. Panigrahi's configurations made in 20th century seem to contain certain amount of enthusiasm for a particular region- the region that includes Chakradharpur, Chaibasa, Ranchi and Manbhum, to the exclusion of other zones. The areas that are spaced in the Northern Tribal region have been specified by Rekha Devi in a different manner in her thesis "*Locational Study of Tribal Settlements of Orissa.* In this study of Orissa's primitive geography, Rekha Devi subdivides the Orissan geography into four morphological zones: (a) The Mountainous Country, (b) The Rolling Uplands, (c) the Subdued Plateaus and (d) River valley and Plains.[3]

Dr. Panigrahi's evidences of the stone-age culture do not signify a civilization, but reflects only on a process of survival in a tropical climate. Dr. Rekha Devi's study on the primitive geography of Orissa, on the other hand, subdivides this Northern mountain region into four sub-units, namely (a) the common interfluves of the river Subarnarekha, (b) the Nilgiri hills, (c) the Baitarani-Brahmani interfluves and the Brahmani-Mahanadi interfluves. This region experienced hot dry summers with a maximum temperature recorded at 41^0 C. and the summer was followed by a well-distributed monsoonal rainy weather.

The possibilities of a civilization in the mountainous region are erased after the publication of an essay in *Dharitri* Dtd. 15-8-2002. The essay predicts about a civilization existing on the basis of river Suktel flowing in the vicinity of Sonepur. The evidences of this civilization have been formulated on the basis of the coins that were discovered during the 1990s. The coins have come to the state museum on 7-8-02 and the historians have periodized them around 10th century B.C [4]

In confirmation with the principles of Human Space Organization, the locations having 50% of tribal population are only enlisted as "tribal core areas."(Rekha Devi) The probability of a civilization on the basis of river Suktel has not been identified as a "core tribal area" so far either by the geographers or by the anthropologists. The river known as Tel was called Suktimati and Suktel at different periods of history, and thus, it seems appropriate to caption it as Suktimati civilization.

This paper aims at focusing on the probable contours of an extant civilization, which is constituted of mere configurations. The authenticity about its periodization needs verification by experts so that the mainstream historians would be able to brighten the twilight zone of this paleo-ontological civilization. However, it is likely to open up a new vista of knowledge in the sense that the earliest civilization of Orissa did never flourish on the mountains, but like all other civilizations of the world, it has taken shape beside a river.

The 325 punch marked silver coins discovered from the valley of Suktel have been identified by the archaeologists as one of the sets of the oldest coins of the world. The experts are of the opinion that these coins were used between 10thCent.BC to 6th Cent. BC. A detailed study of these coins would reveal more interesting facts about the ontology of Orissan culture. The study, would, on all probabilities, prove that certain unexplored civilizations existed in this land about which our historians have not paid attention to because of a cultural politics; and the Orissan historians very often bypass this prejudice with an inefficacious magnanimity.

The 325 silver coins were retrieved by the peasants of Bolangir district and were deposited in the police station during the 1990s. The coins were preserved initially in the treasury of Tarabha and the High Court has ordered to transfer the coins to the state museum on 7.8.02.[5]

The silver coins now available in the state museum bear the marks of sun, trees, river and the six *chakras*. Over the six *chakras* one finds the marks of deer, ammunitions of those days, dogs, elephants, bulls, snakes, rabbits, frogs and fish. These marks may be taken as popular paleo-ontological symbols and they semioticise some probabilities for further interpretations and extrapolations. The proof-based empirical study of history that prevailed in the Imperial Educational system has long been discarded as *passé* and the post modern historians of Europe are found to have manipulated history from multiple sources-from legends, oral sources and interviews.

As we reach the coins, we are instantaneously getting connected to the works of Panini (*Astahyayi*), who mentioned about such coins remaining in currency till his time. Kautilya's *Artha Sastra*, the Upanishadas, and *Vinaya Pitaka*, (the Buddhist text) also mention about such coins prevailing in this part of the country. A single coin weighs 57.07 grams. Some of these coins are cut into halves and this leads to a probability that the coins had a definite value and if the goods purchased were of lesser value, a part of the coin was cut off.

Besides this extant commercial practice, the visual language of the coins opens up a liturgical – ritualistic context of the Suktimati communities. The lexicon embossed on the silver coins also substantiates the language of the Suktimati myths, legends and dominant systems of belief.

The sign-language of **sun** and the **trees** signify the ancient context of sun and tree worship. Such worships were also prevalent in most of the Indo-European practices. The relationship between the marks of the **trees** and the *Chakras* can be traced back in anthropological studies since these are definite features of the worship of the autochthonous gods prevalent in primitive communities. Such practices also continued through the worship of the *Chaityas*, S*tupas* and S*thanu* of the Buddhist, Jain and primitive Aryan religions.

The **snakes** marked on the coins relate to the connection of the Suktimati people with the Naga dynasties that ruled in the Southern part of the mountains of Mahakantara of those days that extended through the district of Koraput and Jagdalpur jungles to the mountainous countries of Andhra and Tamilnadu. Perhaps, the coins were recognized in the politico-economic regions of the neighboring states in which the Naga dynasties reigned. There are multiple references to the *Naga Kanyas (snake-girls, who metamorphosed themselves between a girl and a snake* by a primitive practice of Tantric art) and there was absolutely no fantasy about this legendary practice. It prevailed also in the Tantric belief- systems of the South during the time of Nagarjuna , the greatest promulgator of the *Madhyamika* philosophy. The text of *Madhyamika* Philosophy was written in *pulo-mulo-kili* (Parimalagiri) by Nagarjuna. Now it is identified as Harishankar hills situated in Bolangir district .[6]

The deer engravings on the coins signify that they were relevant to the primitive men of the Middle Pleistocene.

During this period, the Lower Paleolithic man was using his first stone made tools.[7]

Art pictographs and petroglyphs (carvings/inscriptions on the rock) substantiate that animals constituted the major part of such primitive art practices between 4500-3500 B.C.[8]

Deers are found to be the most favorite of the animals of the ancient men. The studies of the fossils, as recorded in the book, *'Deer in Rock Art of India and Europe"* speak volumes about the lives of the lower Paleolithic man (Middle Pleistocene)[9]. Fossils belonging to the Middle Paleolithic (relating to the second period of the stone age) period are found on the Gandeswari at Sisuria in West Bengal. Kurnool caves of Andhra Pradesh have preserved the late Pleistocene fossils of the primates. Since the people of Suktimati civilization used coins with punch marks of deer, it becomes obvious that the people have recorded the paleolithic symbols on the coins as popular icon of their times. The racial memory of the Middle Pleistocene age may be recent or remote. But since the pictographs are on the silver coins, they represent probably a much later civilization belonging to 1000 B.C.

Since no study has been conducted by the anthropologists on Paleolithic Orissa, covering middle Paleolithic, late Pleistocene, Mesolithic and Neolithic phases, I would pick up the example of the fossil studies made in the neighboring states and attempt to configurate a relationship with the punch-marked deer of the Suktimati civilization.

"Mesolithic deposits of Adamgarh in Madhya Pradesh (close to the vicinity of Suktimati zone) have yielded bones of swamp deer, sambar, chital and hare and a few remains of Six domesticated animals" [10].

From the Neolithic phase of Bihar are obtained good examples of bones of antlers xxxx At Chirand in Bihar (4500-3650 B.C) tools of bones of the antlers have been excavated, which may be relevant to what late Paramanand Acharya records in Archaeological Remains of Orissa(Oriya). These tools can be periodized between 4500B.C.-3650 B.C. The study or pre-Harappan cultural deposits of Sind, Baluchistan and Afganistan (1968, P258) has also recorded bones of deer sambar and swamp deer.

"If we consider only the members of cervidae family, we find that deer has been present in India through out the prehistoric past(P 9) xxx "The genus cervus has also been found at Nandaghat (in Mahanadi valley"(P. 9)[11].

In addition to these archaeological evidences on the primordial dominance of deer in the process of paleo–ontological survival, we may look into the forms of art pictographs and petroglyphs to study the pictures of the deer embossed on the Suktimati coins. The rock-paintings of Orissa illustrate different species of wild animals like Sambar, Chital, barasinga and others belonging to different periods and phases of rock art.

Sri Jitamitra Prasad Singhdeo, in an essay, captioned, *"A Bird's Eye view of Anthropological and Archaeological Traces in Western Orissa"* writes, "The earliest art of early man in Western Orissa is found in the prehistoric drawings painted in red ochre and black tint colour at Gudahandi of Kalahandi district. This painting is dated to early stone- age and can be placed around 15 millennium B.C. This primitive art was discovered by the archaeological department of ex Kalahandi state in 1947-48 [12].

Sri Singhdeo had discovered the Jogimath cave painting in 1970 and the Ghat Ghumar shelter painting in 1980 according to his records. The animals painted are dated to be a part of the Neolithic period. The Khariar branch museum stores ring stones of different sizes that belong to the "Stone-Age Culture".

The ring stones are *Chakras* containing different yantras for the worship of the Shakti. The Chakras embossed on the silver coins of Suktimati civilization are similar to that of the Yantras found in Khariar museum. On the way from Rayagada to IMPHA, a way side temple of Siva has some such large pieces of *Surya Yantras.*

These *yantras* made of stone have been discarded as the Aryans began to sculpt the images of different gods and goddesses. The *yantras* are symbolic geometric forms representing different energy-forms of different Gods and Godesses. The Aryans around the Gupta period began sculpting the anthropomorphic forms of Gods and Goddesses. However, some of these images were sculpted during the Buddhist and Jain period and the *esoteric yantras* were brought out of the sanctum and placed outside. This is a sign of irreverence to the tribal mode of worship done through symbolic geometrical forms. The *yantras* are still lying out side and the aryanised visitors accept them as cute pieces of art.

The pale-ontological Odia used stones for different purposes: as tools for hunting, as *yantras* for worship and as utensils. They also used the human skulls for carrying water. Sacks made of the skins of hunted animals were also used for collecting water from distant places.

The "Stilt" dances of Ganjam and Phulbani districts also take us back to the pale-ontological stages of civilization. Late Padmasree Bhagaban Sahu, the great guru of 'stilt dance' of Narendrapur had conducted a field study at Kondhamal hills, Kredimska, Udayagiri, Karachuli and Mahandragiri hills to trace the roots of the dance and discovered that the primitive man invented stilt dancing as an imitation from the peacocks. The primitive shepherds used stilts to climb the hills imitating the birds [13]. I quote this as an example of civilized existence of the remote past . Late Sri Sahu periodizes the dance around 3000B.C.

The worship of the *yantras* made of stone, the stilt dances and the hunting practices of the tribal men are found in the rock arts/paintings of the tribal men. Combined together these sporadic evidences denote the primeval sense of a paleo-ontological cosmology. The high landers of Kodalaks and Khujili Mandala have their own shamans. These shamans believed that the world is divided into different cosmic zones and there are passages from one cosmic zone to the other, form the earth to the sky and from the earth to the underworld. During the field visits of this author to the tribal area in connection with theatrical studies, a Shaman from the

Khinjili Mandala of the Kandh community informed about the conception of a "cosmic mountain" in which they lived. Stilt walking and dancing provided them with a feeling of height and transcendence, perhaps a facility to discover the path to another cosmic zone through this world axis, called the "cosmic mountain". This transcendental experience was also combined with an artistic endeavour of dancing. The birds and the beasts were the models that aroused the paleolithic awareness of the world around them. The awareness could be aroused through their primeval sense of sight and ability to hear.

Similarly, hunting was not an exclusive sport for living. Besides being a metaphor for primitive notion of survival, it has taken on the value of initiation to life, to the point of being identified with the figure of strenuous searching for the invisible worlds. The animals observed at the margin of the glades along the streams, have been transformed into symbols in the cave art. Hunting was a sport, a living and a primitive world view.

While searching for a cultural context of the paleo-ontological Orissa, the cave arts of Bikramkhole and Ushakothi occupy a central place. The caves were highlighted in 1933, when K.P Jaiswal discovered the paintings. The paintings of Bikramkhole shelter are 34.5 meters long and its height is 8.31 meters. The patterns are constituted of circles, squares, oblongs, triangles, straight lines and oblique lines. The pictures are engraved on a lime stone bed and the Mesolithic "*sthapatis*" of Kosala have drawn the figures of the monkey, bulls, birds, serpents, deer and men.

Sri Govinda Chandra Tripathy, in a recent essay periodizes the cave art around C.5000 B.C., which, if not an exaggeration, goes much beyond Suktimati civilization in remoteness. The presence of the deer in cave paintings, as such, must have inspired the Suktimati people to engrave deer in their silver coins. It seems the connection of the deer with men was very intimate. Someswara, in his book *Mansollasa* has divided young woman into six categories *Mrugi, Padmini,*

Chitrini, Vadwa, Hastini and *Sankhini*. Of these, the first two are considered best for making love and the deer type *(Mrugi)* is one of them. *Abijnana Sakuntalam* mentions "*nasta shanka harina sisavo mandam mandam charanti*" as a common sight around Rishi Kanva's hermitage. Much before that Valmiki, too, mentioned about a "Golden deer".

Kashi Prasad Jayswal, who periodises Bikram Khole paintings as Neolithic art, has discovered some pre-Brahmi hieroglyphic writings and has mentioned, "The Characters in Vikram Khol inscription belongs to a period intermediary between the script of Mahanjoders and Brahmin. Some have assumed the Brahmi or Proto-Brahmi form. This throws a flood of light or the history of writings as from Brahmi, the Phonecian and European scripts are deserved.[15]

It is interesting to note that there is another hill named Maheswara Pahad, twenty kilometers away from Bikramkhole and in it is located an old fort called Ullapgarh. A cave adjacent to Ullapagarh is called Ushakoti and some pictographs are found painted on its wall. Ten kilometers away in another direction a cluster of hills called Manikmunda, Lekhamunda, Chichirakhol, Sargikhol, Kendulhol, Sukhamakar and Phuldunguri and in each hillock, there are evidences of cave art that speak of a mountain civilization, in which people knew hunting, primitive art of war, the art of fort-building and cave art. Perhaps, they were the contemporaries of the Dravidians who lived in the valley of river Sind.

Sri Gobind Trpathy has also discovered the remnants of another fort at Kulihaberna village on the foot hills of Laxmi Pahad near Likhanpur of Jharsuguda district in October 2002.[16] A stone slab found (4' x 21' x 2') there has the diagram of a dice board. The complex of forts counteracted in one area justifies the existence of a civilization belonging to the Neolithic period. The people of this civilization knew different games- outdoor and indoor. These Neolithic people, were in no way inferior to the people of Harappa and Mahenjo-Daro.

Late Satyanarayan Rajguru discovered the rock arts of Ullapgarh in 1947. The rock art contains dancing postures.

The next evidence of the ancient civilization of Orissa dates back to the period of king Karakandu, during whose reign the Jain Saint and warrior Parswaratha preached his religion among the tribal people of this region. Ashok kumar Rath, in his book, *Odisare Jaina Dharma* (Jainism in Orissa) determines Karakandu's period around 877 B.C. Herman Jacobi's *Sacred Books of the East, vol XIV* informs that Karakandu became a disciple of Parswanatha during 9th cent. B.C.[17] Bhavadeva Suri's *Parswanatha Charita* records about the strong warrior's role of Parswanatha when Yavana Prasenjit of Kalinga attacked Karakandu. Prasenjit's capital was at Kusasthalapur, now in Ganjam district.[18] Parswanatha was a great warrior and he was married to Prasenjit's daughter Prabhabati.[19]

Mahavira preached his religion in Bhaluyagama, Subhoma, Succheta, Malaya and Hattasisa. B. Mishra in his *Dynasties of Medieval Orissa* (PP 66-72, PP 78-79) [20] mentions about an Inscription of Chola king who ruled in Suvarnapur, the capital of a civilization that flourished on the confluence of river Mahanadi and Suktel. It is probable that the Suktimati civilization continued till Mahaveera's (the 24th Teerthankar) visit of Northwest Orissa [21]. (K.C.Jain, *Mahavir and its Times*, P54)

The 24th Teerthankar was found moving naked on the Streets of Toshali and the people attempted to murder him. Hence he fled to Mosali and then to the Suktimati region as depicted in *Abasyaka Sutra*. [22] Just after Mahavira's return from Kalinga around the last part of 6th B.C, "Kalinga Jina" was consecrated and worshipped. C.J.Shah in his *Jainism in North India* [23] (PP 172-335) justifies the name **'kalinga jina'** since it was worshipped in Kalinga. Mahapadma Nanda had taken it away in the course of his invasion of Kalinga and it was brought back by Kharavela [24].around the last part of 1st. century B.C.

However different historians have interpreted the 'Kalinga Jina' in different ways N.K. Sahu believes that Rishabh Nath's image was worshipped as Kalinga Jina.[25]. Rakhal Das Banerjee and Kasi Prasad Jayaswal identify that as the image of the 10th Trithankar, Sitalnath [26]. Some others are of opinion that Kalinga Jina is the image of Ajitnath, the IInd Teethankar. This guess work is made since his *Lanchhan* was elephant and Kalinga was famous for its gigantic and terrifying elephants [27]. Some others still believe that Kalinga Jina was the deified image of Sreyansnath, the 11th Tirthankara since he was born at Singhapur, the once-upon-a-time capital of Kalinga [28]. Pt. Nilakantha Das has mentioned that the Kalinga Jina was the ancient most image of Jagannatha [29].

The Kalinga of 9th century was famous. It was also famous before the war of *Mahabharata* (c.1000-900 B.C.)

The history of the subsequent period till Ashoka's invasion still remains unexplored from the historical point of view. but the oral history of the Gadabas and the Binjhals conveys that their ancestors were the 12 brothers whom they alternatively call the 12 Iswaras (Barra Iswara) and 12 Oddis (Bara Oddi).These are the twelve **Oddi** or Odiyas. The caste of the *Badhei* or carpenters is derived from the word Bara Oddi. Their legends inform that they used to cut rocks and build temples in Sri Lanka. The ancient city of Srilanka was built by these Oddis. A large number of **Oddi** tribes had migrated to Sri Lanka as artisans and had settled there. Ashoka, in the subsequent years of his conversion into Buddhism could venture to depute his own son Mahendra for the propagation of Buddhism in Sri Lanka because of this Kalingan connection.

The people of the Bara Bhaia tribe are still remembered in the temple of Lord Jagannath on the day of *Odhana Sasthi* (the sixth day after *Amabasya*). If the *Sasthi* falls on a Tuesday, the *Kotha Devata*, Jagannath is offered a 12-fold cloth with five colours and the Bara Bhai Mahavir is offered a special concoction for the ritualistic worship on the day of *Vishuva Sankranti* (falling around mid-April). The concoction is tribal in nature and related to the Barabhai Oddi customs..

If evidence can be built up, following the post modern histriographic methods used in America, like using legends and sources of oral history, the Gadaba tribal legend, gets immediately related to the culture built around the temple of

Jagannatha. But the evidence pertaining to the Gadaba artisans becomes historically justifiable only from K.P. Jaiswal's *History of India 150 A.D to 350 A.D*. The book informs that the paintings of Ajanta caves were done by the Bara Bhaia Oddi, Bhara Siva and the Bakatakas. The Bakatakas had occupied a piece of empire around IInd century A.D, and perhaps much before that was discovered by K.P.Jaiswal. They belonged to Oda Tak clan and called themselves Bakataks. Jaiswal informs that the Oda Taks or Bakataks were great fighters and they conquered kingdoms in Padmvati, Kantipuri, Mathura, Ahichhatra, Antarvedi and Shrughna to spread the culture of the *Odra Desa* out side the state.

The history of the Odias of the subsequent times is recorded in the accounts of the Kalinga war and in the stone inscriptions of Kharvela. The cultural growth from Suktimati period (1000.BC) to the reign of Kharavela, traced in this essay, is a configuration based on interpretations from numismatic studies, rock inscriptions, legends and folk tales. Our colonial historians who were trained under the conservative British professors did not venture to write on this subject since direct historical accounts are not available.

Prof. Nagendranath Pradhan, in a recent essay, captioned *Puratana Dui Juddhare Kalingara Bhumika* (The role of Kalinga in two ancient wars) and published on 1st April, 2004 in *Sabara Srikshetra* calculates the period of Kalinga war during 1464 B.C. Dr. Pradhan mentions how Indian historians were trained by the British Universities to subvert and undermine the ancientness of our civilization. The purpose was political and cultural domination. They intended to compare Hindu civilization with that of the Christians and proved how inferior the Hindus were. The strategy was conducive to their religious conversion projects. This kind of a cultural politics stinks of colonialism that had its roots in a monarchical, feudal, exploitative capitalist logic.

Dr. Pradhan takes the help of Indian astrological calculations, converts the dates into Christian era and periodizes the war. This time his imaginary war of Mahabharata occurs in 3102 B.C. The war began exactly on 20 February, 3102 B.C. at 2' 27"30 P.M, according to Dr Pradhan's calculations [30].

Since our historical mindsets are determined by a pseudo-scientific search for evidences, we credulously disbelieve our Puranic calculations. William Jones did not accept our Puranic calculations because of his colonial bias for Christianity and deposition, extreme faith in the renaissance temper of empire building projects.

Postcolonial studies made by Edward Said and Homi Bhaba have attempted to rehabilitate Indian cultural roots for interpreting history. Micro histories published in Orissa have, thus, calculated regional periods and have dated them basing on palace annals which are also authentic records of history maintained by the *chhamu-karanas* (record keeping caste). The History of Kantilo, available with this author, informs that the tribal king Viswabasu's brother Viswa basava ruled over there around 1700 B.C. That was the time when Lord Jagannatha was worshipped there as Neelamadhaba before a Brahmin named Vidyapati stole the Deity to install at Puri. Perhaps, time has ripened for the historians to deploy post colonial methodology in determining periods of civilization depending on such records. This would obviously generate resistances and counter resistances, but it has to be taken up by the professional historians for correct dating and interpretation..

Bibliography:
1. G.C. Mahapatra *The Stone Age Culture of Orissa*. 1962 qtd in K.C. Panigrahi. *History of Orissa*, Kitab Mahal, Cuttack 1981 P.I.
2. Rekha Devi *Locational study of Tribal Settlements in Orissa*, Lark Books, Bhubaneswar 1993 P.33 (Also See P. 19)
3. Ibid. P 33
4. *Dharitri* Dated. 7. 08. 2002
5. Ibid.
6. Sunit Kumar Pathak. Translating of *Pag-Sam-Lon-Zang*. *Indian Historical Quarterly. Vol XXX. No1. (March, 1954)*
7. Giacomo Camuri, Angleo Fossati and Yasodhar Mathpal. *Deer in Rock Art of India and Europe*

8. Ibid .p. 10
9. Ibid .p. 11
10. Ibid. p. 10
11. Ibid. p. 9
12. J.P. Singhdeo. "A bird's eyeview of anthropological and archaeological traces in western Orissa", *Confluence vol.1*.Ed.Dr. P.M. Nayak and Dr. S.Muduli
13. Padmashri Bhagaban Sahu. "A Brief Sketch or Ranapa Dance" in *Souvenir. Bhagaban Sahu Memorial Committee*. Ed. Bighneswar Sahu, Badakusasthali,. Sept. 2002 .pp. 50-51.
14. Gobinda Chandra Tripathy *"Odisare Prak-Brahmilipi Khodita Giri-gumpha Bikramkhol"* (Oriya) (*"Brikram khol caves: Pre-Brahmi engravings in Orissa). Dharitri . Annual Issue vol.xxx 2003, pp. 40-42.*
15. Ibid. p. 41.
16. Ibid. p. 41.
17. Herman Jacobi   *Sacred Books of the East vol. xiv.* P. 87.
18. Bhavadeva Suri. *Parswanatha Charita* Ed .Haragovinda and Pt. Bachara Dasa. Pp.269-270. *Slokas* 155
19. L.S.S. O'malley and M.M. Chakravarty. *Bengal District Gazeteer*, pub.1908. p. 256.
20. B.Mishra *Dynasties of Mediaval Orissa* pp. 66-72 and pp. 78-79.
21. K.C. Jain. *Mahavir and His Times*. P. 54
22. *Abasyaka Sutra*. P. 219-220. qtd. In A.K. Rath. *Jaina Dharma-o*-Samskriti (Oriya) Tara Tarini Pustakalaya. Berhampur 1991. (p.72)
23. C.J. Shah *Jainism in North India*. Pp. 172-173.
24. A.K. Rath. *Jaina Dharma-O-Samskriti*. P. 69-70.
25. Ibid. p. 70
26. Ibid.
27. Ibid.
28. Ibid.
29. Ibid.
30. Nagendranath Pradhan. *"Puratana dui Mahayuddhare Kalingara Bhoomika"* (Oriya) *Sabara Shriksheta.* 2004, April. 1, 2004. Pp. 3-8

Prehistoric Evidences

Padmashree Parmananda Acharya, in his *Odisara Pratnatatva* (*The Anthropology of Orissa*) records that Ballentine Ball, the famous archaeologist who worked on Orissa, had collected some stone weapons belonging to the prehistoric age in Dhenkanal, Kalia Katakhal of Angul and Kudebaga of Harichandrapur, Talcher. He published an article in the *Journal of Asiatic society*. The stone weapons are now preserved in the museum at Calcutta.

Sri Acharya collected a lot of evidences on the stoneage in 1924 at Badasahi village in Baidyapur, Mayurbhanj. Rakhal Das Bandopadhyay had mentioned about the stone weapons in his book of history published in 1930. Mr.Acharya, then discovered some more evidences in Kuliana village of Mayurbhanj and in Kuchai village also. Now Kuliana, Kuchai; and Baidyapur villages are preserved by the archaeological department asheritage sites. Lots of broken cooking pots made of baked mud were also found in Baidyapur area. Perhaps the art of cooking was known to them. The staple food of these people was fruits, roots, meat and fish. We are not yet sure whether these people knew the art of agriculture/farming like the Bondas of Koraput.

Padmashree Paramananda Acharya reports that while digging a pond at Baidyapur, his native village in Mayurbhanj, a number of prehistoric stone weapons were found. The archaeologist, as a child was attracted by their size and form and preserved them.

In 1923, when he was an apprentice in archaeology, he came to know that these stone weapons were called *Chadaka Pathara* (thunderbolt stones). Such thunderbolt stones were also found in other places of Asia, Europe, Africa, and Australia. It may be presumed that either all these places were not divided by oceans during those days, or the thunderbolt stones were universal. Few years back, some such stone weapons were also discovered at Khandapara, called chadaka stones.

Our archaeologists have discovered paintings in maroon-clay on the walls of the primitive caves at Sundargarh, which shows that these primitives did not know the art of building a house. Similar paintings are also found at Chakradharpur and Raigarh in Madhyapradesh. During my weeklong stay at Raigarh, an Oriya village in Madhya Pradesh, I discovered that they belonged to the same zone of prehistoric culture. These people lived in caves and used fire to cook the meat of different wild animals.

In Bikramkhol hills some pictorial symbols resembling alphabets have been discovered. They have not been deciphered so far. The Egyptologists who have recently claimed the discovery of the first pictographs should be consulted with regard to this for further studies.

Evidences from the Paleolithic Age (Copper age)

Evidences of the weapons of the paleolithic age, like axes, have been discovered in *Gadapada* of Balasore in 1871 by the- then collector Mr. Beams and he had published about this copper plate in *Indian Antiquary*. This copper plate was actually a weapon from the copper age. Late Sri Paramananda Acharya had the occasion of finding these weapons only in Mayurbhanj district. There is a copper mine at Dhalabhumi of Singhbhum district which was in Orissa and has been given to Bihar around 1936. The Oriyas were politically marginalised and they are still being treated as subalterns by the National leaders.

We do not know when the North Indians learnt the use of iron. But in Orissa we have lots of iron mines. The Vedas speak about a metal called *Ayas*. Experts consider this to be copper. But in *Yajur* and *Atharva* Vedas *Ayas* was accepted to be iron and at times it denoted all metals.

However, the transition from the stone weapons to the metals does not seem to be abrupt. Toward the last phase of the stoneage, the Oriya primitives were found using spade-tike stones, which the English men called "shouldered neolith".

During this period, the primitive Oriyas seemed to know the use of three metals only- silver, gold and copper. Later, they used iron for making weapons and agricultural tools. The copper- made tools also looked like the spades. These were discovered in Khiching and Baghada of Mayurbhanj district. Such tools were also found in Yukta Pradesh (the modern Uttar Pradesh) and Madhya Pradesh. We can presume that the North Indians had also known the use of copper. But no such evidence is available in South India as for as my study is concerned. The iron age emerged first in this part of the country and thereafter the stone age. However, after the Mahenjo-Daro excavations, copper instruments were found. We do not know whether that copper belonged to India or Babylon.

Numasmatic Evidences (Coins):

Coins also provide logical explanations about trade culture of a country. Punch-marked round, rectangular and flat coins have been discovered from Mayurbhanj, Sonepur and Khandagiri. We donot know whether these are *Niskas* or *Karshapanas* (names for old coins in India). The punch-marks do not signify any kind of alphabets of the civilized period. Hence, it may be presumed that such coins are either prehistorical or they belong to the paleolithic period.

The later coins found in Orissa have been dated back to Kushana dynasty (100 B.C in Central Asia, from Benares to Yarkand in North India) and I.D.M Belgar, the assistant of Mr. Cunningham has reported in the *Archaeological Survey of India Report-XIII* that he had seen golden coins of Roman period at

Rairangpur, Brahman ghati, Mayurbhanj. These coins had the picture of Constantine (306c), great emperor who shifted the capital to Byzantium and it was called Constantinople after that. (Nehru records his time as 306 A.D and Sri Acharya states it as 323-353). Similar coins had also been found in Tamil Nadu. Perhaps the coins travelled upto Mayurbhanj through Tamluk port and some one buried them under the earth. That was the practice those days, and it was called the system of *"hidden treasures"*. Beglar discovered these golden coins with the wife of the Deputy Commissioner at Chainbasa, who wore them as a kind of jewellery.

Golden coins were also found later in Balasore, Cuttack, Puri and Ganjam districts. These are called *Puri-Kushana* coins. These later coins contained three cars on one side and on the other side, the word *tanka (rupee)* was written. The archaeologists have fixed the period of these coins between the 5th and the 10th centuries. But with the Jaugada excavations such coins were found along with Ashoka's rock edict. Hence an immediate discussion is required with regard to the Jaina and the Buddhist cultures of Orissa.

Odia Culture in and Around 1700 B.C.

Viswa Vasaba was the king of Ranpur in the year 1700 B.C according to the microhistory of Kantilo. The dating seems earlier to the time of Harappan culture. If the war of the Mahabharata is dated between 1500-1000 B.C (This is according to one mode of calculation), the time of Viswa Vasaba predates the war by two centuries. However, the milieu of *Rig Veda* can be found mirrored in Viswa Vasava's era.

About a millennium separates the Vedic era from the Harappan Age. The collection of the Hymns of Rig Veda was not completed before 1000 B.C. (though some of its myths originated in a far remote past). In the *Rig Veda* the bovine species, whether as buffalo or bull, lends its glamour to the evocation of the gods: Agni, Indra, Soma and Varuna - all of whom were invoked as bulls. The Saivite cult and the Sabara

Culture of the Ranapur jungles, the worship of the tribal God Neelamadhaba, the Maninaga hills with Shiva and Durgamba images can be taken as parts of our national culture during the pre-Mahabharata era in a crude and underdeveloped primitive way, though. The bull is related to Shiva and also to the period of transition between the primitive fruit gatherers' society and the agricultural society. The bull is symbolic power in act, in manifestation.

Viswa Vasaba, as a king, was only an archer and Rudra-Agni; the wild archer had always saved him. The commandments of God given in the dreams is neither mythological nor an exaggerated blind belief. The Britishers wanted to deracinate our people from our own rich cultural heritages/power on administrative grounds and introduced concepts like science, reasoning and rationality etc to prove that this latter political religion and culture was an embodiment of progress and what they taught under the umbrella of occcidentalism was Enlightenment and renaissance.

In other words, the belief of Viswa Vasaba in his intuitive dreams, and God's dream commandments would be thrown into the garbage of fantasy since no evidence is available as to whether Viswa Vasaba had really dreamt about worshipping Maninaga Mahadeba and Durgamba. That is a subjective truth and no objective/ laboratory proof can be provided.

The person, who would ask such a question, would be distantiated from the dreamer Viswabasava by about three thousand eight hundred years across time.

Odisa has been invaded by alien cultures several times in the meanwhile. The brand of education introduced during the Imperial times has been accepted as scientific and modern and our ancient knowledge has been consigned to the burial ground by our so called educated folks during and after the colonial period for their own material benefits.

The younger generation is so cleanly cut off from these shaivite and Tantric roots of Orissa, that this early decade of the 21st century, these events culled from the micro history of

Ranapur would appear to them blasphemous and incredible at the first encounter.

The tragic part of our contemporary cultural belief-system is that we fail miserably to identify the tribal knowledge of Viswa Vasaba as a supra- scientific knowledge. If Viswabasu's dream commandments were not true, if the *Yantras* drawn on the Chakasila stone did not convey any truth, how could the facts come true and the evidences stand the test of time till today? How could the ritual worship of Maninaga (Mahadeva) and Durga (the primal mother force) attract the kings of Kangoda and Tosali who made occasional grants of villages to meet the expenses of the continuing rituals ? The survival of the temples and the *Yantras* for 3800 years (From 1700 BC to 2100 AD) might evoke awe and wonder, but the efficacy and the authenticity of Viswa Vasaba's dreams actualising the presence of Shiva and Durga in 1700 B.C. cannot be consigned to the dustbin of fantasies. The advocates of the physical sciences can only venture to attempt such a stupid subversion.

The cultural belief has proved itself as a universal truth and it needs a thorugh discussion on two levels: (a) the relevance of Viswa Vasaba, the primitive Sabara king and his brother Viswa Vasu to the contemporary cultural milieu that precedes the civilization of Mahenjodaro by 200 years, or as a parallel civilization that runs along the Harappan stream and (b) the efficacy of the Saivite and Tantric culture of the Sabara kings of Ranapur in our post-modern era.

Maninaga of Ranapur (in (1700 B.C.) is directly related to the primordial phase of the *vratya* myth of creation and around seven hundred years before the collection of the hymns of *Rig Veda,* or the poetic codification of the powers like Agni, Varuna and Indra, who have later been considered as mythical Gods. In his sacrificial role, however, Angni was equated to Rudra Brahman and both were related to the Savaras (Viswa Vasaba's tribe) as Supreme Archers. Agni was to play an analogous part, though transposed into the orbit of the sacrifice, to that of Rudra, the fierce archer. Agni himself is an archer. His arrows glow with heat (Rig Veda 4.4.1), but his office as a priest, he has no use for them. On the contrary, absorbed in sacred thought centered in his knowledge of the cosmic order (ruta) in its eternal truth, he concurred with the Father when the latter, benefaction in mind, offered up his seed in his daughter, Usas (RV 3.31.1). Then the Angirasas were born (cf Rig.Veda.3.31.3)..

Agni is here treated as the primordial, paradigmatic flame arising as the sacred fire. Agni knows the cosmic order (ruta) for he is its first born in the earliest aeon (RV 10.5.7). In these cosmically and sacrificially ordered universe-to-be, Agni and the Father (Prajapati) are the cooperating powers. The Father (Prajapati) inseminating his daughter performs a cosmogenic rite to which the Angirasas and ultimately Man owe their position in an ordered world (please read the 8th *mandala* of *Rig Veda* to get the full story of the myth of creation).

By the time Agni and Rudra were recorded as powers in the Rig Veda, Viswa Vasaba's era was over. Rig Veda records the history of the universe around 1000 B.C. and the relation of Viswa Visava's dream, the worship of Shiva and Sakti in Maninaga Mountain (which survives even today), the *Yantras* drawn on Chakasila stone, predates by 700 years. The records of Rig Veda are probably enriched by model kings/ archers like Viswa Vasaba and their worship of Mahadeva (Shiva) and Durga. The definition of Durga is given in *Atharva Seersha* and Mother Durga herself declares about her emergence in the primordial times. In Rig Veda (M.10.A.10.Mantra 1-9) there is a *Sookta* called *Ratri Suktam* which reads: *"Orvapra amartyanivato devyudvatah.Jyotisha badhate tamah"*. This Devi (Durga) is eternal and She engulfs the entire creation, from the creepers on the ground to the upgoing trees. Not just this, She destroys the darkness of ignorance by her own glow of light/knowledge).

In *Atharva Seersha* all the Gods come to the Devi and ask: "Oh Great Mother: Who art thou?" Durgamba answers:
1. *Aham brahma swaroopini.*
2. *Mattah prakruti purushatmakam jagat. Soonyam cha soonyam cha.*

[I am the *brahma*. From me has emerged the concepts of gender the anthropomorphic forms of the Male and the Female. I am emptiness and the non-emptiness at the same time.]

3. *Ahamananda nanandau.* (I am the pleasure and the non-pleasure too)
   Ahamavijnana-abijnane. (I am the science and the non science too)
   Aham Brahma Abrahmani Vedityabe (I am the knowable Brahma and non-Brahma too)
   Aham panchabhootani Apanchabhootani. (I am the saturated compound of the five elements and I am also differentiated by the five elements.)

4. *Vedoham Avedoham* (I am the Veda and the Non-Veda, too.)
   Vidyaham avidyaham (I am knowledge and nescience)
   Ajaham Anajaham (I am the born and also the unborn)
   Adhascha, urdhwacha, tiryak chaham (I am the upward, I am the downward, the obliqueward and also do I spread on to the sides)

5. *Aham* Rudrovirvasubhischarami (I flow and get conducted as/through the images of Rudra and the Vasus)

Seven hundred years before this hymn was written, Viswa Vasaba exprienced Her directly within his inner space. There is nothing to feel astonished about it. What Viswa Vasaba experienced in the remote jungles of Ranapur was codified later in Rig Veda, in the Ganges valley. The propagators of institutionalised social religions would be able to build structures for God only to defile them in materialist pride.

This pre-vedic Sabara (Saura tribe) must have been called as *Vratya* by the Ganges Valley dwellers. The Ganges Valley dwellers were outsiders/foreigners and they treated the Natives as the Others. Their education at Taxila (later to the Vedic period) was never indigenous and it was modelled on the Greek curriculum. But a king like Viswa Vasaba had internalized all our tribal knowledge with the blessings of

Maninaga and Durga. He did not know the Vedic religion, but he was self sufficient in his own way. He did not feel the necessity of following the Vedic norms. He was born and brought up in the jungles of Utkal, not on the river banks of Ganges valley. The Aryans, therefore, treated him like a Savara and an Asura.

The Savaras and the Asuras

Viswa Vasaba's *chakasila* (the stone with etchings of a Yantra) is still there on the Maninaga Mountain and numerous attempts of thefts have been obstructed by the Goddess herself. How can a so called empiricist with a scientific bent of mind realise the truth behind such contemporary attempts of theft? The spiritual energy that exudes from this seat protects Itself. The disbeliver may challenge the presence of the Goddess alongwith the efficacy of my statementThere is a sense of adventure also in destroying oneself. This is a fashion with the socalled l**iberal humanists** of the world. Committing suicide is a 'rich' cultural feature in societies that believe in global invasions of commercialism. I remember Hart Crane jumping into the sea because of his alchoholic/homosexual craze.

The power of Viswa vasaba's worship is an evidence of the practice of Shaktism in Orissa during the pre-Vedic and Vedic periods. The *Devi Purana* was composed much later, toward the end of the 7th or the beginning of the 8th century. The *Kalika Purana* was composed around the 11the century followed by the composition of *Yogini Tantra* in 16th century. The evidence of the traces of Tantrism can be descerned in the time of *Rig Veda* (1000 B.C.).

The accounts of Viswa Vasaba state about the tribal sabara civilization of Kalinga. This pre-Aryan civilization is traced back to a period between c.3000 and 4000 B.C. This culture is a contemporaneous culture of the early Sumerian civilization of the Assyrians. The Assyrian emperors like Bonipal and Assurapal were known to the Savara kings like

Viswa Vasaba. The Assyrian-Babylonian countries were founded on the strength of their horrendous invasions. They were a gypsy mobile tribe and lived on attacking the prosperous civilizations. They had also entered into South India and probably attacked them. The faces of the South Indian Dramils and the Sabaras somehow looked similar to the Aryans who came from the delta of river Tigris and had experienced the horrors of Assyrian scourge. They addressed them as the Assuras. Some of the Assyrian invaders might have settled in South India too.

D.A.Mackenzie in his *Myths of Babylonia and Assyria* narrates how the vanquished emperor's skin was peeled off from the body live and later they were burnt. Countries which were aliens to them were burnt. Moret and Davy in their book *From Tribe to Empire* describe the ruthless and excruciating afflictions of the vanquished countries and the beastly behavior of the Assyrians: "This Empire was founded on force and terror, the massacre of prisoners, the destruction of cities taken by storm, the wholesale deportation of populations, were its methods of domination." The primal country of this Assyrian civilization was Babylonia. The brutalities of the Assyrians (the Asuras) were perpetrated from 12th. Century B.C. to 7th century B.C or our historians have traced them from around that period. The Assyrians and the Babylonians were in perpetual war concerning their religions. The Assyrian God was called Assura and the Babylonian God was Merodach. Zarathustra, contemporary of the Vedic civilization in India, had attempted to bring in some resolution to their conflicts.

The priests of the Sumerian Assyrians were naked and clean-shaved their heads. Later they learnt the art of putting on clothes but their heads continued to be clean shaven. One may compare the Sumerian Priests with the Digambara Jain pantheon. Research on 'influence studies' would help discovering greater affinities. The savaras or the kinsmen of Viswa Vasava and his son Viswabasu's tribe worshipped

Jagannatha before the Aryan Brahmin Vidyapati stole the deity and brought to the temple. The Bhairava chakra brought from Suvarnapur was also a tribal tantric tradition.

Pale-Ontological Odisha: Configurations from Suktimati Civilization to First Century B.C

It is an irony that Indian historiographers are still guided by colonial standards. William Jones first documentation of Indian history and culture is centered around Alexander's conquest and this 18th century imperialist has played a political game of power both in his interpretation and manipulative datings. Although he was able to convert the *Kaliyugabda, Salibahana Sakabda* and *Saka Nrupabda* into Christian dates to certain extent, his colonial bias did not allow him to write about any thing that was pre-Alexanderian and pre-Christian. The world, in his narrow religious vision, did not exist before Christ. Indian historical accounts suffer from that western bias till today and the present- day historians are formatted according to that colonial bias

William Jones seems to be guided by the European mediaeval belief –system and he has written everything to the exclusion of the ancient Indian dynasties documented in the epics. This act of politico-religious subversion in historiography has resulted in grave misreading of the coins, rock edicts and copper plates especially with regard to periodization of culture that prevailed at different phases of history in India. German historians like Schwanbeck and Max Mueller have also failed to construct authentic standards of periodization with regard to the events and the watersheds of Indian history.

Records of Orissan histriographic datings suffer from similar colonial misconstructions. In this paper, endeavours are made to reconstruct the culture of Orissa through numismatic evidences, motif studies, rock arts and paintings, folk tales, legends and their semiotic interpretations. The interpretations are made obviously in an interdisciplinary mode and the conclusions taken are purely post- colonial in nature.

Historical configurations about prehistoric Orissa stay limited to the discovery of stone implements belonging to the early, middle and late stone -age cultures. Dr. G.C. Mahapatra observes that "the tools of this culture, taking shape in the secondary laterite pits and cemented coarse gravels of the river sections are generally made out of coarse grain quartzite pebbles."[1]

If these hand-axes, cleavers, scrapers, discoid and irregularly flaked bifaces were used by the primitive men, the historical focus for the pre-historical Orissa goes toward the tribal settlements. Dr. K.C. Panigrahi situates these primitive tribal men in the Northern Tribal Region lying between $21^0 16'$N-$22^0.34'$ latitudes and 83^0E – $87^0.11'$ E longitudes.[2]

Dr. Panigrahi's configurations made in 20th century seem to contain certain amount of enthusiasm for a particular region- the region that includes Chakradharpur, Chaibasa, Ranchi and Manbhum, to the exclusion of other zones. The areas that are spaced in the Northern Tribal region have been specified by Rekha Devi in a different manner in her thesis *"Locational Study of Tribal Settlements of Orissa.* In this study of Orissa's primitive geography, Rekha Devi subdivides the Orissan geography into four morphological zones: (a) The Mountainous Country, (b) The Rolling Uplands, (c) the Subdued Plateaus and (d) River valley and Plains.[3]

Dr. Panigrahi's evidences of the stone-age culture do not signify a civilization, but reflects only on a process of survival in a tropical climate. Dr. Rekha Devi's study on the primitive geography of Orissa, on the other hand, subdivides this Northern mountain region into four sub-units, namely (a) the common interfluves of the river Subarnarekha, (b) the Nilgiri hills, (c) the Baitarani-Brahmani interfluves and the Brahmani-Mahanadi interfluves. This region experienced hot dry summers with a maximum temperature recorded at

41⁰ C. and the summer was followed by a well-distributed monsoonal rainy weather.

The possibilities of a civilization in the mountainous region are erased after the publication of an essay in *Dharitri* Dtd. 15-8-2002. The essay predicts about a civilization existing on the basis of river Suktel flowing in the vicinity of Sonepur. The evidences of this civilization have been formulated on the basis of the coins that were discovered during the 1990s. The coins have come to the state museum on 7-8-02 and the historians have periodized them around 10th century B.C [4]

In confirmation with the principles of Human Space Organization, the locations having 50% of tribal population are only enlisted as "tribal core areas."(Rekha Devi) The probability of a civilization on the basis of river Suktel has not been identified as a "core tribal area" so far either by the geographers or by the anthropologists. The river known as Tel was called Suktimati and Suktel at different periods of history, and thus, it seems appropriate to caption it as Suktimati civilization.

This paper aims at focusing on the probable contours of an extant civilization, which is constituted of mere configurations. The authenticity about its periodization needs verification by experts so that the mainstream historians would be able to brighten the twilight zone of this paleo-ontological civilization. However, it is likely to open up a new vista of knowledge in the sense that the earliest civilization of Orissa did never flourish on the mountains, but like all other civilizations of the world, it has taken shape beside a river.

The 325 punch marked silver coins discovered from the valley of Suktel have been identified by the archaeologists as one of the sets of the oldest coins of the world. The experts are of the opinion that these coins were used between 10thCent.BC to 6th Cent. BC. A detailed study of these coins would reveal more interesting facts about the ontology of Orissan culture. The study, would, on all probabilities, prove that certain unexplored civilizations existed in this land about which our historians have not paid attention to because of a cultural politics; and the Orissan historians very often bypass this prejudice with an inefficacious magnanimity.

The 325 silver coins were retrieved by the peasants of Bolangir district and were deposited in the police station during the 1990s. The coins were preserved initially in the treasury of Tarabha and the High Court has ordered to transfer the coins to the state museum on 7.8.02.[5]

The silver coins now available in the state museum bear the marks of sun, trees, river and the six *chakras*. Over the six *chakras* one finds the marks of deer, ammunitions of those days, dogs, elephants, bulls, snakes, rabbits, frogs and fish. These marks may be taken as popular paleo-ontological symbols and they semioticise some probabilities for further interpretations and extrapolations. The proof-based empirical study of history that prevailed in the Imperial Educational system has long been discarded as *passé* and the post modern historians of Europe are found to have manipulated history from multiple sources-from legends, oral sources and interviews.

As we reach the coins, we are instantaneously getting connected to the works of Panini (*Astahyayi*), who mentioned about such coins remaining in currency till his time. Kautilya's *Artha Sastra*, the Upanishadas, and *Vinaya Pitaka*, (the Buddhist text) also mention about such coins prevailing in this part of the country. A single coin weighs 57.07 grams. Some of these coins are cut into halves and this leads to a probability that the coins had a definite value and if the goods purchased were of lesser value, a part of the coin was cut off.

Besides this extant commercial practice, the visual language of the coins opens up a liturgical – ritualistic context of the Suktimati communities. The lexicon embossed on the silver coins also substantiates the language of the Suktimati myths, legends and dominant systems of belief.

The sign-language of **sun** and the **trees** signify the ancient context of sun and tree worship. Such worships were also prevalent in most of the Indo-European practices. The relationship between the marks of the **trees** and the ***Chakras*** can be traced back in anthropological studies since these are definite features of the worship of the autochthonous gods prevalent in primitive communities. Such practices also continued through the worship of the *Chaityas, Stupas* and S*thanu* of the Buddhist, Jain and primitive Aryan religions.

The **snakes** marked on the coins relate to the connection of the Suktimati people with the Naga dynasties that ruled in the Southern part of the mountains of Mahakantara of those days that extended through the district of Koraput and Jagdalpur jungles to the mountainous countries of Andhra and Tamilnadu. Perhaps, the coins were recognized in the politico-economic regions of the neighboring states in which the Naga dynasties reigned. There are multiple references to the *Naga Kanyas(snake-girls, who metamorphosed themselves between a girl and a snake* by a primitive practice of Tantric art) and there was absolutely no fantasy about this legendary practice. It prevailed also in the Tantric belief- systems of the South during the time of Nagarjuna , the greatest promulgator of the *Madhyamika* philosophy. The text of *Madhyamika* Philosophy was written in *pulo-mulo-kili* (Parimalagiri) by Nagarjuna. Now it is identified as Harishankar hills situated in Bolangir district .[6]

The deer engravings on the coins signify that they were relevant to the primitive men of the Middle Pleistocene. During this period, the Lower Paleolithic man was using his first stone made tools.[7]

Art pictographs and petroglyphs (carvings/inscriptions on the rock) substantiate that animals constituted the major part of such primitive art practices between 4500-3500 B.C.[8]

Deer are found to be the most favorite of the animals of the ancient men. The Studies of the fossils, as recorded in the book, '*Deer in Rock Art of India and Europe*" speak volumes about the lives of the lower Paleolithic man (Middle Pleistocene)[9]. Fossils belonging to the Middle pa-leo-lith-ic(relating to the second period of the stone age) period are found on the Gandeswari at Sisuria in West Bengal. Kurnool caves of Andhra Pradesh have preserved the late Pleistocene fossils of the primates. Since the people of Suktimati civilization used coins with punch marks of deer, it becomes obvious that the people have recorded the Paleolithic symbols on the coins as popular icon of their times. The racial memory of the Middle Pleistocene age may be recent or remote. But since the pictographs are on the silver coins, they represent probably a much later civilization belonging to 1000 B.C.

Since no study has been conducted by the anthropologists on Paleolithic Orissa, covering middle Paleolithic, late Pleistocene, Mesolithic and Neolithic phases, I would pick up the example of the fossil studies made in the neighboring states and attempt to configurate a relationship with the punch-marked deer of the Suktimati civilization.

"Mesolithic deposits of Adamgarh in Madhya Pradesh (close to the vicinity of Suktimati zone) have yielded bones of swamp deer, sambar, chital and hare and a few remains of Six domesticated animals" [10].

From the Neolithic phase of Bihar are obtained good examples of bones of antlers xxxx At Chirand in Bihar (4500-3650 B.C) tools of bones of the antlers have been excavated, which may be relevant to what late Paramanand Acharya records in Archaeological Remains of Orissa(Oriya). These tools can be periodized between 4500B.C.-3650 B.C. The study or pre-Harappan cultural deposits of Sind, Baluchistan and Afganistan (1968, P258) has also recorded bones of deer sambar and swamp deer.

"If we consider only the members of cervidae family, we find that deer has been present in India through out the prehistoric past(P 9) xxx "The genus cervus has also been found at Nandaghat (in Mahanadi valley"(P. 9)[11].

In addition to these archaeological evidences on the primordial dominance of deer in the process of paleo–ontological survival, we may look into the forms of art pictographs and petroglyphs to study the pictures of the deer embossed on the Suktimati coins. The rock-paintings of Orissa illustrate different species of wild animals like Sambar, Chital, barasinga and others belonging to different periods and phases of rock art.

Sri Jitamitra Prasad Singhdeo, in an essay, captioned, "*A Birds" Eye view of Anthropological and Archaeological Traces in Western Orissa*" writes, "The earliest art of early man in Western Orissa is found in the prehistoric drawings painted in red ochre and black tint colour at Gudahandi of Kalahandi district. This painting is dated to early stone- age and can be placed around 15 millennium B.C. This primitive art was discovered by the archaeological department of ex Kalahandi state in 1947-48 [12].

Sri Singhdeo had discovered the Jogimath cave painting in 1970 and the Ghat Ghumar shelter painting in 1980 according to his records. The animals painted are dated to be a part of the Neolithic period. The Khariar branch museum stores ring stones of different sizes that belong to the "Stone-Age Culture".

The ring stones are *Chakras* containing different yantras for the worship of the Shakti. The Chakras embossed on the silver coins of Suktimati civilization are similar to that of the Yantras found in Khariar museum. On the way from Rayagada to IMPHA, a way side temple of Siva has some such large pieces of *Surya Yantras.*

These *yantras* made of stone have been discarded as the Aryans began to sculpt the images of different gods and goddesses. The *yantras* are symbolic geometric forms representing different energy-forms of different Gods and Godesses. The Aryans around the Gupta period began sculpting the anthropomorphic forms of Gods and Goddesses. However, some of these images were sculpted during the Buddhist and Jain period and the *esoteric yantras* were brought out of the sanctum and placed outside. This is a sign of irreverence to the tribal mode of worship done through symbolic geometrical forms. The *yantras* are still lying out side and the aryanised visitors accept them as cute pieces of art.

The pale-ontological Odia used stones for different purposes: as tools for hunting, as *yantras* for worship and as utensils. They also used the human skulls for carrying water.

Sacks made of the skins of hunted animals were also used for collecting water from distant places.

The "Stilt" dances of Ganjam and Phulbani districts also take us back to the pale-ontological stages of civilization. Late Padmasree Bhagaban Sahu, the great guru of 'stilt dance' of Narendrapur had conducted a field study at Kondhamal hills, Kredimska, Udayagiri, Karachuli and Mahandragiri hills to trace the roots of the dance and discovered that the primitive man invented stilt dancing as an imitation from the peacocks. The primitive shepherds used stilts to climb the hills imitating the birds [13]. I quote this as an example of civilized existence of the remote past . Late Sri Sahu periodizes the dance around 3000B.C.

The worship of the *yantras* made of stone, the stilt dances and the hunting practices of the tribal men are found in the rock arts/paintings of the tribal men. Combined together these sporadic evidences denote the primeval sense of a paleo-ontological cosmology. The high landers of Kodalaks and Khujili Mandala have their own shamans. These shamans believed that the world is divided into different cosmic zones and there are passages from one cosmic zone to the other, form the earth to the sky and from the earth to the underworld. During the field visits of this author to the tribal area in connection with theatrical studies, a Shaman from the Khiujili Mandala of the Kandh community informed about the conception of a "cosmic mountain" in which they lived. Stilt walking and dancing provided them with a feeling of height and transcendence, perhaps a facility to discover the path to another cosmic zone through this world axis, called the "cosmic mountain". This transcendental experience was also combined with an artistic endeavour of dancing. The birds and the beasts were the models that aroused the paleolithic awareness of the world around them. The awareness could be aroused through their primeval sense of sight and ability to hear.

Similarly, hunting was not an exclusive sport for living. Besides being a metaphor for primitive notion of survival, it has taken on the value of initiation to life, to the point of being identified with the figure of strenuous searching for the invisible worlds. The animals observed at the margin of the glades along the streams, have been transformed into symbols in the cave art. Hunting was a sport, a living and a primitive world view.

While searching for a cultural context of the paleo-ontological Orissa, the cave arts of Bikramkhole and Ushakothi occupy a central place. The caves were highlighted in 1933, when K.P Jaiswal discovered the paintings. The paintings of Bikramkhole shelter are 34.5 meters long and its height is 8.31 meters. The patterns are constituted of circles, squares, oblongs, triangles, straight lines and oblique lines. The pictures are engraved on a lime stone bed and the mesolithic *"sthapatis"* of Kosala have drawn the figures of the monkey, bulls, birds, serpents, deer and men.

Sri Govinda Chandra Tripathy, in a recent essay periodizes the cave art around C.5000 B.C., which, if not an exaggeration, goes much beyond Suktimati civilization in remoteness. The presence of the deer in cave paintings, as such, must have inspired the Suktimati people to engrave deer in their silver coins. It seems the connection of the deer with men was very intimate. Someswara, in his book *Mansollasa* has divided young woman into six categories *Mrugi, Padmini, Chitrini, Vadwa, Hastini and Sankhini.* Of these, the first two are considered best for making love and the deer type *(Mrugi)* is one of them. *Abijnana Sakuntalam* mentions *"nasta shanka harina sisavo mandam mandam charanti"* as a common sight around Rishi Kanva's hermitage. Much before that Valmiki, too, mentioned about a "Golden deer".

Kashi Prasad Jayswal, who periodises Bikram Khole paintings as Neolithic art, has discovered some pre-Brahmi hieroglyphic writings and has mentioned, "The Characters in Vikram Khol inscription belongs to a period intermediary between the script of Mahanjoders and Brahmin. Some have assumed the Brahmi or Proto-Brahmi form. This throws a flood of light or the history of writings as from Brahmi, the Phonecian and European scripts are deserved.[15]

It is interesting to note that there is another hill named Maheswara Pahad, twenty kilometers away from Bikramkhole and in it is located an old fort called Ullapgarh. A cave adjacent to Ullapagarh is called Ushakoti and some pictographs are found painted on its wall. Ten kilometers away in another direction a cluster of hills called Manikmunda, hekhamunda, Chichirakhol, Sargikhol, Kendulhol, Sukhamakar and Phuldungwri and in each hillock, there are evidences of cave art that speak of a mountain civilization, in which people knew hunting, primitive art of war, the art of fort-building and cave art. Perhaps, they were the contemporaries of the Dravidians who lived in the valley of river Sind.

Sri Gobind Trpathy has also discovered the remnants of another fort at Kulihaberna village on the foot hills of Laxmi Pahad near Likhan pur of Jharsuguda district in October 2002.[16] A stone slab found (4' x 21' x 2') there has the diagram of a dice board. The complex of forts counteracted in one area justifies the existence of a civilization belonging to the Neolithic period. The people of this civilization knew different games- outdoor and indoor. These Neolithic people, were in no way inferior to the people of Harappa and Mahenjo-Daro

Late Satyanarayan Rajguru discovered the rock arts of Ullapgarh in 1947. The rock art contains dancing postures. The next evidence of the ancient civilization of Orissa dates back to the period of king Karakandu, during whose reign the Jain Saint and warrior Parswaratha preached his religion among the tribal people of this region. Ashok kumar Rath, in his book, *Odisare Jaina Dharma* (Jainism in Orissa) determines Karakandu's period around 877 B.C. Herman Jacobi's *Sacred Books of the East, vol XIV* informs that Karakandu became a disciple of Parswanatha during 9th cent. B.C.[17] Bhavadeva Suri's *Parswanatha Charita* records about the strong warrior's role of Parswanatha when Yavana Prasenjit of Kalinga attacked Karakandu. Prasenjit's capital was at Kusasthalapur, now in Ganjam district.[18] Parswanatha was a great warrior and he was married to Prasenjit's daughter Prabhabati.[19]

Mahavira preached his religion in Bhaluyagama,

Subhoma, Succheta, Malaya and Hattasisa. B. Mishra in his *Dynasties of Medieval Orissa* (PP 66-72, PP 78-79) [20] mentions about an Inscription of Chola king who ruled in Suvarnapur, the capital of a civilization that flourished on the confluence of river Mahanadi and Suktel. It is probable that the Suktimati civilization continued till Mahaveera's (the 24th Teerthankar) visit of Northwest Orissa [21]. (K.C.Jain, *Mahavir and its Times*, P54)

The 24th Teerthankar was found moving naked on the Streets of Toshali and the people attempted to murder him. Hence he fled to Mosali and then to the Suktimati region as depicted in *Abasyaka Sutra*. [22] Just after Mahavira's return from Kalinga around the last part of 6th B.C, "Kalinga Jina" was consecrated and worshipped. C.J.Shah in his *Jainism in North India* [23] (PP 172-335) justifies the name '**kalinga jina**' since it was worshipped in Kalinga. Mahapadma Nanda had taken it away in the course of his invasion of Kalinga and it was brought back by Kharavela [24].around the last part of 1st. century B.C.

However different historians have interpreted the 'Kalinga Jina' in different ways N.K. Sahu believes that Rishabh Nath's image was worshipped as Kalinga Jina.[25]. Rakhal Das Banerjee and Kasi Prasad Jayaswal identify that as the image of the 10th Trithankar, Sitalnath [26]. Some others are of opinion that Kalinga Jina is the image of Ajitnath, the IInd Teethankar. This guess work is made since his Lanchhan was elephant and Kalinga was famous for its gigantic and terrifying elephants [27]. Some others still believe that Kalinga Jina was the deified image of Sreyansnath, the 11th Tirthankara since he was born at Singhapur, the once-upon-a-time capital of Kalinga (28). Pt. Nilakantha Das has mentioned that the Kalinga Jina was the ancient most image of Jagannatha (29).

The Kalinga of 9th century was famous. It was also famous before the war of Mahabharata (c.1000-900 B.C.)

The history of the subsequent period till Ashoka's invasion still remains unexplored from the historical point of view. but the oral history of the Gadabas and the Binjhals conveys that their ancestors were the 12 brothers whom they alternatively call the 12 Iswaras (Barra Iswara) and 12 Oddis (Bara Oddi).These are the twelve Oddi or Odiyas. The caste of the *Badhei* or carpenters is derived from the word Bara Oddi. Their legends inform that they used to cut rocks and build temples in Sri Lanka. The ancient city of Srilanka was built by these Oddis. A large number of Oddi tribes had migrated to Sri Lanka as artisans and had settled there. Ashoka, in the subsequent years of his conversion into Buddhism could venture to depute his own son Mahendra for the propagation of Buddhism in Sri Lanka because of this Kalingan connection.

The people of the Bara Bhaia tribe are still remembered in the temple of Lord Jagannath on the day of *Odhana Sasthi* (the sixth day after *Amabasya*). If the *Sasthi* falls on a Tuesday, the *Kotha Devata*, Jagannath is offered a 12-fold cloth with five colours and the Bara Bhai Mahavir is offered a special concoction for the ritualistic worship on the day of Pana Sankranti. The concoction is tribal in nature and related to the Barabhai Oddi customs..

If evidence can be built up, following the post modern histriographic methods used in America,like using legends and sources of oral history, the Gadaba tribal legend, gets immediately related to the culture built around the temple of Jagannatha. But the evidence pertaining to the Gadaba artisans becomes historically justifiable only from K.P. Jaiswal's *History of India 150 A.D to 350 A.D*. The book informs that the paintings of Ajanta caves were done by the Bara Bhaia Oddi, Bhara Siva and the Bakataks. The Bakataks had occupied a piece of empire around IInd century A.D, and perhaps much before that was discovered by K.P.Jaiswal. They belonged to Oda Tak clan and called themselves Bakataks. Jaiswal informs that the Oda Taks or Bakataks were great fighters and they conquered kingdoms in Padmvati, Kantipuri, Mathura, Ahichhatra, Antarvedi and Shrughna to spread the culture of the *Odra Desa* out side the state.

The history of the Odias of the subsequent times is recorded in the accounts of the Kalinga war and in the stone inscriptions of Kharvela. The civilization of Odisa from Suktimati civilization (1000. BC.) to the reign of Kharavela, traced in this essay, is a configuration based on interpretations from coin studies, rock inscriptions, legends and folk tales. Our colonial historians who were trained under the conservative British professors did not venture to write on this subject since direct historical accounts are not available.

Prof. Nagendranath Pradhan, in a recent essay, captioned *Puratana Dui Juddhare Kalingara Bhumika* (The role of Kalinga in two ancient wars) and published on 1st April, 2004 in *Sabara Srikshetra* calculates the period of Kalinga war during 1464 B.C. Dr. Pradhan mentions how Indian historians were trained by the British Universities to subvert and undermine the ancientness of our civilization. The purpose was political and cultural. They intended to compare Hindu civilization with that of the Christians and wanted to prove how inferior the Hindus were. The strategy was conducive to their religious conversion projects. This kind of a cultural politics stinks of colonialism,that had its roots in a monarchical, feudal, exploitative capitalist logic

Dr. Pradhan takes the help of Indian astrological calculations, converts the dates into Christian era and periodizes the war. This time his imaginary war of Mahabharata occurs in 3102 B.C. The war began exactly on 20th February, 3102 B.C. at 2'. 27".30 P.M. according to Dr. Pradhan's calculations [30].

Since our historical mindsets are determined by a pseudo-scientific search for evidences, we credulously disbelieve our Puranic calculations. William Joes did not accept our Puranic calculations because of his colonial bias for Christianity and deposition extreme faith in the renaissance temper of empire building projects.

Postcolonial studies made by Edward said and Homi Bhaba have attempted to rehabilitate Indian cultural roots for interpreting history. Micro histories published in Orissa have, thus, calculated regional periods and have dated them basing on palace annals which are also authentic records of history maintained by the *chhamu-karanas*. The History of

Kantilo, available with this author, informs that the tribal king Viswabasu's brother Viswa basava ruled over there around 1700 B.C. That was the time when Lord Jagannaths was worshipped there as Neelamadhaba before a Brahmin named Vidyapati stole the Deity to install at Puri. Perhaps, time has ripened for the historians to deploy post colonial methodology in determining periods of civilization depending on such records. This would obviously generate resistances and counter resistances, but it has to be take up by the professional historians for correct dating and interpretation..

Bibliography

1. G.C. Mahapatra *The Stone Age Culture of Orissa.* 1962 qtd in K.C. Panigrahi. *History of Orissa*, Kitab Mahal, Cuttack 1981 P.I.
2. Rekha Devi *Locational study of Tribal Settlements in Orissa*, Lark Books, Bhubaneswar 1993 P.33 (Also See P. 19)
3. Ibid. P 33
4. *Dharitri* Dated. 7. 08. 2002
5. Ibid.
6. Sunit Kumar Pathak. Translating of *Pag-Sam-Lon-Zarg. Indian Historical Q uarterly. Vol XXX. No1. (March, 1954)*
7. Giacomo Camuri, Angleo Fossati and Yasodhar Mathpal. *Deer in Rock Art of India and Europe*
8. Ibid .p. 10
9. Ibid .p. 11
10. Ibid . p. 10
11. Ibid. p. 9
12. J.P. Singhdeo. "A bird's eyeview of anthropological and archaeological traces in western Orissa", *Confluence vol.1.*Ed.Dr. P.M. Nayak and Dr. S.Muduli
13. Padmashri Bhagaban Sahu. "A Brief Sketch or Ranapa Dance" in *Souvenir. Bhagaban Sahu Memorial Committee.* Ed. Bighneswar Sahu, Badakusasthali,. Sept. 2002 .pp. 50-51.

14. Gobinda Chandra Tripathy   *"Odisare   Prak-Brahmilipi Khodita Giri-gumpha Bikramkhol"* (Oriya) *("Brikram khol caves: Pre-Brahmi engravings in Orissa). Dharitri . Annual Issue vol.xxx* 2003, pp. 40-42.
15. Ibid. p. 41.
16. Ibid. p. 41.
17. Herman Jacobi   *Sacred Books of the East vol. xiv.* P. 87.
18. Bhavadeva Suri. *Parswanatha Charita* Ed .Haragovinda and Pt. Bachara Dasa. Pp.269-270. *Slokas* 155
19. L.S.S. O'malley and M.M. Chakravarty. *Bengal District Gazeteer*, pub.1908. p. 256.
20. B.Mishra *Dynasties of Mediaval Orissa* pp. 66-72 and pp. 78-79.
21. K.C. Jain. *Mahavir and His Times.* P. 54
22. *Abasyaka Sutra.* P. 219-220. qtd. In A.K. Rath. *Jaina Dharma-o-*Samskriti (Oriya) Tara Tarini Pustakalaya. Berhampur 1991. (p.72)
23. C.J. Shah *Jainism in North India.* Pp. 172-173.
24. A.K. Rath.   *Jaina Dharma-O-Samskriti.* P. 69-70.
25. Ibid. p. 70
26. Ibid.
27. Ibid.
28. Ibid.
29. Ibid.
30. Nagendranath Pradhan. *"Puratana dui Mahayuddhare Kalingara Bhoomika"* (Oriya) *Sabara Shriksheta.* 2004, April. 1, 2004. Pp. 3-8

SECTION-II

OUR MULTIPLE CULTURAL FACES

Kharavela and the Jain culture in Odissa (2nd century B.C.)

But the history of our culture would not take an immediate leap into the 5th-6th century A.D. One of our greatest periods of culture begins in 1st century B.C. with Mahameghavahana Kharavela, who ruled in Kalinga. Kharavela belonged to chedi/cheti dynasty. The *janapada* (state) called Chedi was one of the 16 *mahajanapadas* of *Bharata barsha*. (*Anguttara Nikaya*) The Chedi *janapada* was in Bundelkhand area: (Rayachoudhury 118) Daksha was the founder of this dynasty. According to *Jaina Harivamsa Purana*, Sri Ashok Kumar Rath reports, there were 17 kings in the line - Aileya, Kunima, Puloma, Paulama, Mahidutta, Matsya, Ayodhana, Mula, Sala, Surya, Amara, Debadutta, Mithilanath, Harisena, Sankha, Bhadra and Abhichandra. During Abhichandra's reign, the Chedis left Bundelkhand and came to Vindhya hills to settle there in the valley of the river Suktimatee and Suktimateepuri was their capital.

Vindhya prusthe Abhichandrena Chedirashtram adhisthitam Sukteematyastate adhyayi namna Suktimateepuri

(*Jeena Senacharya 1-38*)

Alexander Cunningham has identified Suktimatee as Mahanadi (Cunningham 69) and D.C. Surcar proves that Suktimatee is river Suktel flowing in Bolangir district. Suktel originates from Gandhamardan hills (Parimala giri) and it joins river Tel. After Abhichandra, his son Vasu (Uparichar) took over and Mahameghavahana established his kingdom in the first half of the 1st century B.C. Mahameghabahana is also known as Jimuta Vahana and he declared himself to be a Jain. Kharavela was the third king of the Chedi dynasty. He was only 24 when he took over the throne of Kalinga.

The Civilization of Kalinga

The *Hatigumpha-Ranigumpha* inscriptions (Bhubaneswer) provide the only authentic evidence about Kalinga of the 1st century B.C. The inscription describes, Kharavela's childhood, his cronation and his rulership for thriteen years. The Hatigumpha inscription was written in *Odra- Prakrit bhasha* in *brahmi* alphabets.

The inscription informs that Kharvela, at the age of 15, was a handsome youngman of pink colour (*Siri Kadasarira bata*) and he was an expert in sports and gymnastics. He learnt *lekha* (alphabets), *rupa* (manufacturing of coins and exchange of coins) *ganana* (accounts- keeping and arithmatic) *vyabahara* (law, sociology and administrative rules) *Vidhi* (ethics), *Gandharba Veda* (theatre, music and dance) Dhanurveda (the science of war). This long list throws some light on the education system of Kalinga in the 1st century B.C.

The capital of Kalinga was *Sisupala garh* and the coronation of Kharavela was held with great pomp and ceremony. The courtiers and other members were honoured and in every part of the empire the occasion was celebrated with *utsavas* (festivals) and *samaja* (that was the term for theatrical performances). The prisoners were released and the subjects were freed from all taxes.

Besides, the achievements made by Kharavela, during the 13th years of his reign has also been recorded. A brief account is given below yearwise

1st Year : There was a great cyclone and the forts, walls, archs, ponds and gardens were destroyed in Kalinga. The emperor spent Rs.35,000,000 for the repairs and renovations.

2nd Year : The emperor gathered his infantry, cavalry,

elephants and cars and attacked the *Satavahana* emperor of Andhra. The King, Satakarni-I was very powerful in Satavahana empire that spread form Maharashtra to Godavari. Asika, Asaka, Mulaka, Surashtra, Kukkura, Aparanta, Anupa, Vidarbha, Abara and Avanti were under him. Their capital was Paithan or Patisthana. Kharavela defeated Satkarni-I near river Krishna.

3rd Year : Kharavela arranged *Vyayogas, Darpa, nritya,* musical shows and boxing competitions for the entertainment of the subjets of Kalinga.

4th Year : Kharavela's expedition to the west. He defeated the king of Vidyadhara on the Vindhyas. Then he conquered Berar and also the Rashtrakas and Bhojakas of Maharashtra.

5th, 6th, 7th Year: In the fifth year he dug a *kulya* (canal) that flowed through Tanasuli (Toshali) to Kalinga Nagara. Actually this canal was originally dug by Mahpadma Nanda 300 years ago and Karavela renovated it. This facilitated trade, irrigation and communication through water routes.

In the sixth and seventh years, he prepared his army for invading Magadh, the traditional enemy of Kalinga. He conducted practice sessions for the cavalry and in the 6th and 7th years he consolidated his army and attemtpted to enhance their capacity in order to test himself against Magadh. Magadh, in the north, was the traditional enemy of Kalinga. So, with this view in mind, Kharavela augmented his resources and engaged them in constant practice session, to keep them fit.

In the 7th year Kharvela's chief queen Heera gave birth to a son. Heera prasad was from Bajirghar, a place known as *Vajradanta desha* in *Kama sutra* (Durgaprasad ed.130)- a place situated close to Kalinga.

8th year : Kharavela proceeded in his expedition toward Magadh. He destroyed Gorath Giri, a fort of Magadh, situated on the Khallatikamountains. (now known as Barabar mountain. It is situated betwen Pataliputra and Gaya In the district of Gaya. Kharavela, then, captivated *Rajagruha*, the capital of Magadh (now known as Rajgir). The old name for *Rajgruha* was *Giribraja*.

Just at that time a Greek commander named Rajdmit (I am not sure about the spelling since I have gathered this account from Prof. Ashok Kumar Rath's Oriya book, *Jaina dharma Samskruti*; 1991) had conqured Mathura and was proceeding toward Magadh from the North-west.

Kharvela chased the Greek commander and drove the *Yavanas* from the famous *Jaina Kshetra*, Mathura. This enhanced the prestige of Kharavela and the Kalingan soldiers were highly honoured. Kharavela brought a branch from the famous *Kalpa brikshya* (the famous sacred tree related to the Jaina and returned to Kalinga.

9th year: In the ninth year Kharavela built a great palace decked up with costly stones at Kalinga Nagar, The name of the palace was *Mahavijaya prasad* and an amount of Rs 38,000,000 was spent over this.

10th year: Kharavela set out for a second invasion of North India and laid siege to the kingdom in the Ganges valley.

11th year: Kharavela attacked the *Dramila Rashtra Sargha* in the far south. This confederation of south Indian Kingdoms constituted of choda/chola, Pandya, Satyaputra, Kerala putra, Tamra Parni (Ceylon) Kingdoms and was established by the Pandyas 1300 years before Kharavela. Great kings like Mahapadma Nanda and Chandragupta Maurya also did not dare to attack this Southern confederation beforehand.

The king of Pandya was subdued and he had offered lots of horses, elephants, pearls and rubies as ransom.

During this expedition, Kharavela also captured an ancient Jain pilgrimage called *Pithanda Nagar* and raised a great area for cultivation. He arranged to till the land deploying donkeys. There is a reason for this new deployment. *Tirthankaras* like *Rushabha* had been insulted earlier and hence the great emperor did not want to commit a sin by deploying *brishavas* (Oxen) for agriculture. This metaphorical action also signfies the emperor's great devotion towards Rishabhanath one of the pioneer saints of Jainism.

12th year: The twelfth year is devoted to the third expedition of Kharavela : This time he invaded the North west and great kings were defeated. His empire spread up to River Sind.

The Hatigumpha inscription further enjoins that Kharvela on his way back defeated *Bahisati Mitra* (Brihaspati Mitra) the king of Magadh. *Bahisati* also had composed a sloka: "Magadham cha rajanam Bahasati Mitam pade vandapayato"

This time Kharavela brought back Kalinga's Jeena icon taken away by Mahapdmananda, the great emperor of Magadh in 4th century B.C. The inscription records: "Nandaraj neetam calinge jeenam samnivesam" (Barua: IHQ). The Emperor also got lots of riches from Anga (Bhagalpur and Mungher districts of Bihar) and Magadh (Patna and Gaya districts).

13th Year: The Emperor devoted the thirteenth year of his reign to religious works. He hollowed out 117 caves in *Kumari Parbata* (Udayagiri) for the Jaina *Bhikshus* (ascetics of the Jain order) and he donated them warm clothes as well as *sukla-vastra* (white garments). He also convened an All India Jain conference near udayagiri. Jain *arhats* and *Shramanas*, Brahmins, Buddhist monks and rishis from all over India flocked here and Kharavela had built a chawl of stupendous size.

As I am copying/ translating these accounts from Sri Ashok Kumar Rath's Oriya book on *Jaina Dharma-o-Sanskruti*, (Jainism and culture)

I might appear like a great historian. I never cherished an ambition to become a historian. I am providing these details since I am greatly impressed by the stupendous amount of research done by this retired professor of history, who is not known even in Orissa to the extent he should have been known and honoured.

To my awe and wonder, I don't find Delhi based Indian historians writing much about Kharavela. Nehru, either in his 'Glimpses' or in 'Discovery' has not even mentioned his name. Does this 1st century B.C. Emperor not belong to India? Hence, I have lots of reasons to presume that all our books of history attempt to structurise facts like an ultimate act of wish-fulfillment, with a desire to establish the national history, as a centre of totalitarianism, which is nothing but a play of powers. At this point, I am also corvinced that historical writings in India, from the colonial days to Mrs. Thapar, reorganise reality to their own advantage. Nehru's centre was Chandragupta Maurya's grandson Ashoka since he devastated Kalinga and it was convenient for the to historians posit him as a transformed Buddhist so that he would be raised to a fictive status called "***Devanam Priya***"(the favourite of the Gods) . Here the concept of the " centre" becomes a concept of a "Free-play" (Ref. Derrida : *Struture, sign and play*) by which any one would, by the free organisation of the historical facts, occupy the centre stage for power-performance.

Kalinga, then, would be pushed to the periphery like a cyclone-hit area of 1999 to generate cathartic melodramas through political performative histrionics. History is, then, not a representation of reality, not something identified with the centre as inner, self-present voice of perennial truth, but also a subversion of all ontological versions of centre, a strategy of decentering.

I devote so much time and space for this 1st.century B.C.- Emperor because his accounts retrieved through Hatigumpha inscriptions signify volumes about the culture of Kalinga. I have not mentioned here about his Ranigumpha stone stage for the performance of *Vyayoga* (a genre of drama in Sanskrit devoted to military spectacles) in 1st. century B.C. That would be incorpotated later, under the rubric of the theatrical performances.

Now, I should mention about his religious convictions. At the beginning of Hatigumpha inscription he inscribed " *Namo arhantanam, namo sabosidhanam*" which conforms to the "*Pancha Namaskara*" principle of Jainism (the five modes of paying ovation: (i) *namo Arahntanam, (ii) Namo Siddhanam (iii) Namo Airyanam (iv) Namo ubhattayanam (v) Namo loe sabba sahunam*). While paying ovation in this manner, the Jainas remember five kinds of saints (i) those who have acquired *siddhi* through knowledge and (ii) those sublime souls who attained salvation (iii) the teachers who lead one through right conduct (iv)the teachers who import knowledge and (v) the ascetics who have attained the knowledge, vision and conduct.

The five sacred symbols *(lanchhanas* of Jainism are etched on both sides of the Hatigumpha caves. They are (i) *Baddha mangala (ii) Nandi pada (iii) Swastika (iv) Rukha Chetiya and Brikshya Chaitya.* By this time, Kalingan culture was thoroughly swept by Jainism. Mahabira, the 24th Teerthankara, had close connections with Kalinga and he preached his religion in *Kumari Parbat* (udayagiri) Toshali and Moshali (*Abasyka Sutra*:30). Mahabira's father Siddharth was a friend of the King of Kalinga (*Harabhadrayavritti*:31. It seems, the name of "Bardhaman Nagar" as it is found written in the copper plate of Tekkali, by king Uma Bardhan of Mathar dynasty stands as an evidence that Jainism was popular in Kalinga. The copper plate (No.33) of Achyutapuram of Kalinga (now in Andhra) also mentions about a village called *Siddharthaka*. This also proves that Mahavira was more popular in Kalinga than the other Teerthankaras. Kalinga sculptedy lots of Jain statices also Pt. Kasiprasad Jayaswal (Jayaswal p,85) and Rakhaldas Banerjee ((Baneerjee :36) identifies the Kalingan Jain state of Udalapur (modern Bhadrachalam in Andhra) with the 10th *teerthankar*, Sitalanath, who was born there. Some other historians presume that to be the statue of the 2nd *Teerthanker*, Ajitnath. Dr. Nabin K. Sahu is of the opinion that the Jeena statues of Kalinga were of Rushabhanath of Pithunda Nagar, which was the capital of Kalinga at that time.

I would not like to comment on Dr. Sahoo's observation since I am not a historian. But Pithunda nagar could never be the capital of Kalinga according to the Hatigumpha inscriptions (see Khravela's activities in the 11th year of his reign). However, it does not matter much for our culture studies.

What we observe from these boring historical details is that Kharavela was a perfect Jain and perhaps he was a *Swetambar Jain*. (A Jain who puts on white dress). This becomes evident from the Hatigumpha inscription pertaining to the 13th year of Kharavela's regime, the year in which he hollowed 117 caves in *Kumari parbata* (Udayagiri) to lodge the naked Teerthankaras (*Kayarisi diyav* (physical rest during the rainy season (*varsha sitanam*) . The inscription says that he distributed fine white clothes (*cheena vatani*) to them.

The conference of the Jain saints held in the same year was attended by 3500 *arhatas*, monks and ascetics of the country. This seminar of the first century B.C., held in Kalinga, signifies a culture that was off-beat in the sense it had an academic/religious milieu and perhaps it also posed a severe challenge to the mainstream power group of Indian culture.

Hence they have not mentioned anything about Kharavela in their history books. Nehru's *Glimpses* is a glaring example of this politics of wiping out the major cultural periods of Orissa (Kalinga). The mainstream history comes down to us through our "totalitarian" histriographers who assert `absences' as `presences' and `presences' as `absences'.

The Indian meta-historical records (*Puranas* and literature) marginalise the indigenous inhabitants of Kalinga, Kosala and Kangoda as the *Vratyas*, the *mlechhas* and so on. The Aryans could not, however, dominate over us. Now, I ocularise this congregation of 3500 naked saints at *Kumari Parbata* (Because Kharavela was also committed to the *swetambara* sect,a sect of the Jaina's who put on whitedress) to discuss the essential problems of the culture of life. What a radical endeavour to dislodge the mainstream assumptions about civilization, mostly the tanets of civilization taught by the Aryans, of the Indus valley! It was the assertion of nakedness over the clothed/masked bodies, the assertion of the **raw** over the **cooked**.

Thus provides us with a very serious allegory to our relationship with the centre. The Centre, normally advocates the Aryan cause of the Hindutva. But who are the Hindus? Are the Odias Hindus? They had stayed as Vratyas all through, through these 6000 years opr more.Even today, when the local politicians and the bureaucrats misspend the centre money, or donot spend the money at all because they do not get a percentage in such money, the Centre does not give us any funding. The ground is that we are basically tribal in our attitude eventhough we have our IAS officers. Our IAS officers are also tribals in their vision and execution. With receding grants from the centre evey year, the Orissan villagers are compelled to live without food and clothes and the centre delegates investigators from the centre who also take bribes and declare that no one has died in hunger.This farcical Aryan attitude to Orissan Vratya poverty seems to be a pungent satire on humanism itself.When the government is not able to clear the bills of NTPC, the Orissans survive with three hours of darkness everyday in 2003, in the beginning of the 21st. century.

They are not dead. The Odias in their hunger and nakedness continuously spit on the faces of the central and the state politicians and the Hinglish speaking bureaucrats.One such great IAS officer spoke to the tribal victims of Sundergarh in English. Thanks to our Chief Minister who talked to his Sundargarh people in Hindi.They understand Hindi better than Odia as neighbours to Jharkhand. Vratya people do spit openly on the faces of these socalled great leaders and politicians. One day, they blocked the road of the Chief Minister to their villages by bringing on hundreds of bullock carts on to the national highway. Yet, the delta dwellers and coastal dwellers of Orissa who reside around the capital, in Cuttack, Puri and Balasore districts have grabbed all opportunities of taking the advantages of power and amassing wealth. The Odias were much better during the rule of Kharavela in 2nd Century B.C. There was also a cyclone during his rule and he managed the aftermath very benevolently.

The 14th line of the Hatigumpha edict states how the *Jeeva* (*Atma* or soul) and the *deha* (the body) are interdependent *[Sariraya asrita]*. The Jain scriptures like *Saptanga* were destroyed by the Mauryans.The period of the Mauryas has been described by the mainstream historians as a golden period.

But they, in their spree of sanskritization of our culture, have destroyed our precious tribal and Jain culture. Kharavela was the only powerful emperor who made sincere endeavors to reassert their values through this Religion Conference in 1st centuary B.C. However, he was never intolerant of the *Brahamnas* and the *Ajibakas* (the followers of Gosala).

His coronation was celebrated according to the Vedic format by the traditional Brahmins. The 17th line of the edict designated him (or, rather he designated himself) as "*Saba Pashanda Pujak*" and "*Saba devayatana Samskara Karako*" (the worshipper of all religions and the renovator of all temples). Thus, Kharavela did not mingle religion with politics. In his last year of reign he also constructed a gigantic palace for Brahmanas, Hindu ascetics and saints from all other sects.

Much before Kharavela, there was a 'relic memorial' (*Jaina vastu vigraha*) at *Kumari parvata*. The Jains of those days were conferencing on religious matters there. Mahaveera propagated his religion from there. This was called *Vijaya-chakra-prabartana* ("Su Parvata Vijay chake Kumari parvata") (a kind of religious conquest through preaching) Kharavela had renovated the "relic memorial".

It is interesting to note that Kharavela never declared, like Ashoka, to renounce war. He contiuned to fight with the other empires, but he was absolutely nonviolent in his personal life. He was never in favour of *Bheri-ghosa* and never declared anything diplomatically as Ashoka did by sending Ambassadors to the kingdoms of Ceylon, Japan, West Asia, Europe and Africa.

Nehru quotes one of the edicts of Ashoka: "Moreover, should any one do him wrong, that too must be borne with by his sacred Majesty, so far as it can possibly be borne with. Even upon the forest folk in dominions his sacred Majesty looks kindly and he seeks to make them think aright, for, if he did not, repertance would come upon His sacred Majesty. For His sacred Majesty desires that all animate beings should have security, self control, peace of mind and joyousness" (qtd. in Nehru: *Glimpses*. 63)

The language of this edict of Ashoka is obviously political and is embedded with a ludic element, a political game that a commoner on the streets would be able to decipher today. Its motif is also transcendental and, therefore, impractical for our contemporary rulers.

Kharvela's edicts are simple and non-political in nature. He believed in the *Digambara* (to stay naked) sect of Jainism, in the unpretentious order of living, closely affiliated to the *vratya* and tribal culture of Kalinga. He never adjectivises them as "forest folks of his dominion".

Kalinga and Odra: Multiple Interpretations

Lots of postcolonial Odias believe that Kalinga is the ancient name for Odissa or *Odra desa*. But that is a deceitful myth created by the people of Utkala, who in moments of euphoria claim that they are the posterity of a tribe called the *Odas*.

Prof. Bemimadhab Padhi contended that in the ancient times, the territory stretching from river Ganga to Godavari was described as Kalinga in religious literature, in the Puranas and in the Hindu, Buddhist and Jain scriptures. The primitive tribes of India used to live in this territory. They were called *Nishada, Sabara, Banu, Vanagu, Kali* and *Bali* tribes. Since the population of the *"Kali"* tribe was more in number, this land was named as Kalinga. These *Sabaras* were divided into three categories according to their locations of living. The *highlanders* like the Bondas were called *Parvatya*, the *jungle-dwellers* were called *Aranyakas* and the people of the *coastal belt* were called the *Oda Sabaras*.

"Oda" in Saura (Sabara) language means cultivation. The coastal land was called *Odra desa*, a land of cultivators. This is an etymological definition.

Kasinath Mishra, another historian, who searches for the roots of the *Odas*, **traces them in the district of Koraput, in which a territory is still named as** *Odabadi*, **the land of the**

Odas. The *Oddis* of Koraput used to go to Srilanka as temple builders during the Pre-Ashokan period. They were also the artist engravers of Ajanta caves. Ashoka could dare to send his son to Srilanka since the *Oddies* tribal people had already settled there before his conversion into Buddhism.

The Odas and the *Oddies* have later designated themselves as the *Odias* and this territory was named after them: *Odradesa*. The *Oda Sabaras* had a language of their own, which was called *Sabari*. Markandeya Mishra, a 16th century author of *Prakruta Sarbasva* mentions "*Sabaryameboudi yogauddesya saurasenadeh*". This means that *Sauraseni* is a regional language and a mixture of '*Sauraseni*' and '*Sabari*'. The Odia language has been created out of such a mix. The linguists discover four kinds of words in Odia language: *Tatsama, Tadbhava, Anyagata* and *Desya*. Words that have been drawn from Sanskrit like *Hasta* (hand), *Mastaka* (head) *Svarna* (Gold) are *Tatsama*. *Hata, Matha, Suna, Pua,* and *Bhauni* etc. are *tadbhava* words, derivations from Sanskrit words. There are certain words, which are not traceable in Sanskrit roots: *gina* (utensil) *tatia* (utensil), *Udhani* (refers to the water boiled for rice) and *Peja* (the juice of rice taken out in the preparation of rice) etc. These are known as *desya* or regional words. They are also called *Abyutpanna* words. These are identified as the real *Oddi Sabara* Words.

We notice a number of such *Sabara* words in the register of Jagannatha's Temple. *Khei, bana* (flag), *Pahandi, Bahuda, manohi, tadapa, hadapa, khatani, daudi, khuntia, sankhudi, pali, madiala, tati* and *Nikapa* are such words which are pure *sabari* in nature used in the register of Jagannatha temple.

It is a pity that the capital of the newly formed state called Orissa (1936) is situated at Bhubaneswar and the grammarians of this area do not know anything about the '*parvatyas*' and the '*Aranyakas*'. **They have been using these words in the temple as traditional usages but they play the game of cultural politics to evade the sabara origin of the words.**

These rootless *Odas* have tried to build up a national

identity of their own by affiliating themselves to Sanskrit roots, the roots that took shape in the Indus valley after the Aryan migration. They have compartmentalized these *'desya'* *sabara* words and simply disposed off them as *anchalika* or dialects.

Still later, during the post-1936 era, the coastal people began to diminish the connotative value of the Kalingan words, used in the southern zone of Orissa. *Debiri* (left), *balita* (used for *salita* or the wick), *Torada* (in stead of Tunduri), *Sira* (Ink), *Maipa* (wife), *barchaulia* (hybrid) and *Kisa* (what) are such words which the people of Utkala ridicule and use as comic touches. The people of Utkala do not know that these are the pure *'Sabari'* words of Kalinga, included in the register of Odia language. They have fatuitously endeavored to preach that Odia has been derived from Sanskrit and deliberately pushed these words into the register of dialectology. It is a paradox to note that the Odias living in the central zone speak the *sabara words* when they are used in the temple, they claimed at times that Jagannatha was the god of their Odia nation, but out side when the Kalingans use those words, they laugh at them as uncultured ones and fidget to asccept Jagannatha as a Sabara god. It is for this reason that Sabara Srikshetra is established in Koraput where the Sabaras worship Him.

The central language of Orissa has, thus, been pushed to the margin and named *upabhashika* (sub-linguistic) or as a dialect. The people of Utkala, in their extreme moments of regional fundamentalism have also marginalized the culture of the Kalingans along with that of their *sabaras*. They have also failed to include any of the words used in Sambalpuri into their mainstream register of the so-called pure Odia. The area that has been consistently devastated by the Moghals, Afgans, Marathas and the British people (the part they call Utkala) has incorporated so much of hybridity, both genetic and cultural, that it sounds funny when the coastal *Odias* claim a 'purity' for the coastal *oda dialect* they speak, and name the Sambalpuri or the Kalingan languages as dialects. The people of Koshala (western Orissa), on the other hand, have maintained their racial and linguistic purity and refuse to accept the coastal signifiers as their mother tongue. Prof. Ashok Das claimed in one seminar in the postgraduate department of Odia that Odia is his "father tongue", is and was never a "mother tongue". The refusal signifies the cultural-linguistic diversity in Odissa. They claim Koshali to be their mother tongue. The Kalingans, on the other hand, have compromised with the power sector that exists at Bhubaneswar

A third opinion as to the myth of Kalinga's origin can be formulated from the *puranic* point of view. The main advocate of this school of thought is Dr. Bhagaban Panda, one of the most dedicated and committed exponents of Orissan culture of the late 20th century and early 21st century. Dr. Bhagaban Panda reports that the emperor of the Eastern India of the Puranic era was Bali. He was issueless for a long time. The blind sage named Deerghatama, the expelled son of Rishi Utathya, lived under Emperor Bali's shelter. According to the tradition of the time, Sudeshna, one of the queens of this king, was deployed to serve the blind sage. In course of time, Sudeshna united with the blind sage and bore five children, who were known as the sons of Bali. The five sons were named as Anga, Banga, Kalinga, Pundra and Sumba and they were given different portions of the empire. Kalinga's portion was named after him (M*ahabharata,* 1-104 and 3-114).

The eastern part of Anava area (from Bhagalpur, U.P. to Ganjam district) was identified as Kalinga. (Pargitar, *Ancient Indian Historical Tradition,* P.158). In addition to this large territory, the area spread from the eastern part of Puri (from river Boitarani) to river Krishna (in Andhra Pradesh) was also called Kalinga. The VIIth *Patala* of *Sakti Sangam Tantra* mentions:

Jagannathaat poorva- bhaga- Krishna-teera-ntaragam sive
Kalinga Desah samprukto vamamarga parayanah.

The Mahabharata mentions that the inhabitants of Pundra, Kalinga, Magadha and Chedi were highly qualified and cultured. (N.K. Sahu, *Buddhism in Orissa).* Though the Vedic people hated these Kalingans as *Vratyas,* the *Brahmana* as well as the Buddhist literatures very often refer to Kalinga.

Panini has described Kalinga as a neighbouring region of Magadha. (*Uttaradhyana Sutra* (S.B.E.) P. 87. and *Astadhyayi* 4.1.170)

Karakandu (9th.cent.B.C) the king of Kalinga was the contemporary of the king of Videha, Nemi. (*Sacred Books of the East*, Vol XIV). Karakandu (9th cent. BC). He was the disciple of Parsvanatha, who was also a warrior – saint. He had saved Karakandu's territory, when Prasenjit the king of Kalinga attacked him. Prasenjit's capital was Kusasthalapur. Now the place is called Bada Kusasthali. The great Ranapa Dance Guru, Padmasree Bhagaban Sahu was born in that village. (Ref. Ashok Kr. Rath, *Odisare Jaina Dharma*, T.T. Book store, Berhampur)

Keeping aside these interlocked historical details, let us veer back to the mythologies. The five sons of Emperor Bali – Anga, Banga, Pundra, and Kalinga, etc. had close contact with each other's territories and lived peacefully. There was no inter-territorial conflict. Kalinga was a region on the bank of river Boitarani. (M.R. Singh, *A Study of the Geographical Data in Early Puranas*, P. 278). The river originates from the Go-Nasika Mountain and flows through Keonjhar and Balasore and merges in the Bay of Bengal at Dhamra. (*Bhanja Mahodaya*. Ed. Banambara Acharya, P.5). Some other scholars are also of the opinion that Boitarani originated from the southern part of Singhbhum. The Puranas, however, mention that the mountain Amarkantak stood on the western side of Kalinga. (i. *Matsya Purana, 5.186, 12,* (ii) *Koorma Purna, 2.39.9,* (iii) *Skandha Purana 5.3.21.7* (iv) *Padma Purana.*)

These various locational references about Kalinga in different mythological records denote that the kalingan territory varied at different points of time. They gained and lost certain territories and the geographical boundary never remained constant.

But Kalinga is mostly referred to as some Janapada on the *Dakshinapatha* and it was in the South- East part of India. *Boudhayana* has mentioned that Kalinga is an impure region and not a single "ashrama" existed there to sustain spiritual learning. (*Boudhayana Dharma Sutra* – 2.2. 16). *Vishnu Purana*, however, mentions that certain *"dvijas"* were also the inhabitants of Kalinga. The king of Kalinga is reported to have joined the marriage ceremony of Pradyumna, the son of Srikrishna. (*Vishnu Purana 5.28. 17*)

The capital of Kalinga was Toshali during Ashoka and Samapa was a seasonal capital. The Hatigumpha Inscription defines Kharvela's Kalinga (150 BC) stretching from Anga and Magadha in the North to Rushika Nagara (on the bank of river Krishnaveni) in the south-east and Pithunda Nagar in the south. However, Kharvela's Kalinga was divided into many small kingdoms where kings of Mathara, Pitrubhakta and Vasistha dynasties ruled. These dynasties ruled till the emergence of the eastern Gangas as a powerful political force. It is interesting to note that the kings of all these dynasties have mentioned themselves as *"Kalingadhipatis"*. Some of the affluent cities of those small kingdoms were Simhapura, Sunagara, Vardhamanapura, Pistapura, Siripura, Devapura, Devarashtra etc. During the reign of the Gangas, places like Kalinga Nagara and Dantapura became the capital cities. The Allahbad inscription (350 A.D.) informs that Kottur, Pistapur, Erandapalli and Debarashtra were famous cities of Kalinga in those days. A large portion of the present Andhra Pradesh belonged to Kalinga.

The territorial borders of Kalinga during the Gupta era stretched from Mahendragiri (Parlakhemundi) to the middle part of Utkala. Pliny informs that Kalinga Nagara or Dandagula was known as the Dandakura and in Pali literature it has been named as Dantapura. Indravarman's (The Ganga King) Jiringi inscription (475-550 A.D) mentions the name of the city as Dantapura. A Jain Muni named Upanga Prajnapana has mentioned a city named Kanchanpur (we do not know whether it is the present Suvarnapura) in Kalinga. The present historians have not taken any interest to identify it. But we are sure that Kalinga had a variegated territorial geography at different periods of history. The *Mahabharata* mentions Rajpur (present Raipur in M.P.) as the capital city of Kalinga. There was, according the Mahabharata, another city called Sobhabati (Mahabharata, *Santi Parva*, 4-2-3)which was Kalinga's capital.

The historians of South India like G.V. Rammurty Pantulu and V.Krishna Rao have identified the present Mukhalingam as the Kalinga Nagar, the ancient capital of Kalinga. But literary works like *Raghuvamsam* and *Dasakumara Charitam* have clearly mentioned that Kalinga Nagar was a coastal city. Mukhalingam is not situated on the seashore.

There is one more Kalinga Nagara on the bank of river Vamsadhara. The coins and utensils retrieved from that place after excavation justify that this Kalinga Nagar was the capital of Kalinga from Kharavela (150 B.C.)to early Gangas of Orissa (Indravarman-1, 496 AD).

The ocean on the eastern part of India was known as the Kalinga Sagara. During the British rule the Bengalies have changed the name as the "Bay of Bengal". The Bengalies, it seems, were intolerant of the glories of Kalinga and availed of the immediate cultural opportunity of changing the name of the sea since the imperial presidency was located at Calcutta and the English merchants knew nothing about the Orissan culture. Colonial records of Indian character appear treacherous at many such cultural crossroads.

Padmasree Satyanarayan Rajguru's lecture at the Ganjam Sahitya Sammelan, 1984, recorded in *Sabara Srikshetra* (June 1, 2003) confirms that Kalinga Nagar was situated on the bank of river Vamsadhara. Samudragupta's invasion of the South terminated at Kalinga Nagar where Umavarma, the Mathara king kept the Kalinga tidy, unified and strong (3rd-4th cent A.D.). Indravarman, the first Ganga king had defeated the Cholas and the Pallavas and commenced his rule in Kalinga in 496 AD. According to the *Classical Age* (Bharatiya Vidya Bhavan) the genealogy of the eastern Gangas is confirmed, and we learn from their inscriptions that they were *Trikalingadhipatis*. This leads to a further discussion about the three Kalingas existing at this historical point.

TRIKALINGA: The Notion of Three Kalingas through Ages

There is no clear record to comprehend what these three-Kalingas meant at what time. Perhaps the Geographical territory of the country was too expansive to manage. Large countries tend to disintegrate since the defeated kings of the invaded areas must have tried to free themselves from Kalingan occupation.

Pliny has mentioned about two Kalingas – '*Macco calingae*' and '*Gangarides calingae*'. Cunningham did not probe into the matter and contended that *Trikalinga* was an ancient name and was also known to Meghasthenes. Perhaps Pliny has taken the idea from the accounts of Meghathenes only.

However, mediaeval literatures mention about Trilinga, Tilinga and Tailinga. Besides, *Markandeya Purana* mentions about Trilinga and *Vayu Purana* provides an account of Tilinga. Raja Sekhara in his *"Bidha Salabhanjika"* (10th cent.) designates the Kalachuri King Keyura Varsha as *Trikalingadhipati*. But this account seems to be a figment of imagination only. Vidyanatha's (14th cent) *Alamkara sastra (Pratapa Rudriya)* eulogizes the Kakatiya king Pratap Rudra Deva as *"Trilinga Desa Paramesvara"*. The Tibbetan historians (like Taranath) and the writers of Persia have also mentioned the word.

Ptolemy in *Geographike Huphegesis*- vii mentioned about *"Tiglastein"* and *"Trilingan"*. But G.E. Gerini in his *Researches on Ptolmy's Geography* of *Eastern Asia* tells that there is a probability that the Telugus, after collaborating with their relative in Kalinga might have created another kingdom called *Trikalinga*.

The copper grants available have given us the most authentic record. The Somavamsi king Janmejaya in his Brahmesvar Temple inscription eulogizes himself as *Trilingadhipa*. Late Dr. Satyanarayan Rajguru reads the inscription as *Trikalinga dhipa*. Since Dr. Rajguru was able to read Telugu and Tamil inscriptions, he informs us about lots of South Indian rock writings in which the word Trikalinga occurs. Raja Singaya Nayaka's Akkalpundi grant (1368 AD) mentions two words: *"Desastrilinganama"* and *"Trilinga deshadhipati."* Later, Alexander Cunnigham mentions in *Archaelogical survey Report, Vol –XVI* that the Greek word *Trilingan* and the Sanskrit *Trikalinga* and *Trilinga* refer to the same territory.

Since the western historians have written histories on guesswork, *Trikalinga* would, thus, it seems, lapse into a fictional territory, which it is not. The Sri Rangam grants (1358 AD) define the borders of *Tiling* (*Trikalinga*) as follows: Maharashtra stands at its west, Kalinga to its east, Pandya to the South and Kanyakubja to its north.

The records of Bajrahasta Deva and Raja Raja -1 state that Guna Maharnava (an ancient king of Ganga dynasty) came from Trikalinga. *Gangavamsavali* provides details of these kings and states their origins at Trikalinga. Such records prove that Trikalinga was a separate country and it was situated to the western side of Kalinga.

Prof. Nabin Kumar Sahu draws our attention to a manuscript of *Brahmanda Purana* preserved in the State Museum at Bhubaneswar. The manuscript defines the borders of Kalinga in a different manner. The territory between river Jhanjabati and river Rushikulya is called Kalinga and the area from Jhanjabati to river Vedamati is called Trikalinga.

Jhanjabati is a tributary of river Nagabali and it flows in the eastern region of Koraput. The present Indravati River is identified as Vedamati. Indravati flows to the western side of Koraput and flows through Bastar (Madhya Pradesh). Its name changes in Maharashtra and finally it mingles with river Godavari. Prof. Sahu is of the opinion that the Trikalinga area, by the 6th century AD, can be identified geographically extending from river Jhanjabati to Vedamati.

Traces of the Culture of Kalinga (between Jhanjavati and Rushikulya):

Rushikulya flows from Rushimala Mountain of present Baliguda near which two kingdoms of Katingia and Gadapur existed. The Rushimala Parvata was a part of the Eastern Ghats and it extends up to Suvarnapur in the west. River Rushikulya, then, flows towards the east touching kingdoms of Badagada, Sorada, Dharakote, Aska and it finally mingles with the Bay of Bengal at the Ganjam coast.

Rushikulya is considered as a sacred river in Boudh, Phulbani and Ganjam districts. According to mythical records, Prajapati, the primal creator, procreated Manu from his own body and a sage named Kardama from his shadow. The reference to Kardama can be found in the *Sri Stotra* of *Rik Veda*. Rishi Kardama married Manu's daughter Devahuti and lived at the foot of Rishimala Hills. Thus goes the mythic account. The fountain, which sage Kardama generated out of his willful energy, was later called Rushikulya.

Rushikulya flowed from a state called Khidisingi. In the days of yore, Vasistha, the royal priest of the Suryavamsi kings, used to live in that area. According to Sri Gouri Shankar Mishra (*Ganjam Itihasa Parikrama*, 2003), a local historian of repute, the regnal power of the kings of Nala dynasty declined around 500 AD at Pushkari, identified as Podagada in Umarkote block. King Skandavarman (C 475-500 A.D.) surrendered Podagada and left the area. The Chalukyas defeated them.

The kings of the Nala dynasty, then, came to Rajim and ruled over there according to the inscriptions of Rajiblochan Temple. A branch of this defeated dynasty entered into the remote forests of Baliguda around 900 A.D. and established a kingdom called Khindirasringa. Raja Bhima Sena Deva of the Nala dynasty has brought out the Pandiapathara copper grant from its capital Bhimpur. Bhimpur is identified as Bhima Nagara or Bhibhinagada of Sanakhemundi estate. One can still discern the remnants of the place of the Nala Kings.

Dhabaleswar temple of Siva, built by Raja Bhima Sena Deba (Nala Dynasty) also stands there as an evidence.

The Khindirasrunga area was under the Bhowmakara's but they lost control over this mountainous zone by the time the successors of Vilasa Tunga (C. 700 AD) like Bhimasena Deba conquered over Khindirisringa. These kings ruled over Koraput and Bastar districts of Madhya Pradesh.

The copper grants found from Chhapali Saranavati village informs that Prithvi Bhanja Dev, Ripu Dhavala and Narendra Dhabala of Nala dynasty ruled over there till 1070 A.D. The 6th king of the Early Ganga dynasty, Devendravarman, son of Gunarnava and grandson of Indravarman –IV conquered Khindirsrunga in 1070 AD The Nalas were driven out and Devendravarman ruled over there.

The Nalas gradually weakened and moved in the jungles occupying small unclaimed areas. The history of this part of Kalinga is available in the palace records of Dharakote, Badagada and Sheragada. The regional records from the above palaces show that Sobhachandra Dev of Nala dynasty established a very small kingdom in 1168 A.D. with its capital at Bajrakona, situated on the bank of a small river called Jarau in the present-day Surada. But he never refrained from calling himself the king of Khindisringa or Khidisingi.(Ref. GourishankarMishra,*Ganjam Itihasa Parikrama,2003*)

King Baliarsingh of this fragmented Khidisingi divided his territory into four parts to distribute them among his sons. Then emerged four independent kingdoms in 1576 A.D: Badagada, Surada, Dharakote and Seragada. The Surada kingdom collapsed in 1833. But the Nala dynasty survives in the other four kingdoms, though their estates have been taken away since 1952.

After 1576 Sorada was called an *Agala* and Rajkumar Abhay Singh, a devotee of Kondhuni Dei, was appointed as its sardar. In 1745, the Nala King (Gadadhar Singh) was assassinated and Kunjabihari Singh was enthroned (1745-1815). Kunja Singh did not have any children and his estate (Agala) was auctioned in 1833. Dhananjay Bhanja of

Ghumusar bought Surada payng 8000 rupees. The fort of the king of Surada was built at Suramoni, a place 8 Kms away from Surada.

Dharakote was another famous estate of the Nala dynasty situated 24 Kms away from Surada to the east. But a copper grant of Narendra Dhabala's time (935 AD-960 AD) informs that there was a feudatory small kingdom under him measuring 24 square *krosas* (around 28 sq. kms), but the name reads either as Gomunda or Momunda in the copergrant. A Nagavamsi King, Ranaka Ghomgaka ruled over that *mandala*. The capital of Gomunda was named after the primal man (*Adi Purusha*) of the Naga dynasty – Dharanendra. Ranaka Ghomgaka named the capital as Dharanai and Dharanamba later, the *mandala* was named like the other Naga Mandalas – *Chakrakote* and *Erakote*. They changed the name to that kind of a rhyming name: Dharakote. To the southern side of this capital called Dharakote, there stands a mountain named Subalaya (locally called Sulia) of the eastern ghat that stretches up to Subarnapur and to the north of this fort, river Rushikulya flows.

The Nala Kings were Saivites. Hence through out the shore of Rishikulya, one would discover about more than 50 temples of lord Siva. Surada's Buddhalingesvara and Dhabalesvara of Singipur were built by Narendra Dhabala of Nala dynasty (935-960 AD). Besides Muktesvar of Putu, Garudesvara of Panibandha, Siddhesvara of Balisira and Suvarneswar of Aska are famous as well as ancient temples of the Nala period.

Raja Jaya Simha (1732-1758 AD) of Dharakote had built the famous Svapnesvara temple on the bank of a huge pond called "Neliabandha". Nelia bandha, situated to the Eastern side of the Nala palace of Dharakote (built in Cuddappa stones and marble) is like a miniature lake situated on the foot of Subalaya mountain range. The Subalaya mountain range is full of mango trees that yield mangoes of different varieties. This jungle of Mango trees stretching for hundreds of kilometers till the kingdoms of Katingia, Gadapur(the temperature falls down to zero degree in the winter and snow falls there)and the present Suvarnapur and sustain the lives of the poor highlanders during the summer. Balukesvara and Visveswara are two other temples of Siba at Dharakote. Tilottamadeipur's Baidyanatha, Sriloknath (Sahaspur), Chandrakalpesvara(Gangapur),Gangadhar (Sindurapalli), Neelakanthes vara (Panchasinghpur), Tribidhesvar, Ramesvar, Pudugesvar, Patalesvar, Belesvar, Brahmesvar, Narmadesvar (Brahmana Chhai), Kuberesvar (Kanjiama), Uttaresvar (Pitala and Pandia), Sakalesvar (Deulapali) Tumbesvar of Pratapur, Astasambhu (Athagada), Mahalingeswar (Jilunda), Kalesvar (Kharida), Dandesvar (Kodala), Gunesvar (Sikula), Bholesvar (Bolasara), Muktesvar (Hatiota), Manikesvar (Fasi), Svapnesvar (Polasara), Dhabalesvar(Bhima nagar) Sakalesvar (Bikrampur), Dakhinesvar (Rambha), Balukesvar (Khallikote) Siddhesvar (Beguniapada), Muktesvar (Bhejiput), Dakhinesvar, Makaresvar, Buddhesvar, Siddhesvar and Batesvars are few temples of Siva that are built on the bank of Rushikulya, the southern border of Kalinga.

The other accounts are not available to this author. But, it is proved that the kings of Nala dynasty were Saivites and Nagas. It is interesting to note that the Naga dynasties ruled in present Tamilnadu and Andhra in ancient times and they had commercial relation with the people of Suktimati civilization (1000 B.C.). Kalinga had strong relationship with Trikalinga and other southern countries.

Pt. Neelakantha Das and some other local scholars have interpreted that the three Kalingas are Kangoda, Kosala and Utkala. This interpretation is euphoric and designed strategically to integrate the political Orissa by investing a sense of false history into their racial consciousness. However, the northern part of Kalinga was known as Kangoda in ancient times and its culture is traceable at Puri and in the temple of Jagannatha. The temple of Jagannatha includes the rituals introduced by a Kalingan king named Chodaganga Deva.

But the historians of Orissa are silent about the northern Kalinga or Kangoda through the history of another dynasty called the Sailodhavas that came to light from nine inscriptions of Kangoda. These inscriptions are (I) Ganjam and (II) Khurda plates issued by Madhavaraja Sainyabhita (III) Buguda and (IV) Malagrama plates issued by Madhava Burman Sainyabhita (V) Parikud plates of Madhyama Raja (VI) Kondedda (VII) Puri and (VIII) Nivina plates issued by Dharmraja Manabhita, and lastly (IX) Tekkali plates issues by Madhyama Raja.

The first of these plates is dated in the Gupta year 300 (619-20 A.D.). The issue of these plates is described as Mahasamanta Madhava Raja, son of Maharaja Ayusobhita and grand son of Mahasamanta Madhabaraja. The humble feudatory titles, "Maharaja" and "Mahasamanta" clearly show that the early Sailodbhavas acknowledged the suzerainty of some over lord.

The Ganjam plates refer to Maharajadhiraja Sri Sasanka, which shows that the Suzerain overlord of Madhavaraja, who issued the plates was the illustrious Gauda king Sasanka, the mighty adversary of Harsabardhana. But epigraphic records show that Southern Tosala, which comprised Kangoda Mandala was in the possession of Parama Mahesvara Sri Sagguyayyana of the Mana dynasty in the year 283 of the Gupta era (620-03 A,D.)

However, records, are clear to the fact that after the death of Sasanka in 637 AD, when Hiuen Tsang visited this part of India, the Sailodbhavas were granted independence. The Buddhist tourist passed through the Kangoda Mandala in or about 639 AD.

Harsavardhana annexed Kangoda in 642-43 A.D. and thus, the rule of the Sailodbhavas came to end by the middle of 7th Century. The Buguga plates of Madhavavarman Srinivasa show that Kangoda Mandala again came to be ruled by the Sailodhava dynasty about the middle of the 9th century. Madhav Burman was the most famous king of this dynasty and "he performed Asvamedha sacrifice", which shows that his eminence among his neighbouring kngs was a fact.

The land he granted by the Parikuda plates was

situated in the *Kataka-bhukti-visaya*, which may be identified as modern Cuttack. In that case we have to suppose that the Sailodbhava Kingdom extended upto Mahanadi River during the reign of Madhyamaraja- I (Hara Prasad Ganguly, "The Sailodbhavas and their contemporaries in Kangoda", *IHQ, Vol.xxxiii, No. 3, Sept, 1957).* The Buguda plates of Madhava Varman describes how Pulindasena, an inhabitant of Kalinga, was endowed with many personal virtues, eg. A lofty stature, strong arms and broad chest, but nevertheless did not convert sovereignty for himself, worshipped Brahman with the result that the God created out of pieces of rock (silasakala) the Lord Sailodbhava, the founder of a dynasty. This story is also repeated in the Parikud plates of Madhyamaraja.

The Pasupati inscription dated the year 153 of the Harsha era informs us that king Harsa of Bhagadatta dynasty held sway over Gauda, Udra, Kalinga and Kosala. Though Kangoda is not mentioned in this list of countries, the simultaneous reference to Kalinga and Udra, the Southern and Northern parts of modern Orissa, may allow us to include Kangoda Mandala in the realm under Harsa. That this establishment of Harsa's power in Orissa was the origin of Kara rule in Kangoda Mandala is made clear by the Chaurasi grant of Sivakara (JBORS, 1928, P. 304), where in the king is described as belonging to the Bhagadatta family. The history of this new royal family is known from several inscriptions of which the earliest appears to be the Neulpur grant *(E.I.XV.PP-1-8)* of Subhakara. The inscription is undated, but Hara Prasad Ganguly fixes on paleographic grounds to have been issued in the 8th century A.D. In this inscription, king Subhakara is described as a "parama Saugata" and "Maharaja". Subhakara ruled up to 795 A.D.

From the internal evidence of the Sailodbhava records, it is possible to determine the extent of their kingdom. Six *Vishayas* are mentioned. Krushnagiri, (near Althagada, according to Rajguru), Khidinagahar (in the Kodala Taluk) Varttani (Boirani or Kavisuryanagar), Gudda (Papuni, Khadira Pattaka and Khairapati Villages), Thorana (Thorabonga) and

Kataka-bhukti. The Sailodbhavas were the followers of the Brahminical faith.

As we journey through the passages of time in Kalinga, we meet on the bank of river Vamsadhara, a city named Kalinga Nagar. It was also known in the ancient times as the *Mukhalinga Kshetra*. Kamarnava-II of the Ganga dynasty (803-853 AD) built it and his grandson Vajrahastadeva (859-874 AD) built Madhukesa Siva temple. Mukhalingam is situated to the south west of Parlakhemundi in the Srikakulam district of Andhra Pradesh. Mukhalingam fort (the capital, Kalinga nagara) was 3.5 K.m.s long and its width was 1.5 Kms. In those days Mukhalingam was known as the Dakshina Kasi Peetha. The lingam that emerged there automatically as a stone appears like the face of Lord Siva. This famous religious centre at Kalinga Nagara was known as "Gobinda Kanan" in Satya yuga, as "Madhukesvar" in Tretaya Yuga, as "Jayanti Kshetra" in Dvapara Yuga and is known as Mukhalingam in Kaliyuga. " Madhukesvara" is also known as "Madhu Kalinga".

The present Bay of Bengal was known as Kalinga Sagara since the hoary days. It is only in the colonial times that the Bengalies changed the name as a part of their usual cultural politics to inflate their own identity. Otherwise, they would not have named the tiger as the "Royal Bengal Tiger". Kalinga Nagara was earlier known as Gokarna Nagar since this Siva temple was called Gokarneswar according to *Kshetra Mahatmya*. Kalinga Nagara, Dantapur (another capital of Kalinga) and Nagari Kataka (another capital) were famous and from these changing names we figure out that the capital of Kalinga changed from time to time to suit the requirements of administration.

Now the place is popularly known as Jayantipur. Dantapur is a demolished heap of soil now, situated on the Srikakulam – Amdalbalasa road. The place is called in Telugu as Dantavrintani Kota. An inscription found from Kalinga Nagar written in nagari alphabets and issued by Ananta Burman Chodaganga Deva reads as follows:"*Svasti Srimad Kalinga Nagarat parama Mahesvara Parama Bhattaraka*

Maharajadhiraja Trikalingadhipatih Srimad Ananta Burma Maharaja Chodaganga Devah Kusali Samasta amatya pramukha Janapadanahuya Samajnapayatih viditam astu vabatam xxx Koti Sthana Nivasi Jajyakula Samudbhuta Karibala Nayaka Putrau Gundyana Potaye Namanau tavyam tayo vangnyuna samakshaya bhogaya trikalinga Deva bhoga nibarddhanartakam Deva ganikaya gundyana varya urna kotinattam guropi putrivyanda, bhartruvyam vadyakara gayika namadhipatyam yavat Chandra taraka asmabhi dattam iti".

It is remarkable in this Sanskrit inscription to note that Madhukesvar is addressed as "Trikalinga deva" and the king has given the grant of offerings to the God. The grant includes a Devadasi, a singer and a percussionist for the daily service of the God. Lord Madhukesvar is treated in the inscription as a king.

Such a statement generates a belief that the kings of Kalinga were great Saivites. Chodaganga Deva had built another temple in the northest border of his territory in Kalinga, at Puri, the temple of Jagannatha. Though this temple has been identified as one of the four *dhamas* of India and the poets situate it in Utkala, its rituals and concepts are Kalingan and the sculptors were, too, Kalingans.

Chodaganga Deva knew it well that in the mediaeval times building up a state was difficult. In the politico-cultural context of Kalinga of those days, it was still greater a challenge. The Mughal power was gathering momentum in Bengal. The Western part known as Kosala was ruled by the Kalachuri kings and before 1212 AD, a Kakateeya leader had already invaded a part of South Kalinga, (Parabrahma Sastry, P.V. *The kakatiyas*, the Government of Andhra Pradesh, Hyderabad, 1978, P. 109-110)

Ananga Bhima Deva – III found it quite a challenging job to build up his position in Kangoda or in Northern Kalinga, which was culturally and linguistically different. The inscriptions available so far in connection with Ganga administration and about the construction of the Jagannatha Temple informs that Anant varma Chodanga Deva and

Ananga Bhima –III adopted the strategy of surrendering their kingships at the feet of Jagannatha by declaring themselves as a "Ravuta" (Rauta"). N. Mukunda Rao, in his book, *Kalinga under the eastern Gangas, ca 900 A.D.-1200 A.D.*(1991, Delhi) informs, "It is even to be seen in that, the king Ananta Varma Chodanga called himself a mere deputy of the God Jagannatha by assuming the title "Ravuta", who, if right, is the first king ever to adopt such a title among all the known sovereigns of the Ganga dynasty thereby initiating such a reckoning unlike Anangabhima – III as opined by the scholars" (P. 173-174). In the "foreword" of this book Herman Kulke has recorded, "Historians were of the opinion that king Anangabhima – III in the early 13th century for the first time called himself a *rauta* or deputy of Lord Jagannatha..." shows that already Ananta varman Chodaganga assumed this title in the year 1139, obviously shortly after he had begun the construction of the monumental temple at Puri."

Prof. Karuna Sagar Behera, has read the inscription of the Nrusimha temple and reached the same opinion that Anangavarma Choda Ganga Deva was the first king to adopt such a "devine-right" theory of kingship. The Vijayanagar inscription written in Sakabda 1061 or 1137 also records, "*Ravuta Raju*" (Telugu). Dr. Satyanarayana Rajguru, in his *Inscriptions of Orissa-Vol-III, part-I, No. 176*, also admits the same thing (p. 198) – that the king designates himself as Chodaganga Rautray. Dr.- Kailash Chandra Dash, however does not admit the interpretation and records that the title, instead of being a symbol of humility may be taken as a strategic pronouncement of his power to assert himself as "*Maharajadhiraja*" and "*Rajaparamesvara*". Dash adds further that the title "Rautray" cannot be accepted as a religious conversion of the king as a "*Parama Vaishnava*". In that case, this author would also not admit Ashoka's transformation from "*Chandasoka*" to "*Dharmasoka*" as a real change of heart.It might have been a pure Brahminical politics or just a political strategy of the court of Pataliputra to expiate Ashoka's sin of his greed for imported goods available in Kalinga, a state full of ports on the "Kalinga Sagara". (Hell with the people who have changed the name as "the Bay of Bengal".) Ashoka's killing of the Kalingans was so beastly an act that without such stone inscriptions he could not have ruled over this land. His conversion into Buddhism and declaration of peace is absolutely pretentious and nothing but a political game. Such examples are plentifully available in the post September-11th Middle East of the 21st century.

Like Ashoka, the Emperor, Ananga Bhima Deva was also tactically able to pool all kinds of support from the subjects of Kalinga. Besides, the consecration of the *Chaturdha Murti* (God with quadruple concept) made Orissa a famous *Purushottama Kshetra* of India. The Mediaeval Kalingans considered *spirituality* a greater power than *politics*. The contemporary politicians, perhaps, hybridized in moral genetics have started assuming themselves as supermen within the prison houses of their subjective ego. A police officer, too, considers him as someone greater than a biped.

To the advantage of Ananga Bhima, Jagannatha became the overlord and Orissa acquired the identity of "Jagannatha Orissa". The king of Nepal, Vasanta Deva was influenced by Samkaracharya and became a disciple of Jagannatha. He offered *Brahma Sila* or *Saligrama* (black stone with a natural hole, worshipped as the symbol of divinity) for Balabhadra and Subhadra and thus, he is authorized to perform the rituals of Jagannatha personally in the temple whenever he visited Puri temple. The musk that is used in the inner space of the wooden images is still supplied from the palace of the king of Nepal. The king of Nepal has also offered a large bell with Nepali inscription on it on the day of *Magha, Sukla, dvadasi* of 1691. The bell is still there on the *Navikata Mandapa* of the temple. The king has also donated an icon of Nrusimha, which is now worshipped on the bank of Markanda pond at Puri.

The kings of Varanasi / Kasi have paid their homage to Lord Jagannatha by having introduced a car festival at Chowmuhani. Besides, to the south side of Varanasi a temple of Jagannatha has been built by Baba Brahmachari, a Marahatta

Guru, financed by the king. Besides the Durga temple of Rama Nagar contains the etchings of Jagannatha. A copper plate issued by Kasiraja Prabhu Narayana Singh mentions. *"Srimad Viswanatheika Nayaka Maharajahdhiraja Sri Kasi Naresa Prabhu narayana Deva.*

Chandrarbhunidhibhu sange vaikramabde tapasmite Jagannatha Puri bhaktya darsanarthe maya sivam xxx Prabhu Narayana singha Kasirajah / Bhurasa samkatakshana vatsare Pingala vidhe / Dadami Mudrita lekha vaisakha seeta pakshatau." Etc.

The Maharajahs of Jaipur, Rajastan have been worshipping Jagannatha since last 6/7 hundred years. King Madho Singh Bahadur used to come to Puri on a horse and used to distribute lots of things to people at places where he stayed. Once he stayed few miles away from Puri and he was caught with cholera. Some of his servitors passed away. The king, weakened in cholera prayed the Lord and an old man with a five-coloured stick appeared at the spot and said, "Dear devotee! The Lord is pleased over you for your devotion. He has given you this five-coloured stick. All the inauspecious sufferings shall be dispelled if you keep this with you."

King Madho Singh reached Puri safely and paid his visit to the Lord. He offered lots of property to the temple and gave the five-coloured stick to his *teerthaguru* (the Guru at the pilgrimage). One Mr. Shadhangi of Bira Gobindapur is still known as *"Pancharangi chhadidar"*. Later he had been to Jaipur, built a small temple of Jagannatha at Jaipur and established a cultural relationship with Puri.

The King of Punjab, Punjab Kesari Ranjit Singh Bahadur, after defeating Lord Delhousie in 1848, had come to Puri, paid a visit to the Lord and has built a Math (Monastery called The Punjabi Math at Puri. After going back, he donated a piece of diamond to the Lord. Later, the British government took away the diamond to England. (Sadasiv Rath Sharma "Rajadhiraja Jagannatha", *Sabara Srikshetra,* Sept 1, 2005). An inscription at the Western gate of the Jagannatha temple reads: *"Teropanth Sudhi Mafiq San 1219 Sambatsya Srimad Jagannatha*

Svami Ka Maharaj Ranjit Singh bahadur ka nidrariketa Smarka Jaddisa Rama Rupasya Paschima dvarake Vanabacha.

The kings of Nagpur, Raghuji Bhosle Sivaji Pandit and Bhavani Pandit used to visit the Lord very often, but the *Chhapana Bhogi Maharashtra Teerthaguru* consecrated an icon of Jagannatha there and the members of the royal family ceased to come to Puri.

Maharaja Keerti Chandra's (the king of Vardhaman) mother was a great devotee of Jagannatha, and thus the king had started celebrating the car festival at Kanchan Nagar near Vardhaman / Burdwan. Keertichandra had donated the images of Radha Krishna and the images are worshipped in *Koormabedha* of the temple premises. He also built the steps of the Markandeya Sarovar (pond) of Puri. Kirti Chandra passed away in 1780 A.D.

The king of Bikanir had developed a cultural relationship with Puri by appointing Raghunath Dash Atmaram as the *Teerthaguru* of Puri. The king of Rewa had established a free food centre on the grand road and Svamigal kings of Andhra had donated land for the Lord vide Record No. 2. Besides, the kings of Mysore, Ranchi and Kashmir have contributed immensely for the daily offerings of the Lord.

The list would be very long for this book. However, the contention of providing such information is to establish that Anant Burman Chodaganga Deva's construction of the temple at the Northern border of Kalinga was a great achievement in the sense that the temple became famous throughout the country and it attracted royal patronage from all around. Further, the temple had become a centre of religious-political attacks at different periods of foreign invasion. But the temple of Jagannatha has remained the centre of Odia Culture since then.

The *Simhasana* (the altar) of the Lords (there are four lords: Jagannatha, Balabhadra, Subhadra, the sister and Sudarsana) is made of a single *Sila-Chakra* and the Vedic figure vaitaneya is consecrated as the *vahana*. The offerings here are called *Mahaprasad* after they are given to Goddess Vimala.

Besides the 4 icons mentioned above, three other deities are also worshipped on the pedestal: Laxmi, Bhoodeva and Madhava. In short, the temple is famous for these *Saptadha moorties* (seven deities).

Dr. Bemimadhab Padhi, making a comparative analysis between Lord Venkatesvara and Lord Jagannatha, states that the Lord Venkateswara is worshipped for *artha* (wealth) and *Kama* (fulfillment of desire) while Jagannatha is worshipped for *Moksha* (salvation)

Besides, the first worshipper of this Lord was a tribal *sabara*, a jungle-dweller of non-Vedic *Vratya* Origin. Visvabasu, (details given in the micro history of Kantilo), the tribal worshipper never thought this Lord as some one larger than him. His conception of God was not only anthropomorphic, but also as some one exactly like him. In summer Jagannatha takes a ritual bath in *Chandan* Pond; in winter woolen clothes are offered and in monsoon he suffers from eye-infection (*Netrotsava*). Nothing is *divya* and supernatural in the temple rituals. Yet its *Prasada* (offered food) is called *"Kaivalya"* and putting it in the mouth is *Kaivalya Prapti*, attainment of the *Svarga*, here, in this temple, in this earth and life, what the Westerners call a *"Spiritual-mundi"* (Paradise in mundaneness).

The most unique feature of this Jagannatha is that its images are made of *"daru"* (wood) and they are changed every twelve years. As an image/symbol made of wood, His worship is related to "tree-worship" of the primordial tribal people. Further, the Lord is worshipped as Ganesha, as Siva, as Krishna and on *Pushyabhiseka Poornima* as well as on Thursday (*Ekadasi*) (the eleventh Day) he is worshipped as Sri Rama. Subhadra turns into Sita, not a sister, but a wife. According to *Skandha Purana (Suta Samhita)* and *Indra Neelamoni Purana*, Nrusimha Mantra worships Sri Jagannatha. The founder of this *Peetha*, the mythical king, Indradyumna envisioned Lord Jagannatha as Nrusimha. Hence Jagannatha is connected to the concept of Nrusimha (the Man-lion God) in everyday rituals. *Nrusimha Mantra* is used as the "archa-mantra" or the *mantaraja* for the *Purushottama Kshetra*. At the Southgate Pandu

Nrusimha, in the North Adi Nrusimha, Chakra Nrusimha in the east and at the Western gate Ugranisa Nrusimha are fixed. On the Vaisakh Sula Dasami, Jagannatha transforms into Nrusimha and is worshipped as Nrusimha.

This compendium of images is religiously admitted by all the sects and He is worshipped by the Buddhists, the Jains, the Saivites, the Saktas, the Vaishnabas and funnily enough, the *Soonya Vadis* (believers of the concept of void) also accept this Lord as their own. In this temple Madhaba (Lord Jagannatha) is worshipped as Bhairaba and conjoined with Durga (Vimala) and yet, on the festival of Rukmini Bibaha (Marriage of Rukmini) Jagannatha transforms himself as Madan Mohan (Srikrishna) and Lakshmi transforms into Rukmini.

As a deity of the tribal Sabara Viswabasu, Jagannatha was worshipped according to Tantrik rituals. So is he worshipped in the temple: *Vimala Sa Mahadevi Jagannatha Stu Bhairaba* As mentioned in *Sadhanamala* (a Vajrayana Tantra book), there are four major *Tantrik Peethas* in India where in the Primal Energy manifests herself: Uddiyana (Vimala – she is also at Kanyakumari), Jullundur (Jwalamukhi), Kamaroopa (Kamakshya) and Poornagiri (Poornesvari).

The most controversial aspect of this temple is the presence of the deity called Subhadra – as a sister and as the consort (Laxmi, Bhairabi etc). She is the *yogamaya* and *Vishnu – Sakti* at the *Purushottam Kshetra*. She is not a mythological character here (as Arjuna's wife). The Primal Energy of creation has always been conceived as the "unitary cause", as (*Hiranya-garbha-samavartagre*, but He, the Energy "desired" to diffuse himself/multiply himself/herself into the collective psyche of his creation: *"Ekoham, bahushyam"*. As a result the first Man Prajapati manifested as the "Desire". We know how in the 8th *Mandala* of *Rikveda*, Prajapati copulates with his daughter *Ushas*.

As this mystery of creation unfolds itself, the boundary lines of the societal relations collapse and there only remain a "Man" and a "woman". The first man and the first woman were being born out of a single *Desire*, who is genetically a brother and a sister. Yet, they operated physically as man and wife for procreation. This root of *Desire* is known in Hindu pantheon as the unification of the *Brahma-Chaitanya* (Supra consciousness) and the *Jiva chaitanya* (the physical consciousness). The centre of this unification is *illusion*. Illusion is conceived as the Yogamaya (*Maya/Vishnu Shakti* / Primal Energy in the image of Subhadra.)

It is reiterated here that the figures of Jagannatha, Balabhadra, Subhadra and Sudarsana are not anthropomorphic. They did not exist earlier in Viswabasu's (the tribal worshipper) consciousness as such. The temple contains only symbolic forms. Samkaracharya was attracted to *Purushottam Kshetra* and composed the *stotra* "*Kadachit Kalindi tata bipino...*" only by this evidence of symbol-worship.

In most of our Tantrik scriptures, Devi is introduced spatially as *"Kampilya-Vasini"*, the inhabitant and queen of an empire called *Kampilya*. Connotatively, *"Kampilya"* means vibration. This means that the goddess of creation stays in the field of vibration. The act of unification of the *brahma-chaitanya* and the *Jiva-Chaitanya* (or the *supra consciousness* with the *physical consciousness)* occurs on a field of vibration only and the "Desire" for creation stays repressed giving preference to the act of unification. This repressed desire surfaces as "Illusion", the unmanifest and the hazy, the twilight. In Vayabeeya *Samhita* the Primal Energy is *"Mahamaya cha Maya cha Prakritistriguneti cha."* (*Mahamaya, Prakriti* or nature and Maya are the three qualities of the same Energy)

At the "Peetha" of Subhadra, a "Yantra" has been kept. The pot of offerings is kept over there according to the *Sastras*: "*Bhoomaupari visarga kampilya bilikhyam tadupari patra-traya samsthapya, jala gandhakshata prakshepahmiti.*" This sentence in Sanskrit instructs the write "visarga kampilya" on the ground (so, there is a yantra), which grammatically defines "*Kampilya*" as a "Visarga" alphabetical sign, a *"matra"*(that functions like a vowel) for joining/unification of two words. The *maya-Sakti* (the power of illusion) exists here as *"visarga-Sajnatah"*, as the grammatical sign of unification. (The Hindu religion and Tantrik science accept geometry and alphabets as energy points; now you may imagine how stupid is Jacques Derrida's theory of Deconstruction! How can you alienate "meaning" from a "word"?)

Subhadra, is, thus "*Bhagini-Stree-Prayartika*", the sister-cum-mother symbolized as *Yoni* (Vagina) for all the "*bhootas*" (earthly beings). The culture of Kalinga and later, the cultures of Utkala and Kosala added to it to formulate a compendium, which this book fails to embody for want of space.

The Odias worship this *Maya*, this Illusion/mystery/unmanifest symbolic vagina, if you prefer to designate it so. To quote *Uma Samhita*: "*Tanmaya Parama Vidya Sarbatra-Vyapini Mune* (Oh, the scholastic sages of the world, that *Maya* is the ultimate knowledge and she is all pervasive).

But the hermeneutics on Subhadra takes a U-turn in Kosala, the Western part of post-1936 Orissa. Late Prof. Prahallad Pradhan situates Subhadra in the Buddhists' space. This great scholar/Professor from the Western Orissa quotes a Buddhist scripture captioned, *Yogavali*, published by *Gaekward Prachya Granthavali* series, wherein we find 26 Buddhist *Mandalas*. Three of those *Mandalas* named *Sambar mandala, Shat-chakravarti mandala* and *Kala-chakara mandala* bring the reference to this goddess (Subhadra).

"Kala-chakara"(There is a Buddhist pantheon called "Kalachakrayana") has a deity called Kalachakra. A Prajnadevi named Viswamata embraces him. She dances on the body of Kamesvara (the lord of desire) and Mahesvar (Siva) and their two spouses Rati and Gouri are found sitting at their feet in a dejected mood and invoke *Kalachakra*. This is the first *Chakra* (circle). Then comes the *Vangmandala* (the circle of uttered words) and the third circle (charka) is *Kaya Mandala* (the circle of the physical body). Subhadra appears in the second *mandala* called *Vangmandala*. There are eight lotus flowers on eight directions and each lotus has eight petals on which lots of Hindu Gods and their spouses are found in embracing position. Most of the Devis and Lords are from

Hindu Brahminical order, but strange counter parts embrace them: Indra embraces Goddess Charchika and Kartikeya embraces Lakshmi. Subhadra figures on the eight petal of the lotus spaced in the Nairuta direction (the angle in between the west and the south is called nairuta). Like all other deities *Kalachakra* Subhadra has four arms and three eyes. She sits in *"Lalitasana"* and her colour is red. Dr. Pradhan reaches at a decision after making multiple references that Subhadra's colour is white.

The description of the six charkas mentions four *saktis*: Shyamadevi, Subhadra, Hayarnoh, Kharakanya. Since these goddesses are found sitting on the dead body of Visvabja Surya, the colour of Subhadra is supposed to be white.]

Subhadra also appears in *Sambar Mandala*. This *Mandala* has theee charkas " (a) *Antarnivista chitta-Chakra* (b) *Vak-Chakra* and (c) *Kayachakra*. The *Vakchakra* lotus has eight petals on which sit eight Gods with their energy consorts. (i) *Ankuraka-Airavati* (ii) *Vajra Bhairaba – mahabhairabi* (iii) *Mahaveera-Vayubega* (iv) *Vajra Humkara –* Sura-bhakshi (v) *Subhadra – Shyamadevi* (vi) *Bajraprabha – Subhadra* (vii) *Mahabhairaba- hayakarna* (viii) *Birupaksha – Khaganana*.

The forms of these Gods and Goddess are described. In short, the Goddesses (including Subhadra) are three-eyed, one-headed two armed and nude. They have fiery shapes and their locks are untied. They take the marks of garlands consisting of human heads. They put on *Mekhala, Saracha* and *Ghurghura* (untranslatable ornaments)

These details of *Kala-chakara* and *Sambara charka tantras* of the Buddhists Mahayanis provide us some notions about the concept of Subhadra, her form and shape as well as the conceptual differences between the Brahminical and the Buddhists orders.

Besides, we are also informed how the temple of Jagannatha was designed to contain the compendium of all faiths – the Brahminical as well as the Buddhist. The culture of Kalinga, too, had a very broad format that was capable of embodying philosophically opposing points of view.

All these details, however, do not complete our study of Kalingan culture. Further accounts shall, therefore be given in the subsequent chapters, especially in chapters XII and XIII.

Kalinga in the Mythologies

The culture of Kalinga was much more ancient. One can find the name of Kalinga mentioned in *Mahabharata*
Tatah Samudrateerena Jagam vasudhadhipah
Bhratruvih Sahito veerah Kalingan Pratibharata.
Lomasa Uvacha:
Ete Kalingah Kaunteya yatra Baitarani nadi
Yatrah Jajata dharmopi devarchharna metyavai
Kalinga was a sacred land and Baitarani was its sacred river.

In an India divided by into cultural oppositions, that of the North and the South, Orissa enjoys a unique position since it neither belongs to the Aryans of the North, nor does it belong to the Dravidian culture of the South. On the contrary, it is a bridge between the two, not only because of its geographical placement, but, it has remained a bridge also from the linguistic, cultural and religious points of view. It has withstood the invasions from both the South and the North and has appropriated the religious and spiritual essences of the rishis from the South and the North.

Evidences from Archaeology: Odiya Culture and History

As we enter into the third century B.C, archacological evidences are available to focus on Orissan culture. Kalinga figured in the pages of Indian history because of Ashoka's battle, for more of its remorseful devastations than for Ashoka's transformation, if at all there was any. This grandson of Chandragupta Maurya (273B.C-236 B.C) slaughtered the inhabitants of Kalinga in the eighth year of his reign.

According to *Discovery of India* "Kalinga lay on the eastern coast of India, between the Mahanadi, Godavari and Kishna rivers." (*Glimpses*: 62). Meghasthenes records that the Indians used shoes to add to their height" (Ibid) and the aboriginals of Kalinga might have fought barefooted. Even today, a person with ten automobiles is considered to be greater than the person who possesses ten thousand books.The army of Ashoka had also learnt how to use an umbrella. I am afraid; the Mauryan killers had frightened the indigenous tribes with their shoes and umbrellas. These tribal men used to show their heads voluntarily and they went on butchering them in a demonic spree.The tribal Odias never had the opportunity to see a pair of shoes or an umbrella. The furore our psedo-patriotic historians tried to make after Shahrookh Khan's Ashoka is a shameless example of minds devoid of performative aesthetics. The sensible Producer of that film on Ashoka had not taken up a project on history and a performative narrativization needs lots of extrapolations, distortions and transformations that would be acceptable to the film's consumers

Kalinga in Sanskrit Literature: The Land of the Hill Dwellers

(a)Kalinga in Literature

Mahakavi Kalidasa, the great Sanskrit poet of 1st. century B.C. directs his cloud-convoy (*Megha dutam*) through the Yaksha to rest for a while in *Amrakuta*. He describes the environment of Amrakuta with the following words:

Sthitva tasmin vanacharabadhu bhukta kunje muhoortam
Toyotsarga drootatara gatistatparam batmareernah
Revam drakshyasyupalavishame Vindhyapade biseernam
Bhakti chhedariva vicharitam bhutimange gajasya.

A functional meaning can be rendered: "Oh cloud! The jungle dweller female folk live in the Amrakuta Mountain. While collecting their forest products they drink and dine under some wild bowers. You'd take rest for some time there and then you'd proceed towards Vindhya Mountain. On the foot of Vindhya you would find river Rewa. It looks like a heroine prostrating at the feet of the hero or like the ash-coloured stripes drawn on the body of an elephant as mark of *bhakti*. Amrakuta is Umarkote of Koraput district.

The soldiers who came with Raghu (in *Raghuvamsam* of Kalidasa) during his expedition are described to have crossed Utkala to reach Kalinga:

Tambulinam dalaistratra rachita para bhoomayah
Narikelasatam Yoddhah Sakraban cha pajurjasah.

The soldiers had stopped at the foot-hill of Mahendragiri and consumed *narikela-asaba* (a drink/ wine made out of the coconut water) From the *tambulies* (beatle-sellers).

Aswaghosa, Sudraka, Magha and Vana Bhatta have described the dress and the customs of those hill-dwellers in their *Kavyas* (poetry) and *natakas* (drama). A distant shot of the visuals of our tribal setting can be seen through the peep-holes of Vana Bhatta's prose-*Kavya* (poem) *Harsha Charitam*. According to *Saptama Ucchwasa* (canto vii) king Sri Harsha moves out with his soldiers toward Vindhya Hills to rescue the kidnapped Rajashree; and stopping for a while in the forest they observe the following scene:

The hill-dwellers carried firewood. Some of them carried wooden rods on their shoulders with two hangings on both sides for carrying their food in leaf-plates. A dog followed them as they proceeded toward the jungle. Small huts were built on relatively high places amidst trees and old men/women supervised their children playing under the eaves. Some of them were hiding with their traps spread nearby to catch parrots, mynas and other beautiful birds. There were cages placed beside them. Others were collecting barks and date leaves to prepare brooms and the peacock's train to decorate them. Some others carried bows and arrows and lived in ambuscades to hunt stags and rabbits. They reared cotton plants, drum-stick trees, brinjal plants, soap-nut plants and trees that would provide them with *sooran* (sweet roots). They constructed their huts with wattle and mud with leaf or hay roofs. Cucumber, gourds, pumpkin, and such other creepers decorated their roofs. Some others cultivated mustard plants. Dried cow-dung cakes and the forest wood were used as fuels." (A plain, thematic translation from Canto-VII of *Sriharsha Charitam*).

These forest dwellers decorated their heads with wild creepers and flowers that hung up to the forehead. They had flat noses, thick lips, fat cheeks and thick necks. Their arms looked like pythons. These dark skinned *Sabaras* looked like the "meteors for the lions, fruits of sin, lovers of the deadly nights and the cause of the *Kaliyuga*".

Sri Bhagaban Panda, one of our senior researchers and contemporary Pundits, is of the opinion that the posterity of the *Aranyaka Rishis*, called the *Vratyas* (sans Vedic norms) were corrupted gradually in course of time and were then called *Kiratas, Savaras, Pulindas* and *Nishadas*.

Viswanatha Kaviraja, the 14th century Sanskrit poet from Orissa mentions about the Bheel women (*Sahitya Darpana*) and kavi Jagannatha Mishra (a sanskrit poet from Orissa b.1725) in his *Rasa Kalpadruma* informs that these hill-women were *"dusta durgandha dehah pasu sama surata schumbanashleshahinah"* (cruel women with foul-smelling bodies, engaged in sex like the beasts, without any kisses and embraces)

Jagannatha also informs that the *Sabaras* are *"chhaga satkulo sobhanam"* (moving with goats) and *"pichhachha parichhadam"* (putting on a dress made out of the feathers of different birds). Kavi Narsimha (18th century) in his play, *Bhanja Mahodaya* (A play in 10 Acts) describes *Juang* and *Sabara* villages, their dances and dresses :*Bhramanti parna vasana gunjapunjeika mandana*

Anavrittasatanah peena varantah savarangana.

[The Savara women (here accepted as the Juang women) move with uncovered breasts and decking themselves up with coloured gunja nuts = small, hard and bright, polished, wild nuts used for making garlands. The nuts are red with a small patch of black. Please refer to Kali Sahasranama and you would notice that Goddess Kali loves to adorn herself with gunja nuts and she loves to stay in

the forest of gunja creepers). In the same play he mentions that the Juangs are very fond of cocks and hens and dogs.

To a deracinated generation of Odias the description of the tribals might appear funny and exotic.It is true that the great Sanskrit poets have given a very acurate picture of the tribals wearing *gunja* nuts and all that. I would just ask them to go through the Sanskrit text of *Kali Sahasranama* (the one thousand names of Kali, the Goddess).The Godess is described as dark coloured,fully naked and having decked herself with *gunja* nuts. Does that mean that the figure of the Godess described is only a *drishyanukruti* (mimesis)? Are our Gods and Godesses only poetic figments of imagination? Well, even today, there are people who would invoke the Goddess and make her appear in front of you.You can see her with your physical eyes, but we can not guarantee your safety and psychic harmony after that.

The tribal women considered themselves as primordial as the Goddess of creation and destruction and as natural as the mother earth. So, they imitated Her features.

(b) The Language of Tri-Kalinga:

The Culture of the Odias can also be examined from the linguistic point of view. It should also be borne in mind that Anga, Banga and Kalinga were not treated favourably by the Aryans who infiltrated through the North-west and could not exercise their powers of culture on these lands. In the *granthas* (texts) of *Arya Samaj*, like *Latyayana Srauta Sootra*, the areas of *Anga, Banga* and *Kalinga* were called *Prachya Ratha*. The *Prachya Ratha* is mentioned as *Bi-Patha* (or the wrong Road) According to *Baudhayana Dharma Sutra* the Aryans were forbidden to settle in these areas.

All our indigenous tribes were treated as fallen people. *Manu Smriti* written around 2nd Century B.C. prescribed that an Aryan had to resanctify himself if he visited this land for any purpose other than pilgrimage. The local inhibitants of Orissa also cared very little for the Aryans and their civilization.

Either they were oblivious of them or they were too obstinate about the culture they lived within.

The Aryans designated them as *Vratyas* or the people who never cared to obey the Aryan norms. When the Aryans advanced toward Kalinga from the Western region, these *Vratyas* were the only folk who resisted them.

The Aryans, who spoke Sanskrit, never tried to learn these local languages. There must have been fights over all cultural norms including language. According to the Aryan scriptures, the languages of those days were divided into four groups: *Souraseni, Maharashtri, Magadhi* and *Udra*. All these were called *Prakrit* languages. *Udra Desa* has been mentioned as *Mlechha Desa* (the country of dirty and irreligious people) in *Matsya Purana*. Since this was the land of the *Sabaras,The Matsya Purana* and *The Vayu Purana* designate them as *"Dakhinapatha Vasinah"* (as if the path of the South or the land of the Southerners are full of sin) and *The Bhagavati Sutra* of the Jains mentions *Udra bhasha* as *Mlechha-bhasha*. On the other hand, Sanskrit was *Deva-bhasha* (language spoken by the Gods).

Be our language a language of the dirty sinners or the flouters, the inhabintants of Kalinga were also human beings who lived since the prehistoric times. Pt. Hazari Prasad Dwivedy, in the process of his enquiry into the reasons as to why the Aryans treated our language as the meanest, assigns two reasons: (i) The Sanskrit Speaking people never wanted to come down from their high pedestal of *Alamkaras* to embrace the pure language in its nakedness (ii) These Sanskrit bards were outsiders and they never tried to assimilate with our culture by learning our language. (Ref. Dwivedy: 29)

Odia is a *prakrit* language. *Prakrit* means the real, the non-artificial language- a language that evolves through the speaker's tongue. It is not a language of the courtiers or of the people who speak from pedestals and thrones. It is never the language of the priests and the elites. Buddha never used the rhetorics of Sanskrit to explain himself. Pali was a *prakrit* language. But later, when it acquired the status of the state language it also incorporated the sophisticated similes and metaphors from Sanskrit.

What I call *Prakrit* languages are technically Indo-Aryan in nature. Although Odia language has borrowed extensively from Sanskrit, it has been marginalised because of the *Vratya* principles of the life of its practitioners. At a particular point of time, Sanskrit also declined and as Nehru writes in his *The Discovery of India*, "...It lost some of its power and simplicity of style and became involved in highly complex forms and elaborate similes and metaphors. The grammatical rules which enable words to be joined together became in the hands of epigones a mere device to show off their cleverness by combining whole strings of words running into many lines." (Nehru: 165)

This is a common fact in history. The power of Sanskrit began to corrupt itslef and its elitist alienation distantiated it from the other Indo-Aryan languages. Nehru has correctly observed that "this continuing use of Sanskrit has undoubtedly prevented the normal growth of the Modern Indian Languages. The educated intellectuals looked at them as vulgar tongues not suited to any creative or learned work, which was written in Sanskrit, or later not infrequently in Persian. In spite of this handicap, the great provincial languages gradually, took shape in the course of centuries, developed literary forms, and built up their literatures." (Nehru:168)

The Sanskrit language was the ancient medium of teaching. Since the books were committed to memory, it laid more emphacis on the sound of the words. Through its musical recitations the knowledge has been handed down to us. The *Vratyas* of ancient Kalinga, mostly tribals, might not have found the Sanskrit rhythm suitable to them. Its rigorous imposition might have been felt a threat of complications to their simple culture. Secondly, our "scheduled tribes" must have calculated no utilitarian value in learning Sanskirt, since they never had ambitions for any cultural power. In their oneness with nature they were closer to infinity, to the eternal principles of creation. The elitist motifs of cultural domination through an ornamental, sonorous language must have appeared petty and trivial to those great individuals who are still capable of renouncing their clothes, and with that the beautifying locks of hair in order to keep the hills green for ever.Won't they spit at your face if you teach them about ecological balance?

It is interesting, however, to note that these *vratyas* and *Mlechhas* and obstinate tribals accepted Buddha and Mahavira more easily than they could do so with the Brahmins. To state it little bluntly, the people of Kalinga rejected Vedic religion to a large extent because of the supremacy of the decadent brahmins, who entered into Orissa as the agents of Vedic religion and asserted themselves on them However, this aboriginal land of the tribals never gave any chance to the *brahmins* to preveil upon them.

Nehru in his *Glimpses of World History* records that during the time of Buddha (600 B.C),the Brahmin Priests had introduced all kinds of rites and *pujas* on a commercial basis, for the more there was of *puja*, the more did the priests flourish. Caste boundaries were growing higher, and the common people were frightened by omens and spells and witchcraft and quackery. The priests got the people under their control by these methods and challenged the power of the *Khattriya* rulers. There was thus rivalry between the Khattriyas and the Brahmanas." (Nehru. 36)(Our contemporary readers should not forget that Nehru was educated at Harrow and was taught by English teachers of the colonial era. They had induced these anti-sanskrit notions into him since the debasement of Sanskrit in India would help the propagation of Christianity).

Perhaps, this casteist rivalry generated a conducive space for Buddha and Mahavira in Kalinga for the ungrudging acceptance of their religions. It is again interesting to note that the life of our culture has been a perennial battlefield for the *Khandayatas* (a degenerated group of the *Kshatriyas*) and the Brahmins. The alternate positions of cultural power they would take can be deciphered in the subsequent pages of this book.Their strategies of vanquishing each other would also vary according to the region they belong to.

What is important now is that with the wide acceptance of Buddhism and Jainism in Kalinga of those days, we are entering into the era of recorded history: archaeological findings, coins, temples and the period of the records of the Western and the Chinese visitors.

Kalinga and its Political Culture

We know about Trikalinga of the past and that name signified that Kalinga was never one and culturally and linguistically they were different entities. Their convictions and the belief systems were three-fold and at many cross roads of history they have fought with each other.

However, it was an independent state between 320 B.c. and 261 B.C.The kings of Kalinga were educated and they followed the administrative system prescribed Chanakya. There were 18 types of officers in the state who took charge of different issues of living. They were called 1 .Mantrin,2. Purohit, 3.Senapati 4.Yuvaraja, 5.Vaivarika, 6.Antarvamshika, 7.Prasasta, 8.Samaharika, 9Sannidhita. Sannidhita, 10.Pradesata,11.Nayaka,12.Paura Vyavaharika,13. Karmantika,14. Chairman of the Mantrins, 15.Dandapala,16. Durgapala, 17.Antapala,18.Atavila It was a system based on strict discipline and reliable detectives to guard and report about lapses if any.

Ashoka had changed this administrative system completely and replaced it with a liberal administration based on love and benevolency.Discipline was no more considered the major focus, the state welfare was prioritized. A king was appointed in carge of Kalinga and different Arakshis were deployed to take care of the problems of law and order. Judges were deployed to take care of the law and order of the state. The other officers of the state were given the following responsibilities.

Officer	Duties
Raj kumar	The administrative head of Kalinga, stationed at Toshali
Pratinidhi	The head of Jaugada zone
Vachanika	Took care of the king's verbal orders
Mahamatra	The Public Relations Officer
Rajuka	State welfare
Pulisa	Supervisor of the works of the Rajuka's works
Pradesika	Law and order, revenue
Ayukta	Law and order of the rural area
Vachabhumika	Agriculture and Veternary
Prativedaka	To report/inform the king on administrative loopholes
Lipikara	To care of the records
Duta	The royal convoy anda representative of the king
Samarhatri	The Revenue Commissioner

Dhamma Mahamatra supervisor of public morality and behavior of the subjects

Kharavela changed this system of administration and followed the dictums of *Manu Samhita*. He appointed military personnel for the security of his country. Separate departments for elephantry,Chariots and also for the naval forces were deployed. The kusuma was the main assistant administrator. Feudal lords were called Chula-Kama, Kama, and Halakhinas. The was considered as the Dharmaraja.(Raicharan Das, Evolution of Administration to comprehensive history and culture of Orissa, Ed.P.K.Mohanty and J.K.Samal,Vol-II, Part-2 Raveni Books,1997,P-98).

The conquest of Kalinga by Ashoka gave a multicultural quality to Kalingan Vratya culture. The local inhabitants who were only flouters and rebels against Aryan standards came under the influence the Buddhist Bhikshus. They spoke Prachya-Prakrit language it later it has evolved into the present day Odia. Kharavela was the successor and he was from Northern Chedi dynasty. He attempted to sanskritize and reform the prakrit Odia

Kalingans believed in Shakti cult and Jajpur stood as the evidence. Ashoka preached Buddhism, but later Hinduism was re-established here. The Kalinga of thse days was divided into Northrn and Southrn Kalinga and Jaugada was the Southern capital. Mahakosala was mainly controlled from Jaugada.

We would begin with demarcating Kalinga's geographical territopry from the accounts of Hiuen Tsang, a Chinese traveller of the mid 7th century. Its history is available from the Western Ganga dynasty who ruled here aound 130 A.D. There was an International Buddhist conference in Kangoda during the 6th century and therefore it was famous for this Chinese tourist, named HieunTsang. A great Buddhist philosopher called Dinnag had come from South Kalinga and had stayed in Buddha Khole of Buguda. However, Kalinga of Hieuen T'sang's time was a land of all religions.

Hiuen Tsang's Records.

Hiuen Tsang's records show "Kalinga at this time comprised the area extending southwards from the Chilka lake to the Godavari river. The Gangas were ruling contemporaneously with the Sailidvabas over the Southern part of the Ganjam district and the northern region of Vizagapatnam." (Haraprasad Ganguli.*IHQ.VolXXXIII. No.3*.Sept.1957 P.209)

Hiuen Tsang passed through the Kangoda country in or about 639 A.D.and had winessed the power of the ruling authorities, obviously, the Salodbhavas who took over from the Gauda Emperor named Sasanka after his death some times before 637 A.D.

But the fortune of the Sailidbhava family declined before long with the conquest of Kangoda by Harshavardhana in 642 A.D. The Buguda plates of Madhava Barman descriobes how Pulindasena, an inhabitant of Kalinga who was endowed with many personal virtues eg. lofty stature, strong arms and broad chest but nevertheless did not covet sovereignty for himself, worshipped *Brahman* with the result that the god created out of pieces of rock (*sila-sakala*) the lord Sailodbhava, the founder of a dynasty. This story is also repeated in the Parikuda plates of Madhyamaraja. The order of the Kings of the Sailodbhaba in Buguda and Parikuda Plates are the same:

1. Sailodbhava
2. Ranabhita
3. Sainyabhita
4. Ayosobhita
5. Sainyabhiota-II
6. Ayosobhita Madhyama Raja

The famous historian of Bengal, named R.D.Banerjea, had some confusions with regard to this chronological order, and that was detected by Ganguly. We donot have the time to enter into such controversies(Ref. Haraprasad Ganguli. *Sailodbhavas and their contemporaries of Kangoda*.IHQ. Vol. XXXIII. No.3. Sept. 1957.P209-210))

Dr. Keilhorn thinks *(E.I.*VII.P.102) thinks that the Buguda plates were issued some time which "cannot be earlier than about the 10th century A.D."(Ibid.211)

The Buguda plates of Madhavaraman Srinivasa show that Kangoda Mandala again came to be ruled by the Sailodbhava dynasty about the middle of the 9th century. Madhava Barman Srinivasa performed Aswamedha sacrifice which shows that his eminence among his neighbouring kings was a fact. This rapid growth of the power of the Sailodbhavas might have been facilitated by the Pala conquest of Utkala and the subsequent decline of the Pala empire after Deva Palo's death enabled Sainyabhita-III (alias Madhaba barman Srinivasa) to establish his supremacy in the neighbouring kingdoms

Madhabavarman Srinivasa Sainyabhita-III was succeeded by his son Madhyama Raja-I who ruled for at least 26 years and performed *Vajapeya* and *Aswamedha* sacrifices. The land he granted by the Parikuda plates was situated in the *Kataka-bhukti visaya*. Kataka may be identified with modern Cuttack. In that case, we have to suppose that the Sailidbhava kingdom extended up to the Mahanadi river in the reign of Madhyamaraja-1

Later, during the rule of the Kar dynasty, known from the Dhenkanal inscription of Tribhubana Mahadevi, the relationship between the Kataka visaya and the Kangoda mandala were strained many times during power struggles. There were instances of fights between the two regions and the weapon was tantra

But elsewhere in Orissa, in a region called Maha Koshala, Tantra or the Sakta culture flourished with a greater commitment and with a broader vision of understanding. These folks of MahaKoshala had already realized that the secret of human happiness in this world is to live always in tune with the song of life, to keep the outer self of action, heart, mind and motive always in tune with the inner self, which is ever at one with the Supreme Self, the Lord of All. They lived in Mahakantara, in the womb of femines, yet, perhaps, they always thought the Goddess residing in their inner space would deck them with gems only.

Famine stricken every year, they dreamt to have lived in the great granary of the cosmos, wherein lies the seeds of new concepts, even though there surrounds a night. As dawn comes, the seed of a new universe germinates as the logos-to-be, as the Purusha.

That is a different kind of Shakti, a power the affluent Europeans would hardly understand. Hence, it is time to discuss about the worship of Shakti in Maha Koshala

Commercial Culture in Ancient Kalinga

Commercial culture is a broad term that includes trade, roadways, sea routes, coins and the business of export and import. We have lots of records with regard to export. But we know nothing about what was imported. More than this is important to trace the roads and other ways of transportation.

The roads in those days were cleared and constructed by the kings during their invasions.

The earliest record of invasion made on Orissa is Mahapadma Nanda's attack in the 4th century B.C. Mahapadmananda, the monarch of Pataliputra, had taken away a throne from Kalinga. This shows that there was a road from Pataliputra to Toshali. Ashoka led the Mauryan army through that road only and he could enter into the heart of Kalinga. Kharavela, in the1st century B.C. must also have used the same road for his expedition of *Uttarapatha* to Magadh, Ganges valley and Sind valley. He brought back the throne of Kalinga taken away by Mahapadmananda through the same road way.

Besides, Emperor Kharavela's southern expeditions extended upto Srilanka. On the way, he defeated the Dramil confederation of kingdoms organised by Pandya kings,who ruled around 1300 years before Kharavela (*terasa basa Satakatam*). This time he had conquered Chola, Pandya, Satyaputra, Keralaputra and Tamraparni (in Ceylon) kingdoms- all these were connected by road.

The Satabahana king Sataparni (106-130 AD) was ruling over Mahendragiri and his father's rock edicts are found in Pune. This shows that Sataparni was the king of eight mountain forts: Vindhya, Parijatra, Sahya, Krushnagiri, Malayagiri, Mahendragiri, Swetagiri and Chakoragiri. The forest routes surrounded by dense forests and wild animals were also open for the traders. This route connected Mahendragiri and Maharashtra through the Vindhya hills. The Mahendragiri area of south Kalinga was under *Satabahana* rule till 2nd century A.D. and this road was used for administrative purposes. Ashoka's *Mahamatras* in south Kalinga were, however, using the forest routes inside the state for their four-monthly visits to the distant areas to read out and explain rock notifications and circulars.

An analysis of the Allahbad pillar inscription reports about Samudragupta's (335 A.D.) expedition into south India through Kosala Mahakantar (Kalahandi) and Kalinga. There was another route that connected Toshali/Kalinga Nagara with *Tamralipi* (Gangetic valley) on its north -east side through coastal regions via Lalitagiri, Dharmashala, Jajpur, Bhadrak, Soro, Remuna, Basta, Amarda, Raibania and Kharagpur.

Archaeological findings reveal another route which stretched from Dharmasala to Pataliputra via. Anandpur, Khiching, Bhanjakia, Brahmanghati (Rairangpur) Bahalda, Saraikala and Manbhum.

Another road passed through Bilaspur, Raipur, Patnagarh, Sonepur, Baudh, Phulbani, and through Kalinga Ghats to Ganjam. Samudragupta used this road for his south India expedition.

Our inscriptions refer to three kinds of roads: *Rajpatha*, (Ep. Ind. xxxi : 109-128) *Dharmaraja Kalinga Marga* and *Sundrika Marga*. Mr. D.K. Borah presumed the *Dharmraja Kalinga Marga* to be the state highway of Kalinga (Borah. 55-60) it was constructed by king Dharmaraj-II of Sailodvba dynasty. The Sailodvabas ruled in Kangoda (Puri and Ganjam together) between 600-750 A.D. Mahendragiri was the cultural centre during their rule.

The Southern Kalinga was connected with different parts of South India by road. The military compaign of Kharavela refers to a route from Kalinga Nagari, his capital to Kaveripatnam which passed through Puri, Palur, Jaugada, Salihumdam, Sankaram, Ramtirtham, Amaravati, Nagarjunakonda and Pithunda.

The location of the Ashokan edicts at Dhauli, Jaugada and Amaravati substantiates this view. The recent excavations show the ruins of monastic establishments along this route. Dr. K.S. Behera's essay,*"Trade and patterns of commerce in Orissa"* shows another route, bringing reference to the southern invasions of the Ganga rulers. The inscriptions of Ananta Burman Chodaganga Deva (12th century A.D.) on the temples of Nirmaljhar near Khallikote, Ganjam, Puri, Alagum, Khilore, Bhubaneswar and Jajpur) indicate the existence of a route which passed through these places (Behera:10)

(a) Water- routes

Besides these road ways, the Kalingan merchants also used the waterways: carrying cargo by boats and ships and travelling through rivers and oceanic routes. Those, who travelled by the roadways, had to hazard accidentsbecause there were dense forests on the way. There were the risks of various robbers and wild animals. The rivers that pased enroute were not bridged. They used bullock carts to carry their cargo on the land.

It appears that the merchants of Kalinga were courageous and adventurous people. They were equipping themselves with security measures and they had very good rappport with the forest dwellers. The forest dwellers did not have any kind of animosity with the plainlanders/civilized people. As such, there were cultural appropriations on both the sides. According to caste heirarchies they were *vaisyas*, but these cultural appropriations paved the way for marriages between the tribals *(Sudras/mlechhas)* and the *vaisyas*. Consequently, the *vaisyas* grew into a robust, warring race like the tribals and the tribals learnt the art of commerce as well as the use of coins. The tribals organised *hatas* (market places) for marketing the forest products. The racial intermixture also allowed the plainlander *Vaisyas* to sell their urban products in the *hatas* of the tribal areas.

The excavations at Sisupalagarh(near Bhubaneswar) have indentified the place with Toshali of Ashoka and Kalinga Nagari of Kharavela. Materials like potteries, terracottas, iron implements, beads of precious stones, punch-marked coins, Kushana and Puri-Kushane coins, rouletted ware (ware used for ""roulelte" or a gambling game in which a small ball/coin falls by chance into one of the compartments of a revolving wheel or disc). and gold coins of the Roman origin (belonging to the time of constantine and Gordius as identified by archaeologist Paramananda Acharya) reveal that Toshali/Kalinga Nagara was inhabited by people of different professions (Pattnaik S.K. 13-19).

Toshali or Kalinga Nagar, as the capital, must have been a fully developed commercial centre, but the trade of Kalinga in those days created a culture in the hinterlands only.

The excavations of Brahmanaghati in Mayurbhnj district and Tamluk in the Midnapur district of West Bengal (in those days Midnapur was in Kalinga) open up the possibilities of our trade with the Roman Empire (Acharya : 533) One gets slightly confused at this distant age to find Roman coins of Constantine's time (306 c) in an interior place like Bamanghati of Orissa. But later, the excavations in Western Orissa at Asuragarh, Manamunda and Kharligarh throw some extra light on such possibilities. The excavations of Samapa (Jaugada) and Palur in south Orissa and those of Ratnagiri, Lalitagiri, Manikpatna, Khalkatapatna and Kalinga patna have further testified our commercial culture.

The *Arthasastra* of Kautilya (Chanakya) and the unknown author of a book, *Periplus of the Erythraean Sea* written in 1st. century A.D. and Ptolemy's accounts (2nd century A.D.) refer to the ports of Kalinga. Besides, the accounts of Fa-Hien (5th cent. A.D.) Hiuen-T-Sang (7th cent. A.D.) I-Tsing (7th cent. A.D.), and the reports of the Perso-Arabic geographers (9th and 10th cent. A.D.) also refer to the commodities of Orissa that were exported outside from the ports of Kalinga. There was also a full fledged growth of the inland trade.

R.D. Benerjee is full of praises for the people of Kalinga since they were pioneers among the Indians in the maritime activities and overseas colonization. It had a great appeal to the great poet Kalidasa, who in one of his plays called *Raghuvamsa* has extolled the king of Kalinga as *Mahodadhipati*(master of the ocean)

The Buddhist text named *Aryamanjushri mulakalpa*, a work of 7-8th.century refers to the Bay of Bengal as Kalinga Sagara. Perhaps it gained importance and was renamed as the Bay of Bengal during the British or Raj period.

Archaeological excavations conducted at various places, i.e. Sisupalagarh,Dhauli,Tamralipti,Bamanghati,Khalkattapat na,Manika patana and Palur etc, the discovery of Roman and

Cylonese coins from the coastal belt and the sculptural pieces depicting the boats in the Orissan temples provide substantial evidence to the maritime activities of ancient Orissa

The depiction of a giraffe, an African animal in the sculpture of sun temple clearly proves the Kalingan contact with Africa. The sculptors of Orissa had also been touring across the globe in ships made in Orissa.The Puranas, the Arthasastra of Kautilya,Raghuvamsam of Kalidasa, the Buddhist and Jain texts, Pliny's accounts,the description given in the Erythraen sea, the writings of Ptolemy, FaHien,Hiuen Tsang,I- Tsing, Ibn Khurdadbih, Alberuni and a host of other writers have referred to the maritime activities of Orissa in their respective works.(Ref.Benudhar Patra.Maritime Heritage of Kalinga. OHC Souvenir, Berhampur University. Oct.2001. p25)

The vast coast line of Orissa in ancient times was studded with a good number of natural ports. Since the portsof anchorage was a prerequisite for sea voyages the coastline of Kalinga gave rise to many natural ports. The floourishing ports were Tamralipti, che-li-ta-lo/ Manikapatana, Khalkattapatana, Palur/Dantapura, Dosarene, Kalingapatanam, Pithunda etc. The port towns were developed as a consequence of brisk trade.Of all the ports, Tamralipti situated at the appex of the Kalingan coast was the most significant one. It has been identified with the present Tamluk on the bank of the river Rupnarayan in the Midnapur district of West Bengal which formed a part of Orissa in the ancient times. It is believed that one of the reasons for the Ashokan invasion of Kalinga was to gain control over the port of Tamralipti for the land locked Kingdom of Magadha. Another important port of Kalinga was Che-li-ta-lo which has singularly been reffered to by Hiuen Tsang. Various scholars have tried to identify this port with different places. But very recently on the basis of archaeological data it has been identified with the excavated port of manikapatana on the northern tip of chilika Lake. The recent Excavation at Khalkattapatana 11 K.m. east from Konark on the left bank of river Kushabhadra where it joins with the

Bay of Bengal has established as an early medieval port. Palur village of the modern Ganjam district. The importance of Palur port was that it acted as the only port of departure to the Malaya Peninsula on the east coast of India. Palur has often been identified to be the same as Dantapura of the Buddhist Jatakas. Dosarene was another port of ancient Orissa. The Periplus of the Erythraean sea has reffered to this port.Though the final identification of Dosarene is yet to arrive it could probably be somewhere in the Chilika coast. Kalingapatanam and Pithunda were two important ports of ancient Orissa. The HathiGumpha Inscription mentions Pithunda as a metropolis which Kharavela Conquered in his 11th regnal year.

The devolpment of ports was associated with many other navigational aspects, i.e, the ships, the routes, timings of the journey, movement of the wind and water etc. The people of Kalinga had proficiency in the art of ship-building. Though very less is known about them, they had their own technique in the construction of ships. Various types of boats have been depicted on the sculptures of Orissa. A sculptured frieze collected from the Vicinity of the Brahmesvara temple now preserved in the Orissan state Museum depicts boats carrying elephants which prove at least two things: (1) that the ships of Kalinga were well built and were strong enough even to carry elephants, and (2) that elephants formed an important item of export. On the Bhogamandapa of the Jagannath temple of Puri, there is a magnificent representation of a boat in Chlorite stone. The Brahamanda Purana, a work of the 9th- 10th century A.D also make some clear- cut references to the boat building technology of ancient Orissa.

From the well flourished ports and with required navigational technology the daring sailors of Kalinga had established brisk comercial-cum- cultural relationship with different parts of the world, especially with the south-east Asian countries like Burma, Java, Sumatra, Bali, Borneo, Ceylon etc.In those days water transport was preffered to the land transport, the later being arduous and troublesome. Transportation by water route was also cheaper which didnot require expences on construction, maintenance and supervision. The sailors of Kalinga used both the coastal route (Kulapatha) and the overseas route (Samyanapatha). The lack of knowledge of the sea, the absence of the Mariner's compass, fear of pirates, unsuitability of the ship to traverse the deep sea etc., however generally led them to take up a route along the coastline. The sailors of Kalinga had taken the help of two monsoon winds i.e. North-east (october- Decenber) and south-west (june - September) during the commencement of the voyage and return journey respectively. The celebration of two socio-religious festivals i.e. Kartik purnimas Boita Bandana (on the full- moon day of Kartik (october-november) and Khudurkuni Osha (on the Sundays of Bhadrav (Agust-september) in Orissa are positive corroboration to the above facts.

By way of the overseas trade the sailors of Kalinga had established colonies in the far off south-east Asian countries. It is a well known fact that the first King of Ceylon came from Kalinga. The Island of Java was first colonized by the people from Kaliga. The island of Bali was completely influenced by the Hindu culture of Orissa. Similarly, Burma was also Colonized by the Kalingans. The close relationship between Kalinga and China is attested to by the chinese pilgrims like Fa-Hien, Hiuen T'sang and I-Tsing, indeed, the people of Kalinga were the pioneers in the colonizing activities in the south-east Asia, and Kalinga became prosperous and powerful substantially because of these colonies.

During the colonial times, a larger portion of Orissa was administered from Calcutta Presidency and the Bengali Officers stopped funding for the renovation and repair of the ports. As a consequence, the ports were destroyed and the sailors of Orissa lost their trade and profession. The Bengalies in their spree sent their fishermen to Orissan coasts and later, the Bengali refugees settled in coastal Orissa to destroy the forests of Abhayaranya to generate more of cyclones in Orissa. Now with Ms. Mamata Benerjee as the railway minister, the same prejudice towards Orissa is being shown and our members of the parliament are unable to raise their voice because they would neither be able to speak in Hindi nor in English. The first qualification of a contemporary politician in Orissa is to remain a drop out from the educational institution and then from the civilized life. He would be surrounded by old hooligans (that was the American style in the 1960s-- promoting violence) would continue to meddle in the small town problems most of the time. One should not expect him to fight for Orissa's railway budget in the Parliament. In which language a hooligan-don would raise his voice?

The same is the case with the ports. The port of Palur/ Palour comes to my mind first. This once-upon-a-time-famous port situated in the mouth of the river Rushikulya in the Ganjam district attracted great traffic as a centre of trade and pilgrimage. A Jaina work named *Uttaradhyana Sutra* mentions this place as Pithunda. The Hatigumpha inscription of Kharavela mentions Pithunda as an ancient metropolis of Kalinga.

With the conquest of Orissa by the Muslims, especially during the time of Akbar, the Southern Ports of Orissa including Chilka and Chitrotpala lost their glory. The Muslim governors in Bengal were more interested in the northern part of Orissa and the ports at Balasore, Pipli, and Harishpur came to limelight. Balasore on the river Budhabalanga, Pipli on the Suvarnarekha and Harishpur on the Patua were also the outlets for the interior tracts during the rainy season. Commodities were collected from these centres for export to the distant places through bigger ports.

The ports at Balasore, Pipli, Harishpur and Ganjam which carried on trade with different parts of the world were also centres for coastal trade. There was the movement of ships between the ports of Orissa and other ports on the Bay of Bengal. It is an irony that the Kalinga Sagara had already been renamed as the Bay of Bengal because of the cultural aggressiveness of the Bengalies and the Odias of Cuttack and Bhubaneswar considered it to be irrelevant to them since the Cuttackies did neither have a prt nor did they have the exposure of going to the foreign countries as the Ganjam and the Balasore people had through these ports. So, due to regional prejudices, the pople of the non-coastal districts did not object to the renaming of Kalinga Sagara.

The situation became more competitive in the British colonial period. The maritime heritage of Orissa(that is the colonial spelling for Odisa) attracted foreign traders and they began to establish factories on the Orissan coast line. This created a cultural jealousy in the West Bengal and they began to clip the wings of the Odias through neglecting the ports by reducing the budget.

The famine in1866 broke the back bone of the Odias. That was the time when the Christian preachers began to convert the hungry brahmins of the Puri district.Thus, the Imperial government because of politico-religious reasons began to pay attention to the ports of the Puri District.

However, John Beams(the famous British Commissioner, who proved that Odia was a separate language and not a "younger sister"(!) of Bengali) , Captain Harris, the Conservator of the Orissa ports and J.H.Jones,the Commander of the British India Steam Navigation Company reported to the government of Bengal about the situation. Accordingly, the government sanctioned some measures of improvements.

The entrance of the Budhabalanga was to be surveyed starting from Balasore to Balaramagarhi house during the closing month of 1873.(See Dr. Harish Chandra Panda."Maritime Significance and Ports of Balasore". GHCB. Ed. Subhas Pani. Bhubaneswar.P.232).Attempts were made to increase the inland communications. Canals and embankments were opened. The coast canal connecting Hooghly and Goenkhali with river Matai at Charbatia(71 miles long) was opened in 1885. Chandbali was declared a port and was named after Ravenshaw. The port was opened in 1872. It was an inland port on the river Baitarani, running between the districts of Cuttack and Balasore. The passangers, in those days, chose to travel to Calcutta by steamers from this port. This port was 25 miles away from Balasore coast.

The British goverment took interest also in another port in the undivided Cuttack district called False Point, situated in the mouth of the river Mahanadi at atance of 70 miles from Cuttack. The scholars on maritime studies consider this to be the best harbour among the coastal harbours of India from Hooghly to Bombay. But there was no means of disembarking the cargo and passengers at the anchorage. The second disadvantage was that there was no communication between the port and the interior of the country. After the inspection of the Imperial team, the harbour was deepened and the channels were buoyed

The work of the Kendrapara canal was undertaken to allow the tidal waters for indirect communication with the False Point.After the famine of 1866, the Lt. Governor of Bengal visited Orissa in Nov. 1874 and sanctioned the following sums of money for the development of the ports."(Brajabandhu Bhatta:"Maritime activities of Orissa in the 19th. Century: A Brief Study".OHRJ. vol.xxxix.No.1-4.pp.1-18)

Name of the port	Amount Granted
False Point	2,89,000
Balasore	30,000
Dhamra and Chandbali	100,000
Puri	20,000

(***Annual Administrative report Bengal Presidency***,1877-78,p.173)

Mr. A.D.Tylor, the Superntendent of the marine Surveys, Govt. of India, declined to sanction any large amount for the development of the False Point, and the report mentions: "Chandbali has become the port for the Calcutta trade and False Point is merely a port of call for coasting vessels and serves Orissa for the trade in rice to Mauritus,Colombo and West coast ports.(W.A.English.The canals and Flood Banks of Bengal.Calcutta.1909)

Although, we had a very good system of waterways, Orissa's road communication was not atall satisfactory. The ancients had to establish a communication between the highlanders and the plainlanders. The *vaisyas* of the plain areas went to the mountains with the agricultural products of the valley areas and in turn they brought the forest products, the medicinal plants,roots, honey,lac,and various kinds of coloured nuts uded for decorating the body. However, the tribals were coming to the plain area occasionally with wild birds,the tongue of a tiger, the nail or the beak of a particular bird and so on, material that can be used for medicinal purposes. The tribal people also used to come to the plain areas to sell cereals,barley, *kangu* and *suan*, typical Orissan hill grains, which I dont find in any other market of the country.

The tribal markets and the *hatas* of the plain lands were linking places for the urban and rural communities. These *hatas* continued till 1950s and there are *hatas* even today at Bhubaneswar as well as in most of the tribal places. There are weekly *Hatas* at Palasuni, Rasulgarh and Bomikhal localities. The *hatas* continue even today despite rapid urbanization and they exist side by side with the super markets.

Perhaps the crowd and the bustle and the dust and the moving bulls attract human beings to these *hatas* every evening for buying vegetables and other provisions. There is also a *haat* at Howrah station (Calcutta) to inspire Odia commercial culture. It would seem strange to an outsider how these people in the Eastern India still love crowd and dust. Our primitivity throbs in such places as life.One can still go to a hata in Keonjhar area to find a man with thousand scorpions crawling on his body and a group of people enjoying a cock-fight at some other corner.

I cannot tell much about the *hata* culture of the new millenium, but those primitive *hatas* were meeting places of the cultivator, craftsmen and artisans. The artisans were of various types:

(a) *Gandhika* (the perfume maker/seller)
(b) *Sankhika* (conch-shell-workers)
(c) Suvarnakar (goldsmiths)
(d) *Tamulika* (betel leaf sellers)
(e) *Kumbhakara* (potters)

(f) *Gudika* (maker of jaggery and sweets)
(g) *Tantuvaya* (the weavers)
(h) *Tailika* (the oil sellers)
(i) *Patakara* (the splitters. of wood)
(j) *Chitrakaras* (the painters) and
(K) *kaivartas* (fishermen)

(Behera:9)

These commercial castes had unions, guilds and corporations and these organistions helped them to conduct their business out side the state and in over- sea countries. The Soma dynasty records of Janmejaya-I refer to a Merchants Guild called *Kamalabana Banika Samstha* (Rajguru. 1950. 96-98).

The records of Ganga dynasty reveal that there were a number of guilds for the goldsmiths (*suvarnakara*), oilmen, (*Tailikas or teli*) milk-men (*Go-kula*), potters (*Kumbhakara*) (These records are also found in *Epigraphia Indica xxvii*: 185). In addition to the above guilds, the xxviii volume (*Epigraphia Indica*. xxviii:235) also provides a list of other guilds like: *the betel leaf sellers guild (Tambulika Sangha), the sweetmeat makers'(Gudias) Guild and patakara guild (Carpenter's Guild), The barbars* (they are hair dressers, nail cutters and they have ritualistic duties in temples palaces, and in Brahmin/Kshatriya families too. Later on, they were found serving the *vaisyas* , the landowner class and the other feuds.

The bell-metal workers (*Kamsaris*) had a special status in Kangoda (the southern part of the present Odissa covering Puri and Ganjam,Koraput and some portions of Andhra Pradesh) which means that the temple of Jagannatha is not in Utkala, but in Kangoda. Some stupid Odia nationalists are trying to rename Odisa as Utkala.By this they are trying to exclude Kangoda and Kosala.I think such a renaming would split Odisa again) They lived in the surrounding villages of Balakati, Puri, Banpur, Samapa and Jagamohan (near Dharakote in Ganjam district), which were the market places for bell-metal pots, utensils, temple bells (*ghanta and ghanti*) decorated stands for lighting insense sticks (*dhoopadani*) designed cup-stands for lighting ghee/oil-soaked wicks (*Rukha and deepa*).

The villages are polluted with the sounds emitted from the bell-metal workers home industries early in the morning. A popular saying of the Odia villages goes like this: *Kamsari-ghara Para-ku Kula dhaun dhaun* ("why do you try to frighten the pigeon of a bell-metal worker's home by sounding the winnowing fan?' This is also used metaphorically for the intimidating braggers).

There were also guilds of washer-men and the fisher men folk. The washermen used to attend to the upper class families for washing clothes.

The custom is slightly different in Kangoda. The washer woman has to wash the clothes put on by female folk during their monthly periods. The practice is still in currency in some families. The female folk do not enter into the kitchen, the worship rooms and the templesduring their periods. They are also treated as untouchables for five days. These periodical clothes and the undergarments were sanctified only after the washerwoman washed them separately.

The fishermen supplied the fish only on the days fish was allowed to be eaten. In many families fish and non-veg. dishes are not allowed on Mondays, Thursdays and Sundays. The worshippers of Hanuman are forbidden to take non-veg. dishes on Tuedays and Saturdays. It was only during the colonial times that some under-previleged classes tried to gain 'class superiority' by celebrating Sundays with fish, muttton or chicken curries.These are the people who got themselves converted into Christianity to climb the ladders of success during the British Raj These are the people who also converted themselves into a new mediocre religion called "secularism". Such colonial notions of modernity have deracinated the Odias from their indigenous culture. There is also an unpronounced hatred for the brahmins in such taboo-breaking newfangled taboos.

This newfangled practice in some of these"modern" families has also facilitated immensely the fishermen's business since the number of "Sunday-fish/meat eaters" has been growing steadily in our neo-modern society. These hybridized fashion-mongers tend to highlight themselves by gleefully flouting the classical dietary regimen calling it orthodox and old fashioned. They do never pay any heed to the scientific study made by our Vedic seers. Macaulay's education has given them the licence to bring in European taboos of science as modern mode of living, as if the pigtailed Brahmins of India did not know science. These followers of the occident quote what happens in America,France and etc. countries and try to prove that they are holders of a giant sized torchlight(pronounced as a bold **enlightenment)**

The potter's business flourished during the days of religious festivals and rituals. The house- holds used to (a current practice, too) change the cooking pots (earthen) during the days of festive celebration that necessiated such a ritual for the sanctification of the kitchen.This is also related to the cocept of 'renewal craft'. The ritual of Nava kalevara or the reconstruction of the wooden icons every twelve years is also related to this concept of changing the pots in the kitchen) An oilman is considered to be inauspicious. One should not see him with his oil pot on the head when one sets out for his profession or business.

The *Tantuvayas* (weavers) the *pathurias* (rock carvers) and the lvory workers had their own guilds, too. The guilds were functioning like local banks/Co-operative Societies and they were being operated with their own rules and regulations.

(b) The Exportation of Odissi goods

Apart from these artifacts- rice, cotton, cloth, muslin, salt, precious stones, touch stones, diamonds, elephants, ivory, timber, honey, bee wax and iron-implements were being exported outside, Kautilya in his *Artha Sastra* has refered to the best type of cotton fabric (*Karpasika* as mentioned in Sastri 1924: 11) available in Kalinga. *The Mahabharata* and *Mana Solasa* of *Someswar Deva* (Shrigondekar 1017-27) refers to Kalinga as the place for production of the high quality of textile fabrics.

Kautilya has mentioned that the touch stone of Kalinga

was the best of its kind in the ancient times (Sastri :Xii). The Indravanaka hill in Kalinga was famous for the best type of diamonds (Mookherjee:210). Kalidasa, in his *Raghuvamsa* has mentioned about the best type of betel nut being cultivated in Orissa. The forest region of western Orissa was famous for elephant breeding. *Artha Sastra*, too, mentions about this. The Orissan Kings were the Gajapatis (kings who were famous for their elephantry in the war fields)

River Mahanadi was called Hiranadi in those days and the area from Harisankar (Gandhamardan hills) to Raigarh in M.P. was known as Hirakoota. It was on the northen side of Gandhamardan. The western side was called Kalakoota, the southern as Kukkoota and the eastern side of the hill was known as Tri-koota. The river, Mahanadi originates from Hirakoota (HiraKuda) and flows through Tri-koota. Plenty of diamonds were available on its bed and these diamonds had a hot market in Rome. According to Hieuen-T-Sang the diamonds excavated from South Kosala (Gandhamardan hills) were transported through the ports of Kalinga. The Britishers cast their greedy eyes on this part only for the diamonds.

The Tri-Koota hills stand on the otherside of Sonepur in Sindhol Thana. This is the dividing line between old Bolangir and old Sambalpur districts. On the foot of this hill stood Kota Samalai or Samalai Kota. The *Madala Panji* records reveal that Lord Jagannath had disappeared into the Sonepur forest for 700 years. Since those years Tri-Koota was also called Daru Kona.

The water ways of Kalinga, Kosala and Kangoda were more convenient for the merchants of those days. Apart from Mahanadi, the Vaitarani, Brahmani, the Suvarnarekha and the Rushikulya rivers provided enough scope for water transport. A large part of the internal trade was carried on through the river routes. As a result, trading centres developed on the coast line and coastal Orissa began to dominate over the southern and western parts.The reason was that they were rich people. They were also widely exposed to other foreign cultures through the riverine traffic.

The only link with western Orissa was through Mahanadi since the bridges had not been constructed. "The epigraphic references", writes Sri Benudhar Patra, a contemporary historian on whose research, my information is hinged, "of the Bhaumakara period to the grant of right over the **ghata** (landing place on the banks of the river) and *naditara sthane* (ferry places) to the beneficiaries indicate the importance of river traffic (Das, B. 174,189) The depictions of boats in Orissan temple sculptures also testify to the significance of the riverine traffic in Orissa." (Patra. 15)

Ptolemy's itinerary refers to Palur as an international port during the 2nd century A.D. Hieun-T-Sang refers to Chelitalo as a thorough fare and resting place for the sea-going traders, The water route was known as *Nuapatha* or *jalapath*. The word *Nuapatha* signifies that the water route was a later discovery. The *Jalapatha* (water routes) was divided into two parts: **Nadi patha** (the river route) and the *Vari patha* (the forest route). The *varipatha (the water route)* had two branches: *Kula patha* (the coastal route) and *Samaya patha* (mid-Ocean route)

The foreign historians inform us that there was an ocean-route from Tamralipti to China along Coromandal, via Ceylon and the Indonesian islands. Fa-Hien, in 5th century A.D. returned from India along this route from Ceylon in a merchant vessel (Legge.100: Beal.147-48), Also from Tamralipti port there were regular sailings along the coast of Banga, Burma and Arakan etc. to the south-east Asian countries. During these days voyages on the coast line was considered to be safe since it was visible from the shore. But during the 2nd century A.D. from the itinerary of Ptolemy, *Samayanapatha* (deep sea) voyages are noticed. Gerini records that the Kalingan merchants were used to set out from the port Paloura (Palur of the present day) and across the Bay of Bengal, they reached Indonesia (Gerini 743). It was the only high sea route during that period on the Coromondal coast. There was another overseas route from Tamralipti to South east Asia across the Bay of Bengal. Sri Benudhar Patra comments,"It was trade that placed Orissa in the mainstream of the Indian civilization and led to the enrichment of its magnificent culture heritage." (Patra 16)

Yuan Chwang's Account

Yuan chwang's account shows that the majority of the people of *wu-cha* (*Odra Desa*) were *Mahayana Buddhists*. He further informs that the country had as many as one hundred Buddhist monasteries and about ten thousand monks. Yuan Chwang had proceeded from wu-cha to *Kon-Yu-to* (Kangoda) where the Sailodvabas ruled. Dr. K.C. Panigrahi's description would be helpful here: "He (Yuanchwang) tells us that Kangoda was about two hundred miles from Odra and it had a capital city about 3miles in circuit. It was a hilly country bordering on the sea. This description tallies with the modern physical features of Ganjam and Puri districts which then constituted the Kangoda country. The chinese pligrim further tells us that the people of Kangoda were of black complexion and their language was not very different from the languages of mid-India xxx Yuan chwang, however, notes that their manner of speaking was quite different and this remark indicates that their manner of speaking had been actually influenced by the regional languages of Kalinga and Andhra, which were not of Sanskrit origin." (Panigrahi:63)

From *Kon-Yu-to* (Kangoda) the Chinese pilgrim proceeded to *Ki-ling-kia* (Kalinga). Kalinga at this time was not a part of *An-to-lo* (Andhra). Making a reference to the people or Kalinga, the Chinese pilgrim remarked (qtd. from K.C.Panigrahi)

"People were rude and headstrong in disposition, observant of good faith and fairness, fast and clear in speech, in their talk and manners they differed some what from mid-India." (Panigrahi: 63)

Yuan Chawang's account of the mountain university at *Pu-Su-Po-Kili* (*pushpagiri*) features another interesting characterstic. A flag was fluttering from the peak of the *stupa* without being tied up or fixed in anyway. It stuck to the peak like a "needle sticks to a magnet". The stoney peak of the monastery exuded some super- natural light that was not intelligible to the ordinary mind. If this account would be accepted as viable, *Pushapagiri university* has to be given a special status. It was different from those that functioned at Taxila and Nalanda that were influenced by foreign system of education. Puspagiri must have been blessed by the Tantric monks to continue with our indigenous and auonomous course of studies.

Yuan Chawang had also visited Mahakosala which included Chhaitisgarh and Bastar regions. The Kosala country was one thousand miles in circumference and was full of forests, high mountains and marshes. Yuan Chwang toured over this country to locate the Buddhist monasteries. He mentioned about lots of *stupas* and monasteries that existed in Mahakosala.

As a Buddhist pilgrim of the Mahayana sect, he was neither interested in the kings of Kosala nor in their capitals. Hence we know nothing about their socio-political condition from Yuan Chwang's records.

Chwang's report informs about a great Buddhist monastery with a *stupa* built by Ashoka in which Nagarjuna lived for some time. Although the account does not tell about the name of the reigning monarch, he mentions about a rock-cut monastery at Po-lo-mo-lo-ki-li which is known as *Parimalagiri vihar*. Nagarjuna had evolved his *Madhyamika Philosphy* at this place. The place was "excavated" according to Dr. K.C. Panigrahi, "for the residence of Nagarjuna by a king named Yin-Chang, but neither po-lo-mo-lo-ki-li nor the king Yin-Chang has satisfactorily been identified" (Panigrahi:64 and Raigarh in M.P.) I have a soft corner for this zone, that could not be hardened through time. Cycling into the villages and living with these forest people (singing and dancing included) was a regular habit with me. What I remember about the women folk of Kosala after three decades appears to me now as "mythical-something" related to Ramayana. One of the queens, of Dasaratha was from Kosala. She was Kausalya, the mother of the eldest son, Ramachandra. The kings of *Aryavarta* used to marry tribal women for political reasons. Kausalya, the daughter of this forest country, Kosala, because of her unflinching commitment to her husband and the ideologies of non-acquisitiveness, fell victim to the palace intrigues of Ayodhya and her son, Ramachandra had to go on an exile for 14 years. The cloud-coloured skin of Ramchandra seems to be a maternal feature and the legends/oral histories I collected from the womenfolk of It is an irony that the history of Kosala is still surrounded in mystery and most of our historians have not devoted enough time to tell us distinctly about the culture of this forest Kingdom.

As my youth has been spent in Kosala (with expriences from Titilagarh, Patnagarh, Bolangir Kosala, Mahakantara (Bhawanipatna, Jagadlpur in M.P. and Koraput) and Bastar area are related to Ramachandra's settlement in these areas. The capacity of this Aryan prince to assimilate the culture of the aboriginals of this area also seems to be natural because these were the areas of Mahakosala, (a cultural zone) belonging to Rama's uncles. The commitment of the army of the monkeys and the bears at the time of Rama's expediction to Srilanka was mostly due to the latter's cultural appropriation of the aboriginal features of living and due to Rama's maternal affinity with this area. Our paleontologists equate Hanuman and the *Vanara sena* (army of monkeys) with the *lanjia sauras* (the tribals with a *lanja* or tail. They did not have orinal tails, but they tied up the animal skins aound their waist that way). The lanjia- sauras tie up their groins with a long piece of cloth hanging like a tail even today. Valmiki's metaphorical and metonymical narrative of Ramayana has been accepted by the later readers as purely literary imagination and hence the sculptors and the palm leaf engravers have drawn the portrait of Hanuman as a pure monkey. All subtelties of human imagination have always been understood by the quotidians as gross things. So is the essence of Hanuman in the contemporary sense. In Orissa, a personal survey revealed that these gross worshippers of Hanuman are also strong believers in anal sex and secularism.

As the marginalised son of a queen hailing from the Kosala country of forests, Ramachandra must have realised the plight of his father, who succumbed to the convention of polygamy, a trait appropriated, from the Aryans who entered into India as seekers of the delta pastures and agricultural land.

The Buddhist version of *Ramayana* found in *Dasaratha Jataka* gives a different version of the story. A translated version is presented here. This Buddhist version of Ramayana is an extant book and it has been translated by Sri Hadibandhu Hali and Sri S.N. Satpathy, two advocates of Bhubaneswar.

- Author

Odissan Theories on Archetecture: *Silpa Prakasa*

Dr. Mahatab was unfortunate enough not to have studied this Orissan *Silpa*-text of 10th-12th century, captioned, *Silpa Prakasa*. Rama Chandra Kaulacharya wrote this text and it is now available in translation edited by Alice Boner, R.P. Das and late Sadasiva Rathasharma.

This valuable treatise on Orissan scrulpture describes that the temple is constructed as a *Purusha (man)* and the thigh of the temple must contain *Kamakala Yantra*, (geometry of erotic art, known as yantra or mandala in the Tantric texts. The symbol of Sakti, for example is a triangle and the Department of Family Planning as a red triangle uses it. A temple without such *Kamakala* (the art and science of sex) images is known as a "place to be shunned" (*tyakta mandalah*). Continuing it further, the *sloka* says that such a temple (without erotic images) has to be taken as a "base, forsaken place, resembling a dark abyss, which is shunned like the den of death...." (Das.9)

Archetecture,however, reflects the deep emotions of a race on stone.Ashoka's inscriptions, Kharavela's Hatigumpha and the construction of temples by Odia archetects prove the quality of the Odia archetects. During Ashoka's time tribal archetects from Koraput were invited to Sri Lanka to build temples. Orissa has a place in the national map of architecture. Indian stone art and architecture is classified into four categories: Nagara,Dravida,Besara and Kalinga.

Kalinga, it seems, had a strong assertive culture. It was an independent region between320B.C and 261 B.C till, when Ashoka invaded the country. And reduced Kalinga only to the level of a province under Magadha the administration of the country was done as per the codes laid down by Kautilya. .

The above two illustrations from literature and sculpture with regard to our cultural notions of sex signify the tension between the dominant civilized Oriya culture and the folk, tribal culture of Orissa.

The position and power of the 'dominants' and the 'subordinates' change through the turns of our civilization. The folk culture dominated during the publication of Ramachandra Kaulacharya's *Silpa Prakasa* in 10th-12th century and also during the time of Upendra Bhanja (1680-1720)

Odissan Attitude to Sex in Sculpture and Medieval Literature

The reactions of the anti-Bhanja critics like Bijoy chandra Majumdar and those of Dr. Harekrishna Mahatab reflect the puritanism of the modern civilization. Sri Bijoy chandra Majumdar emphacizes erotics and the verbal acrobatics of Upendra Bhanja and deleberately neglects his dhwani,alamkara,rasa, auchitya and the dramatic elements in his poetry. Same is the puritanic moral schitzophrenia of Dr. Mahatab with regard to the erotic art of Konarka temple.

It is interesting to note that most of the reactions to our literature and sculpture are registered by the *kayasthas* and *khandayats* of modern era. Their attempt to subvert the sex images by strong puritanic diatribe is an attempt to assert that they, too, are capable of modernity and moral purity, hither to monopolised by the dominant Brahminic culture.To some extent, the critics flout the Buddhist norms though they, on a different level, support the Bhuddhist way of life.

This undercurrent of casteist competitivensess, with regard to the moral norms, has shaped and modified our culture during the last five decades. The *kayasthas* and the *Brahmins* have enjoyed alternative positions of dominating power and during the last two decades the intra-kayastha competitiveness has given rise to a dominating *khandayat* culture to pervade Orissa. In an altered cultural milieu, today, the *Khandayats* have to fight a two-pronged casteist battle: against the *karanas* and against the brahmins, in which, the senior *karanas* talk of an assimilation with the *khandayats* through marriage. But the battle against the *Brahmins* remains constant. The non-brahmins get an edge because the *khandayats* have manipulated harvesting of great fiscal advantages during the post independence times

The extereorization of such casteist politics in shaping and modifying our culture alternately leads one ot contemporary culturalist jargons like "cultural contamination" and "cultural appropriation" While making an attempt to analyse the surfacing tensions with regard to domination and marginalization, one would notice that during the transition from the colonial to post colonial era, the brahmins stayed back from the enthusiasm of getting indoctrinated by the techno-scientific modernity to certain extent though the unorthodox brahmins claimed genetic superiority because they could nurture their children as scientists, engineers and bureaucrats to the irritation of other castes.

The competitiveness on the casteist front was a surrogate game between the 'haves' and 'have -nots', that the Marxists attempted to invoke and failed. Toynbee's observation shows that Marxist ideologues continue to provoke the commoners in our country, but it would never thrive since it is a nation where individualism is avidly nurtured and the common folk would never allow themselves to be shepherded like sheep. Hence, the imperialists, while deploying their divisive strategies to rule India, avoided economical class conflicts and introduced caste-conflicts as well as religious sectarianism to generate an entropy within.

The *khandayats*, who were historically marginalised in Orissa because of Brahminic domination, found here a space through modernity to invade on the cultural front, through economic, political and spiritual passes. The attempt was to falsify the history of the Brahmins. However, Orissa was never a region for Brahmins. It was a land of aborigins/ primitives who had settled mostly on the banks of Mahanadi and other rivers. The civilized people conquered them and they were subjugated by their chieftains and the Gadajat kings (of the feudatory estates). In the process, the non primitives had culturally been 'contaminated' by the primitives.

The *gadajat* culture was in a way 'ethnic' in the modern sense and the people belonging to these feudatory states were kept marginalised by the coastal people. This cultural conflict provided a space for the imperialists to wage religious conversion compaigns in the tribal sector and the natives were treated as the others.But the cultural coercion of the coastal people was so severe that the people in Gadajat areas stayed culturally bonded to the primitives. They were treated inferior even to the Sudras. So, the next option was to embrace Christianity, as an alternative.

Those who did not prefer to convert themselves were subjects inspired by Gandhian thoughts of a casteless society and under the umbrella of Gandhian modernity, the brahminical superiority could no more be accepted.

Thus, the cultural phases of Orissa with such blends of pessimism and euphoria for various castes and different periods, reach a post-colonial era in which our culture tended to forget history with the explosive forces of the 'here-and-now'. It was a leap into the free-air that created a nightmare for the system. One of the inherent contradictions embedded in this paralogical modernity is that, it was neither a particular cultural practice nor a historical period, which underwent the process of cultural appropriations only. Rather, modernity, whatever it might be, opened up possibilities for Orissa disrupting all such historical continuity and cultural evolution of this race.

The Brahmins could not defend their culture since the Vedas were dismissed as nonfunctional and old fashioned. The primitives were discarded as boorish, who can never see the elongated torch-light of *British enlightenment*. However modernity on one side, and the Aryan and proto-Austroloid cultures on the otherside, continues to play a ceaseless game of cat-and-mouse on our cultural ground, in and out of time, because they occupy different ontological sites.

The Brahmins, whether they came from Saka-dweepa or Ujjain were outstanding in this state of primitives and tribals. Most of them who lived in the suburbs of Puri as the dwellers of the *Sasanas* (villages in which these brahmins settled) were *Saktas (the worshippers of Mahamaya or some other Goddess)* and as the higher form of Tantriks they could outdo the tribals and could dominate over them. The culture of the primitives was appropriated first by the Buddhists. The *sudras* were influenced by the primitives on one side and by the Buddhists on the other. The Brahminical revivalism began when the national Vedic culture was jeopardised thoroughly at this point.

In Orissa, the Brahmins could not do much for the restoration of the *vedic* culture since they were diasporas in this land of tribal people. Their disciplined life and habits of cleanliness did not suit the primitives and the other hybridized caste groups. However, they could remain indispensable in temple worship, marriages, and birth as well as death rituals.People had a mysterious notion about these outsiders and as great snobs and sanskrit parrots they went on enjoying some regal influence and power. This facilitated them to do nothing for their living and instead of utilising their leisure for study, they structured their time for pseudo-intellectual gossips keeping themselves out of concentration either smoking canabis indica(*bhang*) or by intoxicating themselves with country made liquor which they eulogized as *soma rasa*.Women from the hybridized castes availed of this opportunity and used these brahmins for satisfying their sexual urges. In those days it was a fashion with these hybridized castes to drag brahmin youngmen into the fold of sex.It was done under the alibi that they were sanctifyng their bodies by availing the opportunity of sex with the handsome brahmin lads. The result was further hybridization and the creation of a super brand of shrewd bipeds, who acquired the brahminic sophistication and a charming agility that was inherited from the primitives. The *dombies* of *Charyapada* got themselves transformed into a neo-intellectual class and the kings appointed them as their account keepers. Those who did not know alphabets joined the royal army. They had, however, a strange complex of inferiority and hence they began to lecture on the importance of sexual abstinence and on high voltage austerity so that under the pretention of this didacticism, they could be able to gather lots of wealth for themselves. They were the people who could exploit and gameplay with the primitives and the brahmins simultaneously

The entire gamut of this cultural transformation gets concretised in the interpretative game of Upendra Bhanja's poetry. The reaction of the *brahmo samaj* and the subsequent responses may be studied from casteist point of view since they ventilate multiple reactions to Bhanja's poetic narration of *sri nagar* in an unintibited manner.

The reaction to Upendra Bhanja's literature by the Brahminic order offers interesting cultural nuances. However, these reactions are triggered off only after John Beams accepted Upendra Bhanja as one of the pillars of our *Reeti* poetry of the mediaeval literature.His rich sanskritised *kavyas* were so much in the south Indian tradition that it did not have a parallel in the Bengali literature.

That was a crucial time in the cultural history of Orissa. The Bengali diaspora of Cuttack pressurized at the Headquarters of British Raj that the Oriyas should study Bengali since they do not have a special identity as a linguistic community. The Oriyas living in Cuttack, Puri and Balasore began to shout in their usual declamatory rhetorics as a contemporary Oriya M.P. shouts when Orissa is discriminated in the Railway budget. These shouts were of no avail.

John Beams, who had studied Odia, could defend the language and literature of the Odias by citing the example of Upendra Bhanja's poetry.So, the literature of the Odias which was almost on the brink of extinction survived feebly. But John Beams is never thanked. The colonial Odias were so ungrateful that they did never bother to retain a photograph of that Sahib in Utkal Sahitya Associations and they donot care to garland him even once in a year, at least on the birth day of this great Sahib if the date of his sad demise is not known.

Worse is the case with the greatest of our poets-Upendra Bhanja. Prejudices were showered on him from the coastal belt because the poet belonged to Bhanjanagar area, which was under Madras Pesidency, and not under Calcutta. With the beginning of the modern era in Orissa,(after 1936) regionalism dominated the psyche of the people of Cuttack, Puri and Balasore (Places where the three Zilla Schools were established by the British government). The first thing they did in Orissa was to marginalise the South Orissans(Kalingan culture) and the Western Orissans(Culture of Kosala). They did it with a vengence. One of the favourite pastimes of these people till today is to ridicule the language of the Berhampur and the Sambalpur people, the languages of Kalinga and Kosala that contributed to form the state of Orissa on the basis of language. This is a hegemonic tradition imbibed from the Calcutta Presidency. In other words, the Bengalis wanted to assert their cultural supremacy over the Odias (of Utkala that was constituted of three districts only – Cuttack, Puri and Balasore. The portions of Oriya speaking areas which were under Madras and Nagpur Presidencies were treated as alien and inferior/marginalised places) by consistently snubbing them in the colonial fashion. This has resulted in the creation of three cultures within Orissa.

No one denies that the Bengalies are very rich on the cultural level because they got the advantage of getting the colonial education much earlier to the Oriyas and they could avail of the opportunities a metropolitan would enjoy today- money and the benifits of an industrial society. But their cultural progress and literary advancement remains confined only to the postcolonial period. They knew it very well that there was no one comparable to Upendra Bhanja in Bengali The Odias of Cuttack,Puri and Balasore who were parasites under Bengal were also fully aware of this unfortunate absence of a poet of Upendra Bhanja's stature in their regions. So, they tried hard to subvert the literary importance of Upendra Bhanja by waging a war against his poetry juxtaposing him against Radhanath Ray, a poet heralding the modern age in Orissan poetry.

Culturally, modernity had so devastating an effect in Orissa that it was considered modern to flout traditions and to go for religious conversions.A larger section of the quotidians enjoyed defiling the traditional values. Liberal attitude toward sex, alcoholism, and feeding the home deity with dry fish were common cultural defiances. I encountered the weeping wife of a lecturer in a government college at Puri who complained against her husband that he placed a bundle of dry fish in front of the deity of Saraswati on the day of Saraswati Puja. I knew a lecturer in chemistry at Titilagarh who told me repeatedly that he enjoyed witnessing a goat being butchered for meat.

Both these cases seem to me psychopathological. But I mention them here as examples of Odia modernity. Religious conversations also come under this category. There are modern Odias who place their Hindu God/Goddess beneath their bed, toward the leg-side. The mute calender gods of these modern households must be enjoying uncensored blue films from the modern nude couples.

This was what the operative modern culture meant for the colonial and post colonial Odias. This was partially imported from Bramho samaj of Bengal and the other part was emulated from the Christian missionaries.Sri Kishori Mohan Patra and Bandita Devi, in their book, *An Advanced History of Orissa* record: "The Baptist Missionary Society undertook the work at Puri in right earnest because Jagannatha or the "Lord of the universe" drew 'national reverence' from the people of India....Naturally it attracted the missionaries to work in Orissa for their cherished desire to abolish idolatry They aimed at destroying our belief in traditional faith and institutions and to supplant them by Christianity . But for long six years, they could not convert a single man from the province. The first Oriya convert, Gangadhar Sarangi was a brahmin and gradually after 1828 more Oriyas accepted the new faith."

In such a scenario of cultural decadence, the modern Odias of Cuttack,Puri and Balasore attacked Upendra Bhanja's poetry. The attack exteriorizes a strong cultural prejudice against an emblem of Oriya literary image who hailed from South Orissa. The charges were that the poet wrote obscenity that might infect the moral health of the coastal belt.

When one talks of moral health, it goes against the brahmins, since they were the gate-keepers of the moral fort now being invaded by the moderns, who included the brahmos, the coverts and the liberal sex seekers. The irony is that these moderns endeavoured to dislodge Kavi Samrat Upendra Bhanja(a Southy) on the grounds that he deployed too much of *sringara rasa.(the erotic)*.

However, two of the famous Brahmin leaders defended Upendra Bhanja and both of them were from the Brahmin settlements of Puri.They were Pandit Gopabandhu Das and Pandit Neelakantha Das. Gopabandhu Das accepted him as "*Kavikula Kanja*" and Pt. Neelakantha Das began the process of revaluating Bhanja poetry by editing one of his texts with his erudite acceptance of *Sringar* (the erotic).

This digression into the poetry of Upendra Bhanja concerning sringar/obscenity opens up another dimension of the casteist-regional bias that corrodes Orissan culture. However, the response from the brahmins shows that they were not antimodern and they had great potency for transcending moral hypocrisyThey were able to judge it from a pure aesthetic point of view. For them, *Sringara* leads to a euphoric state of mind and generates two aesthetic forms: *Rupa Saundarya* (formal beauty) and *Bhava Saundraya* (experiential beauty, eg. the *karuna rasa* (pathos) generating *ananda* or pleasure).

The *Khandayat / kayastha* notions of puritanic morality that generated the attack on the reeti poetry of Upendra bhanja are shadows from the churches as well as from the Christian propagators who operated dominantly during those days as torch-bearers of Enlightenment in an Orissa of Primitives or uncultured people. The only saviour was 'modernity' that entered into our nostrils through the industrial smoke of East-India company, emphacizing logic, reasoning, rationalism and scientific temperament. The cultural strategy of this once-upon-a-time dominating class (the *khandayats belong to a class of warriors who served under the kings, were born in the harems of the kings of the feudal states and occasionally became the feudal lords emulating the Rajputs and the Moghal Subedars)*) was to use morality as a social mask, as a garnishing device, as a behavioural instrument of civilization/ sophistication. They seem to have been influenced by Freud's concept of "repression" as shown in *Eros and Civilization*.

These cheerleaders of morality visualize sex as an instinct and *ripu,which* has to be buried deep so that it would surface either as a mask or as a perversion, or as pulpit talk. Our scientific modernism would lead us to logical, seeable experiments and laboratory orientated truth-findings. Rationalism would rescue us from instinctual black-holes and lift us to ascendence of power, be it a chair in one of the air-conditioned cubicles of the secretariat or in the assembly/ parliament.

The *khandayat* inhibitions for sex may also be an act of cultural appropriation from the Brahminic order. Most of them endeavoured to ascend the ladder of spiritualism and to embrace yogic paths. Bairagi Baba of Asurali set an example for the khandayats of the state and proved that spiritual intensity and the powers of the divine were not the monopoly of the brahmins. Even today, one can identify a contemporary *khandayat* by his keen devotion toward Mahaveer Hanuman.

Since such a civilized, highbrow culture is based on the repression of instincts and scientific experimentation, it would evade the process/ *leela* of life and identify success only in the product, in the accumulative surpuls of commodities, that would ring the death-bell of humanism by banal commodification of human values. As Lyotard has pointed out, the "performative principle" is really all that counts in our contemporary culture. All talks of modernity and games of scientific language are games of the rich, who are *khandayats* and *kayasthas* and since they are the wealthiest class, they operate as the representative of the dominant culture.

But their responses to values, morality and sex are only hypocritical masks, i.e., the gap between their performance and commitment is wider. As a result, they have deracinated themselves from their roots of folk-culture and turned the table toward their benefit, to acquire the position of a dominant culture. They have imitated the post-capitalistic principles and contributed to the productivist aesthetic of the artistic 'representation'.

In a society of capitalistic values, social reality is pervasively commodified, fetishized and libidinized as one notices them in the Lyril soap ad-girl's panty or in the ice-cream ad-boy's garmented genitals. The commodity, in this dominant culture, is less an image in the sense of a 'reflection' than an image of itself, its entire material being devoted to its own self representation. In such a dominant cultural condition, the average college-going Oriya girl prefers not to change the culture but to mimic it. But in fact, in a textured and packaged commodity-culture, there is, in truth, nothing to be reflected; no reality exits there which is not itself already image, spectacle or gratutious fiction.

What I am narrating so far is a casteist politics of our culture through mediaevel times to the beginning of this century in terms of its transformation: from its primitive vision trickled down to folk culture and finally having been banalized by strong influences of pop-culture. It is a transformation that influences our people tremendously, and, yet, they seem to resist it since such a revolutionary stance would keep their masks in tact and unscanned, lending it a layer of sophistication. May be, this cultural paradox is not typically Orissan, it is global.

However, I have provided a wide-spectrum overview of our war of cultural politics through casteism and alternative dominations, but not a traditional format of the definition of our folk culture, its parameters and roots. To reach those roots we have to search for the books on micro histories. The regional historians have always been marooned by the mainstreamers. Hence they have attempted to record their regional versions in different books. Such books would definitely help us to know our roots.

The Mountain culture: Mahendragiri

The micro histories of Kantilo, Nayagarh, Banki and Buguda, while tracing their origins, describe dense forest ranges which provide a contrast to the geographical identity of the Ganges Valley. The ancient myth-writers of India, however, had some sort of awe and reverence toward these mountain dwellers. They have mentioned about 7 mountain ranges that existed according to ancient geography: Malayagiri, Sahya giri, Muktiman giri, Rukshya giri, Vindhya giri and Mahendra giri.

The mythical Mahendragiri is still in Orissa. Since the civilized people grew up on the banks of the rivers and consigned the mountain dwellers to the anthropologists and geologists, the name and the geographical contours of Mahendragiri did not undergo any significant change. We have referred to these mountains and the tribal cultures at different places of this book. But we have never referred to the temples of these mountain ranges.

The Indian historians have a bias that most of our temples are built in the Gupta era since some old North

Indian historian, in his euphoria, has called the Gupta age a "golden age" and has ascribed the art of temple building to them. Their ego echoes only one thing: the river- bank dwellers are more civilized than the mountain dwellers and what gives us heritage-identity today in the shape of temple sculpture belongs only to the civilized Aryans. The dwellers of the Sapta Kulachala or Sapta Kula giri (The seven famous hills of India) have been consistently ignored as far as the temples are concerned.Thus the Europeans are being fed with wrong cultural values may be, with lies.

Mahendra giri, situated in Parlakhemundi or stretching between the present Ganjam and Gajapati districts, figure in the list of seven famous hills of India, and thus, speaks volumes about the antiquity of our culture, Fortunately, a temple called, Bhima Mandira stands there in a dilapidated condition because the Govt. of Orissa had been making consistent endeavours to disaffiliate South Orissa from its heritage zone and the concerned officer, probably a man from Utkala, does not make arrangements for the tourists to visit those places.

The bureaucrats marginalize them culturally because they do not want money to flow on to that area on tourist head. The political representatives of that area are so much immersed in their own self-interests that they do not have any interest in such academic matters. They consider all academic matters as stupid because they themselves are academic drop outs and despite their academic disabilities they could dominate their teachers in matters of posting and transfer. However, it might be of some benefit if the politician executives know that Bhima Temple is the ancient most temple of Orissa and it is situated on the Kubja giri, the highest peak of the Mahendragiri mountain.

The speciality of the temple needs a discussion here since it is the most ancient temple of Orissa belonging to the period of Mahenjodaro and Harappa in its antiquity. The height of the temple is 25' and the largest piece of stone used for this temple measures 9'x4'x3' (L x B x circumference).The temple is built with seven large stones. However, there are twelve other small stones and the total number of stones used in the temple is 19 in number.

Dr. Krishna Chandra Panigrahi, the famous historian of Orissa has referred to this temple in his book on Orissan history. But he consigns it to the Gupta era as a minor temple and has disregarded its antiquity. A local historian named Biswanath Mallik from Goshani Nuagam of Berhampur has protested against such eroneous dating of the temple in an article published in the daily newspaper, *Sambad* (Berhampur Edn. Dated.7th July 2001.Saturday).

Mr. Mallik quotes from Dr. K.C. Panigrahi's book: "The small stone temple representing the shrine of Bhima still to be found on the top of the Mahendra Mountain in the Ganjam district is not only devoid of sculpture, but it is not a *Sikhar* temple also-It is a flat-roofed stone structure, but with no circumbulatory covered path to be generally seen in the early Gupta Temples (p.371).

Sri Biswanath Mallik argues that the Bhima Temple, as the Gupta legends have propagated, has not been built by the second brother of the Pandavas - Bhima. It is built by one Bima, (the Telugu pronounciation for Bhima), the chief of the Saura Tribe living in the Mahendragiri plains. The Savaras or the Sauras have the tradition of implanting stone posts/pillars for the dead in the grave yards. They protect it by a stone henge. A stone henge has three or four pillars with a flat stone kept over it to function as a roof or to protect the dead bodies/souls from heat and rain. One may find quite a large number of stone henges around Rayagada, on the Jagamanda hills of Gunupur and in a village called Maliba near Rayagada. Such stone structures are also found in Nuagada block. The Mallikeswar temple on the Jagamunda hills and the Sikhar Chandi temple of Patia resemble such structures and the Bhima Temple stands as a megalithic structure of the Saura culture. Such structures can also be found in the Nilgiri hills of the South and also in the Naga Hills in the North East. A temple of such megalithic design can also be found on the bank of a tank at Jabalpur (Madhya Pradesh). The stone henge there in Jabalpur is meant for the worship of a snake God. Stone henges are also found in some British islands in which the aboriginal people have settled.

Shri Biswanath Mallick's argument has an undercurrent of protest against the Brahminical domination and their Interpretation of history that the temple belongs to the period of early Gupta architecture. In other words, the North Indian historians belonging to the power group, it is alleged, have misinterpreted our history to their cultural advantages.

Sri Malllik has classified Dr. K.C. Panigrahi as a historian of the Brahminic order, advocating the cause of the Gupta kings as the only harbingers of arts, craft, sculpture sand everything that is dumped under the umbrella of culture. Such historians are close to the government at the centre and their scholarly faces, after being painted with a light coat of histrionic make up, are shown on the small screen of big "Doordarshan". They have researched on the "Short cuts to Successful scholarliness" through compromises and have been able to manipulate the reciprocal award of grants from the most corrupt office stationed in Shastri Bhavan, New Delhi, through their lobbies, or on a 20% *Supari* (the contemporary slang for bribe) given to the Delhi based bureaucrats for a consumer goods called culture.

The temple structure consigned to the debris of early Gupta sculpture (and not to tribal sculpture) has become a codified reference to a point of absent presence, which has subsequently repositioned itself at the centre of assessment. By dislocating it from the centre, the pro-Gupta Era historians of the establishment have given a freeplay to the structural centre.They have attempted a demolition of the *Vratya* sculpture. This is a cultural political game played by the historians of the cultural centres.

The *centre* that the Bhima Temple is modelled on the megalithic burial henges should have been at the *centre* of a historical totality. But, by grafting it on the structure of Gupta colonialism, the *centre* is shifted and given a freeplay with an intention of constituting an assuring certitude. The *centre* that the sculpture, if at all any, in the Bhima Temple of Mahendragiri, belongs to the Early Gupta period is the creation of the "force of desire", the establishment of a fictive status. At this point, history lapses into fiction and fiction acquires the status of history.

On a second level, the attitude of consigning every work of art of Orissa to the Gupta period is a cultural politics played by the histroricists of the establishment relinquishing the innocent origin to the margins.. What Mr. Biswanath Mallik attempts is just a postcolonial reassessment, a protest against the colonial syndrome that acts as a toxicant even in the postcolonial era.

However, the 'absolute origin' or the **primordial** in the context of Orissan culture cannot be ignored, be it dances music, art or sculpture.

The Bonda Tribe: The Hilltop Dwellers

Besides these literary descriptions, one may study the legends of these prehistoric tribals to know more about them. One such primitive tribal race is the *Bonda* tribe of Koraput. The *Bonda* women stay naked even today. Few Years back, I was directing a play at Jolaput, Machkund (Malkangiri district) and I was staying with a police officer. A Bonda father came to the police station with the severed head of his son. "Why did you cut his head?" was the question from the Police Officer. The old man answered, "He stole my date palm wine from my tree.A thief does not have the right to live in my community."

During the last election (Sept '99) not a single *Bonda* cast his/her vote. They refuse to know the meaning of casting votes. The most popular version of an oral story about the naked Bonda women runs like this: Rama chandra, his younger brother Lakshmana and Sita, during the 14 years of their exile, came to *Dandakaranya* (in Koraput) to stay for some days. One day, Sita was bathing naked in a nearby *nullah* (a small streamlet) at Mudulipada (near the Bonda hills). At that time a group or leaf-clad Bonda women looked at her and cut obscene jokes. Sita was angry and cursed them to stay naked for ever."

Modern and Postmodern Responses to Legend

The legends might appear funny to the upholders of rationality. But since the Bonda tribals are staying away from civilization, the story might have been carried over to the present generation uncorrupted. Does this legend not bring in some relationship between the primitives and the Aryans?

Our contemporary attitude to legends, myths and the stories of oral tradition are ambivalent. The Odias who are recently educated, still cling on to the early twentieth century brand of modernism: scientism, industry (the culture of displacement, deforestation and excavation), hypocritical double talk (the art of using suavity to kill) and acquisitive exhibitionism (the illusion that buildings,4-wheelers and mobile telephones harvest status), joining the bandwagon of fashion shows etc. Most of them seem to be oblivious of "post modern culture" that questions not only the efficacy of all these characteristics of modernism, but also reinterprets folk tales, myth, legends and the stories of oral tradition.

Modernism, in its emphasis on logic and historical evidence, attempts to explore the relation of logic to ontology; and history, explores the signification of time. The logic seekers dismiss the efficacy of these oral stories on the basis of their surface metaphors. They ignore the interiority of language of the folk tales. By divesting the legends of all their meaning, they reach a nightmarish impasse "where the promise of the origin indefinitely recedes" (Foucault. 394)

As the quotation from Michel Foucault's *The Order of Things* is used, one remembers Nietzsche, one of the western blindmen who branded himself as a philosopher and misguided generations of readers by announcing the banishment of God (the Westerners do not wish to confuse themselves with 33 crores of Gods as the Hindus do, and so they believe in one commodity called God on whose name religion can be marketed and used for imperialistic hidden agendas. Churches gradually become forsaken places for the average dollar hunters in the USA. It is only an attitudinal construction, used for carnal purposes with greater safety. (I gather this information from an Odia travelogue written by Dr. Umesh Patri, an authentic and original observer of the inside of the greatest democratic athlet of the world playing the game of benevolence.)

In his *Thus Spake Zarathustra*, Nietzsche's Zarathustra descended from the mountains to preach to the mankind about the glories of God. He met a saintly hermit in the forest. This old man invited him to stay in the wilderness rather than to go to the cities of men. When Zarathustra asked the hermit how he passed his time in his solitude, he replied:" I make up songs and sing them; and when I make up songs I laugh, I weep and I growl; thus do I praise God." Zarathustra declined the old man's offer and continued on his journey. But when he was alone, he spoke thus to his heart: How can it be possible! This old saint in the forest has not yet heard that God is dead!" (Qtd. in Martin Esslin: *Theatre of the Absurd*: p389)

With this short-sighted, euphoric pseudo-saint of modernity, contemporary bipeds of the Academia contiuned to banish God from their interior spaces, tore the sky like a disposable sheet of waste paper, drank up the ocean and propagated the idea of modernity in Europe and in all colonial countries including India. Thanks to our un-Enlightened aboriginals of Orissa-they are just trying to become modern in political and bureaucratic sectors only, i,e. only by misappropriating the government money and by cheating the tribal people without any prick of conscience.They think it to be a wastage of time to study Nietzsche. Eschewing everything that is interior (and therefore unseen and abstract) is a legacy that we have assimilated from Delhi or Bombay or some other metro city where the refuges of modernity are being downloaded to contaminate our power sector.

Now, reverting back to Foucault's *The Order of Things*, we would re-examine the oral story of the Bondas about staying naked. Here is a question mark to our epistemes of culture and history, to the notion of validity in accepting oral stories as a historical fact.

Old historians, inspired by modernity, would only accept archaeological evidences as history. I will quote Ihab Hassn, writing about Foucault's book on this point, since written words appear to our intellectuals as truthful as the Lord's words:

Hassan, in his book, *The post modern Turn*, analyses," In *The order of things*, Michel Foucault identifies three major "*epistemes*" of Western history, the last, beginning early in the nineteenth century, is the "modern". Two modern forms of reflection arise: Science, which explores the relation of logic and ontology, and history, which explores the relation of logic to ontology, and history, which explores that of signification to time.

But the decisive trait is this: putting in doubt the reciprocities of being and meaning, modernism finally generates a self-reflexive discourse, a radically intransitive language, which can only affirm its own "precipitous existence", its ludic "dispersal". We call that language modern literature.

The 'dispersal' of language-shall we say its near immanence?- marks for Foucault the "disappearance" of man, not literally, to be sure, but as a particular idea, a concrete figuration of history. This "disappearance" turns out to be yet another Nietzschean prophecy, its realization coming nearer every day." (Hassan: 52)

I relate this idea of 'disappearance' of man to the logic-seekers/ evidence-seekers of "modern" history who take into account only the archaeological evidences as concrete history. This facilitates only the researchers of the wealthy countries. The quotations from the *Puranas* and Sanskrit literature used in the previous pages to configurate the milieu of *Sabara, Juang, Santal, Kondh, Koya* and *Bonda* communities of the prehistorical era would not be believed by the "scientific" historians. The oral histories (as I used them for the Bonda woman's nakedness) would not be accepted as a method to explore the relation of logic and ontology.The story of the Bonda women about clean-shaving their heads goes back to Rama's fourteen years of exile into Malyavantagiri (present Malkangiri, the abode of the Bondas) forest. These tribal women saw Sita bathing in the stream and were cursed to cleanshave in oder to keep the fertility of forest-nature.

Critical histriography simply implies an emphasis on explanation rather than on narrative; all good histriographic research involves both kinds of historical enterprise- a meaningful story and a provocative explanation of the various turns the story takes. Dan Ben-Amos writes about such studies in the context of European Renaissance: "xxx the fundamental questions they posed about the nature of belief and history,language and the imagination, man, nature and society', are crucial to our enquiry today.The challenge they provide to our Folklore studies should be met with modern concepts, methods and theoretical formulations."(Quoted in the "Introduction" to *Critical Studies in Folklore Historiography*" in *Western Folklore. Vol.XLVII. Issue No. 1.Jan.1988*).

As I write about the Bondas, I ransack the interview-papers I collected during 1972-1973 while acting and directing a play of mine in Jolaput, Machhkund, with the initiative taken by Shri Debendra kumar Das, (lyricist & D.S.P stationed at Jolaput,which includes the Bonda hills}. This author discovers from the interview records that there is an authenticity in their voice and they assert their conviction forcefully since they have learnt the story from their grand parents who learnt it from their grand parents and so on. Our contemporary sociologists should resist laughing at me and ridiculing their narrative.

Contemporary sociologists still use interviews as a method for constructing a milieu and social anthropologists may consider it worthy. The postmodern histriographers have also started using "oral history" as an efficacious method for investigation. Today, the *Bonda* calls himself/herself a `remo' which means *human being*. The civilized people call them Bonda (=the naked)

The *Bonda* does not know his/her history as something extraneous to his stories/legends. Verrier Elwin in his *Bonda Highlander* (1950), however, divides them into three locational groups:

(a) **Barjang Community**: The community living at Barjang who settled in the present Barkhandi village situated at the appex of the Bonda Hills. They consider Mudulipada village to be their original place of dwelling. There is an ancient banyan-tree with a cave in it. The god in it is *Patakhanda* whom they worship.During my study tours to other Saura settlements, I could gather that the tribal communities come down from the hill tops and settle in comparatively plainlands, surrounded by the hills though. This might also have happened in the case of the Bondas too.

(b) *Gadaba* **influenced community**: This community is influenced by another tribal community called the Gadavas and they live in around twenty villages. They do not know about the community God called *Patakhanda*.

(3) **Plain area community**.There is another Bonda community that lives in the plain areas leaving his property on the hills above.In early 70s, when I stayed for about a month in Jolaput with a Deputy Superientendent of Police, I lived with these Plainlander Bondas and occasionally met the highlanders. The D.S.P. however, had to inspect the highlands to investigate into the murder cases which were frequentin Bonda settlements.

The civilized people and the tribal development officers consider them to be beasts. But these *Bondas* have preserved their thousands years old culture intact, caring very little for the practices and messages of the civilised people. They even stay indifferent and obstinate to the voting system and other civilizing agencies working in the world outside.

Dr. C. Von Furer Haimendrof stayed with the Bondas for

two months with his wife in 1941. After 40 years, he reached the Bonda Hills on 20.12.1981 and wrote:

"I was delighted to see that the Bondos have retained their independence of spirit and their traditional tribal culture at a time when many other tribal communities have fallen victim to exploitation by vested interests and the alienation of their land."

(*Visitors Book*, Bonda Development Agency, Mudulipara)

The *Bonda* male folk are called *Ingarboe*. They are not black and ugly. Many of them have white skins and their appearance is innocent. They keep uncut curly hair that hangs upto the neck, decked with different coloured feathers. (A contemporary uses clips, too). They don't use any dress. The genitals are covered only with a *ghusi*, a long strip of cloth tied up to the waist. He uses lots of ear-ornaments and rings made of brass. Some of them also put on brass garlands. A pouch hangs from the waist to keep his *dhungia* or bidi. (Smoke sticks made of leaves for rolling them). But the Bonda is used to keep four weapons-battle axes, a bill-hook or chopper, a dagger and bows and arrows with a quiver. In prehistoric days they used stone-weapons. Mostly they live on drinks called *Sagur* (made out of fruits and grains) and *Sapung* (made out of *salapa*, an indegenous tree of the palm-family).

The *Bonda* females are called *Selani*. They clean-shave their heads and do not put on any dress since Sita of Ramayana days cursed them. The *selani* believes that the Bonda hills would go bald if they violate the words of Sita. She prefers to stay naked and bald and ugly in order to keep her forests glow with greenery. But she does not look ugly and naked, in fact. Her bald head is decked with strips of *ludaya* (beads). She uses *ndainda*,an improvised hair clip prepared out of palm leaves. Her naked bust, from the neck to the naval is covered with *lubadya* (garlands of yellow and red beads or coins). The waist is covered with a piece of *ringa* (a piece of home spun coloured cloth). The thighs and the legs and the buttocks are bare. They put on ten/twelve metal bangles and a *limbilu* (ear-rings)

These italicized words are derived from Telugu as the

Bondas live closer to Andhra Pradesh, seperated by the river Machhakunda, and from Andhra. The Bonda women would never put on a sari and develop a hair style. Such beautificated women cannot be married. However, the female folk run the family, look after the cultivation and spin the strips of clothes. The male members move about fully drunk and they work according to their moods. The women preserve their homes, their forests and their culture.

Marriage in *Bonda* communities is a matter of the girl's choice. They meet in the *Selani dingo* (the club house for the young folk) and the young ones sleep there in the night. Widows, elderly ladies and divorcees of the Bonda female community watch them. But they would never marry in the same village. Young and old men from distant villages would come in dark nights crossing the mountains and holding flames. They would blow their *Singa* (a blow instrument made out of horns), *Kintisagar* (their dhol or percussion) and *Phine* (an indigenous *Sahnai*).

There would be altercations through songs. The girls' team would say in songs: "We have houses like yours. Also we've paddy and rice. We have also *beda/dangar* (fields in the mountain for cultivation) like those of yours. We've mango and jack fruit trees. If you feel like coming - come. If you don't - go away."

The male team would, then, start coaxing female ones : "*Anang naul sagnai* (we've come because you're so good) "Dini sari sibsiti digla" (You're as beautiful as a flower) and so on. The bondas believe in free sex, but premarital sex is not allowed. No illegal baby is ever heard to have been born on the Bonda hills. A boy is married at the age of 7 or 8. A fifteen year old boy who comes to marry would be teased as an "old grown groom" (*budha bara*).

This lengthy diversion into the *Bonda* tribal style of living may be taken as my nostalgic infatuation, my personal acquaintance with them. However, I have also lived with the *Kondhas* and the *Parajas*. I also know a Kela community (a community of snake charmers) living near Bhubaneswar.

Instead of using vermilion on the forehead as an auspicious mark, the husband puts a mark on the forehead of the wife in mud. These gypsy tribals hate people who build houses to enclose the sky with a roof and those who store materials for their personal use. They treat these house-builders as untouchables.

What I attempt to describe through these glimpses of tribal life is expected to be a pointer for our aboriginal culture for which I do not find "modern" historical evidences. However, my account should not be set aside with an alibi that this is a faddist endeavour to prove that the culture of the Odias is one of the most ancient cultures of India. There is nothing controversial about it.

The History of Koraput (Odra Desa)

Shri Jaladhara Swain, the famous local historian of Koraput, traces the history of Koraput to the Mesolithic times, but admits that this district of the primitive tribes has not been able to preserve anything to authenticate his observations. However, there are mythological evidences. Ramachandra, the prince of Ayodhya, had spent his youth in the jungles of this district. Sita has sanctified its small river Tamasa after taking a dip in it. The Bonda (the most primitive of Koraput who do not believe in clothes even today) legends and oral history still retains the memory of Sita. The river Indravati was known as Mandakini of the Ramayana fame.The river Nagabali has been named after the princess of the Naga kings. Similarly, the river Machhkund has been named after the Matsya kings.

In a district that has nothing but the jungles and the rivers and the mountains, the evidences can be inferred from such names only.The primeval kings had implanted bamboo trees to keep up the memories of their family(*Vamsa*) alive, and later, they had named the river as Vamsadhara.

The sixth son of Bali, the great donor of Ramayana fame,

ruled over this forest region. His name was Odra and since then the land was called Odra Desa. Raja Dandaka of the *Satya Yuga* reigned here and after him the Dandakaranya forest has been named.Shri Swain, in an essay published in a souvenir of the *Cultural festival of Koraput* (1999) mentions that this was the place of the Astadasa Vidyadharas, the eighteen Vidyadharas (intermediaries between the Gods and the human beings, who had the capacity to fly. If you dont believe in such a concept, read the inscription of Kharavela in the Ranigumpha of Bhubaneswar and see for yourself who the Vidyadharas were.Your 20th century rationalism, scientism and logic ceases here and gets nullified.The Vidyadharas were worshipped by the kings of the Naga dynasty. The Vidyadharas can be accepted as the tribal equivalents of the Buddhist Yakshas, who could also fly.(The ignorant moderns should hold their rationalistic attitude and cynicism in abeyance for a moment. We are talking about Koraput, a district where a tribal man even today, in the twentyfirst century transforms himself into a tiger, lives as a ferocious beast for some days and again reverts back to manhood. If you dont believe, please go and chek up. The *Vidyadharas* are still alive in ther tribal Tantra.)

Koraput gave us the first concept of paddy as a crop, reports Sri Swain.The *Maha Bharata* mentions this land as the <u>Nishada Rajya</u> , while the Vedic people named the tribal men of Koraput as the *atabikas*. Pliny, too, mentions this region as the land of the *atabikas*.Valmiki's Ramayana, however, describes Dandakaranya in detail. Kali Dasa's *Megha dootam* mentions about Ramagiri hills.

The region was called Mahakantara, or a part of it around 300 B.C.King Vyaghraraja was ruling over here around 350 A.D. Samudra Gupta defeated him and began to rule over here after that.The Salia rock edicts etched around 5th.century informs that Samudra Gupta, got his son Chandra Gupta (Vikramaditya-II) married with king Kubera Naga's daughter. Prabhavati. . She was the queen-in-chief of king Rudra Sena of Bakataka (between c.375-414 A.D.) The historians still believe that Chandra Gupta (Vikramadityta-

II)used to depute Kali Dasa to Nandapura to look after the well being of his daughter, since she was married in a remote area. Kali Dasa's occasional visits to Nandapura might have inspired him to mention Ramagiri in his *kavya*, *Megha Dootam* since it was the main tourist site of Nandapura kingdom, inhabited by different forest tribes in those days

. Friendless and away from home, this North Indian poet used to visit the Ramgiri hills to enjoy the tourist- friendly clouds. In the 70s of the twentieth century, this author has seen clouds softly entering into the Koraput bus, wetting the passengers and silenly passing by the next window. It seems Kali Dasa had spent a memorable monsoon in this exotic wild zone one thousand and seven hundred years ago.Presumably, the idea of sending the cloud as the emissary might have struck him at that time.

Nandapura was the capital of the state called Bakataka. The natural beauty of Nandapura (in Koraput) might have pulled him many a times, and the Ramagiri hills was, perhaps, the major attraction. Sri Jagannatha Saraf, a local historian writes, "the caves at the appex of Ramagiri hills, the green trees all around, the murmuring music of the forest foiuntains kept the poet enthralled. In one of the monsoons, the great poet, away from his motherland and the family, imagines himself donning the role of a cursed yaksha, and sends the cloud emissary(*Saraf*"Megha doota re barnita Ramagiri"*(The Ramgiri hills as described in *Megha Dootam*)Tr. Ramesh Panigrahi,*Sabara Sreekshetra,* Koraput, Sept.1,2003 P.11)

A rock edict found at Podagada of Umarkote division and written in Sanskrit language reads like this: "Bhavadutta, the king of Nala dynasty was able to get back the states lost by his father and he paved wide roads in the country. His highness has built the temple of Harihar at Podagada and he has taken all responsibilities of its maintainance and has sanctioned money for the smooth conduct of the Lord's annual rituals."(Tr. from the Oriya text of Sri K.N.Mishra)

Umerkote was the capital for the kings of Nala dynasty: Arthapati, Narendra sen, Skanda Burman and Chalukya Keerti

Burma. They ruled from 400 AD to 450 A.D. and during their administration the knowledge of Tantra was spread among the tribal people of Koraput.

The period between 450 A.D. to 498 A.D. was domainated by the kings of Mathar dynasty. A rough account given by Bira Vikram Dev of Jeypore reveals that Bisakha Burman, Uma, Sankara, Shakti, Chanda, Nanda prabha and Jnana Burman were the kings of Mathar dynasty and Umarkote was their Capital.

Before we discuss the impact of Buddhism and Jainism in Koraput, we should know something about the Dongria Kondhs, one of the ancient most tribes of Koraput, who would show us the light toward the primitive inner space, the cultural space that actually predates the Vedic age. The Odras were never the Aryans. Whenever the Aryans have stepped into this *atabika* space(the forest dwellers), they have been compelled to admit *the* superiority.of the *vratyas*

As we probe into the history of Koraput, we not only discover a major chunk of our cultural antiquity, but also get a glimpse of the religious bel;ief-system of the Orissan primitives. This situates Orissa in a comparative space of culture, juxtaposed with the so called hoary Aryans, who are known across the world as great Vedic philosophers. But long before the Aryans arrived and settled in the delta of the Ganges, the Dongria Kondhs of Koraput lived in the deep forests and they never wanted to know about the Aryans. They lived in their own style, and were never bereft of a spiritual vision. .

The Languages of Primitive Odissa

But before that we must complete the disscussion about the prehistoric languages. By the time, our highlanders rejected Sanskrit, *Kalinga, Kangoda* and *Kosala* (called *tri-kalinga* or *tri-calinge* and also as Toshala, Moshala and Koshala) had sixty two tribal groups living in different parts of our state. All of their languages were oral languages and a couple of them had alphabets too.

These languages can be divided into two language families (a) Munda langauge family (b) Dravidian language family. The Munda language family consists of Gatah (Didayi), Gutab (Gadaba), Juang (Juang), Koda, Mundari (Munda) Birhor (Mankadia) Santali (Santal), Saura (Sabara) Garum (Parenga), Remo (Bonda) Kharia, Korua Bhumija, Ho (Kolha) and Mahali languages.

(b) Among the Dravidian language groups we have Parji (Dharua), Kui (kondh), Kubi or Kanda (kondh), Olari (Gadaba), Kurukh (Oraon), Gandi, Madia, Pengu (Penga Kondhs) and Kisan languages.

However, there are regional variations. The Munda groups of language speakers do not stay in one concentrated area. They are spread all over the state. The Southern Mundas are of five types. Saura, Pareng, Gadaba, Bonda and Didayi, who speak their own languages. The Mundas of the central Orissa speak Juang and Kharia languages. There are lots of Mundas on the Northern part of Orissa who speak Santali, Ho, Bhumija, Mundari (Munda), Birhor (of the Mankadias), Mahili and Korua languages.

Languages of the Dravidian families like Tamil, Telugu and Kannad have also influenced different tribal sects who are spread over the Southern, Central and Northern zones. Among the Southern tribals we notice pure Tamil, Telugu and Kannad being spoken in their distorted pronunciation. The centrally located tribals who speak *kui*/kuvi/kanda variations of Kondh language have the influence of South Indian languages. The Pengu, Gandi, Koya and Modia languages of the centrally located tribals are also influenced by the Dravidian group of language. But it is strange to note that the South Indian influences are also there in the Northern Orissa tribal languages like Oraon, Malto, Kisan and Brahui.

The Santalies and the people of Kui group have their own alphabets. Pt. Raghunath Murmu (1905-1982) has created the Santali alphabets (1935-36), which are called Olchik. These alphabets look like pictures and printing presses have these letter types in Mayurbhanj district. The Sauras have their own alphabtes which are pronounced almost like Telugu. The inventor of the Saura alphabets (*Sorang Sompeng*) is Guru Mangei Gamang (1916-1980) and these alphabets were created around 1936. Sri Loka Bodra of Jhinkapani, Singhbhum (Bihar) has invented Ho scripts. There is an All Orissa Kui Society Union at G. Udayagiri and its president Sri Dayanidhi Malik has devised the Kui alphabets mixing up Oriya and Devanagari styles in it. Some other tribals are using a mixed language that can be studied under Oriya dialectology.

In the Southern Odissa *desia, jharia, matia, utri, halbi* and *bhunjia* langauges are used as tribal dialects. Samilarly, *bathudi, bhuyan, kurmali* and *saunti* are the northern dialects. The people from the western Orissa speak a totally different dialect. However, *sadri, laria, aghoria, kandhan* and *baiga* languages are considered to be pure dialects of the western Orissa.

These days the Governemnt of Orissa has founded an Academy for Tribal langauges and culture. The Academy has taken up translation projects from the tribal languages to Oriya and vice-versa. Once these books are available in the market more information would be available to us about the tribal ways of living.

This sketchy study about the languages of Orissa reveals that our culture has more of Dravidian roots than those of the Aryans. The state God of Orissa, Lord Jagannath, is also a *Sabara* God, and his floral decorations (*Tahia*-etc) are purely South Indian. Lots of sweets made in the temple are South Indian. *Makar Sakranti* is celebrated in the temple and the typical rice soaked in butter milk and mixed with sugar and coconut is offered to the Lord on that day in the South Indian style. What are the Odias then as a cultural community?

Village System and Agriculture

What I have traced through these pages is only a silhoutte of the prehistoric past, the days of the Odia *Vratyas*, the naked folk of the mountains and the jungles, their appearance and food habits seen through the description of the Aryan invaders, the civilised, disciplined and code-abiding power groups.This reminds me of Jacques Derrida's construction of the bipolarity between Nature and Culture.Orissa was Nature and the Indo-Europeans/Aryas who codified their notions of civilisation became Culture.What am I writing about in this book? Is it only Nature? Not Culture? If my vratyas/ tribals were not invested with a culture, I'd throw away all Indo-European hybrids as cultured people into the dustbin of civilization. People clad in a bikini called rationalism and logic would call me a belated romantic and diagnose me as someone suffering from "spontaneous outburst of emotions". But what does that scientific terrorist do when he engages himself with the invention of destructive weapons? Is it not a romantic Frankenstein syndrome? Perhaps it is a postmodern retribalization of the self. It occurs in the United States and this phenomenon is imported to New Delhi and other metro cities. It is beyond the parameters of logic and rationalism to conceive retribalization as a trendy concept. In that case the Bonda Hills and its clothe-hating tribes are more advanced than the bipeds, who freak around Ansal Plaza in the evenings of the capital city of India. Since this proposition would be unteneable to many, hence I build up my own independent rationale of culture in my own primitive Nature. My Nature is my Culture. I care little whether the Indo-Europeans approve of it or not.

There were no glaciers in Kalinga to bring reference to the ice Age. Geologists, the people who study the history of this earth, tell us that the ice-age was succeeded by a warm spell. The picture of Kalinga we get through this silhoutte belongs to this warm spell that generated the dense forests where the pre-historic men and women lived in their blessed nakedness, in the pure "state of nature".

When the Aryans reached central Europe (they were the Greeks and the Mediterraneans), they looked upon the people of central Europe and Northern Europe as barbarians. By this time, America was discovered and Gondwana land was separated by a great earthquake, a part of it was retained as the triangle-shaped south India and the other part was split up to become Africa.We do not know what was happening there. Egypt was, during this period, declining out of her great and ancient civilization. In Mesopotamia and Persia and Asia Minor empires were created and destroyed. There were the Assyrian Empire, The Median, the Babylonian and later, the Persian.

At this point, before we focus on the scenario of agriculture, we may look at the roots of the Aryans. Romila Thapper's *Cultural Past* (OUP, 2002) proves that the concept of the *Aryans* and their racial superiority emerged only during the colonial times. But the word Arya was used in Sanskrit since a very long time and its meaning is "honourable person/women". Zarathustra was also called Arya, and that was more related to his biological birth. It is connections with his blood. Emperor Cyrus of Persia was called Kuruh (and the Kurus of Mahabharata were of Persian blood) and the Jews who lived to their West believed that they were the dearest ones of God. They came to Assyria as prisoners and after bthe death of Cyrus, Darius released them. Later, Persia was split up and later Jehova emerged as the Father of Jesus Christ. Later, around 622 A.D. Allah emerged as the emissary of the Creator.

The concept of God, the Sumerians believed, emerged from their culture and it travelled to India.They were, of course, a highly cultured race by 4000B.C. They knew the use of metals; they shaved their beard and head, used very complicated alphabets and dominated over the mountain range of Persia.They were naked. Pt. Nilakantha Das, the only cultural anthropologist of Orissa argued that these Sumerians were the Dravidians of India and had sailed to the distant land through sea route. They travelled from Sind area(where the Mahenjo daro excavations were made)also by land and reached the banks of river Tigris. Later the Aryans defeated them, but the Dravidians have kept the Aryans enthralled by their highly polished culture, language and style of expression. The Aryan civilization has been built on the skeletal infrastructure of the Dravidians. Das argues that the Puranic Ila was the original ancestor of the *Ailas* or the Somavamsis. The contemporary Pamir plateau, China and Turkey area was the once upon a time Aila varsha and the ancient Sumerian area. The Persians had come to India after getting afflicted by the Asuras (the Assyrian Gods) and ulltimately these people were compelled to admit the these Asura Gods: *"Mahaddevanam –asuratvam-ekam"*. They had their own ways of pleasing the Gods-Indra, Agni and Varuna. They used to invite them to their lunch and dinner. But the subsequent generation developed contempt for the Asuras and designated them as demonic creatures. Thus they differentiated themselves as Aryans. The Asuras in the Persian religions also appear as cruel and subhumen. All the religions and agricultural sciences emerged from this Aryan-Non-Aryan bipolarity.

About 5000 years from now, there was also an invasion on China and the invaders were from the west- the tribes of central Asia. They knew the science of agriculture and kept large folks and herds of cattle. They settled down near the river Hoang Ho. The Chinese people of this priod were largely farmers and their chiefs were patriarchs, though at times, they behaved like emperors.

As a contrast, the naked people on the Bonda hills were also found to be rice-eaters and *suan*-porridge eaters (*suan* is a grain cultivated in the Saura mountains, not available in the plain area), which presupposes that they also knew the art and science of agriculture. *Suan* is a kind of seed which can be cooked like rice. But the cultivation was done by the women folk. Besides, they knew the art of making bead-garlands. They could spin narrow and long strips of loin-clothes for themselves as well as for their male folk.

Although I have not stated it clearly, these naked people had already developed their own village system. The western researchers have classified them into three groups basing on their village system, that had a *Nayaka* or a chieftain who controlled the village affairs, the *Selani dingo* (the club house), the deity to be worshipped and based on the differences in marriage rituals.

The chieftains, however, were not the autocratic administrators. There was a spirit or democracy and the folks were given the full liberty to exercise their own choices. Such a practice can be evidenced from the marriage system of the Bondas in which the choice of the girls in selecting their husbands was to be voted by the elders with the consent of the Nayaka. The 'collective' was the culture for the tribal.

To appropriate a phrase from Sri Chittaranjan Das's study (and to translate it), the umbilical chord of the tribal individual has not yet been severed from the society. The villages named Dantipada, Bandhaguda, Baunsapada, Krisanpada, Patiguda, Chalanguda, Goparaguda, Sirelguda, Baraguda and Mudulipada, in which the Bondas live, are living evidences of their ancient village system.

The *Parajas* of Koraput had caste system. A *paraja* cannot marry in *Dama* caste. In an essay captioned '*The parajas of Orissa*, Ram Das classifies the *Bondas* as the fifth clan of the *parajas*. The *Bondas* like the *parajas* have a caste called *Bhandari* (the barbar) who is deployed during their *Patakhanda* festival, celebrated during the month of February as a fertility ritual, after the harvest. The ritual signifies the practice of farming.

Patakhanda Mahaprabhu (The God of the sword) is their lord of Lords. According to a legend prevalent in the area about the genesis myth, God had to undergo an intense inner termoil because of the reckless exploitation of the earth by human biengs. Completely exasperated, God was trying to reach a place for his peaceful habitat and he selected Mudulipada *village* in Koraput hills. He was pleased with the environment and stayed there. By this time God was old and therefore he disappeared after showing a glimpse of his arrival to the villagers. Next night, he emerged again in a dream to the *sisa* (the village priest) in the shape of a sword and directed him to worship him in that material form. He was placed in the shape of a sword and was brought down. The *Sisa* (Priest) worships him by offering rice almost equivalent to a quintal. A cock was sacrificed and its blood was poured on to the rice. The bloodstained rice was distributed amongst the villagers and they threw the rice in their fields for higher yields.The practice still continues as a continuity of that legend.

This aboriginal practice is connected with the *Kedu Parab* (the kedu festival) and the "Meria Sacrifices" of the Kondhs, which has come down to the folks in the plain land, as *Dharani Puja* (worship of the mother earth.) These are all figments of their fertility rituals, that prove their knowledge about agriculture.

With these ritualistic practices, we retrieve a glimpse of the social organisation of the tribals of the distant past.We need not, therefore, focus exclusively on the Bondas only. There are other tribes about whom we should know.

Odia Tribal Culture

Odia Tribal Culture stands as an antithesis to the Vedic culture.The cultural characteristics of our tribes, therefore, differ from those of the Hindu culture in several ways.Besides tribal endogamy, they have got clan systems of their own with varying rituals of marital and sexual norms.Their caste heirarchy differs according to their professional occupations and levels of acculturation.Clans are generally totemistic and are followed religiously by different groups. These totemic objects (be it a sword or a tree or a plant or an animal) are believed to have helped the remote ancestors of the group and are treated as sacred.

Clan exogamy is common and marriage within the same clan is strictly prohibited. Any attempt to flout the norms of the clan are treated severely and it results in ex-communication. Because of such strict rules, they could not convert themselves into the Vedic Hindu norms and the Aryans treated them as the Vratyas.But during the 19th. century, the Christian preachers could convert them. They could convert them successfully hitting at their poverty by providing them with fiscal aids, medical help and rare comforts of modernity.This has taken place under the pretext of purging the tribals of their taboos and superstition. It could also be renamed as an extension of humanism. Now, after the expiry of the era of scientism and logic, we re-examine their life style and discover that the greatest taboo the westerners suffer from is science.What the tribals practise as exogamy seems to be a high order of social organisation.

Besides the practice of clan exogamy, certain tribes also followed the principle of village exogamy. Marriage within the same village is not permitted.Village exogamy is prevalent among the Kondhs,Bondas,Juangs and the Bhuyans. In some other tribal societies, marriage within a group of villages is prohibited as men and women are treated as brothers and sisters in that area.

The tribal society was, thus, constituted taking a group of villages andthe entire group was treated as one family. The seasonal rituals were being performed by rotation in different villages. The Kondhs used to observe Meria sacrifice(human sacrifice) as a part of the fertility rite.As the Goddess Kali was a part of their life experiece and habitat she was also a part of their dream experience(for your information, dream is not a part of the subconscious, it is a strata of the effulgent consciousness and a level of awakening in tribal psychic space. Freud is much inferior in his understanding of the structure of dreams, to the tribes who practised human sacrifice and equated agriculture=mother earth=the Goddess painted in blood as the source of creation in their shamanistic practices.

It is also interesting to note that the Imperialist government, in its spree of showing us its renaissance-brand modernity, took severe steps to ban the Meria sacrifice. I consider this British sociological project more as an act of politico-religious subversion than an endeavour of social reformation.(COmpare this with U.S.A. and England's recent attack on Iraq) The tribals of Orissa were also aware of this British strategy and though no Mahatma Gandhi had an occasion to inspire them, they revolted against the imperialists vehemently.The congress brand historians should not boast that the speeches and the journalese of the FATHER of the nation ignited in every Indian citizen's mind the fire of national love and then the country became independent. Gandhi did hardly have any impact on the tribal uprisings of the highlanders of Orissa. Their role in the freedom struggle has been totally dehistoricized in India. Our stupid historians found it less lucrative to document the contribution of the tribal society to the freedom struggle of India than those white caps occupying chair in the central governments. Their fights and sacrifices are more dramatic and thrilling than those of the most mainstream freedom saheeds and perhaps more than that of Saheed Bhagat Singh. Their cases go unrecorded because they did not belong either to the North or to the South. Patriots of capitalism do not sponsor their case either in small oron big screen. We can recount the names of Dharanidhara Bhuyan(Keonjhar) Laxman Nayak(Koraput) and Chakara Bishoyi(Ghumusar). The playwrights of Orissa have depicted their events and staged shows, but the historians are almost silent about them.

However, we do not like to digress here by recording their history. We are concerned here mostly about the pre-Aryan social organisations existing in the tribal settlements of Orissa, and not with the colonial history.

The practice of the marriage rituals speak eloquently about their social organisations.A tribal marriage is a major social institution.It posits the individual event in the large context of the universe as it was known to the tribe. The songs are attempts to universalize the marriage. We can take, for example, a Santal marriage song called *Binti*, which continues for three to four hours and the song is rendered through professsional singers.The song begins with the creation of the world, the original human settlement, the need for a social organisation, and then it moves to the evolution of the society through historical time. It is strange to note here that the song acts like a Hindu marriage mantra, in which different gods are invoked to stand witness to the marriage.

The ceremony is also a space for social gathering and the dances and other performances done in the presence of the old people transform the performance space to a ritualistic space and then to a sociological space.The young ones also use it for selecting their future brides and grooms. Thus the interaction between the villages is enhanced and it paves the way for a compact and harmonious community.

The tribal social organization is also discernible from the agricultural rituals, birth rituals, name-giving rituals and bone-drowning rituals.These rituals will be discussed in detail in a separate chapter.

However, we can discuss about the position of women in the tribal society, which can also justify its matriarchal nature. They do not recognize any FATHER of the nation because they conceive a nation in terms of a mother. This is the reason as to why the government situated at New Delhi or Bhubaneswar does not like to make direct funding to the tribal people. The NGOs with foreign funding exploit them sexually.

This observation on the contemporary tribal societies would not help us much about their roots and about their social organizations. Everyone must have seen them dancing in circles to a 3-beat rhythm and that is basic to most of the tribal dances.Dr. Sitakant Mahapatra, a celebrated poet, anthropologist and a *jnanpeeth* Awardee in a book captioned *The Tangled Web:Tribal Life and Culture of Orissa* designates a chapter as "Circles of Togetherness". Though he uses the phrase in a different context, I decipher a visual thinking in his phrasing, and I would like to borrow the word to use it in the context of the cultural ontology of the Odia tribals.

This pre-Aryan and the pre-Vedic village organisation was autonomous and "self sustaining human institution. They have looked at it from the points of view of political institutions and processes, social and cultural interactions, interpersonal and inter-family relation They have also looked upon it as an economic institution and a sociological structure."(Mahapatra.p.29)

As I deal with the tribal awareness of the social

organizations of the ancient times, I tend to get overpowered by a bias that as non-Vedic *Vratyas*, the Odia tribes were never inferior to the Ganges valley- dwellers who came from the European stock. They designated us as *mlecchhas* and have been humiliating us as inferior to them.Thus, even today we are discriminated by the centre in terms of funding, railway communication and other things which would have made Orissa one of the major sources of primordial knowledge. Instead, they have fallen victim to the Imperial strategies of pseudo-revolution and have totally marginalized this tribal state. As a result, the centre misses a major chunk of global post modernism, that could have been extracted from the tribals in terms of primitive knowledge. The tribal people of Odisa would have guided the directionless European scholarly bipeds in an era of post postmodernism.It is a time, in which, the western creative people feel euphoric and attempt to break all boundaries and fail ; yet they obstinately continue to limp toward the limitless, perhaps boasting of cyberspace.

They would have been just amazed to dicern the cyberspace in the cave-like huts of these highlanders. Of course, they ought to have the right kind of eyes to dicern it, otherwise, they should readjust their scholary lenses for an inner focus. Their economic affluence has led them toward an alternative beastliness, which they endeavour to hide with a newfangled secular value called "value-neutrality" This is moral schitzophrenia, which our tribes do not suffer from. There was no diplomatic fence for the Odia tribes to sit over and change their points of view according to their own conveniences.

But another question perturbs us at this point. Are these tribal people the real natives of this land? I would quote Prof. Suniti kumar Chatterji, one of the ex National Professors of India in Humanities:

" The racial composition of the Odia people, as that of the people of any other part of India, is still a matter of controversy or of diversity of opinion. The latest view pronounced officially by the Anthropological Survey of India, through the writings of the late Dr.B.S.Guha suggested that in Eastern India, including Bengal and the coast lands of Orissa, the basic races were "Palae-Mediterraneans" and in the interior the people were mainly "Proto-Australoids" and "Negritos". These various racial names are more or less abstractions which had to be created by professional scholars of the Science of Man.(Mukherji.A.B.Mohanty *Memorial Lectures*.P6.)

This discussion on the roots of culture emerged as a digression from the belief-system and the myths of the tribes who had a pre-Vedic social organisation.The religious belief system shows the world view of their society. The world view has three dimensions: the natural, the world of the ancestors and that of the gods.All the three worlds are interlinked. They also believe that the homosapiens have been created out of happiness and for happiness. They should enjoy life in fun and play. Thus the homosapien turns into a homoluden in the tribal society. They could not accept the Aryan grammar of life and prefered to stay as the *Vratyas* or the flouters of the Vedic system of life. In other words, they could not be dominated by the Aryan ethics of abstinence. At a later stage, Lord Buddha came and embraced them The Khandayatas of the contemporary Odisa almost live a *defacto* Budhist life.

One can analyse the ancient tribal belief-system as a three layered construction: (a)man's relationship with man(b) Man's relation with nature and (c) Man's relation with the spirits. The first is related to the sociological plane of life and the other two are cultural in nature. However, Franz Boas and Kroeber, who emphacize on the technological progress of the western cultures would not be able to understand our tribal culture because they believe only in materiality and horizontality of life, not in verticality, that has either a depth or a height.They would not be able to understand the belief system underlying the Meria human sacrifice as a part of the fertility rituals.

When a self-complacent 'modernist' would read this book (born in colonial period, and believing credulously in 'logic' and scientific analysis of the 'moderns, without knowing that science and rationalization are outdated modes), he would take my account with a grin, cancelling out all its evidential efficacy as an advocacy for irrationalism, and not scientific analyses.How can a modern humanist(this is a dubious term, that has been used since renaissance for colonising the naive oriental) believe that the Meria human sacrifice is a part of a rich culture? But such beliefs of fertitity embedded in their collective unconscious, and directly or obliquely articulated through the "legend/myth of creation" signify the protoplastic pattern of the race, not any illness or neurotic state of their mind. No one can refute these symbolic actions with his weapons of scientism.Science cannot analyse Shamanism.

The Meria sacrifice was banned in Orissa by an Imperial Act and this discontinuity was given effect to propagate the western cult of humanism, a humanism, that at one stage, explored an Emile Zola- brand realism in the gutters and called it modernity. This stupid scientific movement inspired Satyajit Ray to sell the moving pictures of the hungry generation of half naked women in the bleakest possible way to the western world to bag few awards for something called the "new arts" and experimental cinema and realism. Satyajit Ray had violated all Indian norms of aesthetics to support the Zola-brand Realism and that facilitated him to bag prizes.

This colonial motif in Satyajit Ray severed the link of many from the rich experience of Tagore's Chandalika, in which Prakriti waits for Ananda, the Buddhist monk, to salvage her. Prakriti's experience is a quasi-shamanistic experience.She hailed from a family of the untouchables and her mother was a lady shaman. Tagore recaptured the story of the Buddhist era and treated it as a contemporary theme since he himself believed in the cosmological dimension of the Buddhist shamans.

Jean Houston, in his foreword captioned "The Mind and the Soul of the Shaman" for a book called *Shamanism*(1987), writes,"Why is there so great a renewal of interest in one of the oldest forms of the religious life-the practice of shamanism? I believe that agood part of its fascination lies in the fact that it is prepolitical, for all religions begin as spiritual experiences which then become politicized and bureaucratized. Shamanism, in both its most ancient and most modern forms, recalls the democratization of the spiritual experience, in which hierarchies are reserved for levels of experience rather than for priest and bishops. Each level and dimension of reality is available to the one who will make the effort to learn and practice the ways and means of the spiritual journey.Thus, in shamanic practice one can have one's spiritual experience and revelation direct and unmediated by strutures ordained by church or doctrine. This appeals immensely to those who seek autonomy in the spiritual journey."(P.vii)

If this seems esoteric and incredible, I will quote about some of the quasi-shamanistic ludic elements in the writings of the twentyfirst century scientists.The first is Ray Kurzwell, the principal developer of the first omnifont optical character recognition technology, the first print-to-speech reading machine for the blind, and the first music synthecizer capable of recreating the grand piano and other orchestral instruments. I read him in a news paper. Kurzwell writes:"I have two ideas, although their full impact won't be felt for decades.The first is a three dimensional molecular computer, possibly based on nanotube technology. Molecular computing will keep the exponential growth of computing going past the anticipated life span of Moore's law.

The next idea is a system for sending microscopic intelligent robots into the human bloodstream. These robots will fight pathogens,rebuild bodies, provide full immersion virtual reality from inside the nervous system, and establish direct mental connections to the internet.

Mr.Kurzwell's project does not amaze me.The tribal shamans of Koraput used to do miracles which no scientist has yet thought of. I was teaching in Vikramdev College,Jeypur in the Koraput district and I havetoured over the interiors of the tribal district and interacted with the tribals. That was easy for me because their children were my students and they were with me every time. Most of the tribals with whom I dined and chated were their relatives. One such character used to transform himself into a tiger and was moving/jumping around the jungle and after experiencing the tiger-life for some days he would reconvert himself into a biped and return home to his family. If the Western scientists are competing with our tribals, let them do this trasformative magic through shamanism and show his "crazy wisdom" to the world.

Mary Schmidt has written an essay captioned, " Crazy Wsdom The Shaman as the Mediator of Realities." in a rare book edited by

Shirley Nicholson and captioned *Shamanism*. The book has a wonderful compendium of essays written on shamans by anthropologists, mental health practitioners and shamans themselves. I want to quote the experience of a shaman from Siberia who was regularly being visited by the spirit of a small child. The young Karagasy shaman says," The little one, the little spirit used to come to me. He had flown into my mouth and then I used to recite shaman songs."(p.63)

Douglas Sharon, in his book, *Wizard of the Four Winds:A Shaman's story*(Newyork.The Free Press.1978) writes about the concept of shamanism with which I juxtapose the concepts of new science and place it before my readers who are currently going through the chapter on Orissan Tribal Culture. The tribals had their own notions of power and the *palata bagha*, or the transformed tiger of the Paraja tribe of Koraput, about whom I am reporting here, was also exhibiting that power. Probably the central concept of shamanism, whereever in the world it is found, is the idea of power.Here is a tribal notion that semioticizes that underlying all the visible forms of the world,animate and inanimate, there exists a vital essence from which they emerge and by which they are nurtured.Ultimately everything returns to this ineffable,mysterious,impersonal,unknown. The varied religious expressions of humanity are attempts to develop a meaningful and/or practical relationship with this power.

The government of Orissa, which has a Tribal

Development Department functioning under the shadow of imperial rules(sans its discipline though-Ask any old timer and he would nostalgically recount how good the British regime was) attempts to cheat them into modern culture and they are extremely resistant to them. For more than two and half years I lived with these tribes as a family member. By the time I used to come back to my rented house at about 11P.M. in the night, a tribal adult from a remote village would be found sitting on my verandah without disturbing my wife. He would be happy to find me late in the night and he would request me to go to their village to address a cultural meeting. He would refuse to sleep in my drawing room and would also refuse to use a pillow. He would sleep in the verandah area on a mat made of grass. He would refuse to eat a late dinner at my residence. Oneday, I pressurized one to eat. But he felt very uncomfortable with my food with rich spices. Perhaps, he felt like vomitting it out. Later, a student of mine informed that they are not used to eat curry cooked with mustard oil.

What wanted to emphacize through this subjective experience is that the *paraja* tribe of Koraput have a discipline of their own and a culture with a moral code much superior to us.When I used to go to their villages, the same thing happened to me. During a recent to a Saura tribal village in Ganjam district, a woman behaved with me so well that I was compelled to take glass of *serbet* made of squeezed lemon and sugar. But, the water was contaminated(there was no fountain nearby)and my stomach was upset. But the village was so democratic and organised that a socalled civilized person would be simply amazed.

Jawaharlal Nehru, in his *Glimpses* of *World History*, claims that the Aryans had a well planned democracy and village system. He also claims that the Aryan villages had *Panchayat ghar* (the house for the village *panchayat*).On the contrary,our naked *Bondas* of the high hills were never informed about the Panchayat house. But they had their own *selani dingo* (the dormitory where the young folk, men and women sleep) in their hilltop villages which was the centre for discussing all kinds of village affairs.Such dormitories are also found in *Paraja* and *Saura* tribal villages also.

The contours of the hidden culture which I endeavour to trace become distnict now as the alien Aryan culture is juxtaposed against the indigenous tribal culture. There is nothing to feel inferior about the culture of the highlanders. Our pre-historic culture was like a cascade pouring itself down the hills. The plain lands and the river banks were slimy to them, as slimy as the characters of civilization it produced. The highlanders of Orissa were almost like the ascetics, indifferent to the enticement of civilization and hence they cared very little for the mainstream and never thought of bowing down before the dominant culture. They are very proud of their culture and if they are hurt, they would murder you.

Mahakosala in the History

We have already established Mahakosala as a civilization of the Vratyas that existed before the Aryans who migrated from the delta of Euphratis. The *Baudha Yatakas* mention the name of Telvaha river which is river *Tel* of this area and it was used as a river route for commerical purposes in the hoary past.

Most of the kings who ruled over this area were tribal rulers. Mahakosala was known as the *Atabika Rajya*, during the time of Kharavela and Ashoka. The Allahbad inscription records that during Samudra Gupta's Deccan expedition in 350 A.D. Mahendra Kurala, the king of Bolangir (Mahakosala) was defeated. Raja Manta Raja and Vyaghra Raja of Mahakantara (Koraput and Kalahandi) were also defeated. The local historians identify Vyaghra Raja as a tribal king and his capital was Manika Garh (present Komana).

Asura Garh (Narla) was the capital of Mahakantar. The Kings of Nala dynasty ruled over Koraput and Kalahandi during the 5th century A.D. Pushkarigada (Potagada, near

Umerkote) was the capital of the Nala kings in Koraput and Marda Garh (the Maraguda valley of Nuapada) was the capital during the Nala rule. The gold coins belonging to the Nala dynasty provide evidence with regard to this. The Nala kings were Saivites (Phallus worshippers). The Nanda Kings were ruling in this area during 400-500 A.D from Pushkarigarh (near Umerkote) and lae the capital was shifted to the valley of Maraguda. The Nanda kings, who were saivites, called them selves as "Maheswaras". The golden coins of that period bear the mark of *Vrishava* (a bull) and *ardha-chandra* (a half moon). The Rithapur Copper grant of Bhavadutta Burma (Ganga dynasty) reads:

Maheswara Maha Senapati srista Raja vibavah nanda nrupa Vamsah prasuta tripataka dhwaja Sri Maharaja Bhavadutta Bruma

Hence, it is evident that the "Maheswar-Siva" tradition was promulgated as the royal religion. This is the cultural aftermath of Samudra Gupta's invasion. The land was designated as Trikalinga and the evidences are found in descriptions of the Brahmins. The Kesari Beda copper grant of Arthapati mentions that the Koutsava *gotra* Brahmins like Durgacharya, Rabicharya and Rabi Dutta were given the Kesaleka village (*Epi. Indica. Vol.IX*.P.170).

The last king of Nanda dynasty ruling over there was Skanda Burma and he was a Vaishnavite. His podagada inscription informs that he built a Vishnu Temple for the worship of His feet and an Agrahara village was donated for the maintenance of the temple. The Rithapor Copper grant mentions *"Swasti go-brahman prajavyah siddhirastu"* (*Ep. Ind. Vol XXI*. P.155)

The Terasimha Copper grant informs that king Tustikara and Kaustuveswara, the two kings of Parvata Dwaraka dynasty ruled over there during the 6th century A.D. and they worshipped *stambheswari* (the Goddess of the Pillar) Their capital was situated at Parvata dwara, which according to Prof. Nabeen Kumar Sahu, is Patadaraha or Boden of the present times. Kaustuveswar had his capital at Tarabhrarmaka or Palabhramara. This copper grant also informs that King

Tustikara had granted the village named De Bhogaka to a Brahmin named Drauna Swamy. The grant proves that-during this period (6th century) the Aryan Brahmins entered into this Vratya land for the first time.

Mahajaya Raja's Amaguda copper grant and Maha Sura Deo's Khariar Copper grant prove that the kings of Sarabhapuriya dynasty ruled in South Kosala during 7th-8th century. The Copper grants also enlighten us about the interaction of the Brahmins with the tribals. The golden coins of the Kings, Prasanna Matra Mahendraditya and Kramaditya have been discovered from the archaeological findings at Maraguda. Their kingdom was Sripura (in Madhya Pradesh) and Sarabha Garh (Sundargarh). These Kings were Vaishnavites. But by 9th-10th centuries the Somavamsi Kings took over South Kosala and they were converted from Vaishnavites to Saivites. The Great King of Soma dynasty was Mahasiva Gupta and he built Someswar Temple of Lord Siva at Ranipur Jharial. The Siva Temples of pataleswara, Mohangiri, Khariar Dadapur (Neelakantheswar Temple of Siva) are built by these somevamsi kings. A local historian talks about the Kosali archetectureal techniques deployed in the consturction of these temples. But this author knows little about this style.

After the Soma kings the kings of Chindaka Naga dynasty of Chakrakote ruled over the area for few years. A feudatory king of Rajendra Chola Samanta was someswara. He began the tradition of worshipping Lankeswari in Kalahandi and Bolangir area. The ruling deity of the Chindaka Nagas was Manikeswari and her temples were bilt in Bhawanipatna of Kalahandi and in Bastar area. The other name of Manikeswari is danteswari and she was worshipped as the Godess of the Bastar palace. According to another historical interpretation, Manikeswari was brought form Sanakhemundi of Ganjam in Kangoda by a king of Ganga dynasty and was worshipped in Kosala. It shows that there was an intimate cultural contact between Kosala and Kangada. The cult of pillar worship was also imported from Kangoda. The Ganga king used to marry their daughters in Naga dynasties of South and later, the daughter of the Ganga kings wer married in the royal family of Chhotanagpur who belonged to Naga dynasty.

The kings of Ganga dynasty ruled over Kamala Mandala or Kalahandi since it was under Trikalinga tlll mid-13th century and the Ganga-Kalachuris ruled over for some time in west Kamala Mandala. It was a battle ground for the Gangas and the Kalachuries. The inscriptions of the temple of Siva at Narla show that Madan Mahadeo, a feudatory king of Ganga dynasty ruled over Kamalamandala (Kalahandi) till 1252 A.D. After him the kings of Chhotangapur belonging to Naga dynasty would ove Kalahandi.

The Chauhan kings of Gada Sambar of Chhatisgarh invaded a part of Mahakosala during the 13th-14th centuries and it is reported that one Hamir Deo, a mythic hero from Sambargarh came and took shelter in Manik Garh of Khariar. Then, his son Famai Deo defeated one Asta Mallikka, a local tribal king at Patnagarh and laid the foundation for the Chauhan dynasty in Orissa. The Chauhan tradition can still be found in Komana Garh, Guda Garh, Khola Garh and Manki Garh. The clan Goddess Sambareswari was brought to Sambalpur during this Chauhan rule and was worshipped as Samaleswari since those days.

What was found in the succession of such dynasties was that the kings alienated themselves from the tribal people and the gap between them was so wide that their administration could not bring any socio-cultural change in Mahakosala. The common folk lived in their own traditional pattern, totally unconcerned by the change of the dynasties and the governments. The Govt. of Orissa, which means its Ministers and Bureaucrats, have looted Mahakosala for the last 54 years (after 1947) and the people die unconcerned and yet orally lamented. The government at the centre considers Odias as the Vratyas or the unholy people and the M.Ps. from Orissa are not able to speak either in Hindi or in English. Hence cultural matters are suppressed.

The invasion of the Chauhan kings on Mahakosala during the 13th and 14th centuries created an interface of the high and the low culture since the process of Aryanization began with them. The face of the Odia culture is distorted and multiple alien cultures claim their rights over this land. The *little* and the *high* traditions are mixed up.

As we delve into the roots of Odia Culture, this study seems to have concentrated into a major investigation of our history, from the unrecorded past to the recorded epochs: The investigation, in other words, has sought to discover our multiple cultural faces, buried and unseen for a long time. In the process, icebergs of our culture have also surfaced through such excavations, readings of the inscriptions, charters, rock edicts, texts, *Puranas*, oral history and other material evidences.

These faces and surfaces reveal three major cultural sources - the proto-Austroloid, the Dravidian and the Aryan. Even though the investigation has been conducted under various sub-headings, a discerning reader would notice lots of interfaces, i.e. spaces with overlapping boundaries of cultural roots and their manifestations in phenomenal life of the Odias through ages.

(a) Mahakantara: A Brief Account of Kalahandi

The district of Kalahandi was formulated in 1949. Khariar (Khadiala) which was in Madhya Pradesh till 1936 was tagged to Sambalpur in 1936 and then the place was included in the Kalahandi district. Kalahandi had different names at different periods of history. The place was called Maha Vana, Atabika Rajya, South Kosala, Trikalinga, Kamala Mandala, Karunda Mandala and finally it was evolved as Kalahandi.

Panini's *Astadhyayi* mentions about a commercial *Janapada* named Taitilaka which has later been identified as Titilagarh of the present times by Prof. Nabin Kumar Sahu, the famous historian of the place. This pre Aryan political entity called Mahakantar had one of its capitals at Asuragarh. Asuras were the people whom the Aryans hated. Kalahandi is the habitat of 46 varieties of tribes out of which Gonda, Kandha, Bhunjia, Paraja, Mirdha, Dal, Munda, Savara, Sahara, Binjhal, Banjara, Bhatara and the Paharias are the main ones. However, the ancient kings had imported Aryan Brahmins, milkmen, oilmen, fishermen, snake charmers, goldsmith, wine sellers and fighters from the Aryan region and they have settled in Mahakantar.

(b) The tribes of Mahakantara (Kalahandi)

The largest number of Gonds (the name of a tribe) lives in Kalahandi and their number is 1, 23, 778 according to the last census report. They have migrated from the Gondwana land, which, by an earthaquake was split up and the split up part of it is now called Africa. The imigrants from Gondwana are called *Laria Gonds* and the originals are called Odia Gonds. They are identified by the eight original clans of Gondwana from where they have migrated: Markam, Netam, Morhi, Sori, Ot; Porti, Naek and Jagata and they are called *At-sagas* (the eight friends/kinsmen) Every clan has its own capital, presiding deity, the Perceptor of the clan, the original place of birth, the primal man born in the clan and its mythic heroes. The ethnic culture of the Gonds has influenced the other coexisting cultures of the forest (*Maha Vana*)

The next largest tribe of Kalahandi is Kondh tribe which has shaped the contours of its culture. Their total population is 1, 14,644. The tribal legends inform that the mother of the Gonds and the mother of the Kondhas were two sisters. The Kondhs of Mahakantar were of 3 varieties: (a) the *Desia Kondhs* are the plain lander Kondhs. (b) the *Kutia Kondhs* or the forest dwellers (c) the *Dongria Kondhs* or the highlanders. A part from this division of the Kondhs are put under six classes: (1) *Ganga* (2) *Gagram* (3) *Yadu* (4) *Kadam* (5) *Reteko and* (6) *Teteko*. Out of these six categories innumerable sub-categories have proliferated. Madhu Majhi, the spokesman of the Kondh community, has listed 172 classes among them in Kalahandi and Bolangir districts, which constitute a major portion of Mahakosala. But the *Desia Kondhs* never established any marital relationship with the *Dongrias* and the *Kutias*.

The culture of Mahakosala is also shaped by the Savaras who are 40, 950 in number. They are divided into 12 classes:

(a) Mundari: The people of the Mundari clan have forgotten their original language and they have assimilated themselves into the Hindu country.

(b) Savara: This sub-clan of the savaras has not undergone the upward mobility which the savars have achieved in course of time. Out of the eight categories of Savaras, who are also called Sauras/Saharas, five are the inhabitants of Kalahandi;

(i) Paraja: The Paraja tribe of Koraput is different from the Parija tribe of Kalahandi. The Parajas of Koraput divide them into seven classes. The Kalahandi Parajas are of four categories :(a) Bada Paraja (b) Bareng or Jodia Paraja (c) Chhelia Paraja (d) and Kondha Paraja. The Bada Parajas claim that they are the best amongst the four. They are originally of a mixed parentage - of the proto-Austroloid and the Melanid. Similarly, the Kondha Parajas are the hybrids of the Kondh and the Parajas.

The *Banjaras* have migrated to Kalahandi from Madhya Pradesh. This is a shifting community of business men. Their number in Kalahandi is around 3,362. The Bhunija tribal are 5, 673 in number. Out of the 21 varieties of the *Bhunjia Tribes*, *only* two categories of Bhunjias live in Kalahandi: (i) Chinda and (ii) Chaukhuntia. They have twenty one clans. The *Chiuda Bhunjias* live in the plain lands. The *Chaukhuntia Bhunjias* are very conservative and they still live in the isolated valley at Sunabeda, in Koraput district. They have peculiar customs to preserve their notion of purity. If a new comer would enter into their houses, they would demolish their houses and build new ones. They would not allow the dust under the new comer's feet to enter into their houses. Every house has its own totem deity and this "signifier" (deity) is likely to be defiled if a new comer (from the other clan, alien society) steps into the house. The Aryan Brahmins, too, have appropriated this peculiar habit of conserving their own purity. The notion of purity, it seems, has been understood as "superiority" and "cultural ego" in the culture of certain European races also. It is difficult to distinguish them from the Bhunjia tribal people.

The cultural compactness of the Binjhal tribes in Mahakosala is unique. They are of four categories: *Binjhabar, Sonjhara, Biranjia* and *Binjhia*. Besides these four categories, they have seven more subcategories: (1) *Son bana (2) Saria (3) Naga (4) Bagha (5) Amera (6) Semee (7) Boja. These tribes still live in Madhya Pradesh also.*

The total *Bhatara* tribal population has been computed to 3853 in Kalahandi. They are divided into two groups - the *Bada Bhatara* (the big clan) and *Sana Bhatara* (the small clan). The *Paharias* tribe has been classified as a scheduled Tribe in Madhya Pradesh. The folk language of South Kosala is mostly influenced by the Bhatara language.

Besides, the *Mundas*, divided into *Lohra Munda* and *Mahali Munda* have a small population of 2695 the Kalahandi. Similarly, the *Dal* Tribes (2020 the number) and the Mirdha Tribes (1125) are also two minor tribes living in Kalahandi (South Kosala).

It has to be reiterated here that the culture of Mahakosala dates back to the Pleistocene and Hallocene ages. (very distant prehistoric periods when the evolution of life had grown from the unicellular amoeba to the Dianossaurs.)

The Tribal inhabitants of Mahakosala belonging to a much earlier period than the Mahenjo Daro era had a developed village administrative system with a Chieftain as the head. The practice is still continued as a cultural heritage. They are called *Gountias*. But the headman, found today, is not always a tribal person. During different phases of Aryan administration the Brahmins, the Muslims, the Paikas, Gardner, oilmen and milkmen have become the Chieftains.

The tribals have a village committee in which the tribal priest, the witch doctor, the *nariha* (the milkman), Khabaria (one who circulates news) and *sians* (oldmen). During the post-independence time, the village administration has been taken over by the government organisations and the decision with regard to the festivals is taken by these village committees

(c) A Different Systems of Belief: Mahakosala

The religious belief system of the people of Mahakosala is guided by the four-fold notion of deities-(a) the Supreme God (b) the Earth Mother (c) the Primal mother and the (d) Sun God and the emblem of Truth. Besides this four fold heirachy, they also offer their prayers to the deities that are worshipped not in the anthropomorphic form, but as symbols: stone made phallus, tridents, swords and iron instruments inserted in the vagina-shaped earth. The shamans invoke them and perform the rituals. In most of the places, as it is discussed, the pillar is a characteristic element in their dwellings.

The universe is conceived by them having three levels- sky, earth and the underworld, connected by a central axis. This imaginary axis, as the "pillar", is worshipped to express symbolically the inter connection and the inter communication among the three cosmic zones. The axis passes through an 'opening' or a 'hole'. It is through this hole that the Gods descend to earth and the dead to the subterranean regions. They, too, have a symbolism of the centre. The Juang tribes of Keonjhar, (not in Kosala, though) consider their mountains as the centre of the world that connects the earth with the sky. But the tribals of Mahakosala (Koraput, Bolangir, Kalahandi, Sundargarh and Sambalpur districts) believe the world as a tree. Their deity is connected with the leaves and branches. The tree provides them with the wood to make their drum and their deity. According to the cosmology of their belief, the World Tree rises at the centre of the earth, the place of earth's "umbilicus", and its upper branches touch the place of God. The World Tree becomes the Tree of life and Immortality as well in the archaic civilization of Mahakosala. It expresses the sacrality of the world, its fertility and perenniality and it relates to the ideas of creation, fecundity, and initiation rites, and finally to the idea of absolute reality which manifests the eco-motherhood, eco-feminisn and Sakti Tantrism.

The oral stories and the symbolic interpretation of the *stambha* (pillar worship and the cosmic, symbolic Tree) are innnumerable and the present pysiognomy of the folkloristic mythologies are immensely influenced by this notion. In the National Seminar on Saktism held on 28-29 March 1992, Dr. K.C. Mishra addresses: "The State abounds in Sakta Temples and shrines. In each village, there still remains a Devi Temple, often of queer character, inter woven with mythical accounts. In the hinterlands, particularly in the tribal pockets, goddesses in multiple forms are still being worshipped." (Mishra: *Studies in Saktism: 1)*

(d) Rituals

It is interesting to notice that in addition to these principles of public worship, the tribals of Mahakosala have their own private deities that conform to the norms of their domestic religion, too. The following four types of rituals need mention

(a) *Birth rituals*: The people of Mahakosala perform a ritual to know which ancient soul has taken rebirth as the new born baby.

(b) *Marriage rituals*: During the marriage ritual they keep a *Joga Khunta* (the lucky branch of the *mohul* tree) and *Joga Kanda* (the lucky bow-arrow). These objects symbolise that the newly married groom would go to the jungle for hunting to sustain the wife and her children.

(c) *Death rituals:* On the third day of the death *Tela* (oil) a *Sana Karama* (small ritual) will be done. On the tenth day, the *Dasa* (the 10th day ritual) will be done The ritual of invoking the spirits of the dead back to home involves a complicated series of rituals. The Gond community would light eight wicks for the eight primal companions (*Atha Saga*) of the dead.

(d) *Kana Bara:* The initiation rite of a girl is called *kana Bara.* They believe that a girl attaining her puberty in the paternal home would consign the father to hell. Hence, before the attainment of her puberty she would to be married to an arrow. Previously the girl was exiled into a forest on the day of attaining puberty and she was brought back after the ritualistic celebrations are over.

Cultural Osmoses: Vedic, Buddhist & Tribal Cultures

However, the people of Mahakosala have also appropriated some of the Aryan rituals in course of time with the multiple Aryan invasions on to this land. The little tradition has, thus, been assimilated in to the great tradition. Budha Raja or Budha Deo (The old King) has become Lord Siva. Ganga Dei has become Durga, Bhima of *Mahabharat* accepted as the Lord of Rain, The blacksmithsare acknowledged as the progeny of Viswa Karma. The Aryan rites of human sacrifice has been appropriated as *Meria* and the *Buffalo sacrifice* of the Kondha tribes. The *Toki Parab* (The Toki festival) has also been appropriated from the Vedic rites.

The confluence of the Saktism of the archaic tribes of Mahakosala and the mainstream cults of Vedic culture shows that none of these rituals can be viewed with contempt or as practices of a superstitious nature. However, some of the scholars of Vedic culture interpret Saktism with philosophical justification.

Saktism reveals the principle of the union of the universal soul, the *Purusha* with the primordial essence, *Prakriti* the root-evolvent. The documentations in the Vedic Texts is not only the culture of the Vedic Times, but they also preserve the traditions belonging to pre-vedic or of a time that pre-dates the Indus Valley civilization. However, one can find ample evidence of the worship of the Mother Goddess during the Vedic period.

The *Devi Sukta* and the *Ratri Sukta* of the *Xth Mandala* of the *Rik Veda* appear to give indications to the worship of *Sakti* (mother energy) in the Vedic period. The *Vajasaneyi Samhita* (18-15) of the *Black Yajurveda* speaks of Devi Ambika as the sister of Rudra while the *Taittireya Aranyaka* refers to Ambika as the wife of Rudra. Ambika is first conceived as the sister of Rudra in the *Taittiriya Samhita* (1.8.6 : *Svasrambikaya* Saha jusasva) *Maitrayani Samhita* (1.10.20), *Vajasaneyi Samhita* (3.57).

Then Goddess Ambika has been identified as the spouse of Rudra, the Vedic counterpart of Siva, or the Primordial Man *(Taittiriya Aranyaka x.18)*. *Taittiriya Aranyaka* (10.1.7) also expressed the daughter aspect of *Sakti* as Kanyakumari.

The *Buddhist Tantras* have also accepted this three-fold identity of *sakti*. The *Dasaratha Jataka,* an extant Buddhist version of *Ramayana,* found in Orissa,(translated from the Jataka stories ,published in Bengali by Surendranatha Satapathy) desribes Sita as the sister of Rama.The alternate version of *Ramayana* as given in the *Dasaratha Jataka* has been translated by Mr. Hadibandhu Hali of Bargarh village, Bhubaneswar and the translation has been included in this book. The Odissan deities of Jagannatha, Balabhadra and Subhadra conform to the notions of *Black Yajurveda*. Subhadra is the sister of Jagannatha in the temple.Thus, the concept of Jagannatha embodies lots of Buddhist notions-like nondescretion in sex and nonbelief in casteist divisions.

In the *Mahabharata*, Arjuna addresses a hymn to Durga under the advice of Krishna, in which the goddess is prayed for granting victory to him in the ensuing war:

Namaste Siddhasenani arjye mandaravasini
Kumari Kali Kapali Kapile Krushnapingale.
Bhadrakali namastubhyam Mahakali namostute
Chandi Chande namastu bhyam Tarini Varavarnini.

The *stotra* (prayer) identifies Durga as a powerful Mother Goddess during the time of *Mahabharata*. The primordial godesses addressed in Arjuna's *stotra* refer to many other names like *Katyayani, Kantaravasini* (Kalahandi in South Kosala was also called *Mahakantara* and Kausiki etc). Although the prayer of Arjuna refers to one Goddess, the other names of the Goddess seem to have been borrowed from these names of Devi in other parts of India; one may assign their conceptions to different historical conditions.

While defining the contours of the Vratya culture of Odissa found in Mahakosala and Mahakantara through the practices of Saktism, a reference to Lord Siva, the symbolic phallus, can not be avoided.

Siva or Rudra was a Pre-Aryan God and a *Vratya*. The entire book of *Atharva Veda* (Book XV) is dedicated to a *Vratya* and his transfiguration. According to a study made by J.C. Heesterman in *IIJ* (1962) (Pp 1-37), the *Vratyas* were a host of consecrated people within the Vedic Tradition. Little is known about them in classical books apart from *Book XV* of the *Atharva Veda*. The Vratyas were clad in black, fringed garments; the black colour distinguished their attire, as it did that of Rudra when he appeared on the site of the sacrifice by the *Angirases*.

The *Vratyas* wore a turban and carried lance and bow (*Atharva:* 15.2.10.)Their name is derived from *Vrata*, a host, which in turn, may have been derived from *Vrata*, a vow or observance of a sacred ordinance (Ref. M.Mayrhofer *Concise Etymological Sanskrit dictionary, S.V. Vratah)*. In the *Sata Rudriya* hymn to the hundred forms and powers of Rudra, the leaders of hosts (Vratapati) are invoked. This ecstatic litany imbued with the presence of God opens with a homage to his wrath, to his arrow, to his bow.

The archaic marriage rituals of the pre-Aryan tribals of Mahakantara, their custom of marrying the young, immature, girl to an arrow may be compared to the litany in *Rik-Veda* in which Siva's transfirguration takes place from a Vratya to a Mahadeva (the Great God). The transfiguration of the Vratya has three phases: the birth of a God, the vision of that god and the building of his monument, the Great God, with the mark of the third eye on his forehead.

The Vratya, a roving ascetic, was roaming about and stirred Prajapati, the Lord of Generation. The Vratya stirred him toward the act of generation. As an ascetic, the Vratya had magic power and acted not unlike *Agni*, the Fire, who had prepared the seed for the Father. The Father became sexually excited and was about to emit the seed into his self-created daughter, but some of the seed fell down on earth. Prajapati, stirred by the Vratya, was similarly impelled toward generation.

Rudra-Siva emerged from Prajapati. He was his son by the agency of Vratya. The birth of Rudra is told as it happened in the rupture of the Vratya. When he knew that he had stirred Prajapati, he identified himself with his action and with the outcome of his action.

In mystic realisation, the Vratya brings about the birth of Rudra form Prajapati and recognizes in Rudra his own divinity. The miraculous generation of Rudra as son of Prajapati is the mythical aspect of the mystic realization of the Sole Vratya. Now the Sole Vratya took up a bow: "That was Indra's bow. Blue its belly, red its back" (*Atharva Veda* 15:16-7- Tr. W.D. Whitney. 1962. P 773). The new born God takes over the rule of what had been Indra's domain: the cosmos.

It is difficult to assume whether the Vratyas of Mahakosala appropriated the symbols of the bow and the arrow in marriage rituals or the Aryans appropriated and codified the myth (its symbol, transfiguration, meaning and literary representation in *Atharva Veda*). The latter seems to be more reasonable.

How could then the North Indians hate the *Vratyas* as uncultured? It seems more like a slander of power politics from the North, from the Gangetic valley. Later, a historian of the stature of Jawaharlal Nehru could wipe out the name of Kharavela from the pages of history (of Orissa) and the super-cyclone in 1999 could not be declared as a "national calamity" where as in 2001 the Vratyas of Orissa had to pay a surcharge of 2% in the income tax to help the people of Gujarat after the earthquake.And the highplaced Oriyas think that it is a kind of right for them to defame the Odias to stay glued to the national stream.

One may visit the forest lands of Mahakosala and Mahakantara today and still detect the same limitless forbearance. One may choose to visit Kalahandi even today to decipher how the *Vratya* and the *Vedic cultures* have created a mosaic, each standing out as separate and yet mixed up, at least, toward a workable synthesis.

The people of Ganges valley were rich. They allowed the Greeks and Mongoloids to enter into their bed-rooms and kitchens. The cross-fertilization gave them the obstinacy to call them the "purest" of the world and to hate the *Vratyas* of the eastern India because they were black in colour and they put on black clothes. Constant invasions from the North West and their biological interaction with the Western countries made them fairer and handsomely built characters and as hybrids they were the people who framed the law of drinking the cowdung water for self purification, when they came down to Anga, Banga and Kalinga, which included the Vratya land of Orissa.

The North Indians learnt the shrewd art of manipulation and cultural domination to exploit the *Vratyas* consistently through different phases of history. Mahakantara is the zone in the contemporary map of 21st century India, where the parents sell their girl children in the North West to work as slaves. Kalahandi, Sundargarh, Sambalpur and partially Bolangir constitute the area, in which the government, in this welfare state, is unable and unwilling to provide water for cultivation. At this point culture and politics become one and the centre dominates over the periphery.

The Mahakantara suffers from consecutive famines and deaths due to starvation. The govenment money is taken home for personal flourishment of the government people. Humanitarianism, be it a word in the public talks or a phallic extension of carnality (through out the history, women have been exploited under the petticoat of humanism) has been proved as hideous as the Ganges Valley civilization penetrated into the loop-holes of other subaltern cultures.

Dasaratha - Jataka: One more version of Ramayana

The extant script of Dasaratha Jataka was available with our historian Sri Hadibandhu Hali of Badagada village(Bhubaneswar) and he did not like to part with the book. Instead, he has summarized the story in English and has given it to me. This Buddhist verson of Ramayana retrieved from the moth-eaten Odia script is interesting and is relevant since the Buddhist subversion of the story of Ramayana in the form of a *Jataka* tale evidences how the Hindu epic is distorted. The summary is produced verbatim:

In ancient time a great king was ruling over Varanasi. He was maintaining his subjects as per law without the sin of fraud, jealously, charm and fear. In his harem he had sixteen thousand queens. Out of them the Chief Queen had given birth to two sons and a daughter. His eldest son was named Rama Pandit, the younger son was Laksman Kumar and his daughter's name was Sita Debi.

In course of time the Chief Queen died. After her death Dasarath bereaved for a long time. At last by the advice of his ministers, he performed her death rituals and selected another Chief Queen.

Dasaratha also had much love for the new queen and after some days she conceived. After the conception rites were performed she gave birth to a son. This son was named Bharat Kumar.

The king being very much pleased for filial love one day asked the queen, 'Darling, I shall grant a boon to you. What boon shall I give?'

The queen said, "I accept your boon bending my head. But I shall not ask now."

Bharat Kumar grew up to a seven years old prince. One day the Queen asked, "You had promised to grant a boon to my son. Now grant it to me".

The King told, 'Ask the boon.'

'My Lord, grant my son kingship.'

The king was furious, and asked her to check out of the room immediately."

The queen was scared and retired to her harem. But afterwards she also frequently asked for the boon. At last the King granted the boon; but he realised: "women are ungrateful, and unfriendly. The queen, by writing a fraudulent letter or by bribing a stooge might kill my sons to fulfil her evil desire."

Afterwards, the king called his eldest son and Laxman kumar and informed them everything and said, 'My sons, there is danger for your life here. So, you go to a vassal territory or to a forest and reside there. When my body will be reduced to cinders, then come to conquer your ancestral throne."

After telling this, the king summoned the astrologers, and asked, 'Tell me how many days I shall live.'

They told, "Great king, You will live for another twelve years.;

The king said, 'Sons, comeback after twelve years and ascend the throne.'

'Yes our Lord!' They nodded, prayed to his feet and descended from the royal palace with tears in their eyes.

At the time Sita Devi also, came and said, 'I will also go with two of my brothers. Thus she prayed to her father sitting under his feet and then obtaining Dasaratha's permission, Sita also followed her brothers- Rama and Laxmana.

When they went from the royal palace thousands of subjects- men and women, accompanied them. But Rama sent these people back, and after some days, reached the Himalayan Range. They built a small hermitage, where water and other facilities were available and they settled there.

Laxman Pandit and Sita Devi told Rama Pandit 'You are like our father. You remain in the hermitage. We will collect fruits and roots for you.

Rama Pandit agreed. From onwards, he remained in hermitage and Laxman and Sita brought fruits on which he lived.

Rama, Laxman and Sita lived like this sustaining on the fruits of the forest. Here King Dasaratha breathed his last after nine years consistently yearning to his sons and the daughter. After the death rituals were over, the mother of Bharata told: "Now, it is time for drawing the royal parasol over the head of Bharata.

But the ministers did not confer royalty to Bharata. They told, 'The rightful owners of the throne are living in the jungle". Thus they did not allow Bharata to sit under the royal parasol.

Then Bharat decided , "I will go to the forest and bring back elder brother and restore him on to the throne"

He took with him five kinds of royal symbols with four types of forces and reached the same forest. At a short distance from the hermitage, they erected tents and with some ministers he went to the hermitage when Laxman and Sita were absent. He found Rama Pandit at the doorstep with his usual yellow, golden coloured costume. Bharata went to him, saluted and informed him about father's death. He cried bitterly with the ministers prostrating under his feet. Rama Pandit, however, did not cry. Nor was there any visible symptom of sorrow on his face.

Bharata sat at the feet of Rama. Evening descended and Laxman and Sita returned to the hermitage with fruits and flowers.

Seeing them Rama Pandit thought, 'they are too young. Till now they had not matured in intelligence . Suddenly if I would break-out the news of death of our father, then they might not be able to tolerate the impact of the sorrow and their heart might fail. So, I would send them to the pond anyhow, and after they take a ritual bath, I shall divulge them the shocking news of death.'

Ram Pandit thought like this and said, "Why did you return to the hermitage so late? I shall punish you both. Now, Laxman and Sita! Go to the pond and stand in waist-deep water.'

'Hearing this Laxman and Sita instantly went into the pond and stood in the mid-waist-deep water. Then Rama Pandit divulged the news of sorrow by reciting the mantra.

Bharat had come to inform, 'King Dasaratha has ascended the heaven,' Laxman and Sita fell unconscious. After coming back to sense when they again heard it, they became senseless. Like this they heard three times and became unconscious for which the ministers brought them to ground. Regaining the sense they all began to wail.

Then Bharat Kumar thought; 'My brother Laxman and sister Sita could not tolerate the sorrow of our father's death, but how it was that Rama Pandit was not affected? How could it happen?.

Then he recited the second verse:
'Brother dear, What secret power made you so strong?
How could you withstand the shock of our father's death?
Then, Rama Pundit explained by reciting the following verse:
If one cries day and night
Child or old, rich or poor,
Unwise or wise!
Death would perish them all.
Yet people shudder at
Death frightens them
They are dead every night
and born next morning.
He who's seen in the morning
may vanish by the evening.

They're swallowed by Time
By God of death.
We mourn in vain
Sunk in sorrow
It weakens the body, it withers
Skin and skeleton remain
Can you you resurrect the dead by mourn?
We'd finally burn;
as the houses in fire
Are doused by water
The wise suppress sorrow.
As cotton is scattered by wind

Wisdom drives the sorrow away.
Human beings must
Face ordeals, it's the fruit of Karma
Some die, others take rebirth

Our father has reached his terminus, met his end.
Some one has to succeed him
Take up his charge
Donate to the poor and
Honour the magnates
With care.

Reciting these verses Rama Pandit explained how the life is transitory. The people who stood around and gathered there listening to the explanation regarding the futility of life at once felt relieved Then, Bharat Kumar, offering Puja at Rama's feet, said, "Please come back to Varanasi and take over the charge as the successor."

Rama said, "Brother! Go back with Laxman and Sita and rule over the kingdom".

"But how can an exile be the king? I shall take over after the completion of twelve years. I cannot flout my father's behest. Let three more years pass. I will return after that."

" Who will rule over the Kingdom till that?"

"Why, you will"

"Then this pair of shoes made of grass would be kept enthroned as the King till I return."

He handed over the pair of grass sandals. Bharat came back to Varanasi with thousands of followers.

The sandals of Rama ruled over Varanasi for three years. In case a legal case was instituted, and a judgement was needed, the ministers put it on the throne. If the oders were not fair,and there was some wrong decision, the pair of magic sandals stroke each other and the ministers refrained from passing the orders. If the decision proved correct the sandals remained steady.

Three years passed like this. Rama Pandit returned from

the jungle and reached the royal garden of Varanasi. Bharata went to the garden and welcomed Sita as the Chief Queen. They also performed the coronation ceremony of both. After the coronation, Rama was taken to the city in the decorated car in a procession After parading the whole city he ascended the topmost story of the palace (named Suchandrak). After reigning over the kingdom for sixteen thousand years as per canon, he took leave of this world to have a place in heaven among the gods to increase their number.

The following information is taken from *'Abhisambudha'*. It reveals:

Thousand times of ten and hundred times of sixty
Add the two members
Whatever years the result was
To that extent of years Rama ruled properly Jambu-Dwipa

(Like this Buddha delivered the sermon through Jatak after speaking the truth to the landlord Srotapati who got the result *samabadhan:*

At that time Maharaja Suddhodan was Dasarath, Anand was Bharat, Sariputra was Laxman, and the followers of Buddha were other people and Rama Pandit was understood as Buddha.

(The father of a certain landlord died; for which he was in dismay. Then Buddha told this story to that Bhikhu as a sermon. After the death of the father, he was so much indulged in grief that without doing any work he was only weeping. One morning, Buddha was observing the cosmos and he saw that the land lord named Srotapati has attained time for a maturity and is fit for getting a result. Knowing this, the Lord begged in Srabasti for the whole day and after taking the lunch, he sent away the other Bhikshus. He only took one Bhikshu as the follower and went to that particular land-lord. The land-lord was delighted to see the Lord at his door. He offered proper salutation and begged him to sit down.

Buddha asked him sweetly "Bhikshu! Have you been perturbed too much? The landlord said : yes, Lord, after the death of my father I have been overwhelmed with grief."

The Lord's sermon given to the Bhikshu(the devotee called Stotrapati) is translated as the annotation. As I understood it, this is a critical appreciation of the *Dasaratha Jatataka* written in Oriya. The translated version of the annotation is given below:

ANNOTATION
1. Eight types of people's conduct: gain, loss, fame blame, praise, reprobation, pleasure & sorrow.
2. It is comparable with *Ramayana* of Valmiki.. In Ramayana, Rama and Laxman are not uterine brothers, Rama is son of Kausalya and Laxmanis son of Sumitra. But here Rama and Laxman are the sons of Kausalya.
3. In *Ramayana* Rama, Laxman, Sita were in Deccan but in Jatak they were in the Himalayan region.
4. In *Ramayana* Rama and Sita lived in hermitage and Laxman collected fruits for them.
5. In the description of *Ramayana* Dasarath died after the banishment of Rama due to grief. In Jatak story, he died after nine years.
    (a) In kingship progenitor's system prevailed
    (b) The ministers strictly adopted this
    (c) The king or queen could not violate the rule of the state
    (d) The ministers had power to elect rulers.
    In the *Mahabastu* of Buddhist Canon (3/206/1) the role of the King maker has been defined and from that the duties of the ministers are presumed.
7. Sword, parasol, Sandal, crown and fly-whisk. This is called 'Panchakalud" see *Mahabastu* (3/11/7)
    The four types of army called *Chaturanga* are the riders the chariot, rider of elephant, rider of horse and the infantry.
8. The Ramayan and jatak story refer to the sandals.
9. In Ramayan, Bharat came with sandal but in Jatak story Bharat came with Laxman and Sita.
10. It was known at the time that the brother and the sister

married. It was in vogue among the Sakyas. They are very proud of purity of blood for which marriage was performed within the family. *Mahabastu* (1/351/3). Yasodhara was a cousin to Gautama or Siddhartha. One can compare this notion with the Vedic notion in which sexual relationship with a sister is treated as incest. In South Orissa there is still a practice of getting married to the daughter of the sister, i.e. a neice. This is a continuation of the Buddhist notion of sexual indiscrimination.

In the Jagannath temple of Puri, Subhadra, the sister of the two brothers, is worshipped also as the Bhairabi, or as one of the root forces of female energy. I do not know since when the concept of Krishna was extrapolated on to Jagannatha. With this practice, the meaning of the icon of Subhadra is overlooked. To me it seems that Sankaracharya, with his sloka beginning with "*Kadachit kalindi tata bipino*" attempts to defend the Vedic idea of asexuality of Subhadra and at the same time tries to subvert the Buddhist notion of treating a woman without any relational ideology.

11. According to Ramayana *(Adi Parba)* Rama attained heaven after ruling for eleven thousand years. In the *JatakaStory*, it is sixteen thousand years.
12. Kindly note that out of the 447 Jataka stories, *Dasaratha Jataka* is one and it is originally written in Bengali and has been translated by Sri Surendranatha Satpathy.

Rama's travel through Kosala and Mahakantara had also embodied a zealous educative mission. He intended to teach the art of ploughing to the aboriginals who knew nothing about farming. They were fruit gatherers. Valmiki's story of Ahalya (*A-halya*=not ploughed) transformed into a fertile woman at the touch of Rama's feet (a metaphor for travel, and the use of the plough). The geographical conditions of Kosala and Mahakantara still reveal stony features.

Valmiki's allegory and metaphorical language have been interpreted as purely literary and metaphorical in course of time through which our capacity for decoding the metaphors and symbols have been lost. Hanuman has been imaged as a pure monkey and Ravana as a man with ten heads. (Perhaps, he was a highly intelligent Brahmin. My Western readers are requested to treat the narratology and the mode of characterization in *Ramayana* in conformity with the rhetorics of Fantasy and not with any logic of the empirical/realistic mode of narrative as deployed by the Christian Missionaries for conversion of the Hindus).

(N.B. This translation of *Dasaratha Jataka* is done from the original by Sri Hadibandhu Hali, an advocate and historian of Bargad, Bhubaneswar and is provided to me. *Dasaratha Jataka* is a rare collection and most of our scholars and historians do not know about this ancient book of Orissa. The author is facinated to give this account in Mr. Hali's language since this Buddhist narrative of Ramayana goes contrary to the Aryan interpretation of Valmiki and provides an alternative. This ancient Orissan Buddhist account also reflects how the Oriya Vratyas rejected the Northern Indian mythologies and provided their own Vratya and Buddhist alternatives to the national myths. It seems they summarily denounced the Ganges Valley culture.

The Vratya Culture

Kulluka Bhatta, in his commentaries on Manu classifies our traditional language into the Vedic and the Tantric, the latter based on the anti-Vedic doctrines. The flouters of the Vedic rituals are called the Vratyas. They had their various local traditions and cults that seemed to be indifferent to and unaffected by the Vedic norms. The Vratyas were primitives, drunken and nomadic ascetics, aggressive and erotic people, but there were few brilliant seers and thinkers also amongst them. Some of our classical scholars identify them also with the Samkhya and Yoga ascetics, from the nomadic tribes.

The cocept of the worship of Grama Devata(s) was popular among the Pre-Vedic tribes and such worships impacted the Brahminic belief systems. These non-Aryan practices got blended with the Vedic series of rituals gradually. The Natas, Karna, Khasas and the Dravidian races were called the Vratyas. Manu was of the opinion that the Dravidas were the outcome of a racial mixture of the Aryan *Kshatriyas* and the Austric women. Thus, they are also taken as the Vratyas. The amazing community of the Vratyas included magicians, medicine men, shamans, mystics, mendicants and other pleasure seekers. Some of them were also very austere and spiritual men.

The XVth *Khanda* of *Atharva Veda* is captioned *Vratya Khanda*.

Paul Charpentier, in an article published in *Vienna Oriental Journal* established them as members of the Vedic tradition, but as the worshippers of Rudra Siva. Siva was worshipped by them in his dreaded forms and some fallen Brahmins had also accepted Rudra Siva as their God.

The *Kesi-sukta* of the Rig Veda brings a reference to *Eka-Vratya* in contrast to the pancha-vratyas. The Rig-Veda uses the term Vratya to denote the break-away group of the Vedic tradition. Jaimineya Brahmana describes the Vratya as a group of ascetics roaming about in an intoxicated state. *The Tandya* (24:18), however, addresses them as divine Vratyas. The *Vajaseneyi Samhita* refers to them as physicians and as guardians of truth. They seem to have been a community of ascetics living under a set of religious vows (Vrata). Atharva Veda (V.22.14) denotes a *jana* (tribe) called Magadha as the vratyas. Gradually, the Magadha tribe named their country as Magadha.

It is interesting to note that the concept of Atma was not conceived of in the Vedas. It appeared in the Upanishadas toward the end part of the 5th. Century B.C. and it is evident that the Vratyas of the Eastern India nourished the idea of spirit in our body. The basis of Vratya belief was that the spirit allowed us to feel some elevated levels of thoughts as well as imagination as the highest level. The idea of Atma that flourished in the eastern part of India was of Vratya origin.

SECTION-III

RELIGION, EDUCATION, ART, AND ARCHITECTURE

The Spiritual Life of the Dongria Kondhs

The spiritual life of the Dongrias can be known from their religious pantheons, sacred centres and their myths of creation. But what was religion to them? Was it a knowledge that protected them from the inexplicable, unpredictable failures and hence mysterious? In that case, every society develops certain patterns of behaving designed to guard, by one means or the other, against the unexpected. This is a strategy to improve and control his relationship to the universe in which he lived. Perhaps religion to them was a system of symbols which acts to establish powerful, persuasive and long standing moods and motivations. But more than that, religion was a binding force, by which the primitive maintained his solidarity and ensured its continuity.

Some of the anthropologists maintain that religion in such societies is related to animism, which is belief in anthropomorphised spirits.They had a firm belief in the concept of soul or consciousness that was detachable from the body and could travel to distant places where he had strange experiences. Since images of the dead are common in dreaming, early men could have also developed the notion that the soul outlived the body and survived after death.(I would like to remind the Aryans that their Rishis were not the only embodiments of spiritual knowledge. The Vedas are not the only source of ancient knowledge.Much before they arrived through the North-West, this tribal state had its own spiritual codes and hence our naked tribal people did never care the intruders. Even today, a politician in Delhi gets a vicarious pleasure by ignoring/cheating Orissa and considers him self wise, diplomatic and shrewd, while the Odia tribal people either boycott the election or spit on the photographs of the Aryan *Netas.)*

However, animism did not cover the spectrum of truly basic and pervasive religious phenomenon, for it omitted reference to supernatural powers. Anthropologists like Tylor and his critics like Marrett had coined the word "Animatism" to refer to belief in impersonalized, disembodied and transferable force that may become infused in people, animals, or objects. The ethnographic prototype of such power is the Melanesian and oceanean concept of Mana. A great Chief's person may become imbued with Mana, making contact with him dangerous to commoners.

Before we come to state about the religious belief system of the Dongria Kondhs, let us take a look at the definitions of religion given by anthropologists like Frazer and Malinowski etc. For Frazer religion is a propitiation or conciliation of powers superior to man which are believed to direct and control the course of human life. He further belives that religion personifies the universe in the form of a deity or spirit who can chgange or manipulate the natural law for the good of their favourites.

Malinowski saw religion as man's principal means of coping with anxiety. Sigmund Freud's contribution to the study of religion found its origin in the extirpation of guilt for the primal crime of parricide. Religion, in the Freudian world view, is a system of projections of unconscious, expressed experiences that are characteristics of a people; they are expression of the wishes of the people. Jung, on the otherhand, considered religion to be therapeutic. Recognizing the anxieties that people are subject to as a result of their socialization experiences, he suggested that religion provides help for the resolution of inner conflicts and attainment of maturity

While reporting about the religious belief-system of the Dongria Kondhs, I heavily indent material read from a book captioned ' *Culture and 'Developement'*, and my quotations justify that I am interested to give my readers different versions of opinions with regard to religion. Most of these opinions are either from the Western anthropologists or from the Western psychologists. In the pretext of behaving in a socalled rational and scientific manner they tend to think in an egoistic, gross and empirical manner about Gods. Most of the contemporary Odia thinkers also define God as a creation of Man. Chittaranjan Das, who is claimed by the younger generation of Odia critics as one of the pioneering original thinkers, has written in many essays that God is nothing but a figment of human imagination. This audacious and stupid secular logic of defining God is a blind imitation of the avantgardist trend of the 1960s. Such occidental radicalism did not hold much water and the anti-god, avantgardeism was thoroughly shaved off by the post modernists.

I attempt here to define and categorize the religious belief-system of one of the World's ancient-most civilizations established much before the Aryans and they are the Dongria Kondhs.The religious belief of the Dongria Kondhs begins with the celebration of the story of creation.

It is interesting to note that the Aryan mode of worship, the notions of Pranava Mantra and the multivalent religious symbolism embedded in the sound of OM signify creation and nothing but creation.The Hindu theory of creation, as mentioned in the Vedas, is contained in this mantra. The theory states that (i) Creation is not a linear process, beginning and ending at particular points of time, but it is a cyclic process going on eternally; (ii) God creates this universe out of Himself by Himself. To put it in a technical language, He is both the material cause and the efficient cause; (iii) (iii) Before beginning any particular cycle of creation, He utters the Vedic words denoting the various classes of beings and objects; conceivesof the corresponding forms(remembering them from the previouscycles of creation) and creates them.

This leads to the notion that the form (rupa) is preceded by a name, which is composed of letters that have sounds.

Contrary to this Vedic notion, the primitive Kondhs of Koraput have conceived of a Creator Goddess named Dharani Penu, meaning the Earth Goddess who is otherwise also known as Jakeri Penu. She is recognised as the creator of this universe and also as the sustainer. She protects from the evils and brings about happiness and prosperity in their society.

Dharani Penu resides in every Dongria village. She is represented by three long pieces of stones posted upright and another two pieces of stone placed horizontally over it. Sixteen pieces of stones lay scattered all around Dharani Penu representing her 16 disciples, who work for her. The abode of Dharani Penu is known as the Kudi or Sadar Ghar which is situated in the centre of the village in the village street and is a small thatched hut.

Koteyavali Penka is the cosort of Dharani Penu. He is represented by a big slab of stone, 2 to 3 feet in height, and a wooden plank or munda, both posted upright vertically and another wooden piece placed horizontally over it. On both sides of this horizontal piece of wood are hung coloured thread balls and small triangular pieces representing combs. This is the reflection of the fact that the Dongria males sport long hair tied in a knot in which they adorn wooden combs, Koteyuvalli Penka guards each Dongria village and protects the villagers from any sort of mishap.

At the entrance of every village resides the Jatrakudi Penka who protects the village from drought, epidemics and other natural calamitiesa. He is represented in a small, square piece od earth, enclosed by four bamboo posts, 2 to 3 feet in height and covered on the top by a perforated umbrella made of leaves.

Bima Penka is Lord Indra's equivalent in the Dongria belief system. So, he represents Thunder. Obviously, he is worshipped for adequate rainfall, which, in the absence of irrigation facilities, is essential for good harvest.

Lahi Penka or the Lord of the *Dongaras* (the mountains), is worshipped before the falling of the trees for shifting cultivation. Lahi Penka protects the Dongria's swidden.

The felled logs can only be taken home and/or burnt in the swiddens after Lahi Penka is propitiated.

The Aji-budhi Penu or Basanta, the Goddes of Small pox resides near the Jatra Kudi Penka. She is propitiated when the villagers suffer from any epidemic diseases like small pox, cholera and other similar diseases. She is otherwise also known as Takrani Penu.

Hira Penu, another Goddes, is also worshipped along with Takrani Penu. She protects the children of the village from different types of diseases and unnatural deaths. Both Takrani and Hira Penu are also worshipped by each Dongria households

Lada Penu is worshipped before the annual ceremonial hunting operations. She is propitiated to enable the Dongria to get good games as well as to protect them from wild animals that are found in the forests.

Ghungi Penu is the Goddes of the stream, the gadgada, which is the Dongria's only source of water. Therefore she is revered and propitiated.

Satara Penu, a bronze figure mounted on top of a long bamboo is worshipped and propitiated during the meria festival alongwith Dharani Penu.

The Dongria Kondhs who believe that they are the descendants of the Niyam Raja or Neba Raja , also worship him as an ancestor. This is a hightened version of what we call a *sraddha*. The Neba Raja Penka was traditionally represented by a traditional sword. He was worshipped annually during Dussehra in the temple of Goddess Durga at Bissamcuttack during the rule of the Rajahs of Jeypore. The practice is, however stopped because of modernization. The Niska Mutha, who are the original descendants worship him in the Neba kudi and Neba Raja Penka is revered and propitiated by all Dongria Kondhs.

Besides, there are innumerable Gods who are beneath the above Gods and little above the common folks. These constitute the plethora of unnamed spirits. Most of them are the guardian spirits, and others who become known for efficacious work, may be promoted to the rank of named gods and goddesses. Some spirits who are known, but never invoked by the people, are of the hobgoblin type. They delight in miscjief and can be blamed for any number of small mishaps. Other spirits take pleasure in deliberately working evil for people

In addition to the village Gods and Goddesses, every Dongria household has a residing spirit, who is given the status of a God/Goddess. For example, Lai Penu is a female spirit and is supposed to reside in the western corner of a Dongria house. She is the Goddess of wealth. Sita Penu, another female spirit, is also worshipped with Lai Penu. She is represented by a dry ground or a Tumba containing all the kinds of seeds sown in the swiddens. After all the crops in the shifting cultivation fields are harvested, these are ceremonially put inside a tumba wrapped in a new piece of cloth and hung from the ceiling of the house on a sikka. This tumba is the representation of the Goddess Laxmi.

It is interesting to note that in most of the traditional civilized houses this tradition is being followed during the *Laxmi Puja* held after the harvest in the month of *Margaseersha*. But no one knows that the ritual of hanging the grains on a sika, or filling the grain in a tumba is taken from the Dongria tradition. Even today in Kalinga the female folk use *ada, gouni* and *tumba* knit in cane during the *Mahalaxmi Puja* of the month of *Margaseersha*. This bears the proof that the Odias still continue with the vratya rituals and there has been a cultural osmosis between the two races- the civilized and the primitive.

Another female spirit known as Danda Penu is represented by a small wooden post or *munda* and worshipped in the kitchen. She is the guardian spirit of the *doli/duli*, a bamboo-knit big basket painted by soil and cowdung for storing their grain.She is worshipped and propitiated by each Dongria household.

During the Meria festival, the Dongrias worship three male deities: Chhatar Penka, Bhario Penka and Banjari Penka. They are also represented by mundas or small posts, indigenous phallic symbols and are worshipped in the households.These gods protect the members of the Dongria family from diseases, epidemics and accidents.

Banjarian Penu and Haru Penu are two female spirits who are worshipped along with Sita Penu. Banjarian Penu is represented by a ladle, a wooden box with bells (such bells can be seen hung around necks of the cattle). The ladle is hung in a corner of the house and is supposed to ward off evil eyes on the household possessions. The Haru Penu is worshipped to ensure a good harvest.

There are some evil spirits who intentionally do harm to the people if they ar not properly appeased. A female spirit, known as Miali Penu, causes illness the people and is worshipped at night during Dussehra. Bura Penka and Suka Penka are male spirits whose acts are malevolent. Bura Penka brings cholera to the village and Suka Penka destroys crops. Both are propitiated at night in the burial ground.

The second category of supernatural beings is of human origin. Ancesotor spirits and ghosts are among the spirits who were once human. Some communities believe that everyone has a soul and that the soul survives after death. There are many interpretations of what the soul does after death. Some societies believe that the spirits of the dead remain nearby and continue to take interest in their living kin.

Swanson has found that people are likely to believe in active ancestral spirits where kin groups are important decision making units. The kin group is an entity that exists over time, back into the past as well as forward into the future, despite the deaths of the individual members. The dead feel concerned for the fortunes, the prestige and for the continuity of his kin groups as strongly as the living.

This concept of veneration for the dead has several effects on the society. It keeps serious fights from developing within the family. The living may grumble at the behaviour of the young, but the punishment is left up to the ancestors. The man who eats rich food and does not invite his kin to share, or the man who shows off his ability at a dance and impresses the woman while his kinsmen stand alone, may not be rapproached directly, but may have the ghosts invoked against him. The invocation of the ghosts is particularly useful where there is a power struggle for authority within the lineage or clan.

The ancestor spirits of the Dongria Kondhs are known as Dumbas. The Dumbas of each Dongria household are thought to live inside the house and are represented by a small wooden post near the *tuli munda*, the central post of a Dongria house.. The post representing the Dumbas is known as the *Hadada Munda*. It is the most secret and sacred object inside the house and no Dongria house can be complete without the *Hadada Munda*.

These ancestor spirits guard and protect a Dongria family from all unforeseen situation and take an active interest in the well being of their future generations. The descendants of these ancestral spirits, in turn, respect and propitiate them. The Dumbas often appear in dreams and tell their descendants to appease them. Failure to do so may incur the wrath of the Dumbas. Generally, however, the Dumbas are benevolent spirits and will not like to harm their descendants.

People who die unnatural deaths are believed by the Dongria to become *mahates* or ghosts. The souls of these persons move about the cremation ground and the house in which they lived. Sudden deaths in Dongria Kondh community include death by tiger maul, death by hanging, drowning or falling from a tree, suicide or murder.

If a man dies when mauled by a tiger or a leopard, he is cremated at the site of the accident. He is not touched for fear of contamination except by his nearest family members. Similarly, all other types of accident and sudden deaths are viewed s prone to contamination, awful and fearful. The members of the older generation report that all these forms of death result in the infection of an inheritable condition whereby the "blood jumps" especially within the family. For example, murder is thought to be an inherited trait and may miss one generation, but reapper in the next. Thus, in the lengthy and complicated purificatory rites for all these sudden deaths, one of the main duties of the priest is to symbolically and repeatedly suck out the blood from each kin member, who may otherwise become future targets.

In case of accidental deaths, mortuary rites are observed, on the seventh day after the death. After three or four days, the *dishari* is called and given a new winnowing fan, a piece of new cloth and a fowl or pigeon. Then he goes to the forest to collect medicinal and magical herbs from the forest after which he sacrifices the bird to the *dangar* (forest) deity. On the day of purification, the *dishari* powders the herbs and mixes it. He proceeds to the place where the person was cremated, and pours the herbal mixture. If a uniform sound comes out of it, then it is believed that the spirit is there and soon after he encircles the area with new yarns and drives an iron nail approximately in the throat of the body. The belief is that by encircling the area, the spirit is arrested there and by piercing the nail, it cannot move on its own.

There is absolutely no reason to laugh at this belief system. The Aryan application of *keelaka* in tantric literature and practices is exactly like this. Tha Aryan death rituals are almost equal to these rites except for the chanting of some Sanskrit mantras, which the *dishari* does not recite. This author has a strong conviction that the Aryans who came from the Caspian lake area had, by and large, appropriated all these Dongria beliefs in their death rituals.

The long years of Muslim and British rule has sucked out all our collective memory and at this deracinated stage of culture they are not in a position to connect themselves with the tribal practices. Further, the Brahmin diaspora that came from Kanyakubja were mostly illiterate and rejected bipeds who played shrewd roles to grab the opportunity and dominate over the dongria kondhs culturally. In their *yajamana*-friendly business deals, they could not evade the tribal ritualistic practices. These practices were deeply rooted in the collective psyche. The present belief system of the Odias is, thus, a hybridization of the Dongria beliefs and that of the Aryans. The Aryans for diplomatic and political reasons cannot avoid Orissa and yet cannot embrace it with warmth and honesty. The present government(s) at the centre is unable to delete the Odias from the political space since they are getting money from Orissa. But unfortunately they are not able to accept us as human beings, too. Like the advisors of Ashoka, they would, one day, write stone inscriptions that they changed their religion after murdering millions of Odias and in their new political strategy, they too love to be designated as *devanam priya like Ashoka*.The Odia M.P.s shall be afraid of the criminal ministers from other states and would not voice a word of protest in the sessions of Parliament against the injustice done to them.

To continue with the belief system of the Dongria Kondhs in conncetion with the death rituals, a shaman or a *bejuni* performs her/his rites and calls the spirit to speak of his/her (the dead man/woman's) future desires. On the seventh day, a feast is prepared out of the sacrificial cows and pigs and meat is cut into small pieces so that no one is inconvenienced with the bones while eating. The Brahmins, in their purest form in the *Sasanas*, cook fish on a Sraddha/Pitri-tarpana day. But this non-veg practice is forbidden in the families of Kalingan Brahmins (South Orissa).It seems transparent that the Aryan Brahmins of Puri have inherited kondh habits. However,the Dongria children are not served with this meat. If bone is stuck in some body's throat, further misfortune is apprehended to befall the village.

The belief in the death rituals and in the Dumba/Dombi concept immediately connects the reader to the milieu of the *Charya* literature of 8th to 10th century. I consider Charya to be literature of a cultural interface. The Bengalies, the Assamese and the Biharees also claim that *Charya –geeti* is also their earliest form of literature. I do not know whether the Dongria Kondhs have influenced their cultures too.

Religion and Magic in Odia Vratya Culture

Religion in tribal culture is a repertoire of assimilations of the belief-systems about spiritual beings and animism. The rest of the supernatural of the tribal is left to magic because the vratya savage understood a relationship of causality in terms of analogy. Tylor termed this as magic, 'Pernicious delusion'. However, despite his western rationalism, this anthropologist feels compelled to see the **magic** as logic of association.

Sir James Frazer formulated a distinct and coherent theory of magic on which all subsequent studies were largely built. Frazer said that the savage perceived sympathies between things and expressed the idea in terms of the "law of sympathy" or "Homeopathic Magic" Theis law has been divided into two sub-types – the 'the law of contact' or 'contageous Magic'. Magic is, thus, a distinct human art and it is practiced only through man's agency and for his benefits.

Magic may involve manipulation of the supernatural for good or for evil purposes. Many societies have magical rituals to ensure good crops, the replenishment of games, the fertility of the domestic animals and the avoidance and cure of illness The Dongria Kondhs also believe in magic and the services of a *Bejuni* or a shaman to affect a cure. (Ref. *Culture and Development. Pp.211-218)*

The magic healing system of the Dongria Kondhs may be considered as a taboo,something incredible in an era of scientism.during the 1950s and 1960s Odia society generated a lot of professors and bureaucrats who were influenced by colonial notions of empiricism. They deracinated themselves from our cultural roots. , I shall refer to an essay by Jeanne Achterberg, captioned. "The Shaman: Master Healer in the Imaginary Realm" embodied in a book, *Shamanism: An Expanded View of Reality (Ed.Shirely Nicholson. The Theosophical Publishing House. Wheaton, III. USA. 1987).* Achterberg writes: "In the shamanistic traditions, avoiding death is not necessarily the purpose of the practice of their medicine. Our Western mistrust of these systems often comes from the observation that shamanic healing may not have resulted in an extension of life. Healing, for the shaman, is a spiritual affair; Disease has origins in and gains its meaning from the spirit world". (P.105)... Illness, as conceived even in the modern sense, is regarded as some virus entering the body from without, some thing that needs to be removed or destroyed or protected against. In the shamanistic system, the primary problem is not the external element, but the loss of personal power, the spiritual immunity, which permit the intrusion in the first place. It may be an arrow or an evil spirit. Actually, this is rather advanced thinking, since recent discoveries in medical science support a description of the disease process in similar terms."(P.105)

In Dongria Kondh system of magico-religious healing witchcraft occupies a major place. The bewitched person dies and then he is cremated in a normal way and his soul is brought back. Thus a part of the soul's consciousness is indestructible by witchcraft and it becomes an ancestor spirit or Dumba.

Mahabira And Buddha's Influence on Odia Culture

Here is a little space for a bit of comparison between Buddhism and Jainism-between Ashoka's diplomatic prosperity and Kharavela's marginalization in the books of our contemporary history. This is esential for our study of culture. Though both the ruler- preachers were very popular in Odissa, they revolted against the Brahmincal/Aryan order. Both of them advocated for righteous living, good conduct etc. But there was a difference in terms of costume and their regional spacing. Ashoka operated from Magadh which had international exposure and Kharavela was regional.

Indo-Greeks were spread from Kabul to Pujnab. King Menander succumbed to the spirit and atmosphere of India and became a Buddhist to rename himself as Milinda. Thus he earned a name in the Buddhist legends. From the fusion of Graeco-Buddhist styles of art was generted the Gandhara school, and this region(Gandhar) covered Afganistan and its frontier.

Heliodorus, son of Dion came as a Greek Ambassador from Antialcidas to king Kashiputra Bhagabhadra and stayed at the boarder of Taxila university.

On the contrary, Kharavela was from Kalinga, surrounded by forests and far away from the invasion of the foreigners. He was not Kanishka to become a hero in any of the legends. But Orissa was congenial to him though he stood victorious over Pataliputra three times and chased out the Greeks from Mathura (8th year).

During the Kushan period a great schism divided Buddhism into two sections-the *Mahayana* and *Hinayana*. Nagarjuna (1st.cent.A.D.) helped a lot to popularise *Mahayana's* doctrines in China while Ceylon and Burma adhered to the faith of the Hinayana. The impact of Kharavela and his national conference on religion seems to have induced this schism. The *Vratya* style of life in Kalinga had influenced the Buddhists since Orissa was also a great seat of Buddhism.

The Impact of Jainism in Koraput

This was the time when Mahabira considered Kalinga to be a fertile culture for sowing the seeds of Jainism. Buddhism had also become popular during that period and it was splitting into Mahayana and *Hinayana* almost during that period. Indian History reveals that Nagarjuna had taken the lead to nurture the Mahayana sect that was accepted by Kanishka of the Kushans emperors. He was a Mangoloid and although he operated from his capital, Taxila, there was a contiunal flow of traffic of Chinese and Mongolian people to interact with Buddhist culture.

The *Hinayana* sect was made popular in ceylone.

This short digression into the history of Koraput reveals that during this period of Satabahana (Vasisthaputra Sataparni

(106 AD-.130 AD) and Yamana dynasties the worship of the trees and poles were prevalent and the Nala and Mathar dynasties had propagated the Sakta Tantric sects of religion.

As we find in North India the *Stupas* and the *Chaityas* being worshipped by the Buddhists and the Jains, this seems to be an influence from the tribal culture of Orissa. The cosmopolitan Magadhans and the Videhans, who were hybridised by the Aryan races through foreign invasions, had enough of reasons to look down on the Kalingans.

But on the other hand, they were threatened, too, by these *vratyas* and *Mlechhas* who were affiliated to the Dravidian races and the primitives of Gondwana land, a part of which was separated by a great earthquake of the primordial days. The inhabitants of Koraput, (the Southern part of Kalinga) had therefore cultural affiliation with the African tribes. The earthquake had created a geographical scism between Africa and south India.Udra Desha was on the interface.

The kings of Koraput who ruled during this period were from the Satabahana dynasty. Basisthaputra Pulamabi's Nasik cave edicts inform us that his father Gautamiputra Satakarni (106-130 A.D.) had conquered the eastern states. The edict describes the geographical condition of those days through the eight mountains: *Vindhya* Parijata, Sahya, Krishnagiri, Malaya giri, Mahendragiri, Swetagiri and Chakoragiri. Out of these eight *Giris*, Krishnagiri, Malayagiri, Mahendragiri, Swetagiri and Chakragiri were in Kalinga.

The cave edict describes Satakarni as:

"*Himavat meru, mandara parvata sama sarasa, asika, asaka, Mulaka, Suratha, Kukuraparanta, anupa, Bidabha akarabanti gajasa bita chhabata parichata Sahya Kahanagiri machasiri tana malaya mahinda Setagiri chakora parvata Satisa.* (Ratha 79) After Gautamiputra Satakarnis death, his son Basisthiputra Pulambi (130-154 A.D.) was the king of Mahendragiri in Ganjam under whom Koraput was placed. (*Epigraphia Indica, vol. viii (a) (b) (c) (d)*).

It is also known from *Vishnupurana* (*Puranas* were also considered to be *Upanyasa* and historical records) that

Bhauma and *Pulinda* tribals were living together with the Aryan diaspora in Mahendragiri hill area (V.P.24:62). They were known as *Guha* or *Guhyakas*. The *Mahishas* who are also known as the descendants of royal families (from *Matsya* and *Vayu Puranas)* were also the inhabitants of South Kalinga (M.P. 50.76, *Vayu Purana*, 45, 126, 47, 48). The Aryans termed them as *mahisha, Bhauma* and Pulinda. The Brahmins, with their tendency to pull everything toward the main stream, made them known as Guha rulers. A sloka from *Vayu Purana* would look more authentic;

"*Anuganga Prayagamcha Saketam magadham Statha / Etan Janapadan sarvan bhokshyanti Gupta vamsajah Kalinga mahishaschaiva Mahendranilayaschaje/ Etan Janpadan Sarvan Palayishyati Vaiguhar*".

The Sloka, quoted in Pargiter's book (Pargiter 53-54) informs that while a king named Guha ruled over Kalinga, Mahisha and Mahendra of the Gupta dynasty ruled in the valley of Ganga circumscribing states like Prayag, Saketa and Magadh. This was during the time of Chandragupta-I.(319/320 A.D.)

By this time, the King of Ceylon was Keertishree Meghavarna. (310 A.D.) A Buddhist document of that time named *Datha Dhatuvamsa* records the name of King Guha Siba ruling over Kalinga (Rath:80) during his time.

Different historical records reveal that king Pandu of Murunda dynasty ruled over Pataliputra by the end of 3rd century and Guhasiba of Kalinga was a subordinate to him. He was a contemporary of Mahasena, the son of Kirtishree Meghavarna of Ceylon (*JASB*: 186) Pandu was a Jain and Guhasiba was a staunch Buddhist who was worshipping the Tooth relic of Buddha at Dantapura, the- then capital of Kalinga. Dr. Nabin K. Sahu is of the opinion that *Dantapura* was near Mahendragiri and according to his predictions, Mahendragiri was supposed to be a Buddhist kingdom by 3rd century A.D. (Sahu.116)

The Gandhamardan hill of Bolangir (the present Harisankar) was a great seat of the *Mahayana* sect of Buddhism in Orissa. Qutoting Dr. Nabin kumar Sahu, , Shri Kasinath Mishra states in an Oriya historical essay that a *bhikshu* named Ratnakar had presented a *Bodhidruma* (plant of a banyan tree) to Buddha at Gandhamardan hills. (*Divyadana* 157)

Sri Mishra (p.56) refers to a Buddhist document named *Divyavadana* in which he finds a reference to Gandhamardan hills.

A *mantri* (Minister) named Rudraksha lived on the foot hills of Gandhamardan (Divyabadana: 320) and Lord Buddha used to visit him frequently. Thus, as an important place of Buddhism, the hill is described in detail in *Bodhisattva Vadana Kalpalata* (p.25 and 31) and *Lalita Vistara* (p.39). Sri Mishra refers to a Tamil classic called *Manimekhalai* (V. Swaminathan Iyer, Canto vii, 11-43,63) in which it has been stated that Lord Buddha had been to Lanka for three times and he found the King Mahodara and his nephew Chulodara of Naga dynasty waging a war against the king of Gandhamardan for a bejewelled throne. The Lord (Buddha) intervened and was able to settle the issue. The king of Gandhamardan gave the bejewelled throne to the Lord and he took it to Ceylone. He sat on the throne and imparted spiritual knowledge to Mahodara.

Lots of Naga soldiers were converted into Buddhism after listening of these spiritual discourses. During the 1st. century A.D. Nagarjuna wrote his Madhymika philosophy at Harisankar. But the place was called Parimalagiri or *Pu-lo-mu-lo-kili* (as called by Heuen T'sang).

Another version of the legend says that the Kingdom of Sonepur or Suvarnapura was called Lanka till 10th century A.D. According to the copper plate of Kumar Someswara of Soma dynasty, Lanka (*Lanka vartaka Sannidhara*) was situated on the bank of the river Chitrotpala (*Mahanadi*). A goddess named *Lankeswari* is still worshipped at Sonepur.

These half historical and half legendary/puranic evidences prove the popularity of the Buddhist culture in Orissa. It is interesting to note also that the Northern Kalinga was influenced by the *Mahayana* sect while the southern Kalinga adopted the *Hinayana* sect of Buddhism.

It seems, the Northern Kalinga apropriated most of the cultural traits from Magadh and Videha Schools of Buddhism, while Buddhism itself appropriated the tribal traits of Tantra in the South. But the prejudices of regionalism and Brahminical order continued. A short discussion is needed here with regard to brahmanization and tribalization of the Buddhist culture.

Jainism and the Jain gurus: An Introduction

Mahavira chose Odissa (Kalinga, Kosala and Toshali of those days) and the Odias chose the concepts of Jainism on a common ground – that both flouted the Vedic notions. The primal Vedic culture was nothing but killing animals and offering the meat to their Gods with wine. Later, the Vedic people, having commingled with the *Asura*s invented the idea of casteist separation.

The native Indians knew how to synthesize contrary principles of religion to diagnose truth. That is how the Rik Veda expresses two concepts only; the presence of a universal "manhood" on one side, and, on the other, the notion of the "void". There was "nothing in the beginning". Both these ideas converged on the Vedas.

The Jains understood both the concepts in a different way. The presence of the Universal "Manhood" (*Purusha*) was a feeling of the Asuras – which connotes that everything was "full" in the beginning. The earliest form of Jainism manifested this idea in South India in multiple ways.

'The word Jain has been derived from *"Jina"* or the "conqueror". Jainism was transparent as a religion most probably after Kharavela's conference at Khandagiri (1st Cent. B.C.). It seems to have originated, as Pt. Neelakantha Das points out, from Rishabhnath. The legends say that Rishabhnath came from the Himalayas after deep meditation and realization in order to preach his religion.

The *Purana* literature declares that Rishabh Dev's

son was Emperor Bharat. But the Hindu *Puranas* announce Bharata to be the son of Shakuntala. Pt. Nilakantha Das was of the opinion that Shakuntala emerged from the myth of the western Asura queen Semirasis.

The unification of the myths of the western Asuras and the Hindus does neither formulate nor confirm the purity of the Aryan race. We know it from the myths that primitives like Vyasadeva and Srikrishna had also been aryanized. The "unification" is purely Indian – an example of the Indian power of synthesis. The native Indians had the largeness of heart to accept all men as one and equality / humanism as their religion. The cardinal principle of this equality emerges from the concept of the "soul". The idea of the multiplication of the soul or, the emergence of the "universal soul" is rooted in the experience of "motherhood" – the experience of delivering a child, who inherits a part of his/her mother's life. This is one of the fundamental principles of Jainism, which Mahavira preached in India. This is what we broadly understand as the *"Jina"* or as the conqueror. The idea of "conquest" comes when we understand that all men do possess a "soul" and are therefore, equal internally; though there are external, gross differences.

This notion of "fullness" (Purusha) must have generated the concept of the void, the concept of the "absences" and the "lack" known as the *"shoonya"*. Like the colourless soul, the *"shoonya"* too is without any divisive idea – like the Muslim, the Christian, the Hindu and the "superior –inferior" and so on. Such an idea gave rise to Godhead like "Purushottama", conceived as Jagannatha in Kalinga.

The concept of "Jagannatha" or "Purushottama" (The best of Purusha or the idea of fullness) has thus, emanated from a Jain concept, and the idea can be referred to in a book captioned *"Jnanasiddhi"* by Indrabhuti, the King of Uddiyana (C. 7/8th cent). One may decipher Buddhist ideas in this concept. Indrabhuti was a king from the Kosala and he ruled over an ancient civilization on the banks of river Suktimati. The first *sloka* of Indrabhuti's *"Jnana Siddhi"* invokes Jagannatha.

"Pranipatya Jagannatham Sarvajana Vararchittam
Sarva Buddhamayam siddhi vyapinam gaganopamam."
[Indrabhuti offers his salutations to the symbolic Jina, "void" or a Jagannatha conceived as the Buddha. He is like the sky in matters of *"siddhi"* or, the ultimate realization]

The *"shoonya"* is basically a concept of the *'Nishadas'* a tribal group living in Kalinga and Koshala). The *Nasadiya Sukta* (10, 129) explains how there was nothing called *'Sat'* (The Right) and *'Asat'* (The wrong) at the beginning and how there existed *Kama* (desire for procreation) only. *"Kama"* expressed itself in the figure of the woman. One can decipher one more evidence in *Kenopanishad,* (Kena-Upanishad)-Part-III also. Indra searches for the primal man of the universe and discovers a woman, who was "Haimavati". The *Rishis(the sages)* interpret this woman as *"Brahman"*. Thus Brahman has never been conceived as a male-centric concept.

After a millennium Varaha Mihira imagines Brahman in terms of icons. He has created three figures and the *Madhyama* (The middle) icon is called Ekanamsa. There icons are preserved in the museum at Lucknow. After around four to five hundred years, the concept of Ekanamsa manifested as "Subhadra" in the temple of Jagannatha in eastern Kalinga. Later this flourished as Tantra.

Uddiyana (Mostly the present western Orissa of our contemporary times) has emerged, therefore, as a major seat of Tantra.

One more powerful concept called *Aikantika Dharma* (the notion of a unitary God) entered India during the post Vedic period. Consequently in Mahabharata Vasudeva or Krishna was accepted as the unitary God of this universe.

Later, the *Bhagabata* established a religion called "Narayaneeyam". Pt. Nilakantha Das is of the opinion that such an idea emerged from the *Sveta dveepa,* a place from where the Brahmins and the astrologers emerged. The story depicts that Narayana/Vishnu/Krishna slept in the ocean of milk on the snake called Vasuki, under its hood. Two young wives-Lakshmi and Sarasvati serve this God. Narayana thought of conceiving a child. Hence from his naval point emerged a lotus (a symbol of *yoni* or a vagina) and Brahma was born from this lotus.

During this long sleep, Narayana fought with two Asuras / Daityas named Madhu and Kaitabha. Narayan killed them and built this *Medini* (earth) out of their *Meda* (fat) and *Mamsa* (flesh etc.). The story is embodied in *Chandi-Purana*.

The idea of the Asuras baffles us at this point. As mentioned in D.A. Mackenzie's "Myths of Babylonia and Assyria", we know about the cruel king of Assyria, who conquered alien states, burnt their bodies and maimed them. The idea of the "Asura" emerged from him. H. R. Hall in his *Ancient History of the Near East* (7th Edition P, 415) described about the violent and cruel rule of the Assyrian King.

Jainism flourished at a time when the Vedic people talked in contradictory codes. There was disagreement between the two rival schools of Veda – one recommending "animal sacrifice" and the other holding *Ahimsa* as the *summum bonum*. One may find evidence in Vedic literature in which one expression propagates *"Ma himsyat sarva bhutani"* (do not kill any living creature) and *"Sarva-medhe sarvam hanyat"* (kill all kinds of animals in the *"sarva-medha"* sacrifice).

Mahameghavahana Aira Kharavela (C 150 B.C.) was most probably a svetambar Jain, and he called for a Jain conference at Khandagiri. According to the Jain school the svetambar schools is subdivided into three sects: (I) *Mandira Margi / Murti Poojaka* or the image worshippers II) *Dhundias* or *Sthanakbasi* sect and III) *Terapanthi* Sect. All these sects are opposed to the Digambara School; they recognize the wearing of while clothes on the part of the ascetics, women's right to *Moksha* and the possibility of *Moksha* for the untouchables and house holders. The *Mandirmargi* sect worships the dressed idols and their monks live in the temples. The *sthanaka-basis* do not believe in idol worship and their monks and nuns live in *sthanakas* or houses especially set apart for them. The *Terapanthi* monks and nuns wander about from place to place.

The Jain scripture *Jambudvipa Panannatti* mentions

Kalinga as one of the 25- ½ civilized countries (*arya desa*) of India. Toshali (Dhauli of Bhubaneswar) was one of the major seats of the wandering Jain sages. The 18th Teerthankara Aranatha transformed himself into a *bhikshu* at Rajpur (present day Raipur in M.P.which was a part of Kalinga in those days). Parsvanatha (the thirteenth Teerthankara) and Mahaveer had visited Kalinga for the propagation of Jainism.

The *Uttaradhyayana Sutra* and the *Kumbhakara Jataka* mention how the King of Kalinga named Karakandu (9th century BC.) was converted into a Jain. A Jain scripture captioned *Bharateswara* (*Ancient India, Vol-1*, Pp. 118-132) inscribes the life story of the ancient most Kalingan Jain King of the 9th century BC.

Mahaveera passed and preached through Valuyagama, Subhoma, Suchheta, Malaya and Hattaseesha before he entered into Kalinga. Shri Ashok Kumar Rath, an eminent scholar and authour of a voluminous book captioned *Odisare Jainadharma* mentions that these places are likely to have been situated in the present day Western Orissa. The place called Subhoma, according to the inscriptions of the Somavamsi, Bhanja and Chola dynasties was Suvarnapur of the present day Orissa. We have located the ***Suktimati civilization*** of 10th. Century BC at Suvarnapur. It is the place where Mahanadi and Suktimati (River Tel) have commingled. Mahaveera moved from Toshali to Moshali(the Western Odisa) to preach his religion. The people of Toshali considered this naked preacher and a Robber had arrested him and thrown into the prison as a lunatic. Later, they released him. Mahaveer,then, had to move toward Moshali. Even the present day Koraput is full of *sasanadevis* that have later been appropriated as Hindu Temples. Actually, Mousalia/Moisalai/Maisalus of Ptolemy's *Geograhy-vii-1* extended from the Southern part of Ganjam to the delta of river Godavari. Pihunda or Pithunda was one of the famous ports of Kalinga of those days since the *Uttaradhyayana Sutra* mentions this to be also an important place/seat of Jainism.

The Hatigumpha Inscription of Kharavela mentions that

Kharavela invaded Magadh and brought back the 'Kalinga Jeenasana'. Mahapadma Nanda had taken it from Kalinga in the 4th cent. BC. Pandit Neelakantha Das considers Lord Jagannatha to be this Kalinga Jeena and traces the culture of Lord Jagannatha in this ancient Jain icon/concept.

Buddhism in Odissan Culture

Buddhism, as such, rose into popularity and esteem in eastern India after the era of the *Upnishadas*. Kalinga was full of forests and forest dwellers. There were few Brahmins around the capitals for performing the rituals, which were done in the vedic style. we could know it from Kharvela's education and coronation-Kharavela's teachers of *veedhi* (ethics). *Vyavahara* (study of law and administrative ranks) and *rupa* (the science of coins/money) must have taught him in Sanskrit and the curiculum must have been modelled in the pattern of the courses imparted in Taxila University. The influence of Taxila was felt upto Pataliputra in the east and the kings of Kalinga were keeping a close eye on the experiments made in the field of Pataliputra. The academic knowledge of Taxila, thus, came to the capital of Kalinga, with a little distortion. So was the case with Buddhism.

But Pataliputra was nearer to Lumbini, Magadh and Videha, where Buddha's initial preachings began.These were multicultural places.The people of these cities appropriated the cultural traits from Greece and Middle East and had adopted multi-culturalism. The Nandas and the Mauryas and the Kushanas were outsiders and India had already absorbed their culture. Buddha's concept of doing away with the idol worship and the Vedic rituals had a very strong appeal to the foreigners who had settled between Kabul and Punjab and Greece and Punjab.

The cities of Pataliputra and Videha were cosmopolitan in nature and they generated a situation for a mulicultural milieu.Once upon a time Pataliputra and Videha were also considered to be the great seats of Upnishadic culture.

Padmashri Paramnanda Acharya's text on archaeology informs that by the time Buddha began to preach in those areas, the impact of Brahminic rituals (*homa* and *yajna* etc.) were not as much powerful as the death rituals. In those days the dead bodies of the great men were burnt and a *stupa* was built, to be worshipped later. A *chaitya Brikshya* was also worshipped as the abode of *yakshas* and *yakshinis*.

The *yaksha* is an ancient deity and a powerful mythological figure which has its depiction equally in the three prominent religious arts in India, namely the Hindu, the Buddhist and the Jain art. Dr. Shyamalkanti Chakravarti writes, "An array of etymological attributions have been adduced to explain the mysterious term yaksha. The word is derived from root Yaj (to sacrifice) and *yaks* (to reveal or to move quickly) are *prayaks* (to honour). The term is almost equal to the Iranian word *yaxs* denoting a sense of appearing. The Atharva Veda signifies Yakshas as *punyajanah* or *itarajanah* (sacred people or the Other people).

In some cases, the word *Yaksha* is used in the sense of the mysterious or the secret. In the Rigvedic passages, in which the word occurs (RV. 4:3:13:8:6:5; and 10:88:13), it is used as proper noun or adjective which denotes mystery, secrecy, formlessness and the invisible. In the verses of the Atharva Veda, *Yaksha* has been taken for a living being, a great spirit, an animating being and so on". (Chakravarti:38)

The *Vamana Purana* differentiates the functional aspects of the *Rakshasas* and the *Yakshas*. Both of them are worshippers of Siva, but the former is known for notoriety as to raping other men's wives and coveting other's wealth while the latter is noted for egoism, aggressive nature and fondness for the study of the Vedic lores.

"The Jains had the *Yakshas* as *Vyantara Devata* denoting a demi- god who lives on trees inside caves or protects the water bodies" (Chakravarti:39) This belief is comprable to the belief of the *Bondas* of Koraput. The *Patakhanda Mahaprabhu* is kept in the cave of a Banyan tree in Mudulipada village. The abode of the *Yakshas* is *Chaitya*, It seems the worship of the

Chaityas in Buddhism and Jainism are appropriations from the tribal culture of Orissa, specially from those of Koraput and Bolangir districts.

It is very important to note that one of the top thinkers of Buddhism Dinnaga, was born and stayed in ancient Kalinga of those days. Dinnaga, as per the Tibetan tradition, was born in Simha vaktra near Kanchi, lived in a cave on Bhorasalia in Orissa and sojourned in Nalanda.. These accounts of the micro-histories are differently reported in Yuan Chwang's report.(Ref.P.S.Sastri, *Some Buddhist Thinkers of Andhra, IHQ. Vol.XXXII No.2 &3 June-Sept. 1956, Gautama Buddha 25th Centenary Special Issue*)

Yuan Chwang entered the Antolo (Andhra) country, saw its capital P'ing-k'i(Vengi), and found a hill 200 li further southwest of the town. On the ridge of this isolated vhill, he observes, was a stone tope where Ch'en-na (Dinnag) P'usa composed a treatise on logic. "Manjusri summoned him to develop for the benefit of posterity the *yogachara-bhumi-sastra* originally delivered by Maitreya. It was on this hill near Vengi in the West Godavari district that the *Pramanasamuchhaya* was composed. All this happened around Kalinga.

Nagarjuna was in Pu-lo-mu-lo-ki-li (Parimalagiri) or Harishankar for about one hundred and fifty years and the Madhyamika philosophy was written here. Most of the tribal mantras of Bolangir area still contain the name of Nagarjuna. The inclusion of the name of Nagarjuna makes the mantra efficacious and it cures chronic diseases which are not cured in great hospitals. 80% of the cases of jaundice are still cured at Bhubaneswar through Tantra even in 2003. Educated people call the Baba of Barmunda to the hospital to cure the severe cases of jaundice and he cures them risking a quarrel with the great professors of medicine. Orissa is a strange province.

The tradition of Nagarjuna continues inmost parts of Orissa. The Aryans (and the Northern Indians, too) always hated the Vratyas of Orissa since they were great flouters of Vedic belief system. The Orissan people did not believe in the concept of Vedic sacrifices. They did not observe the rituals and ceremonies. They did not believe in the notions of a self. On the contrary, they believed in the effacement of the self. During the killing spree of Ashoka, myriads of these tribals offered their heads to be butched and as they were effacing themselves, the great Aryan Emperor declared himself to be a great warrior.

Then he handled everything diplomatically, accepted the tutelege of two Buddhist merchants of Orissa and suddenly rose up to fame as a "messaiah of peace." The historians have politically bulldozed the Indian plebians by designating Ashoka as an apostle of peace.This is an irony. One can just imagine what the tribal men of Orissa think when they find Ashoka -wheel on the centre of the national flag.

This is the reason why the Bondas of Orissa still refuse to vote during the elections and we call them illiterate people who are ignorant of their democratic rights. Perhaps we are inhumanly widening the hiatus between the tribals and the civilized ones(this is also a binary opposition between Nature and Culture) and that would grow as long as we would continue to educate them with our democratic/bureaucratic rationale and logic.All our International projects fail in Koraput and Kalahandi because the executors tend to do the work without knowing the tribal vision of life. That is an alternative space we refuse to know about.

The fight between Ashoka and the Kalingans is a war of cultures or a war between the Aryans and the Vratyas. To make it a little contemporaneous, the Kalinga war was a fight between the North Indians and Orissa. The fight continues even today in budget sessions, especially when there is an invasion on Orissa for the destruction of its Raiway sector.

It is idle to say that Buddhism issued out of the Upanishadas and was a phase in the evolution of the Upanishadic thought. It is just an euphemistic concept of the naive Sanskrit scholars.On the otherhand, it may be stated that Buddhism was a revolt against the Upanishadic thought and it was the denial of soul, which undermined the belief in the efficacy of the sacrificial rituals and ceremonies.

The three primary Vratya beliefs of the Odia tribals which also make a true Buddhist is the elimination of the belief in the existence of a self (sakkayaditthi) and the efficacy of the rituals(silabbataparamasa) to which is to be added the implicit faith in the Triratna by discarding all doubts(vichikitsa) about their excellence.

These radical concepts of Buddha appealed the Vratyas of Odisa and the tribal areas became the fertile ground for their promotion and propagation. Later, the Christians started to convert them. However, the commonness between the Tribal people of Koraput and the Buddhists leads us to be curious about the people and culture of Koraput.

Between 106 A.D. and 202 A.D. Koraput was ruled by Satavahana, Ikshyaku, Guna, Mathore, Sailodvaba and Nala dynasties. The Sabaras, Gonds and other tribals were their active leaders in the socio-political and cultural celebrations. The kings of Ikshyaku dynasty ruled between 202 A.D. and 300 A.D. and they had their capital in Koraput as well as in Bastar (Now in M.P.) Biddhyasakti was the name of the king who conquered Korput and Bastar in 300 A.D. and he ruled till 350 A.D.

Sri Kasinath Mishra, a contemporary historian records that the people of that area had deep religious faith .Most of the inhabitants of Koraput were either the devotees of *Siva, or they were Saktas*. Koraput and Bastar were under Samudragupta (350-400 A.D.) and the tribals adhered to *Sakti* worship in various Tantrik modes.

The trees and stones were worshipped as incons of *Sakti. Stambheswari* (a goddess that looked like a pole) was the most popular Goddess. The Chaitya worship of the Jains and the worship of the Stupas by the Buddhists are appropriations from the tribal practices of Koraput.

A brief digression into the history of Koraput would benefit us here. But the readers might question as to why this book on culture would digress toward history. At this point, I should point out that histories are of three kinds. The first is of the general kind which is merely chronological. The second variety of history is the exemplary one which takes its stand "on some moral point". The third kind is the history most truly grounded on philosophy. This final kind tries to describe human nature itself on a great scale as a portion of the drama of providence. Eliciting a redemptive pattern from history was typical to the German philosopher, Schelling, and it leads to a scheme which seems unavoidably pantheistic, identifying God with his immanence in history. Schelling writes in 1804 that history is an epic composed in God's spirit, a theme which had exercized him towards the end of his "system of trannscendental idealism"

As we proceed through our cultural milieu of the 1st century, through the Buddhist radical notions of soul alongside the vision of the Vratya tribal people, we need to re evaluate the primitive culture of Koraput.

Oddiyana: The Centre of Buddhist Religion

Schools of Buddhism

The naming of a branch of Buddhism as *Hinayana* signifies hatred, cultural marginalisation and racial prejudice. 'Hina' is mean, fallen etc. This is termed so because of its incorporation of 'Tantric' and *'Sakta'* (worship of Mother Goddess etc.) elements.In such worships, the southpole of the human body is given priority.

But Mahayana had also equally appropriated the Tantras. The Mauryan Empire had culturally accepted Buddhism because of a clever Brahminic Policy. It has to be remembered here that after Ashoka's death, the Mauryan Empire fell apart and South India "Over-shadowed the North." (Nehru. *Glimpses* 78). Ashoka's descendants continued to rule the vanishing empire for nearly 50 years till they were forcibly removed by their commander-in-chief, a Brahman named Pushyamitra. With this Brahmanism was revived.

The Buddhist monks were persecuted. The Brahamanization of Buddhism had a poliical motif too.

Nehru writes, "The great Buddhist *Sanghas* were powerful organisations and many rulers were afraid of their political powers, hence they attempted to weaken them. Brahminism ultimately succeeded in almost driving out Buddhism from the country of its birth by assimilating it to some extent and absorbing it and trying to find a place for it in its own house." (Nehru. *Glimpses* 78) The Buddhists who compromised with the establishment were called *'maha-yanas'*. Others who succumbed to the *vratya* and *mlechha* practices in Kalinga were called *Hina-yanas*.Lord Jagannatha at Puri is also worshipped as Buddha and in the Dasavatara song of Odissi Dance Kesava(Lord Visnu) is supposed to have incarnated as Buddha:*Kesava dhrita Buddha Sareera Jayajagadisa Hare.*"

My short digression into the history of Koraput and Bolangir is not only an attempt to unfold hidden chapters of our history, but they substantiate our cultural position too. The notions of *Hina* (the fallen) and *Maha* (the sublime and the great) as cultural codes were foisted by the Aryan Brahmins. The teachings of Mahabira and Gautama,in regard to the demolition of the casteist order, however, was acceptable to our radical vratya culture.

Casteism in India has been introduced by the Aryans, who were outsiders to India. A Mileander from Greece changed his name and became Milinda and we have accepted him as a great king. The historian,who eulogises Mileander must have been a great yesman of the polical strategy called globalization,that lays the foundation for a cultural imperialism.Cultural imperialism begins when funding agencies try to dominate a culture. I know one Anmol Velani of Bangalore who does this by funding the south Indians only through a funding agency called India Foundation Arts. During a meeting of the IFA at Bhubaneswar in 2001, a very senior and reputed research scholar of the state asked him as to why projects from Orissa are not being sanctioned and he snubbed him by retaliating that Orissan scholars do not know how to prepare a project. The IFA has turned down 4 of my genuine projects and I came to know that Mr. Vellani takes away these ideas to sell them in the foreign countries to get more funding from the Foreign Funding Agencies.

Globalization and the process of osmosis in cultures creates lots of hybrids in the field and the division of Buddhism into Mahayana and Hinayana and its acceptance and rejection in different regions of Kalinga gives us insights about the regional attitudes to culture. After the birth of a new state called Orissa in 1936, the people of Utkala have been trying to wipe out the Buddhist legacies of Kalinga and Koshala in order to bring fundings only for Lalitagiri and the (golden) triangle. Parimalagiri, Sonepur and Jaugada have been marginalized in the tourist map because the officers of the central Orissa do not want the tourist money to flow to either Koshala or Kalinga.

The relics of the fort Jaugada in Ganjam and its inscriptions reveal that the Buddhist culture was very popular in South Kalinga. The fort acted as a gateway for travelling from Kalinga to Dakshinapath. A rock edict in its interior reveals lots of hidden facts about Ashoka's invasion of Kalinga. Ashoka invaded Kalinga in the eighth year after his coronation, i.e. in 261 B.C.

The war of Kalinga was one of the most atrocious events of the history of the world. The war was mostly cultural and a product of regional fundamentalism. The grandson of Chandragupta Maurya, Ashoka operated from a cosmopolitan city called Pataliputra, which flourished in those days because of their appropriation of Greek and Middle-east cultures. It was also a seat of Brahminical dominance. Ashoka attacked Kalinga because its inhabitants were mostly forest dwellers and they were considered to be *vratyas* (who flouted the Vedic norms) and *mlechhas* (dirty people with no disciplined religion).

According to the **Aryan interpretation of history**, Ashoka's feeling of horror and remorse at the slaughter, after his conquest of Kalinga, brought a transformation of his heart and he abandoned warfare after victory. But Ashoka's own words reveal a political game with a mask of transcendentalism to exteriorize a Brahminical cultural supremacy.

We can examine the words of Ashoka: "Even upon the *forest folk* in his dominion. *His sacred Majesty* looks kindly and he seeks to make them think a right for, if he did not, repentence would come upon his sacred Majesty" (qtd. in Nehru: *Glimpses*:53)

Ashoka's language denotes more of cultural politics than of any authentic transformation of heart. The genesis of the invasion is not political annexation with economic benifits since Kalinga was inhabited by "forest folks". Three phrases in this edict deserve interpretation: "forest folks" "His sacred Majesty" and "think aright" Ashoka's language, if taken as an expression of his 'remorse' is an ideologic schitzophrenia leading toward an internal disintegration of the self. He exteriorizes cultural superiority by calling the Kalingans forest folks' since they did not choose to get Aryanised *and Brahmanised* with the Taxila brand of western education followed at Nalanda whose scholars were executive officers at Ashoka's Pataliputra.

'His sacred Majesty' can hardly claim any 'sacredness' since the guiding instinct of the invasion springs from hatred and envisages a fake superiority. The hatred underlying the cultural war manifests in the atrocities of violence, the demonic urge to exterminate the *Vratya* culture of the 'forest folks'.

This great theme of conflict must have circumscribed his Royal Majesty with innumerable unsolved questions: "Who should hold power in the organised community? What relation has that community to the rights and duties of that individual? How should the Monarch, the protector, justify assassinations? Does his action not offer a supernatural basis for royal absolutism? Is it the example of upholding the rule of law? Did not the vratyas have the power to nurture the Sakta Hinayana faiths for understanding the problems of life? What is the connotative meaning of the term "think aright"? Is the idea of right thinking only inherent in the Brahminical order of Pataliputra?

Ashoka could not have answered the questions to the advantage of perpetuating his political power. His professors of *vidhi* (ethics) might have themselves been awe-striken at the sight of devastation, and might have induced a feeling of pity", (Victory generates this pseudo-moral catharsis to prove the victors' superiority) into this monarch, drunk with cultural fanaticism.They would have tried it for restoring the prestige of this beastly biped called Ashoka, the Emperor.

Hence the Aryan Brahmins must have suggested another strategy of power- rock writing-to inform to the posterity about the Magadhan notions of "right thinking". Writing rock edicts is also an agenda of acquiring power, meant for (mis) informing the`absences'to the posterity. It (mis)informs about the wrong `presences'also (presence of a moral transformation for attacking the secular culture of Kalinga) which a contemporary French cultural critic calls "necessary evil". Ashoka and his *Vidhi*-advisors must have foreseen the impossibility of coming together to talk out their differences in a common communal forum. So, the diplomats of Ashoka's court have manouevred this pseudo-historical melodrama of repentence to perpetuate Ashoka's remorse that was never visible to the wailing women who lost their sons and husbands in this vratya land.

The readers should remember that this is the land(Harishankar in Bolangir) in which Nagarjuna wrote his Madhyamika philosophy. This is the land in which the concept of *Duhkha* has been analysed.

However, I would like to make a thorough cultural analysis of the motifs that led to the invasion of Ashoka. It was an attack of the Aryan/vedic Brahmins over the secular *Vratyas* of Kalinga, who were not only the practitioners of Buddhist Mahayana and HinaYana, but also the followers of many unsystematized fragments of Buddhist Tantra, namely, *mantrayana, kalachakrayana, nathism and vajrayana* etc.Since most of our readers are not acquainted with the above branches of Buddhism, I should brief on these subsects.

In the *Tattva Ratnavali* (Collected in the *Advaya-Vajra-Sangraha*) we find Mahayana subdivided into two schools: *Paramita Naya* and *Mantra Naya*. The principles of *Mantra*

Naya are said to be very deep and subtle. Such philosophy is inaccessible to ordinary readers. However, scholars are of the opinion that the *mantra sastra* is much superior to other philosophical treatises of Buddhist Tantra.*The Mantra Sastra* is free from delusions and it is accessible only to people of higher intellectual calibre. *This Mantra Naya* or *Mantra Yana* school of Mahayana seems to be the the introductory stage of Tantric Buddhism from which all the other offshoots of *Vajrayana,Kalachakra Yana and Sahaja-Yana etc*.grew up / arose later.

In the *Laghu-kala-chakra-tantraraja Tika*, entitled *Vimalaprabha*, we find that the doctrines of the *Paramita Naya* are wholly written in Sanskrit, while those of the *Mantra Naya* are explained in Sanskrit, Prakrit,*Apabhramsa* (the corrupt forms) and even in the non-sanskrtik languages like sabari(language spoken by the sabara tribes).

"Early Buddhism was a religion of rigorous moral discipline, practices and contemplation. But such a religion of purely ethical codes and deep meditation could not appeal to the masses and the systems of moral discipline and the methods of the *jnanas* were not acceptable to them." writes S.B.Dasgupta in his book *An Introduction to Tantric Buddhism*. He continues,"To the ordinary mind religion is something full of rites and ceremonies or other paraphernalia of esoteric practices.It is for this reason that for the sake of the common run of the people, the mantras, the mudras,and the mandalas(the mystic circles or jhoti or alpana of our folk/tribal culture mostly drawn on the grounds every morning by the women either in the liquid rice paste or in chalk stone water paint). These mantra,mudra and mandala are introduced for the realisation of the ultimate truth. These practices were followed by many other rituals and Buddhism began to put on a different air, which is generally known as tantricism. We may recall in this connection the later *Mahayanic* idea of *Trailokya Vijaya* or the religious conquest of the three worlds. The idea behind the whole drive was the idea of bringing people of all calibre within the Buddhist faith by making Buddhism acceptable to all classes of people."(P.60-61) (the bracketed explanations are mine).

Although these practices had lots of Upanishadic influences, Emperor Ashoka's Brahmin ministers considered such practices of Orissa as flagrant violation of the Vedic norms and defiling of national(?) culture. When Ashoka came for killing these Buddhist tribals, the people in the Sonepur and Bolangir area(pu-lo-mo-lo-ki-li of HeuenTsang) had offered their heads for getting killed and the rivers were flooded with the human blood) The North Indian historians have depicted this cultural war as the victory of a mighty emperor, not the beastly attitude of a maniac killer, who wanted to save a decadent brahminic culture in this way.

His conversion into Budhism is also a showcase of absent values. No amount of postcolonial euphoria about his morale and principle of nonviolence would convince the younger generation of Odias who have watched and analysed the visual image of the September-11-violence in Newyork and its follow up peace mission.In all diplomatic games of perpetuating power, the agenda makers of peace can only continue with violence.

The notion of "right thinking" as enjoined in Ashoka's rock edicts opens up multitudinous vistas of cultural philosophy-broadly boiling down to a conflict between openendeness and closure or `Nature' and `culture'. Rousseau considered `Nature' as the source of all goodness and virture, while `culture' represents "an inherently corrupting influence, a perpetual fall into error and bad faith." (Norris. 103),

The *Bondas* and the *Santals* and the *Juangs* can hardly be influenced by any notion of 'right thinking'. If they are able to pull down the entire phenomenal world into their interior, if their affinity with innocence and nature can generate a cosmos within them, why should they care for Ashoks's diplomatic edicts? A hookworm cannot differentiate beween a doctor and a decoit.

Our archaeologists inform us of the strange stories of these Buddhist edicts. Some of them have been discovered from the eaves of the village head, who used the rock-edicts either as a step to their mud houses or as stones for rubbing their feet in the village pond. However, these are not stories of history. These are current events of twentieth century that will soon pass on to the next millennium. All writings are necessary evils to our cave dwellers. They did not know anything about agriculture or about farming.

They were fruit gatherers. Valmiki's story of Ahalya (*A-halya*=not ploughed) transformed into a fertile woman at the touch of Rama's feet (a metaphor for both: for travel, and for the use of the plough). The geographical conditions of Kosala and Mahakantara still reveal stony features.

Valmiki's allegory and metaphorical language have been interpreted as purely literary in course of time through which our capacity for decoding the metaphors and symbols have been lost. Hanuman has been imaged as a pure monkey and Ravana as a man with ten heads. (Perhaps a highly intelligent Brahmin. My Western readers are requested to treat the narratology and the mode of characterization in Ramayana in conformity with the rhetorics of Fantasy and not with any logic of the empirical/realistic mode of narrative as deployed by the Christian Missionaries for conversion of the Hindus.

Ramayana and Mahakosala

Mahakosala is still inhabited by people who depend on farming and agriculture. Dasaratha's marriage with the daughter of Kosala is also a marriage between a proto-Austroloid and an Aryan. This political marriage might also have taken place for achieving a greater racial harmony. Rama's Character (viewed without religious connotations) seems to have imbibed both the proto-Austroloid and Aryan features. As a Young, handsome, dark coloured prince, educated in Aryan *Gurukula* (residential school), his visions of eco-feminism must have expanded him to the heights of Godhood. In the most intense and crucial moments of his life, he has prayed the mother Goddess and sought for Her blessings. The worship of the mother-principle, despite its later Aryanisation, belongs mainly to the proto-Austroloid race, which had migrated into Kosala and settled there unobtruded by the Aryan civilization. So, the race knew little about the art/science of cultivation. Rama's link with Ahalya (the uncultivated) signals toward notions of fertility and agriculture

The middle Ganges-plain known as "transitional regions" (24 30 N-27.50', and 81.47' E-87.50' E) is a large physical area (1,44, 409 kms) and it is its immense human, cultural and economic significance that makes it the heart region of India. Shri Krishna Kumar Mandal, a contemporary historian, writes, "...from the middle of the 2nd millenium B.C. one notices a gradual but perceptible process whereby numerous but separate primitive communities inhabiting the indo-Gangetic plain were broken down and foundation was laid for a new type of society. This new type of society makes a meaningful beginning from 600 B.C. ..."

He lays emphasis on the use of iron plough share technology and paddy transplantation. Both literary and archaeological findings suggest the appearance of a new agricultural technology and the iron plough share which enabled better ploughing. The *pali* texts describe the process of cultivation and the techniques of irrigation." (Mandal.1-2)

This recorded evidence of the historians slightly tally with our periodization, but there is no mention about the Upanishad era and our Gurukulas in which training was imparted on agriculture and cow-rearing(Please refer to *Chhandogya Upanishada*). However, Ayodhya, from which came Ramachandra had a feudal system with peasant labourers.

But Mahakosala, the forest region about which we are concerned, had a society of fruit gatherers with no social stratification. However, Nagarjuna wrote his *Madhyamika* in Parimalagiri Vihar of Kosala about which Patanjali referred to in his *Mahavasya* (Majumdar. 106-7) This historical refernce leads one to infer that the cultural milieu in this forest country was either congenial for philosophical discourses or its proto-

Austroloid inhabitants were influenced by Buddhism. If Buddhism was the root of the belief system and the content of their oral education, Kosala must have eschewed the Brahminic system of education and consequently, this land must have been cut off from the mainstream curriculum imported from abroad (Taxila and Nalanda Universities). But Mahakosala had definitely some indigenous system of education about which detailed reports are not available. These are not available because the Vratyas, in their cosmic expansion of minds did hardly believe in the idea of recoded history.

In those days Mahakosala extended upto Bastar of Madhya pradesh and Bastar area was influenced by Dinnag, the Buddhist philosopher of Andhra-Pradesh. South Kosala was ruled by the Panduvamsi-Somvamsi kings during 6th to 8th century A.D. and under the patronage of its last king, Balarjuna Sivagupta, a monastery(*Vihara*) was built at Sirpur (The capital of south Kosala) which was famous as a centre of learning. Later, the Panduvamsi Kings were ousted by Kalachuris and the kings of Bana dynasty. Thus, a detailed discussion is needed on the cultural milieu of Kosala from the time of Nagarjuna through Dinnag to the regnal years of the Kalachuries since these years' fostered Buddhist philosophers of a very high order.

Kosala and Nagarjuna (Nagarjuna's life story)

Nagarjuna was a great Buddhist philosopher. Mr. Sunit Kumar Pathak retrieved his life story from the Tibbetan book *Pag-sam-Lon-zang* and published it in the Indian Historical Quarterly vol. xxx. No.1. (March, 1954). The record tells that he was born "in a place south of Vidarva" in a Brahmin family. The "sooth sayers advised his parents to entertain one hundred Brahmins and *Bhikshus* with feasts for the prolongation of the life of their son from seven days to seven months and even to seven years." (p.93). Nagarjuna was seven years old and the parents, thought that it would be unbearable for them to see the deadbody of their son. So they allowed him to go abroad. Nagarjuna came to Nalendra (Nalanda) after travelling over various countries and met Saraha, a great teacher of Nalanda University. By the utterance of mantras in invocation of *Amitayus*, his life span increased.

On his 8th year he began to study *Sarvastivada* doctrine from Rahula and was given initiation. After being associated with Sarah he took insturctions on the *Guhyadikshetra* and other texts. He was ordinated by Upadhyaya Sarah and was called Sriprajnadhara. Meditating on the goddesses - Mahamayee and Kurukulla, he attained various *Siddhis*, (attainments) particularly in chemical (i.e.medical) sciences, and was named *Vajrakaya Siddha*. In the monastery he picked up from Bhalaba the knowledge of alchemy for changing colours and metals, but being unable to do that practically, he learnt it again from a wine-seller woman.When a famine broke out in Nalanda, he, as an attendant of the monastery, saved the people by the alchemy of changing the metals (other than gold) into gold by the propitiation of Goddess Chandika and maintained them for twelve years.

He had a missionary zeal to reconvert renegades and he changed one Sankara by explaining the religion rightly. While he explained the religion, the daughters of Nagaraja Takshak heard his religious discourses on the human world. He was called to Nagaloka where from he brought the complete *Tripitakas* and various *Dharanis* in 16 volumes for which he was named Nagarjuna.

Nagarjuna learnt the Tantras of the goddess Tara from Hayaghosa a disciple of Hayapala, a Scholar of *Tripitakas*. Hayapala was Guhyasri's disciple. In the *Dhanya Kataka* monastery he obtained the texts of *Mahakala Tantra* and *Kurukulla Tantra* from Goddess Tara. It is said that no one received any other new *Mahayana Sutranta* in India after this. He erected one hundred temples in the Madhya Desa for the propagation and development of *Mahayana* and he placed an image of *Mahakala*.

At *Vajrasana* he placed railings made of stones to save the *Bodhi* tree from the attack of an elephant. At Jatasam ghara he defeated about 500 *tirthikas* (scholar pilgrims) and earned a great distinction by preaching his doctrine.

Pathak writes: "It is said in Tibet that he spent two hundred years the Madhydesa, twelve years in the northern countries and in the countries where non human beings were inhabitants (mi-min), two hundred years in Southern countries and one hundred and twentynine years in Sri Parbata. Thus he lived for more than five hundred years" (p.94)

Like Lord Buddha, he attained the *Chittotpada* in the presence of Dipa of Naga family. Nagarjuna's contribution to the Buddhist missionary service can be summarized as under:

(1) He rectified the doctrine of practicing *Vinaya(humility* as a moral value) that was corrupted by Sankara in Nalanda University

(2) He composed the major texts of *Madhyamika* doctrine and he advanced the doctrine with in the line of *Prajnaparamita*

(3) On his way from Uttarkuru to Jambudipa, he went to King Pujatakal and presented his text by Ratnamala.

This biographical text translated from Tibbetan language appears partly eumphemistic and partly belonging to the *para* and *pasyanti* group of linguistic articulation prevalent in those days and later subtitled as *Sandhya-bhasa* (twilight language of mysticism). Language in those days of India had four gradations till it reached the external shape of articulation. *Para* form of language is mere sound: *Sabdabrahman*, the potentiality of growth in the seed; *Psyanti* language is the seed beginning to sprout, *Madhyama* stage of language occurs is when the first two small leaves appear, but are not yet separated. *Vaikhari* language manifests when these two small leaves are separated, but joined at the root.

The time of writing this biography was the era of Buddhist Tantra. Hence the language, distantiated from our gross level of western linguistics, appears exaggerated, But it is not euphemism. The reference to his longevity is also not exaggerated. By uttering the mantras for invoking Amitayusa, the longevity increases and there is nothing to feel skeptical/cynical about it.

Nagarjuna was trained in Tantra and his Goddesses were Tara, Kurukulla and Maha Mayuri. Tara and Kurukulla, as mentioned in the Tibbetan text, are forms of *Shakti* (energy) and their names appear in *Rudrayamala* and other scholarly books on Tantra. The *Shakti* called Mahamayuri does not find a place either in *Dasa maha vidya* (the ten forms of feminine energy) or in *Rudrayamala tantra*. *Rudrayamala* mentions the names of the female energy icons like *para-sakti, Adi-sakti, Ichha, Jnana, Kriya, Bala, Annapurna, Bagala, Tara, Vagvadini, Gayatri, Savitri, Siddhalakshmi, Svayambhara, Nakuli, Turagarudha, Kurukulla, Renuka, Sampat kari, Samrajyalakshmi, Padmavati, Siva, Durga, Bhadrakruti, Kali, Kalaratri, Subhadrika, Chhinnamasta, Bhadrakali, Kalakhandi, Sarswati* and many others.

Although the mother energy, titled *Mahamayuri*, is not mentioned, She is related to *Ichha(the godess of desire), Jnana(the godess of knowledge)* and *Saraswati(of knowledge and prosperity)*. Nagarjuna's ideas of philosophy have been fully lifted by Jacques Derrida of our time and most of his postulations on 'deconstruction' are hinged on his texts. In an era when knowledge is treated as auxiliary to many and readymade answers are bought in packaged form to be mugged up and regurgitated in the examinations, Nagarjuna's philosophy would appear as irrelevant as his knowledge trickles down in the form of a blessing from the Goddess Tara.

Nagarjuna's initiation into Tantra not only helped him to prolong his life for a miraculously extended tenure, but it also provided him with a perennial source of knowledge. Although a staunch believer in the *Mahayana* sect, he learnt the science of changing colours of the metals (transforming cheap metals into gold) from a wine-seller woman. This women did not belong to the Vaisya group or to the caste of other business men. They were almost untouchables those days. Learning such sciences through Tantra implied sex-ritualistic worships and the other four gross activities like taking wine, meat, fish, and offering appropriate symbolic gestures to the goddess (**mudra**).

It is strange that Nagarjuna as a Mahayana Buddhist could perform such gross rituals for the ultimate realisation of of knowledge through Mother Energy, (*Vidya* in Tantrik devotional texts is identified with the Goddess). Secondly, one would question as to how Nagarjuna, being a brahmin, could follow the path of the Vajrayana and could evade the traditional *samskaras* of the Aryan sect of the Brahminic order. The long years of his tour in India, from his early childhood, must have induced these secular traits into his life-style that blended nature and culture into a synthetic mould.

Maha Kosala of those days was described in the Tibbettan text as Madhyadesa. The territory of Mahakosala (which extended from the modern Bilaspur of Madhya Pradesh to Koraput district of Orissa) tallies with this geogaphical area. The Tibbettan biographer states that Nagarjuna stayed for 129 years in this area. The Parimalagiri Vihar, identified with Harishankar and Nrusimhanatha of Bolangir district, was his cave-abode. The seclusion and the peace of that area provided him with the epiphany to construct the **Madhyamika** philosophy.

Harishankar is a picnic spot now with a broad cascade, at times leaping within deep woods and exuding serenity all around. One can imagine how lonely and bewildering the place would have been in Nagarjuna's time.One can configurate it with the milieu of Kharavela, who used to convene National conferences on religion and thousands of naked saints congregated in Khandagiri area. His inscriptions record that the Samrat/Emperor built caves for their shelter and distributed rugs for protection from cold). That was a time of religious crises and the Emperor of this land used this cultural space for free discussion on the efficacy of the multiple belief systems-eg.capitalism,terrorism, roots of human suffering and functional modes of overcoming them. Perhaps that was a time of sundown in the sky of Hinduism. Nagarjuna was fighting a battle in his interior space sitting in one of the caves at Parimala Giri (Maha Kosala). He was codifying the canons of Madhyamika Philosophy in this deep forest. This remote place would have never corroded his mind with untruth. Culture and philosophy must have sprouted there like nature.

As he was used to travel alone in the dense jungles since his childhood, he chose Parimalagiri as a place where he could move untramelled. But the episode in the Tibbetan text in which he was taken to Nagaloka (the territory of the snakes) by the daughters of the Nagaraja (the snake king) seems to be slightly fanciful.I had to struggle for about a month to decode this metaphorical narrative of the Tibbetan Text in translation.

During the long period of his stay in Parimalagiri Vihar there was a country called Siddha Badi in Tamilnadu where the Kings of Naga Dynasty ruled. Late Padmashree Satyanarayan Rajaguru had written a history of these kings. The title of the book is *Naga Itihasa*.(The History of the Naga Dynasty) Dr. Rajaguru's book quotes from a rock edict of Yerrakota to trace the geneology of the Naga kings. But since we are dealing with Odisan culture, a digression into the history of Dramila country would be viewed as extraneous.

However, the rock edict of Yerrakota informs that the first king of these Chandika Nagas was Nrupati Bhusana and he ruled over Koraput-Bastar state. His capital was Chakrakota (the present Chitrakuta on the delta of river Indravati).

Another rock edict from Barasura informs that after Nrupati Bhusana, his son Jagaddeva Bhusana alias Dharavarsha became the king of Chakrakota. The regnal period was 1090 A.D.(So, it is not relevant to us)

Another rock edict from Narayana Pali states about king Kanra, who was Jagaddeva Bhusana's grandson and Somewara's son. There was a large state called Bhengi on the south of Chakrakota and a famous state called Kinali on the north-east of this capital. Kinali included Orissan estates like Ghumusar and Boudh. One can still find some residual Tamil families in these areas, who have been odianised in course of time. But their surnames (Iyengers etc) identify them as extant diasporas.Now they are pure Oriyas and no one can be able to, identify them as Tamils

South Kosala of Nagarjuna's time included Bastar and

Koraput. The Tibbettan text narrates how Nagarjuna was taken away by the daughters of Naga Raja, Takshak. The biographer of Tibbet must have added some magical element for deification of Nagarjuna. The use of mythical words like Nagaloka and the mention of the name of the king as "Takshak" might have been a part of the fertile metonymic narrative of the ancient Tibbetan Buddhist disciple who might have collected the data from some oral history. That has come down to us - xeroxed from a moth-eaten, *Indian Historical Quarterly* to be ignored by our younger generation of readers in the Kanika library of Ravenshaw college.

They belong to a generation of website explorers and would never read a printed book. If an unfortunate, old fashioned scholar, would, by any mischance, encounter the essay translated from the Tibbetan, he would brush it aside as *Purana*.

The Purana is a metaphoric genre of history written in Jambu Dveepa (India) and a deracinated generation of modern historians inspired by the Western ideologues of 'rationalism', 'logic' and 'empiricism' would dump them out in the garbage heaps as unbelievable creativity of esoteric races. I would advise them to read Rajasekhara and his definition of *Purakalpa* for reconstructing a postmodern histriographic methodology for the people of contemporary Jambudvipa(India).

Thus I put a temporary pause to this heuristics for my analytic operations, to trace the cultural ontology of Kosala through Nagarjuna's Parimalagiri Vihar. The author is aware of the fact that in the absence of a chronicle of our ancient system of education, a historical representation through evidential hermeneutics would be impossible.

Though this Vidarbha-born Brahmin Buddhist/Tantric/Philosopher called Nagarjuna, is a 'non-Oriya', his 129 years of stay in Mahakosala defines his aptitude, and that of the Kosala dwellers.

They are a race of people who roll like pebbles under a leaping cascade of their mountains, like the one that flowed (and still flows) beside Parimalagiri. They are like pebbles those are rubbed off into layers of sedimented sand to be buried anonymously beneath the flux of time and yet, they would be endeavoring to structure the contours of eternity. never being able to find a still-point in the gyration of changing visions. *Duhkha* (suffering), if at all it is in the postcapitalistic epoch, still embodies the faded effulgence of Buddhist philosophy. *Vinaya* (humility), one of the major ethical postulations of Buddhism was/is their creed. So are the Kosala dwellers.

Nagarjuna, the deviser of Madhyamika Philosophy that influenced Jacques Derrida later, stood at one of the interfaces of our cultural geography, that claimed conflicting spaces : the Aryan, the Dramil and the proto-Austroloid. This spatio-cultural battle ground had so synthetically mixed up nature and culture, the brahmin and the buddhist, the brahminic inhibitions and the liberated instinctuality of the Sudras to such an extent that the polarities were vaporised to silhouttes of the void, and configurated 'something' at the *Soonya* (void) of *Ajna chakra*.

If Kosala did not generate this Buddhist philosophy, it lent its womb for its germination. This womb of Mahakosala was itself the University, greater than Nalanda and Taxila, the universities that were corrupted by Greek invaders long back. Hence, inferences can be made about the enlightened educational culture of Orissa. If the Odia people were not capable of containing Madhyamika philosophy, how was it ever engineered in Kosala ?

The *Madhyamika-Brutti* of Nagarjuna, commented upon by Chandrakirti, begins with the declaration that the Madhyamikas have no thesis to prove, their business is to contradict any and evey *thesis that may be offered by any school of thought.*

Nagarjuna, having studied at Nalendra (Nalanda) entered into this womb of nature to write about the principle of "dependent origination" realised and preached by Lord Buddha. Madhyamika names it as *Pratitya Samutpada*. *Samutpada* can be explained either as the origination of some existence *(bhava)* obtaining some cause or conditions (*hetu pratitya*) or it may be explained as the origination with reference to each and every destructible individual.

The theory of causation generates confusion with in us. For example, this author feels disturbed and irritated because a mosquito stings him at the wrong place that caused the itch. What is the cause of irritation? Is that the itch or the mosquito? The search for *samutapada* would lead to multiple layes of related causations, none of which are true. They might be just seeming causes *(Samvrutti)*. Thus, the theory of *Pratitya samutpada* propounds a law about the relation of interdependence among the illusory appearances as things, called *Samvrutti satya*, . These illusory appearances which constitute the realm of our experience have their origin in a law of inter-relation of dependence. As one reads *Madhyamika*, one would discover ultimately that there is no origination. Neither is there any cessation. There is no destructibility, no permanence, no reality, no unreality; no coming, no going, no subjectivity - no objectivity, no knowledge- no knowable; everything is free from all the disturbance of birth, decripitude and death. There is neither real origination of the thing by its own nature, nor by others- nor by a combination of both- nor by any unreason. There is origination no where-at no time- and of none.

Na svato napi parato na dvabhyam na dvabhyam napyahetutah
Utpanna Jatu vidyante bhavah kvachana kechana
(Madhyamika Vrutti. Levis Edn. P.12.)

One can still go to Mahakosala that spreads from Bailapur (M.P) to Machhkund and Bonda Hills (Koraput) and examine the most illiterate of those people living under short tiled roofs with clean painted walls and clean verandahs. They do not know about any of the comforts given by science. But they would talk in their own dialect a philosophy that would sound like the theory of *samutpada* of the Madhyamika school of thought. According to Nagarjuna things can not be self -originated for "self-origination" implies the existence of a thing before it originates itself. If a thing exists already by itself, there seems to be no satisfactory reason, why it should produce itself once more. Moreover, if the existent again requires self production, this will involve the fallacy of the vicious infinite.

There is no space here to discuss elaborately on Madhyamika philosophy since it does not provide us with the concrete evidences of the ancient education in Orissa. To elaborate on Nagarjuna and his philosophy would sound not only a circumlocution, but also a bragging about the culture of Kosala, the present western Orissa. The people of western Orissa, today, do not seem to have emphacised education in their culture.However, our entire discussion shows that the people of Koshala did never suffer from any poverty of wisdom during those periods of ancient history.

The unwillingness to pursue the philosophy of Nagarjuna is not a negative quality in Western Odissa. Any philosophical mind set, perhaps, it is thought, would retard the material progress of the place. But Nagarjuna is not forgotten by them. His one hundred and fifty years of stay in *Po-lo-mo-lo-ki-li* has raised him into the status of a God. He is an incarnation of God to the tribal people of western Odisa.

Nagarjuna was not a cave-bound philosopher. He moved out into the primitive society and his presence cured diseases caused by unseen demons. The people of this tribal area believe in "demonology" even today and it is not **at all** a superstition. The greatest of the crimes are being committed by such occult practitioners in India and most of these crimes are done for the people in power.

Sakta Culture in Mahakosala

In the Western Orissa, this knowledge is known as *Dusta jhaden mantra"* (the mantra to drive away the cruel spirits) and one such Mantra reads *"Na jau boil kahara ajna, kuanri debinkara, Nagarjuna Mahadevankara koti koti ajna"*.

[This part of the tribal mantra says: you, the evil spirit you have to go ! Who commands you to go? This is a command from the virgin of the Fire and a command from Great God, Nagarjuna:]

What happened to my personal life is a different story. What is important here is that Nagarjuna's name is deployed here as a Great God (Maha Deva, also Lord Siva) since last 200 years. Nagarjuna's life-story informs that he studied the science of Tantra in Nalanda University around 1st. century and he had learnt the science of alchemy (transformation of stones into gold) from a wine-sellers woman of Madhya Desa (Kosala constitiuted the major part of madhya Desa and was being called Maha Kosala during those days). His philosophical life-style and saintly style of living must have generated a great belief amid the folks and the later codifiers of Tantra have used his name as a magic-dispeller of the evil.

Modern scientists would think that I am recycling the taboos of the tribal people of Kosala. In short, anything connected to the *Shakta* cult is rejected in the coastal area for scientific reasons. The scientists of the world, it seems, have an ego that they can explain the world in a laboratory and anything that is unexplainable can be dumped into the waste-paper-basket of taboos.

On the other hand, the coastal people, who had the exposure of going out to Java and Sumatra islands as business men, earned great amount of money and exploited the highlanders through ages. All that is preserved in the highlands and plateaus of Orissa should therefore be taken as elements that suited the political and commercial needs of the plainlanders.

Tantra is rejected as tribal and unscientific.. That is why there is a great political resentment today with regard to cultural supremacy and the citizens of Kosala voice protests against the coastal people without knowing it definitely that culture is only politics. The basic difference is in the vision of life.The coastal people can never understand the supremacy of the highlanders since they discard, like the Britishers,all Tantric notions of life on the ground that they do not conform to the standards of European knowledge.

Orissa continues to have two major physiographic divisions - the coastal plains in the east, and the plateau in the west and central tracts where lie the conspecuous tribal areas in the middle mountainous region and the rolling uplands. The second physiographic unit is conducive to tribal habitats and their culture goes back to the Pre-Vedic era. Orissa has a total area of 6640 sq. kms classified as forest-land and therefore 42.65 of the total geographical area is under forest of one kind or other, occupying lands which are hilly, undulating or mountainous. The people of Kalahandi (527 thousand hectars of forest constituting 45.5% of the total land), Sambalpur (701 hectares of forest) and Koraput (1400 hectares of forest) belonged to Mahakosala and most of the tribal settlements are found in these areas.

Mahakosala comprising of the tribal settlements exteriorize the spirit of the *vratya* culture. This culture, though partially antithetical to the Vedic spirit, is essentially a culture of the *Sakta* religion. The *Sakti* cult, according to B. Srivastav, can be traced back to 3rd millennium B.C. (Srivastav. 1) The clay figurines and seals have been discovered from the Indus-valley-excavations and these figurines represent Sakti in anthropomorphic and aniconic form. (Sharma: 6-8)

The mother Godess *(Sakti)* was the beloved deity of the primitive pelple. The *Savaras* and the *Pulindas* worshipped her at Mahendragiri around 6th century A.D. She was worshipped as Kandhuni Devi or Khambeswari. The Ananta Gumpha (Ananta cave) rock-icon testifies that king Kharavela patronised the cause of Saktism in the 1st century B.C. J.N. Banerjee reports that the Mother Godess was worshipped as Aparna (Godess of the leaves) and Nagna Savari (The naked Savari) (Banarjee 120)

The Cult of the Yoginis in Western Odisha

The 64 *yoginis* of Ranipur Jharial in Western Orissa, thus, testify that the Kosala country was essentially a place for mother worship. A part of Kosala was called Mahakantara which is the undivided Kalahandi district of the contemperary times. There is a mountain called *Gudahandi* situated amid deep forests and cave paintings are discovered there that belong to the plestocene age. These paintings are geometrical drawings and they are related to the *Tantric Chakras* (Geometric Figures representing the energy of the mother spirits) (Ref. *JKHRS. Vol-II*.P.243).Similarly, three circular paintings have been discovered in the Jogimath Dangar of Khadiala which are dated back to the Holocene age. These circular figures represent the "waves of the divine light" or *Brahmajyoti Taranga*. Besides, the ring stones (stones with holes) discovered from various places reminds one of a pre-vedic *Sakta* culture prevalent in Kosala. A *Yoni* stone or a stone representing a vagina has been discovered by Jitamitra Singh Deo in Maraguda valley, and the mother-worship of this area is dated around the time of Mahenjo- Daro. (Sing Deo qtd. in Mahendra K. Mishra: 2)

Mahakantara and the Cult of Stambheswari

The tribal population of Mahakantara (Kalahandi) used to worship a pillar, a trunk of the tree. But the strong influence of Hinduisation was felt during the Gupta rule in the 5th century A.D and the tribal people began to accept the mother Godess as *Isvari* or Uma of the Vedic pantheon. This shows the cultural osmosis in the orbit of transformations, that took place in the Sakti cult around 5th century. The Goddess of the Pillar" (*Stambheswari*) was formless autochthonous deity and she was worshipped by the king Tustikara, the Sulkis and the kings of the Bhanja dynasties. She is still the presiding deity of Sonepur, Angul, Talcher and Dhenkanal. King Tustikara ruled over Kalahandi, Sonepur, Boudh and Ghumusar in the 5th century A.D. These were the areas that belonged to the earlier Mahakosala.

The excavation of the Asuragarh Fort in 1973 by late Prof Nibeen Kumar Sahu, (at Kalahandi) revealed a temple of Mother Goddess wherein the terracota figures of different animals and articles for magic- cure were found. The ruins of the fort are assigned to 5th century A.D based on archaeological studies.

The Terasinga plate reveals that the tribals worshipped Stambheswari (the Godess of the pillar) at Asurgarh.

The Bhaumakara Kings popularised the cult of Sakti worship in Kodalaka Mandala, (now known as Dhenkanal) during 8th and 9th century A.D. The inhabitants of Kodalaka Mandala were the Gond group of tribals. The Kings of the Tunga dynasty also patronised the Goddess of the Pillar in Yamagartta Mandala which was the historical name for Pallahara and Keonjhar of the present Odisa. The Bhanja kings who ruled over Mayurbhanj, Keonjhar, Ganjam, Phulbani and Bolangir districts as the feudatories of the Bhaumakaras, claimed that they were born of the egg of a pea-hen. The Bhanjas also claimed that they were also of the tribal origin and they worshipped the Godess in the form of a pillar.

Khambeswari (the name of the Goddess who appears like a *Khamba* or pillar) is now found worshipped at Sambalpur, in western Orissa. She is the tutelary Godess of the Duma people. But the practice of worshipping the post or pillar as the Godess is also prevalent in Sonepur, Boudha, Athamallik and Redhakhole, the borders of contemporary western Orissa.

B.C. Majumdar, in his *Orissa in the making* informs that the Dumals of the Western Orissa had migrated from Khemidi in Ganjam (Bada Khemundi and Sana Khemundi). Prof. S.C. Panda and Dr. D. Chopdar, in an essay captioned "Tribal Religious Faith in Orissa: A case study of the Stambheswari cult" inform us about the details. The Dumals never wear any cloth or ornament which is black in colour. They always wear border and they put on the red coloured bangles made of lac. The Dumal women never put the mark of vermillion on the forehead xxx. Their houses are painted with red clay (*Geru mati*) (Panda and Chopdar-70)

The Cult of the *Sixty four Yoginis* emerging as a major belief-system of the Western Odisa during the 6th-7th century

A.D. reflects some of their major cultural traits. Historians like Dr. H.C. Das identify the 64 *yoginis* of Ranipur Jharial temples with *'Sakti tantrism'* (the occult related to mother-energy). Such temples are also found in Bheraghat of Khajuraho in Madhya Pradesh and Coimbatore in Madras.

Sakti Tantrism has a subsect callded the *Kapalika* (carrying a skull) and Kalamukha, who worship Yogonis of the same name. One can find the name of *Kapali*, a yogini mentioned for the first time the *Yajnabalkya Smriti*. There is a Buddhist text named *Lalita Vistara,* belonging to early Christian era which speaks of *Kapalikas* besmearing their bodies with ashes, wearing red garments and carrying tridents, a bowl made of big, dried up gourd skin etc. However, by the time the Bhaumakaras ruled over Odisa (6th-7th century), the *Kapalikas* emerged as a major sect. That was also a common pan-Indian phenomenon by that time. Hieun Tsang's accounts give a picture of the Digambara Jains and the Buddhist ascetics: "the dress and ornaments worn by these "non-believers" are varied and mixed. Some wear peacock feathers; some wear ornaments, necklace made of skull bonessome have no clothing but go nakedsome wear leaf or bark garments, some pull out their hair and cut off their moustache; others have bushy whiskers and their hair braided on the top of their heads. The costume is not uniform and the colour, whether red or white, not constant." (David: 15-16).

The Tribal Culture and Tantrism

But Prof. S.C. Panda and Dr. D. Chopdar, in an essay captioned, " Tribal Religious faith in Orissa - A case study of the Stambheswari cult " report that " The Sakti cult with its multi dimensional manifestations has a long, varied history traceable to 3rd millenium B.C. The non Aryan tribes like the *Sabaras* and the *Pulindas* who lived between the Vindhyas and in Mahendragiri in the South Eastern part of Orissa worshipped the mother-Goddess in their own styles.

The Sabaras and the Pulindas were the inhabitants of

Mahendragiri (now in the present Gajapati district). The hill is referred to in the inscriptions (Verse 3 of Banapur plate of Madhyamaraja, line 9. 1. 0. vol.1, part 2. Ed. S.N. Rajguru Pp 192-195) of Orissa of the early medieval period.

Later, the Aryans have desingnated this tribal *Vidya* (knowledge) as *Sabari Tantra* (The tantra of the *Sabaras*.). The Aryans have called these Goddesses of the hills, rivers and caves as " Aparna" and " Sabari" etc. The Mother Goddess is still worshipped in the form of a log of wood (stambha or a post) and has been designated as Stambheswari,.Khambeswari or Kandhuni Dei (the Goddess of the kondh tribes).

The new generation historians of Orissa have made critical analysis of *Aryastava* and a study of the epigraphical records of Orissa in the Gupta and the post Gupta period has concluded that the later Tantrism is a fusion of the Tree worship, proto-historic *Yoni* (vagina) worship, the worship of Ratri and Uma in the Vedas and the Upanishadas. However, there is big gap of time between the regnal years of Viswa Vasaba(King of Kantilo and brother of Viswa Basu) and that of the Vedas, Upanishadas, and Puranas.

The depiction of the sculpture of Gaja Laxmi in the doorway of the Ananta Gumpha (Ananta caves) augments the hypothesis that Kharavela had also patronised the cause of Saktism in the 1st. Century B.C. There is no record of the growth of this religion after the fall of the Chedi dynasty. But the Bhadrak inscription throws some dim light on the Brahminical form of Hinduism in Orissa in the 3rd century A.D. (D.C. Sircar. *Select Inscriptions vol.1*.1965.pp 99-100 and .*Epigraphic India Vol. xxix*.p.169)

However, the worship of the mother Goddess has spread over almost all the villages of Orissa within the forest belt and one can find the names of the Goddesses who are not mentioned in the *Dasa Mahavidya*, or the ten classified deities for whom *strotas, kilakas, argalas, kavachas* and *Vija-mantras* have been written by the Aryans.

The most prominent of the unclassified tribal deities is Mangala Bauti, Baunti, Baurani, Pitavali, Bhalukuni, Palasuni,

Kharakhai, Saunlei and Khambeswari are some of the names which can be mentioned. The mother goddesses of tribal origin enshrined in different villages have been dealt extensively in a book captioned *The cult of Jagannath and the Regional Tradition of Orissa*. (Ed.Eschmann and Others Delhi 1978). In a place called Surada lying between the estates of Dharakote and Badagada in Ganjam district Konchuni Devi is worshipped as a log of wood. Scholars who would like to know more about the practices of Sakti cult may refer to:

    (i) S. Patnaik: "Kodala Mandala - O - Stambheswari ", *Utkala Sahitya (Oriya). Vol .xxvi .No. 3 and 4.* 1922. pp7-15.

    (ii) J.K.H.R.S. vol ii. No.2.pp.107-10.

    (iii) B.C. Pradhan. *Sakti worship in Orissa*. Sambalpur University. 1984.

Out of all the tribal Goddesses mentioned above, Magala needs a discussion since the *Navakalebara* ceremony (Once in 12yrs, when the neem-wood log of Jagannath is changed) is connected with Mangala. The history of Neelamadhaba, Kantilo shows that the Lord Neelamadhaba had been shifted to Puri temple and the rituals of Lord Jagannath are conducted according to the-then tribal principles. What the Odias boast today of Jagannath culture is a continuation of the tribal God Neelamadhaba of Kantilo and the Sabara king Viswa Vasaba.

Sun -worship in Odissa

A study of the primitive cave paintings on Sun Gods mounted on horse driven Chariots prove that Sun worship was also related to the primitives and the worship dates back to 2nd century B.C. Dr. P.K.Nayak reports in an essay, captioned, *Sun-worship in Orissa, As gleaned from Archaelogical sources:* In Western Orissa, sun-worship can be traced to the 2nd/1st. century B.C. In the punch-marked coins discovered at Asurgarh in Kalahandi district and in the potsherd procured from the excavation at Manamunda in Bolangir district, we find the representation of the Sun. Here the sun is represented symbolically i.e., by a circle with radiant rays from all sides. The rayed -disc device of sun-worship was widely prevalent all over India. The representation of the anthropomorphic form of the Sun-god is met with on certain coins of the Indo-Greeks and Kushanas (Ref. J.N.Banerjea, *Development of Hindu Iconography*. P. 139). Human representation of the sun-god is also found in some of the potteries of the Mauryas. But we donot find this form of representation on potteries and coins of Western Orissa. The earliest occurence of the Sun -god in human form is found in the Khandagiri hills. In Anantagumpha of Khandagiri there is an image of the sun shown in a big chariot drawn by four horses. The God is attended by his two wives and on the top there is a parasol. Another icon of the Sun is noticed in the middle of the backwall of the Tattva Gumpha. The Khandagiri and Udayagiri complex was a Jaina site. Probably the tribal cult of the Sauras was also popular with the Jains in the early days.(*Confluence. Vol.-1* Ed. Dr. P. M.Nayak xxx P. 12-13)

The *Agama Sastras* like *Mahalaxmi Tantra* indicate that it was also a part of ancient Vaishnavism. These practices were discontinued with the rise of Buddhism and it was revived again in the 9th century A.D. with the emergence of the SomaVamsi Administration.

The Lingaraj Temple of Bhubaneswar also embodies a small temple for the Sun God. The *Aruna Stambhas* (Posts with the image of mounting Garuda meant for the worship of the rising Sun) built at the gates of different temples, indicate how the worship of Sun is a part of the worship of Narayana or Vishnu.

Madala Panji (the almanac of the Jagannath Temple) reports that, out of the 44 kings of the Kesari dynasty that ruled over Orissa, the 30th king, Purandara Kesari built a Sun temple and established brahmin villages around that temple. Dr. Harekrishna Mahatab, in his *History of Orissa* Part-ii reports that the Ganga and the Kesari Kings were worshipping the Sun God at Konark even before the temple was built.

A rock Edict form Sumandala of Khallikote informs

that Dharmaraj, the king of one Abhhaya Vamsi dynasty, worshipped the SunGod as his home deity around 570 AD (Tripathy 82.) The legend of *Mahabharata* reports that Sun God Killed one demon named Arka and hence the place is called Konarka, But the *Surya Purana* informs that Shrikrishna's son Samba was cursed by him and he suffered from leprosy. Samba had to meditate on he Sun God at Konarka and he was cured.

One day, Samba was passing by a pond in which Srikrishna's wives were swimming and bathing. Samba felt tempted after witnessing their naked bodies and his sexual desire was aroused. The desire tentamounted to mating with the mothers and he was cursed by his father   (Srikrishna) to be infected with leprosy. Samba prayed his father Sri Krishna and he was advised to meditate on the Sun God at Konark.

Konark was also called *Padma Kshetra* (the field of lotuses). The Puranas inform about 4 *Kshetras* (fields)in Orissa, Which are considered sacred : (1) *Sankha Kshetra* (the field of the Conch shells) : Puri (2) *Gada Kshetra* (the field of the club): Jajpur (3) *Chakra Kshetra* (the field of the wheel) Bhubaneswar and (4) *Padma Kshetra* (the field of the lotus) Konark .

This subsection on the micro-histories has helped us to probe into the ontological status of Odia culture. Mythologies are considered today as supernatural legends and the contemporary historians, who have been nurtured under empirical schools, do not accept the deeper level of inner experiences (as narrativised in the Puranas) as authentic historical data. The paradox is that in India there was no conception of history and the Puranas were considered as the only records of the experience of ancient times. *Puranas* are treated as history even today.

Time surely does pass by and the circumference of our faith is receeding with overdominating scientism. But if the Puranas of India are *faded fairy tales* according to the Western notions of history, why should they celebrate Christmas? Is it only a post capitalistic cosmetics and megalomaniac exhibitionism? Never. It is the continualtion of the actual practices of real people and incedents, who were our ontological parents. We should feel like toddlers endeavouring to go ahead holding the hand of our parents. The faithful relationship with God is much the same: we are like the 3year-old toddlers proceeding through life with our parents/ancestors, needing and trusting them to provide everything. The events are narrated in our Puranas in such a manner. If we, in our disbelief, begin to discard our parents/ancestors, it would be a negation of our own existence, a Satanic revolt at God since the disbelief presupposes that we are grown ups and we donot need a God and a Purana simply because their glow spills over the boundary of naturalism. Such manifestations of pride would rebound and destroy us.

The Beginning of Education in Odissa

Reputed historians of India have written about Nalanda and Taxila as the two exclusive educational centres. What was happening then in Orissa? Were these people naked tribals only? If so, how could Kharavela, in the 1st. century B.C., study *lekha* (alphabets), *rupa* (manufacturing of coins and exchange) *ganana* (maths), *Vyabahara* (law, sociology and political administration), *Veedhi* (ethics) *Gandharba* veda (theatre, music, dance etc.) and *Dhanurveda* (science of war). These were neither indolent fancies of a culturally marginalised race nor were they compensatory braggings of a race suppressed under inferority complex. Since I am not dealing with Adlerian psychology of power, I would not elaborate on it.

Kharavela's education in Orissa was a truth and his confessional accounts are written on rock. (The *Hatigumpha* cave inscriptions) The Delhi-brand historians patronised by post independence politicians have twisted/interpreted Indian history, perhaps, to the advantage of North Indians only. I have absolutely no prejudice to discover this cultural politics. It might also be the insincerity of the Indian historians, a lack of interest in comparative history. However, there is no doubt about the fact that Orissa has been marginalised because of its geo-cultural impenetrability. The government of Orissa could not also afford to hire historians by providing them research fundings to highlight the contribution of Orissa to the history of the nation or, to manipulate fictions about themselves to pass on as history to the posterity. As a result, our contemporary regionalists in other states are endeavouring to rub off the contours of Odissi culture from the Indian map. The post-cyclone activities in Orissa proved that most of our administrators are tricky thieves and indolent lotus-eaters and the few that that take their job as a *seva* do feel estranged from the mainstream of power. Otherwise, they couldn't have embezzled the money that flowed from the compassionate sources and they could not have hurled tricky slogans to declare the cyclone as a "national calamity". The only *national calamity* for Orissa is that the state is being administered by a set of corrupt and inefficient operants. I wonder whether our education and culture have taught us inhuman tricks only. Hence I would like to search the roots or Oriya education in the subsequent paragraphs.

Fortunately I could discover that Hieuen-T-Sang during his visit in the 7th century, landed at Tamralipti port and from there he went to Karna Suvarna.

After visiting Karna Suvarna, Hieuen-T-Sang visited Puspagiri University in Orissa and then he travelled through Kangoda toward Mahakosala (toward Raipur). The present Ratnagiri in Cuttack district was called Pushpagiri in those days. Karna Suvarna was not modern Rangamati in Murshidabad of West Bengal as indentified by the Bengali historians. According to Cunningham it was situated on the bank of river Suvarnarekha in Manbhum district. Mr.I.D.M. Beglar reports that legends about Sasanka, the king of Gauda Desha (the present Bengal) were very popular in Karna Suvarna and hence the historians might have been confused about the location of the place. Secondly, Sasanka was a very powerful king in India of those days and he had conquered Utkala and Kangoda. Harshavardhan in the North India and

Pulakeshi-ii in the south India were also considered to be the other two contemporary major forces of Sasanka during the days Pushpagiri University functioned in Utkala. Hieuen-T-Sang's account informs that Harshavardhan had donated the collection of taxes from 80 villages as a contribution for Pushpagiri University.

But we do not know anything about the courses that were taught in Pushpagiri. He was connected with Nalanda and Taxila and the Professors were traind from Taxila and Nalanda universities. Thus we may presume that there was almost a uniformity in the curriculum that was taught. Secondly, that was the time when the Mahayana school of Buddhism was very popular among the mainstream elitists. Yuan Chwang's accounts would be helpful at this point, though with Chuwang we would switch over to 7th century A.D.

Yuan Chwang, the Chinese pilgrim visited *wu-cha* (odra). *Ki-ling-Kia* (Kalinga) and *Kong-Yu-to* (Kangoda) about 639 A.D. Dr. K.C. Panigrahi summarises the account of this chinese pilgrim.

"From the pilgrim's accounts we get an idea that majority of the people of the Odra country were Mahayana Buddhists. He tells us that the country had as many as one hundred Buddhist monasteries and about ten thousand monks. The Deva temples according to him, numbered only 50, in which the followers or different sects worshipped together. It may be noted that Yuan Chawang was a devout follower of Mahayana. Buddhism xxx The chinese pilgrim mentions two places of Buddhist importance in the Odra Country(Odissa). One of them contained a famous monastery called *Pu-sie-po-ki-li* of which the transcript is Pushpagiri..." (Panigrahi 64)

Ancient Disciplines of Education in Odisha

Our historical records do not say anything about our educational curriculum in the post Kharavela era. The main source of education, however, was through religious teaching. Kharavela's pan-Indian religious conference in Kalinga and the relic memorials around Toshali identify *Veedhi* as a popular subject of those days. Ashoka's Mahamatras were reading out the administrative notifications written on the rock plates every fourth month on *Tishya Nakshatra* days in all parts of Kalinga. and Kangoda. Although Brahmi lipi was prevalent, the illiterate subjects were not able to read them. However, Hieuen-T-Sang's account on Odra Desa says, "they (the Odias) love learning and apply themselves to it without intermission." (Apte, Qtd. in A. mohanty. 63)

However, it should be remembered here that the education in those days was different from today: eg. the process of writing examinations etc.Smt. Prativa Devi, a research scholar on the educational system in Upanishadic era writes:

"When there was no script, no alphabet and no written form, the seers through *Svara* (Phonetics), *Chhanda* (meters), *devata* (Subject matter, *Rishis* (Seers) alongwith *Nava-vidha patha* (the nine methods of recollecting), protected the vedas. By this it could not be interpolated and could reach us almost in the same manner as we read it today.

It is a common belief of the Hindus that *Rigveda*, the social sciences, was first conceived by Agni Rishi, *YujurVeda*, the practical science by Vayu Rishi, *Sama Veda*, the psalm by Aditya Rishi and *Altharva*, the metaphysics by Angirasa are the unlimited sources of knowledge, So they trace their authorship to Supreme Divinity." (Pratibha Devi:31) It is quite interesting to note that most of our contemporary educated men disbelieve the word "supreme divinity"since divinity is not available in the science laboratories to stand the test of logic by a group of hybridised empiricists.

Faces of such disbelievers still flash before my eyes. They are senior citizens of the state(their age being between 70-80 yrs now). These once-upon-a time professors with colonial hang-ups attacked the Vedas and all such ancient knowledge as a dustbin of imagination. I still salute these colonial bootlickers who could infect our posterity with pseudo-intellectual logic and western empiricism (empiricism encourages scientism,belief in materiality which is horizontal and never vertical, and empiricism promotes industrial smokes and trickeries of cultural imperialism through a newfangled verbal rhetoric for subjugation under the umbrella of *globalization*).

But by the 1st. century B.C. *lipi* (alphabet) was developed. We do not know how efficiently *lipi*, or, the art of writing was operating without paper and ink. Hence, it is presumed that the *navavidha patha* or the "nine methods of recollecting" was followed.

The art of teaching was oral. The students had to memorise the lessons. They deployed concrete examples to enable the students to comprehend and realise the abstract ideas. The teachers mostly belonged to the Brahmin caste and they allowed the students to ask question for clarification. The presentations were, therefore, made in dialectical method. Although the commoners did not know much about the vedas, the method of teaching was elitist since they followed the methods adopted in Nalanda and Taxila universities. *Vidhi* contained *Vedic* and *Upanishadic* ideologies. The problems that were discussed in *Chhandogya Upanishad* may be taken as an example to explain the dialectical method of teaching.

(a) Where does a creature go from here?
(b) How do they return here?
(c) Why does this region not get filled up?
(d) If the whole earth is filled with riches for me, do I then become immortal?
(e) Since all this is enveloped by death, how can one escape death's grasp?

The abstract questions were answered through concrete examples. In *Taittiriya* the teacher (Varuna) explains to his student/son Bhrugu how the Supreme Reality can be realised through food. From *atman* or self rose space, from space the wind, from wind fire, from fire water, from water this earth, herbs, food, semen and from semen, the person.

The brahmin teachers were given grants by the kings

and they acted as the messangers of education. The copper plate records belonging to different dynasties of Orissa testify that grants of lands or *agrahara* villages were given to attract scholars. Visakha Varman's son Uma Varman of Mathar dynasty (C. A.D. 360-395) had given grant to 36 *agrahara* villages which formed a large scholarly area equivalent almost to a district (*Ep.Ind*-xii. 4-6). The copper plate grants provide us with lots of information about the brahmin teachers (Gurukulas) of those days.

The Sumandala copper Plate of Dharmaraj (*Ep.In*.xxviii-pp.79-85) mentions about a distinguished Scholar named Upadhyaya Muthuswami and the Tandivada grant of Sri Prithvi Maharaj (Rajguru : 48-53) refers to a distinguished brahmin named Bhavasarman, who had studied "three thousand sciences and had written twenty commentaries." (Rajguru 48-53) Accepting these *Prasastis* as euphemistic though, one cannot fancy to ignore the scholasticism of these Gurus.

The epigraphic records of the Sailodvaba kings(6th century A.D.-8th cent. A.D.) provide us with the information that most of these brahmins were 'Bhattas' and they received *vritti* (scholarship) from the kings for imparting knowledge in Kalinga, Kangoda and Kosala. S.K. Aiyengar explains, "*Bhatta vritti* is usually a piece of land given to a learned Brahmin to provide for his living with a view to ensuring the pursuit of his calling, i.e. namely the propagation of learning (*IHQ*: 380). He further points out that according to *Dharmasastra* a Bhatta should not be the native of a village, and he should be well versed with Panini's *Astadhyayi* and with *Alankara Sastra* (*IHQ*. 380)

The copper plate grants of the kings belong to the Sailodvaba dynasty. But the dates assigned to them are approximate. Dr. K.C. Panigrahi in his *History of Orissa*, however, traces a geneology of the Sailodvaba kings, amongst whom Dharmaraja is one:
1. Ranavita
2. Sainyavita

3. Ayasobhita
4. Sainyabhita Madhava Varman Raja-ii
5. Madhyama Raja-1
6. Dharma Raja.
7. Madhyamaraja-ii
8. Ranakshova
9. Allapa Raja
10. Madhyama Raja-iii (son of Tailapanibha)

In the Ganjam plates dated in Gupta Era 300 (619 A.D.) It is clearly stated that Madhava Varman Raja-ii had an overlord named Maharajadhiraja Sasanka, "who can be none other than king Sasanka of Gouda, the rival emperor of Harshavardhana" (Panigrahi:52). Entering into these intricacies of history is not our job since we are engaged here in tracing the educational culture of Orissa during the Sailodvabas around 619-620 A.D.

But, much before that, around 4th century B.C., during the Nanda rule (most probably after Mahapadmananda's attack since I am not aware of any Nanda after that) a village named Battapalika was considered to be a famous *Agrahara* in Trikalinga. Prof. Amiya K. Mohanty writes, "It is learnt that Hari Swamy and Bappa Swamy of Bharadwaja *gotra* managed an educational centre". (Mohanty :64. qtd. E.1.vol.ix. pp.32 and 342-45)

If the educational centres during Mahapadma Nanda would be admitted historically, the role of Chanakya or his influence on Kalingan educational system cannot be ignored. Dr. Gian Singh Mann writes, "Kautilya was a Brahmin adventurer who reached the ancient metropolis of Pataliputra after completing the education at the ecclesiastical university of Taxila. He took service under the Nanda emperors, at Pataliputra, as controller of a charitable trust endowed by them." (Mann:x)

But the copper plate records (though they belong to a later period) delineate about South Indian Scholars, running such educational centres. These were unknown places since the mainstream historians have not recorded clearly about them. Since we endeavour to trace the culture, we should know what type of institutions/centres were they. Unfortunately, we have no records.

The educational centres run by Muthuswami and Bappaswami etc. were residential schools and were totally financed by the king. These schools were held in the residential quarters of these South Odissan (Kangoda) Brahmins of *Bharadwaja gotra*, which were in the forest. But since the provisions would have been sent by the kings, it is presumed that these Brahmin professors did not stay in the dense forests. They would have settled either in the outskirts of the capitals, or in a bucolic *agrahara* complex of villages or a little away from the outskirts of the capitals surrounded by green trees, fountains and pastures etc.

The schools were very informal. With the *Vratya* atmosphere all around, and a hatred for the brahmins, the academicians would have preferred to stay away from the society like the untouchables. The situation could not change even today since most of our politicians are academic dropouts. These professors must have had an adequately secular mind-set to accommodate the ten varieties of students, those who were eligible for admission (i) *acharya putrah* (teacher's son) (ii) *Susrusuh* (those ready to serve) (iii) *Jnanadah*, (those committed to impart knowledge, later) (iv) *dharmikah* (intent on fulfilling the conditions of law (v) *suchih* (the pure) (vi) *aptah* (connected by marriage or friendship to the guru) (viii) *saktah* (the capable) (viii) *arthadah* (those who could pay) (ix) *sadhuh* (noble and honest ones) and (x) *Svah* (teacher's own kith and kin).

Education was entirely free and *gurudakhina* (honorarium) was purely optional. The teacher-student relationship was not regulated by utilitarian needs and the teacher acted as a father, guide and friend for the pupil.

The teachers took lots of pain to improve the phonetic ability of the students and trained them in recitation, which included modulation of voice. Shri A.K. Mohanty records that one Narayana Senapathee, Governor of Kalinga province during the time of Narasimha Deva-II, made provision in the temple at Simhachalam for instruction in the recitation of the *Taittiriya* branches of Yajurveda by two brahmin professors. The same provision also made arrangement for imparting training in *Purana, kavya, Nataka, Chhandas, Vyakarana* and *abhidhana* (*S.T.I. vol.vi*-904). He also provided maintenance allowance for four scholars who were to teach in the school of philosophy and grammar attached to the temple. Thus, it can be inferred that the system of education in the *Vratya* country had also adapted the Upanishadic mode of teaching as it was conducted in the *Gurukulas*.

These residential schools (*Gurukulas*) and the training centres in the temple premises offered courses that continued for twelve years or more.

It is evident in *Chhandogya Upanishad* that a students named Svetaketu (Chand : 6:1:2) and Upakoshala Kamalayana (Chhand 4:10:1) spent 12 years at the Gurukula. Satyakama Jabala, another student, had to stay till his four hundred cows proliferated into one thousand in number. In the same Upanishad it is also mentioned that some students were foundf spending 32 years (8:7:3). Some scholars also have extended the period to 101 years. These accounts are not exaggerated. Such students, after getting the formal courses, had perhaps, devoted their entire life to teaching by living in the wild, bucolic environment of the *Gurukula*. Prof. Radha Kumud Mukharjee describes the life of a student in the *Gurukula* in the following words :

"Tending the house was training the pupil in self-help, the dignity of labour, of mental service for his teacher and the student brotherhood. Tending cattle was education through craft as a part of the highest liberal educations. The craft selected was the primary industry of India. The school and the homestead centre round the cow whom the Indian counts as his second mother, whose milk nourishes the child and is the best food even for the grown up. Three acres of land and a cow has been the average Indian's economic plan through the ages. The pupils received a valuable training to rear up cattle and diary farming. With all the other advantages it gave of outdoor life and robust physical exercise, which was more fruitful in every way than the modern barren game of Football and Hockey." (Mookerjee :XXIX)

Dr. Mookerjee's accounts inspire one to presume that the *Gurukulas* also offered vocational training - in farming and cow rearing. In Orissa, there is a brahminic sect called *Halua Brahmins* who are wedded to their ploughs- which means that they accept the tilling of the land as their creedIn Bihar, they are known as Bhoomiharas.

. The cowherd castes in Orissa are still allowed to supply water for all religious rituals in Brahmin families. It has already been explained how the Upanishads explained the Indian consciousness to realise the Supreme Being in food. *Karshana* or ploughing is still considered as a fertility rite as experienced in festivals like *Raja Samkranti* (the day on which the female beings are given rest and are not allowed to walk on the earth barefooted as the mother earth is supposed have run her periods.) and *Garbhana Samkranti* (the day on which the paddy plants are found pregnant). The cows were also considered to be second mothers. There is also a brahmin sect called *Jhadua Brahmins* in Western Orissa. Either they are products of *Jhada* or bushy jungles or they were brooming (*jhadu*) the fields or temple premises as savants.

At a later stage, when the Odras identified themsleves as *Oda Chasha* (Odia cultivators), the *Sudras* took over the job of farming and began to underestimate the *Halua* and *Jhadua* brahmins. The farmer brahmins emerged as rivals of the tribals and the Sudras and they did not like the emergence of the brahmins as technically trained cultivators and also as the qualified cow-keepers to dominate over their dominion - the fields. This must have led to a cultural as well as a casteist conflict between the *Sudra* and the tribal farmers on one side and the Brahmins on the other.

At this point, the Brahmins were treated ontologically as outsiders (Aryans). The Sudras attacked them on the ground that a brahmin is one who knows '**brahma**' (*brahmam janati iti brahmana* etc)and not the one who cultivates the fields.

The 'knowers of brahma' were mere meditators between the micro and the macro levels of consciousness and perhaps their contribution to the society was not recognised on the utilitarian level/on the level of materiality. They were accepted only as theoreticians. Even today, a business executive, an engineer/ doctor, an IPS / IAS officer considers himself as a more useful 'commodity' than a teacher since the former ones are sold at a higher price in the job-emporiums, while the latter is not.

The great professor-saints of the Upanishadic era like Yajnabalkya and Jabala were cattle keepers (around 100 cows) and perhaps they generated their own funds for the maintenance of their residential schools. Although a country inhabited mostly by the mlechhas and *the Vratyas,* our Odissi education also embraced some of the Vedic norms of the mainstram.

In a verse of Rigveda, a parent-son dialogue explains that the caste was not very much related to the profession: "We, different men, have different aptitudes and pursuits. The carpenter seeks something that is broken; the physician a patient, the priest some one who will perform sacrifice. Then the son tells "I am a poet, my father was a physician, and my mother a grinder of corn." (9:112)

Since the practice of education brought in paradigmatic notions of culture, such conflicts were inevitable. But the conflicts were synthecised in Orissa because of inter-racial marriages. The Vratyas and the Aryans intermingled in Orissa through inter-caste marriages.

The kings of those days, however, were orthodox with regard to education. They did not like to mix up the tribal Vratya system and the Aryan system in the educational institutions. So, they brought some *brahmins* for the dissemination of the mainstream education.

According to our oldest copper grant of Korasandha, Maharaja Visakha Burman brought five pure Brahmins of the *Atreya* clan. They were Vishnu Burma, Sresthi Burma, Agni Burma, Naga Burma and Siva Sharma. The King gifted them with a village named Tapoyaka in Korashodaka (now called

Korashanda). This is a village situated 15 kms. away to the north of Parlakhemundi *(J.B.O.R.S.) Vol XIV.* P. 282 and *Ins. Or. Vol 1. Pt-II.* P.3)

The grant recorded in copper plates belongs to the Mathara dynasty of Orissa to which Visakha Burman belonged. The gift of this village is important for our educational culture. But the inscription also bears an evidence of the Orissan knowledge of mathematics and astrology.

(b)Mathematics, Astrology and Almanacs

Perhaps astrology as a subject was not much developed during this period in Orissa. The copper grant record does not point out the exact year. It has been written: *Sambat /Hemam / "divasah 20"* (The twentieth day of the *Hemanta* season or the month of *Kartika*, which is the 5th day of the bright fortnight or *Sri Panchami.)*

The Bobbili copper grants of Chanda Burma, another king of the Mathar dynasty also reads *"Sambatsar 4, Grishma 2 Day 5.* This means, the 4th year of the kings's accession. It was the second day of *Grishma* (Summer Season) or the month of *Baisakha* (Around April), 5 (Krishna) or the 5 th day of the Dark fortnight. The next copper grant about the gift of another village in the 6th year of Chanda Burma's accession, records *"Chaitra masa Sukla Panchami"* or the fifth day of the bright fortnight of the month of *Chaitra* (March-April). The alphabets for denoting the numbers were also quite different from the contemporary Odia style. These alphabets were in currency till the 10th century.

The kings of the Mathara dynasty ruled here in Orissa at the time of the Gupta invasion (380 A.D.-570 A.D approximately) in India. However, Samudra Gupta expired in 380 A.D and the historians find no link of Orissa with Gupta empire. However, the copper plate grant of Sumandala was made by Prithivi Nigraha and it was dated Gupta year 250 (AD 569-570) Its donor was Maharaja Dharmaraja, a subordinate Chief under Prithivi Vigraha who ruled from Padamkholi near Khallikote."

The second grant, as reported by our historian, K.C. Panigrahi is dated in 200 Gupta era, is that of Loka Vigraha and the third grant is of Madhavaraja II of the Sailodvaba dynasty dated in the Gupta year 300 or 619 A.D." (Panigrahi 43-44)

All these copper plate grants lead scholars like Dr. D.C. Sircar to presume that Orissa was "within the orbit of the Gupta empire" (Panigrahi 44). But as we discuss about the study and application of the mathematical-astrological studies in Orissan educational system, we are to find the evidences from the Mathara and Sailodvaba dynasties, who wrote the copper grants during 569 A.D. onwards. As the grants are written in Oriya, we trace the use of Odia alphabets and numbers etc of the early stage and also know that the kings of Mathara dynasty did hardly acknowledge the supremacy of the Gupta kings. Here is another instance of Odia cultural attitude that evidences a resistance to the national culture.

However, this Vratya land was not immune to appropriation of alien cultural traits. The Sakas, Kusanas and the Yavanas had captured some portions of Kalinga on the coastal line. The Odia almanacs written prior to their invasion had to undergo a change by different mathematical calculations. As the copper grants testify, the indigeneous Odia mathematical calculations included the year, season, month, lunar days (*Tithi*), the movement of moon and sun etc. As a result, the almanacs used the lunar as well as solar calculations with regard to an individual's birth, the days of the social festivals, marriages, coronations and other important religious performances. The scholars of such calculations were designated as *Joshi* and *Pattajoshi* by the Kings. They were astrologers recognised by the Royal Court.

The astronomers of Orissa had established three different centres to calculate and ascertain the time of sun rise. These three fields of study are called (a) Viraja Kshetra (b) Neelachala Sri Kshetra and (c) Sri Kurma Kshetra. The *pundits* who were engaged in formulating the "birth charts" were called *Graha Bipras*. But they could not be taken into the caste of the *Bipras* (the Brahmins). They believed in the ancient principle :

Janmanajayate sudrah samskara dwijamuchyate
Vedavyasi bhavet Bipra bramha janati bramhanah.
[Rough/inadequate translation : Every one is a Sudra by birth. Refinement makes one a bramhana. By practising the principles of Veda one becomes Bipra and by realising the meaning of the "Bramha", the micro-principles of life and their cosmic connection, one becomes a bramhin]

In an India (in the world, too), highly strung by casteist sentiments, one finds it difficult to make this *sloka* relevant to the contemporary life that proleferates moral dementia and sprawls across grossness to the complete exclusion of the subtelties. How would it be possible establish on the sociological plane whether someone has realised the efficacy of the *Bramha*, the abstraction that connects between the microcosmos and the undicipherable macrocosmos ? Any teenager studying in an English medium school of any metro city would find these words esoteric and not "trendy"since the trend is to see the seeable only and nothing beyond that. How would one be capable to articulate the poetry of this concretised self-consciousness, the fullness that is auto-permeated ? Thus, any such endeavour to define the role of a brahmin in terms of mediating between the microcosmos and the macrocosmos would be risky and incommunicable. Some of the supporting fanatics would also try to catapult me to a height of transcendentalism. This would,consequently leads us into the orbit of a perennial binary set of oppositions.

Coming back to our *Graha Bipras,* our indigenous texts report that they had migrated into Orissa from *Saka Dvipa* (the Saka islands) in which the Sun was being worshipped. They were also worshipping the nine planets of the solar system. The birth-chart, for the non-believers of astrology, may be difined as a map of the heavens, which, at the time of birth of an individual, shows the Ascendant rising at that time and the position of the planets in the 12 houses or the signs of the horoscope. The temporal scheme is spatialised here or the vice-versa.

As the *Graha Bipras* of the Orissa of the 6th century point out, the *Rasis* or the signs are spaced in the zodiac. The Zodiac is a broad belt in the heavens extending about 9 degrees on each side of the ecliptic. The ecliptic is the path of the Sun which passes exactly through the centre of the zodiac. The zodiac is an imaginary circle of 360 degrees and the Graha Bipras divided this circle into 12 equal parts of 30 degrees each. Each equal part of 30 degrees is known as a sign (*Rasi*)

The Orissan sculptors were influenced by these Graha Bipras and they carved out the different shapes of the Grahas (Nine in number -Aries, Taurus, Gemini, Cancer, Leo, Virgo, Libra, Scorpio, Sagittarius, Capricorn, aquarius and Pisces). There is a Sun-temple at Konark and it has been built strictly according to the geometry of the zodiac. It was accepted in the Vedic system and into the fold of Bramhinism.

I would like to reiterate here that the Bramhins are diasporas in this *Vratyaland* and their immigration to Kalinga, Kangoda, Utkal and *Kosala* (all these four countries are now combined into one integrated state called present Orissa) during the Gupta age was more frequent. They carried with them the belief-system of the Aryans. The importment of the Bramhins for educational practices and the grants of villages to them initiated the Aryan mode of education in this part of the country.

Varaha Mihira, the father (?) of Indian astrology or, at least, the first codifier of the system, wrote *Brihat Samhita* (The Great Treatise) the major astrological treatise during the Gupta period, i.e. when the Matharas and the Sailodvabas ruled over this land. The Indian astrologers, after interaction with the foreigners, had learnt the science of the movement of the planets. Bhaskaracharya was a great mathematician of those days. Some of our cultural historians are of the opinion that the "Sun-worshippers" or the worshippers of the "thousand-rays" (*Sahasranshu*) were the immigrant Brahmins. Sri Satyanarayan Rajguru writes in a vernacular book, that around 1st and 2nd century B.C the astrological knowledge of the native primitives and the Bramhins could enrich the standard of education in general. Kharavela's inscriptions testify that he, too, had studied *ganana* (calculations) as a subject.

The astrologists who came to this part of India had travelled through the ocean routes and they could calculate time through the movement of the stars. The people of Kalinga were also aware of the movement of stars even during the time of Ashoka, in the 3rd century B.C. Ashoka's, *Mahamatras* had to visit the remote parts of the state with his official orders engraved on stone slabs on the day of *Tishya Nakshatra* (Star) to read them out to the subjects of Kalinga. It is presumed that the orders of Ashoka were read at the rising time of the Tishya star. The Sakas, the Huns and the Yavanas, who invaded India from out side had also travelled through the sea-routes and they had to locate their direction by observing the stars at night. During the Gupta era the astronomers were patronised in India and Varaha Mihira (Mihiracharya) wrote *Brihat Samhita* during those days.

The great Orissan text on Astrology, Captioned *Bhaswati* was written by Pundit Satananda in Orissa in the 11th century and most of the writers of the almanacs of Orissa continue to follow the text till today. Pt. Satananda was born during the early part of Ganga rule and Chodaganga Deva instituted a laboratory at Neelachala Puri Srikshetra to forecast time. King Udyotkeshari of the same dynasty patronised a group of *Graha Bipras* in the *Nava Muni* cave of Khandagiri (Cave No. 14) and in the 18th year of his rule two famous astrologers called Sri Kulachandra and his student Sivachandra used to live in that cave (*Ep. Indica Vol. XIII.* P.166). The festivals and the rituals of the temple of Lord Jagannath are conducted according to such calculations and in collaboration with the *pundits* connected with the *Mukti Mandap,* an institution of the temple adminstration that decides on the spiritual matters festivals/rituals.

(c) Studies in Ayurvedic Medicine

The Ayurvedic study in Orissa was also initiated by the scholarly *Graha Bipras* who migrated from the *Saka Dwipa* (the Saka islands) and settled on the sea-shores. However, the Orissan tribals, highlanders and the Dravidians had great knowledge of Ayurveda before the Aryans intruded. The Vratyas and the primitive dwellers of Orissa knew the medicinal values of the trees, leaves, roots and the barks and they offered the forest products to their Gods and Godesses. *Dalkhai* is a goddess in the Western Orissa who is fond of the branches of the trees. Sakambaraa is the name of the Goddess Durga in the month of October. She is supposed to have worn the green leaves as her dress. However, the development of the Ayurvedic Science could be possible in this country because of the contribution of the imigrants at different periods of history.

The ancient *vaidyas* (medical practitioners) of Orissa learnt the science from their forefathers and they emulated the spirit of service from the days of their apprenticeship. They had to develop a deep spiritual attitude and they used to cure the patients by the power of the *mantras* and simultaneous application of medicines.

The modern scientists are extremely skeptical about the efficacy of *mantra* healing. I would suggest these science-freaks to study a book captioned *Mantras : words of power* by Swami Sivananda Radha, a German lady. She writes, "When I went to India in 1955, I heard about *Mantras* and the marvellous power they have, but I was Western and very skeptical. I asked my Guru what good repeating the same words over and over would do. He replied that I would have to practice chanting mantra and find out." (Radha :*Mantras:Words of Power*. Sterling Paper back p.x)

There are two main divisions of *mantras*. Under the first division come *the Vedic Mantras*. To the division belong the *Tantric Mantras*. The etymological meaning of Mantra, according to the Vedic design is *"Manamat trayate iti mantrah"*

(Mantra is that devoted recitation or chanting which frees the persons from all troubles and miseries. The necessity for devotion to *mantras* has been described by Maharishi Patanjali as follows :

"*Iswar Pranidhanadva*", "*tasya vachakah pranabah*", "*tajjapastadartha bhavanam*"

The mind can be controlled by devotedly worshipping the God or by constantly praying in the language of God (Iswara). His symbol is the holy monosyllable *Om*. It is this holy and divine word 'Om' that should be recited and its meaning should be understood and well thought of.

On the other hand, the Tantrikas have also interpreted the *mantra* as follows :

Mananam viswa-vijnanam tranam
    Samsara bandhanat yatah
Karoti Samsiddhih mantra ityuchchate Sah.

[Mantra as a word means the knowledge of the world and freedom from worldly chains. Therefore, what bestows accomplishment in both worldly and ultra mundane affairs is called Mantra]

The meaning of the Vedic Mantras is comprehensible to ordinary minds. When one says *Om Namah Sivaya* people understand that as "I offer salutation to Lord Shiva." But the meaning of Tantrik mantras cannot be easily understood becase they are written in "twilight language", an esoteric, secret language which should be kept hidden like the mother's vagina. All mantras are semblances of *Shakti* or energy according to the Tantrikas.

The chanting and the incantation of the *mantra* words denote *Vak-Shakti* or the energy of the speech-act. *The speech-act theory* of Searl and Austin should not be confused with the chanting of the mantras. Jaques Derrida received strong opposition from India when he wanted to prove in his theory of deconstruction that the word is separated from meaning. I officiate as the President of a literary organisation named *Vagartha* (the relationship between *Vak* (speech, words) and *artha* (meaning). In India, words are not used as instruments of gameplaying except by the politicians, bureaucrats and businessmen. We accept the embedded meaning in the word as *Parvati* and *Parameswara* combined together (Kalidas, the Indian poet and playwright) and inseparable.

The *Vak*,(the speech), has a special role in the healing of the diseases because all diseases are considered as the consequences of the evil influence of the malefic planets. Bertrand Russel has a poor Western mind and he might have misunderstood the existence of the planets as it is evidenced from his book, *Impact of Science on Human Society*. The taboos of the scientific minds and the reason-seekers are mysterious. They do not prove themselves to be efficacious in a post modern era.Hence, many such rationalists of the Western category residing all over the world, including India would consider my statement as an audacious lie.

In a mantra offered to Sun, the prayer is made to keep the devotee away from eight kinds of leprosy which include the skin diseases also. There is a *Maha Mrutyunjaya Mantra* which can pave the way to win over untimely death. But these are vedic mantras and there is nothing indigenous about them.

The Odissi methods of primitive treatment was based on the *tantric mantras* and on the medicines prepared out of the wild roots and barks etc. The Ayurvedic medicine about which the professors of the modern Ayurvedic colleges talk, are products of the knowledge given by the imigrant *Graha Bipras* from Saka Dvipa. The Orissan mode of treatment is classified under *Guni-Garedi-Sahitya* (Literature of the Occult Sciences. The witch doctor,or a shaman being mostly a lady)

The manuscript of a Tantric Treatise written in Odia (T/33 in the State Museum) titled as *Kumara Tantra* depicts about the different pedriatic diseases caused by malefic planets. It also suggests about the tantric treatments. The treatment is called *Ravana Sadhana*.

This indigenous tantra records :

A planet called *Niruta Graha,* which is also a *matruka Graha* (a mother planet) becomes malefic and generates diseases in children either on the 10th day, or in the 10th month, or at any time in the 10th year after his birth. The child would not sleep, and weep continuously. The malefic planet causes fever and inflicts pain in the body. A Tantric sacrifice is needed with a *pooja*. The *pooja* ritual should be done as follows :

"Bring some clay from the seashore and make a doll. Place it in the *Vayabya* direction (North West) at the outskirts of the village in midnight. Light five wicks. Offer fish, mutton and wine and chant the mantra *om Ravanaya Namah* while cutting off the live fish or the animal. Call five brahmins for blessings. Collect cat's hair, the horn of a cow, *gorachana*, garlic, ghee, the stool of a cow and the leaves of a *neem* tree to burn them as incense. Feed four brahmins on the fourth day of the ritual. Thus the *niruta graha* (the malefic planet) would be propitiated and the child would be cured *(Odia Sahityare Tantra ra Pravaba (Oriya). The Influence of Tantra in Odia Literature,Orissa Sahitya Akademi. 1982. P.186)*

What I intend to establish is that the practice of Tantric treatment is as old as this *vratya* culture and it cured innumerable ailing children around 1st century B.C. or before that in this *Vratya* land. This was the practice before the *Graha Bipras* arrived here from Saka Dvipa.

The kings of this land cultivated medicinal plants and raised forests of medicinal trees. Sometimes they brought rare plants from outside and planted them in their forests. During the reign of the Bhaumakara dynasty (C 600-700 AD) Biraja Nagar (Jajpur) was the capital and a family of Bhatta Brahmins was given a grant of land to serve as the royal doctors. The inscriptions etched out the name of Vishaka Nannata as one of the most famous *Ayurvedacharya* of his time. *Maharaja Jaya Barma Deva alias* Maharaja Unmatta Keshari permitted Maharaja JayaBarma Deva of Kangoda (belonging to the Svetakara Ganga dynasty) to take Nannata Bhatta to his country. (Kangoda was the Southern part of Orissa and Biraja Nagar or Jajpur is hundred kms. away from Cuttack, in central Orissa). Vaidya Nannata Bhatta was granted a village named Vartini in Kangoda *(E.p. Ind. Vol.XIX (1927)* P. 263 and *Vol. XIII (1915)* P.165). The Puri Copper grant of the

Sailodvaba king, Dharmaraja mentions the name of the village Vartini *(JBORS, Vol. XVI.* pp.176-188). The Southern part of Toshali was called Kangoda and its capital Kangoda was on the banks of river Salima (salia) near Banpur. According to the Dharakote Copper grant, Dharakote was in Kangoda Mandala *(JAHRS.* Vol.IV.pp.189-194), which had lots of non-brahmin Ayurvedic doctors. Late Ananta charana Barada was one. The Barads were from Maharashtra and they had come to Dharakote during the Maratha invasion of Orissa.Dharakote was originally a state belonging to the tribal Kondhs and it was invaded and won over by a branch of Mathara dynasty(3rd-4th cent. AD)

Nannata's wife Lijja gave birth to a son, Bhimatta who grew up as a great Ayurvedic doctor during the reign of Santikara Deva, the king of Bhaumakara dynasty. Late Satyanarayan Rajguru dates his life around the end of 8th century and the beginning of 9th century A.D. One of the rock edicts at *Ganesh Gumpha* (caves), Udayagiri Hills near Bhubaneswar, records that Bhimatta was a great devotee of Lord Ganesh. The edict writttten in Sanskrit reads as follows:

Ijjyagarva samudvuto nannatasya sutyei vishak
Bhimato yachchato te dhanya-prastham sambatsarat punah.

Bhimatta's son Loyomaka was also a great doctor. In a rock edict written in Bhaumabda 93 (830 A.D) at Dhauli Hills, Bhubaneswar, Bhimatta has recorded that he arranged to build a monastery for 12 Goddesses *(Ep. Ind. Vol IX P. 29* and *Ind. Art. Vol. 49 (1920) P.28)*

Nannata Bhatta, the grand father of Lomaka earned great reputation as a royal doctor in Toshali. Our history is silent about the date when Toshali was formed as a state. But a Jaina Text called *Abasyaka Sutra* records that Mahavira had been to Toshali for preaching his religion at first. Then he went to Moshali. The text records :

Tato bhagabam Toshali gou XX Tattha suma gaho nama
rathio piyami to bhagabao So maei. Tato Sami Moshalimgou."
(Hist. of Orissa. Vol.1 Utkal University Publication and *Dhaulira Itihasa (The History of Dhauli.* Kedarnath Mahapatra. 1875. p.1)

The records prove that Toshali, during the time of Mahavira (6 cent A.D.) was an important city in India. The city was established on the delta of river Daya. Similarly, Ptolemy's *Georgraphy of India* records that Maisolam or Moshali was situated between Krishna and Godavari rivers. Ashoka ruled over Kalinga from Toshali for 28 years (261-232 B.C) according to Dr. Nabin Kumar Sahu as he has recorded in *Buddhism in Orissa*. J.W. Mc Crindle records in *Indian Antiquary, Vol. XIII* (1884). "Tosalei, called Metropolis, has become of great importance since recent archaeological discoveries have led to the finding of the name in the Asoka inscriptions on the Dahuli Rock. The inscription begins thus : "By the orders of Devanampiya (beloved of the Gods) it is enjoined to the public office charged with the administration of the city, Tosalei. Vestiges of a larger city have been discovered not far from the site of this monument and there can be no doubt that the Toshali of the inscription was the capital in Asoka's time of the province of Kalinga and it continued to be so till at least the time of Ptolemy from Greece visited India. The city was situated on the margin of a pool called kosala-ganga which was an object of great religious veneration through out the country. A rare Buddhist Treatise called *Gandabyuha* or *Avatamsaka sutra* written in the 3rd century A.D. contains some information about Tosali. The *Surava Parvata* (Surava mountain or Dhauligiri) that stood to the north of the city, had a medicinal garden and a park for public entertainment." (qtd. in *Dhauli (Toshali) ra Itihasa (Oriya) The History of Dhauli (Toshali) pp.8-9*)

The purpose of digressing to the short history of Toshali is to assert that Nanna Bhatta, the royal Ayurvedic doctor lived in one of the famous capitals of India which was connected with Ujjain, Pataliputra and other important cities of the country. The contribution of the Odia Ayurveda doctors, therefore, cannot be ignored in the Indian context. The Odia Ayurvedic Acharyas covered the eight important medicinal fields namely (i) *Kaya Chikitsa* (General medicine), (ii) *Salya Tantra* (General Surgery), (iii) *Salakaya Tantra* (Opthalmology, including other ENT departmens) (iv) *Bhoota Vidya* (Psychiatry and Demonology (v) *Kaumar Bhrutya* (Pedriatics and obsterics) (vi) *Agada Tantra* (Toxicology) (vii) *Rasayana Tantra* (Immunology and Geriatrics) (viii) *Bajikarana Tantra* (Science of aphrodiasic and sexology).

As the Orissan Ayurvedic doctors were in charge of the medicinal gardens and they were preparing the medicines by the help of the tribal people, who were supposed to be experts in *Trisuja-Ayurveda* also, the threefold knowledge, i.e. *Hata-Jnana* (Aetiology), Lang-jnana (Symptomatology) and *Aushadha-jnana* (Pharmacology).

Although *Ayurveda was known to the Aryans through Saint Bharadwaja* (earlier to 5000 B.C), the primitives of the *Vratya* country called Kalinga knew the science prior to that. The history of the Ayurvedic education, as it has been traced in this chapter, does not go beyond 1st. century B.C. since our historical research in this field seems to be silent about it. Nagarjuna, the great Madhyamika philosopher knew much about *Rasa Sastra* (Science of alchemy etc) and he is known for his alchemic practices which he learnt from a wine-seller woman of Madhyadesa (Sambalpur, Koraput and Mahakantar area)

Ayurvedic education in Orissa was, therefore, not purely a part of the Vedic educational system. The Orissan tribals had their own *Aushadha Jnana* (pharmacology) and the practitioners were also some scholarly ladies of those days. The rituals of the temple of Lord Jagannath also testify such practices. In the month of *Jyestha* (June) the deities take a ritual bath on the *Snana Mandapa* (the stone pedestal for bathing) with 108 pitchers of water from the temple well. After that, the Lords suffer from a ritual fever every year and the deities are given a herbal concoction by the non-Aryan servitors of the temple for fifteen days. The Aryan Priests are not allowed to enter into the temple during those 15 days when the Lords are cured. The wooden deities are painted after 15 days and then the car festival takes place.

This primitive practice of administering the herbal

medicines leads to a temple legend that registers a conflict between the Aryans and the primitives as recorded in Dr. Ramesh Prasad Mahapatra's book, *Temple Legends of Orissa*.

"Once during the reign of King Chodaganga Deva there arose a conflict between the leaders of two religious sects regarding the supremacy of their tutelary deities. One of them was Acharya Someswara, the advocate of God Markandeya and the other was Nitei Dhobani (a tribal washer woman who conceived of the deity of Jagannatha. She came to Orissa from Andhra or South Kalinga), the worshipper of Lord Jagannatha. Each one of them was adament in his/ her conviction with regard to the authority of his/her beloved deity. Both the leaders, too, had a good number of followers at Puri. The esoteric practices of Acharya Someswara were patronised by the Keshari Kings (Kings of the Keshari dynasty) and more particularly by Uddyota Keshari. He brought him to Puri and allowed to settle there. He had a right to defy the authority of Lord Jagannath.

Nitei Dhobani (the tribal washer woman), on the other hand, was fully patronised by King Chadaganga Deva. It is believed that he was allowed to occupy the throne of Orissa at the advice and assistance of Nitei Dhobani. Chodaganga Deva constructed the temple of Jagannath at Puri and installed its deities. Naturally, he had a very soft corner towards his presiding Deity, Lord Jagannatha. Nitei Dhobani was an ardent devotee of Lord Jagannatha. She considered Jagannatha as the supreme deity and everything else as his manifestation only" (p.43)

As the conflict could not be settled Chodaganga organised an open test for both to prove the supermacy of these two Lords.(This seems to be an old rivalry between the Vaishnavites and the Saivites) Mr. Mahapatra reports :

"Some quantities of husk were brought to the spot xxx It was desired that whomsover will produce rice from the husk by pounding in a wooden mortar through a pestle would be declared as the winner of the test and his or her Lord will be accepted as the supreme Lord of the universe. x x x Someswara offered his prayer to his Lord Aghorasiva Markandaya " (p.44) and failed. But Nitei Dhobani could produce rice from the husks.

"To testify the veracity of this legend, one can find even at present the mortar and the pestle under worship in a shrine at Chudanga Sahi of Puri. Local people generally attribute thepeople of this street to Nitei Dhobani.

As Nitei Dhobani was from South and she came with Choda Ganga Deva (a prince from the Chola dynasty), She could generate the miracle by Tantric applications. She was recognised as one of the most celebrated Tantric practitioners of Odissa and was also included into the fold of Buddhist *Sahajayana Tantra* of Orissa.

The museum of Sambalpur University (Jyoti Vihar) preserves some of the stone images of the 4-handed and 6-handed Durga as Goddess Mahisa Mardini, obtained from the excavations of Saintala. In South Kosala, Lakshminkara, the lady Tantirk, was a great Preacher of the Buddhist *Sahaja yana Tantra* and she introduced the worship of *Sapta Kumaris* (the worship of the 7 Virgin ladies) in which Nitei Dhobani's name figures. The seven virgins worshipped in the Buddhist Tantra of South Kosala includes Nitei Dhobani, Pitei Savaruni, (a Saura trbal lady with great potency) Jnanadei Maluni(the maluni is a lady who picks flowers and makes garlands for the Gods and the queens etc). *(Paschima Odisara Loka Samskruti, The folk culture of Western Orissa. p.4)*. Most of the witch doctors/ shamans of the contemporary Orissa also use the name of Nitei Dhobani in themantras they deploy for healing practices.

The younger generation of the Odias, who are nurtured under the new-fangled scientism and educated by silly English medium systems (I am connected with these species for the last 30 years as a college teacher of English and I am convinced about their shallowness through generations. Except for their ability to speak fluently and impress the vernacular speakers for a short spell, these game players of words are totally deracinated from Indian culture and they are trying to build up an alternative cultural island for themselves now) are likely to ridicule the tribal culture of Orissa and its shamanistic healing methods.

For them I would quote few lines on Shamanistic practice from a book captioned *Shamanism* published from USA. Jean Houston, in his forward to the book, writes, "Shamanism, in both its most ancient and modern forms, recalls the democratization of the spiritual experience, in which heirarchies are reserved for levels of experience rather than for priests and bishops. Each level and dimension of reality is available to the one who will make the effort to learn and practice the ways and means of the spiritual journey. Thus, in shamanistic practice one can have one's spiritual experience and revealation direct and unmediated by structures ordained by chruch or doctrine. This appeals immensely to those who seek autonomy in the spiritual journey." (P.VII)

If the aim of education is the attainment of a liberated state of mind, and not a confinement in the post-capitalistic norms of fiscal imperialism showcased under "globalization", then the ancient educational system in Orissa had definitely carved a niche for itself, an autonomous identity that never cared for the recognition from the mainstram, but that could contain and fulfil all the requirements of an individual's living in the face of aggressive and inhuman Aryanisation.They remember how an Aryan like Ashoka could be a beast . These tribals had shown their necks to the sword of that Aryan - beast called Ashoka, who was on his spree for beheading the tribal human beings.All his propaganda with regard to his religious conversion is diplomatic filth, a face saving Aryan politics. The historians of the world who have eulogized his missions of peace are cultural mafias, seekers of padmashree awards and position mongers in an Aryan power lobey.

However, Toshali, Kangoda and Kosala have never disrespected the Aryan Brahmins in their states. The Ayurvedic doctors of Viraja (A Goddess who is *vi-raja* or does not undergo the process of monthly cycles) Kshetra at Jajpur are recognised as Vedic Brahmins of *Vatsasa gotra* and are accepted as *Kanva-sakha-dhyayis*. Their research and the vision of treatment had enriched the study of Indian medical science. The feudatory states and the kings of the small estates developed their own medicinal forests under the guidance of these *Veshajas* (doctors). The Orissan Ayurvedic doctors had also developed their own laboratories at home collecting three kinds of ingredients : (a) Forest products like leaves, barks, roots, flowers and fruits and oily substances (b) Organic ingredients like bile, urine, milk, meat and bones (c) minerals like stones, clay, iron, gold, copper, mica, sulpher, zinc, alum, mercury, rock salt and yellow orpiment etc. Burning and making different kind of ashes, concoctions, steaming, frying and drying in the sun were some of the modes of their functioning in the laboratories and some outsiders and foreigners were also engaged in those home laboratories.

A Jain Saint named Malli Sena was living in Orissa and it is suspected that he was a south Indian doctor.

A famous Ayurvedic doctor named Ugraditya lived in the court of Queen Dandi Mahadevi of Bhaumakara dynasty. Ugraditya designated himself *as Guru, Mahaguru, Munindra* and *Pundit* at different times. Doctors with the title of Pundit lived in Orissa as *Rasa Vaidyas* (doctors with knowledge of the science of minerals, metals and alchemy). These Ayurvedic doctors did not confine themselves to their laboratories only. They moved out into the rural sector to treat the unattended diseased people with a missionary zeal. They were the Jain Saints following the spiritual path of Mahavir, who began disseminating his religious ideas from Orissa.

The Odissi Scholars have discovered an Odia treatise on medicine, named, *Kalyana Karika* in two parts written by Ugraditya. He has mentioned the name of one Kumara Sena who belonged to 10th century. Pt. Satyanarayan Rajguru has discovered the stone image of Kumar Sena in Gandibeta village near Sora(near Balasore) in 1853. The following two lines are written at the end of the feet of the Jain image. The language is Odia :

Deba kahi bhagati karuna
Achhanti vo Kumara Sena.
(OHRJ. Vol. II (1953). No.3. pp.-21-23)

But our historians are not yet confident enough to announce that Ugraditya of *Kalyana Karika* is the same Ugraditya who lived in the court of Dandi Mahadevi as Her *Sandhibigrahi*. But many such texts of Ayurveda have been written in Odisa. Charaka, Susruta and Madhavakar were the important scholars among them (Rajguru. 55)

Acharya Sulapani, a disciple of Prathamacharya, received a village as grant from Mahasiva Gupta, son of Harshagupta, a king of Somavamsi dynasty in western Orissa. The Name of the village is Vaidya Padraka. The Vaidyas (doctors) lived there and studied Ayurveda from the Acharyas (Professors). Mahasiva Gupta granted the village on the fullmoon day in the 57th year of his reign *(Ep. India,. Vol. XXVIII. Pp.319-25)*

The religious institutions established by the Buddhist and the Brahminical kings had the facility of boarding, lodging and also for medical treatment of the Acharyas who were working as religous teachers. These Ayurvedic Pundits were given villages as grants.

Hanumana of the Ramayana had brought the life-giving herbal medicine from Gandhamardan hills when Rama's brother Laxman was fatally injured in the war and was almost on the verge of death. *Gandhamardan* is the hill in the South Kosala and the Somavamsi kings had raised a medicinal forest there.

Boudh, an estate of South Kosala was ruled by Maharaja Satrubhanja. A copper grant found from Boudh and given by Satrubhanja inscribes a sloka, which is important for the Ayurvedic studies

Ma parthiva kadachintyam brahmasvam manasadapi
Asesha dharma vaishajyam etat halahala bisham
Abisham bishamityapah brahmasvam bishamuchyate
Bishamekakino hamti drahusvam putra pautrikam
Louha choornasma choornam cha bishamcha harayannara
Brahmasvam tu sulou kashtam kah pumman jara ishyati.

The sloka depicts the dangerous consequences of looting the property of a brahmin. Taking away such properties is equal to drinking poison. It causes severe pain to the body and the *sloka* depicts in the metaphor of medicines about the consequences of plundering, its reactions and the mode of , treatment by administering *choorna* (powder, mode in Ayurvedic laboratories by burning metals). The Brahmin *Vaidyas* (doctors) who composed the verse in sanskrit belonged to 8th century and the composition proves that the medical practitioners had the knowledge of moral law, literature, religion and medical science and the Vaidyas, were capable of blending them together.

However, all the Brahmins of Orissa did not lead a scholarly and spiritual life. The intermingling of the Vratyas and the Brahmins leads to a kind of hybridisation in our educational culture. But it cannot be considered as degradation. It, rather, led to a different kind of vocational education in the state.

(d) Vocational Education in Ancient Odisha

As some sects of the brahmins eschewed their yogic or subjective practices for the realization of 'Brahman' and came down to the functional level (*Karma yoga*), some of the Sudra artisans also started *Gurukulas* or the residential schools for training pupils in palmleaf engravings, wood engravings, stone work and *dhokra* art etc.

The courses of their *Silpa Sastras* varied from region to region. Terracota horses were moulded in brown clay and then klin -fired in some region and in other regions, where the Silk-worms were cultivated, the craft of *Tassar* (silk) painting developed. In some jungle areas of Kangoda, clothes were woven and two pieces were stuck up by tamarind gum. The stuck up cloth acted as a *cania* and the *chitrakara gurus* trained them in *patta* painting. In some areas of south Kalinga (Paralakhemundi, Koraput, Nowrangpur) the tribal *gurus* taught the art of making toys and lacquer-boxes decorated with threads and beads. Others made painted wooden boxes.

The *Kansari* (brass ware, bell-metal ware) *gurus* in Kangoda, Utkala and Kosala provinces conducted courses on brass ware. Even today, the tribals of Dhenkanal and of western Orissa make cast-metal figures in the ancient method. The craft is handed down to them through generations. The craft *gurus* of those days also trained pupils in horn-craft. Since Kalinga was a repository of soap-stones, sand stones and serpentine stones, lots or *Pathurias* (stone carvers) conducted schools. Similarly, in the coastal zone crabcraft had developed.

This brief discussion leads to two distinct diversities-regional and casteist. The casteist diversities emanate from the Aryan and Vratya cultures lead toward an open conflict between the Brahmins and the Sudras. The Brahmin gurus attempted to Indianize our education while the Sudra gurus were preserving the regional crafts and technical education. However, during the Buddhist period the culturgal conflicts were resolved to some extent. It is interesting to note that the people from North Kalinga had accepted Mahayana sect of Buddhism while the south Kalingans joined the *Heenayana* sect. The regional and cultural polarities can be focussed clearly from Yuan chwang's records.

(e) Architecture:

I don't refer to Odissan architecture as advertised in the tourism brochures: temples, golden triangle etc. I refer to Ramachandra Bhattaraka's *Silpa Prakasa*, the typical Orissan *Silpa* text of 10th-12th century. Alice Boner and Sadasiva Rath Sarma are the first post-independence scholars of the *silpa* tradition of Odissa. I would quote from *Silpa Prakasa* part-II, V 801-802 in English translation: "In the understanding of the various best *sastras* there are differences due to local customs. The temples are of various types, according to regions and canons. Since there are different methods in the local ways of work, these *sastras* are founded on the practice of *kaulacharas*." (Das R.P.)

Kaulachara is related to Tantra. Its influence is discernible in *Silpa Sastra* since this treatise was written in the post-

charya period. *Silpa Sastras* in Oriya were written during the Bhaumakara dyanasty of Orissa (736A.D.) and the palm-leaf manuscripts have been published by late Sadasiva Rath Sarma procuring them from Raja Jagannath Rajamani, the- then king of Manjusha, a feudal state in North Andhra-South Orissa border.I would like to quote from the "Introduction" written by Alice Boner, in the translated version of *Silpa Prakasa*.

"The Silpa Prakasa has the rare merit of providing instruction into the art of temple building on all levels, on the religious and ritualistic, as well as on the architectural and technical plane. This gives a feeling, that, with an adequate disposition of mind and heart and the availability of trained workers, it would be possible even today to build a temple according to its directions.

The text of **Silpa Prakasa** *exists, as far as we know today, in four copies only. Three of these were consulted for working out the present translation. The existence of the fourth copy came to our knowledge only recently, and therefore couldnot be included in our studies. It is in the custody of Sri Goswami, Arisandha Math, Nimapada (dist. Puri, Orissa).*

The three copies, on which our translation is based, carry each a colophon, in which the copist mentions his name, the king under whom he lived and the date, on which he completed his work. These copies have been numbered by us in the order in which they are found.

Colophon of Ms. No. 1

I declare this **Silpa Prakasa** *to be one among the Silpa Sastras. In the village of Sobanapura situated on the banks of the Rsikulya (river), thos book was transcribed by me, the best Brahmana Narasimha of Kapinjala gotra, in the reign of king Gopinath Deva. In the eleventh year of his reign I have transcribed it.*

According to Dr. Harekrishna Mahtab, Gopinath Deva reigned from 1720-1737 A.D., and in consequence, the eleventh year of his reign would be 1731.

Colophone of Ms. no. 2, which is illustrated and was mainly followed in this translation:

Born in a high Brahmana family of the best town of Manjusa, in a village surrounded by the Mahendra mountains, called

Srinivasapuram, entirely inhabited by Brahmanas,

My name is Govinda Dasa, born in the Kausika kula, well versed in the Niti Sastras (ethics, social life, polity)

Bowing to the feet of Mahasakti Durga, I transcribed this excellent book for King Srinivasa.

In the Saka era, bana (5) Indu (1) sindhu (7) Naksatranayaka (1)= Saka era 1715, which is 1793 A.D. I have transcribed this book, as it is in the Sastras.

(This copyist added his colophon in slokas in continuation of the text of the book).

Colophon of Ms No. 3

Tanscribed by Bhuvanesvara Mishra of the Kausika gotra, living in the village of Narayanapura in the Asoka mandala in the fourth anka (year) of Divya Simha Deva, Utkala era 1198 (1791 A.D.) On the tenth day of the bright fortnight of Kanya on Wednesday, this true transcription was completed.

The dates of Divya Simha Deva's reign are given by Stirling as 1786- 1798 A.D.

Inside the text the author himself reveals his name, his geneology, his qulifications and his residence. He mentions no date, but gives some clues as to the time in which he lived, by mentioning the name of the King under whom he worked. These notes are found at the end of each one of the two chapters of the book, in slokas that run in continuation of the text of the book."(Silpa Prakasa.pp xv-xvi)

Alice Boner records in her personal diary about another Orissan Silpa text called **Saudhikagama** in which the *yantras* of various *devatas* are mentioned. Reference to *Kamakala Yantra* has been given in the first part of this essay. For more elaborate study, Devangana Desai's *Religious Imagery of Khajuraho* and Vidya Daheija's *Yogini Cult* may be studied.

Alice Boner's introduction reveals that "this Silpa Text should belong to the Tantric period of Orissa, between the 9th and the 12th.century, perhaps rather to its later part, and this for the following reasons:

1. Because the language of the Silpa Prakasa appears typical of that period with its free admixture of Oriya words in the Sanskrit, especially in the technical terminology.

2. Because a perfect example of the temple, whose costruction is described in the *Silpa Prakasa* has been found in the Varahi temple of Caurasi near Kakatpur, this temple belonging to the Vadabhi type, which, according to Nirmal Kumar Bose's book *"Canons of Orissan Architecture"*, was in use in Orissa from the 9th to the 12th cent.A.D.

3. Because the groups sculptured on the *anartha pagas* all around this temple are no ordinary *mithuna murtis* (erotic idols) but textual illustrations of the *vira- puja* ritual, the *astakamakala prayoga* prevalent amongst the Sakta community of that time. This is described in an unpublished text from Orissa, *Kaulacudamani Tantra(* This is not the *Kulacudamani* Tantra edited by Arthur Avalon in his series of Tantrik Texts) which is at present under study by Prof. Jitendranath Banerjee.

To these reasons we should like to add the remark that the tradition of considering Lord Jaganath as another form of Daksina Kalika, as he is invoked by the author of our text, goes back to the time of Sankaracharya. It is said, that when Sankaracharya came to Puri, he found the temple broken and the sacred core of the image removed to Sonepur near Jajpur. He is said to have dug it out from underneath the tree where it was buried, to have brought it back to puri, to have erected a shrine and to have established the tantrik worship of the divinity under the name of Daksina Kalika. According to the *Saudarsini Vamadeva Samhita*, which might havebeen written by the disciple of Sankaracharya, Padmapadacharya, Lord Jagannath is the very self of Kalika: *'Tarayantra pralambagno Subhadra Bhubaneswari. Syama yantra Madhava che Dakshina Kalika Svayam*

Tantric worship is traced back to the *Atharva Veda*. It was prevalent in Orissa between the 9th and 12th century A.D. and declined only after the advent of Ramanuja and the greater spread of the Bhakta form of Vaisnavism, although in some form or other it is surviving to this day. The author of the

Silpa Prakasa made it clear in every way that he belonged to the Tantrik community and that he was a devoted worshipper of the Sakti.

The first *prakasa* or the first chapter of *Silpa Prakasa* begins with invocations to Viswakarman and Yantrakalika, since the latter is supposed to have been embodied in the instruments of the artist. This chapter details about topics like: five kinds of arts, selection of a building site, determination of the cardinal points, examination of the grounds, different shapes of building sites, testing of the building site, *nagabandha*, layout of the ground plan, divisions of the *mukhasala*, *yogini yantra*, construction of the portal, different types of *vajramastakas*, construction of *mukhasala* wall, *Bhairava yantra, torana Lakshmi yantra*, ornamental composition of the portal, front-wall of the *mukhasala*, the plinth, the pillars, *na*ga pillars, the *konaka*, the *anartha, avarana devatas, sakti yantra*, different types of ornamental creepers(*Kumchita, hamsa,vartula*), flower ornaments and the Alasa Kanyas. The most interesting part of the First Prakasa is its grammar of *Alasa Yantra* over which all the *kanyas* would be etched. The *Alasa Yantra* has been given in the plate XXI(a).

Ramachandra Bhattaraka prescribes:

Without a rectangular ground -panel the movement of the **Alasa** will not come out properly. In an upright rectangle a middle vertical line (should be drawn) according to rules.

Horizontally, divisons should be made by three lines. From the left prastha- bindu two obliques go in opposite directions.

Above and below they are joined as an open triangle (to the outer lines) to both sides of the **madhyarekha**. Again on the right side two (such) lines go up and down to the (outer) corners (from half the side of the **madhyaprastha**).

In the same way a line based on the side of the **madhyaprastha,** beginning from the side of the horizontal (middle- line) reaches to the two (inner) corners (from above and below of the right side to the middle horizontal).

This wide triangle is on the right side. This is the **Alasa-yantra,** which is suitable for all the **Kanyas** (maidens).

On the left side of the middle- line is the head. The breast is to be made with care in the third horizontal division. (The sentences are wrongly joined in both manuscripts.)

In the centre of the upper division along the obliques, the arms should be placed above the head. The navel is on the central **bindu**, and the hip is on the left side.

Beginning from the **madhya- bindu**, the right leg should be beautifully made (bent, Ms.), the left leg, in an elongated beautiful shape is along the oblique. The author explains the details of the words Chandita and Spandita as follows:

Chhandita (chhandita= palms turned upwards) or **Spandita** *(palms turned downwards), these are the two movements of the Alasa.*

The author, then, proceeds to classify the different *kanyas* according to the Odisi modes of sculptural perception:

* *Mugdha:* She is an innocent, simple girl. Her figure should be carved like this:"one hand with the *naga sira* (snake-head) *mudra* goes in front of the face. The *naga-mudra* is on the right the left arm is along the line. Along the side of the triangle, it is placed on the hip. The two legs are slanting towards the right side like those of the *Spandita-Alasa.*

* *Manini:* This is the posture of a resentful or offended girl, whose head is in the last division, turned or slanted towards the left side. The right arm should be made along the upper oblique above the heads. The right palm should be on the head, the lefty is on the lower lip, the left leg is straight, the right leg is bent, the shank goes backwards and touches the wall. She should wear *alambas*, hanging from the hip, a beautiful *kanchala (*breast band) and attractively tied hair. Both the eyes are half opened and on the lips there is a mood of love (*lasya-bhava)*

* *Dalamalika*   This is a girl garlanding herself with a branch. Her head is in the lower part of the triangle seen in beautiful profile. There above the right-forearm goes along with the branch. The right upper arm lies on the right side triangle. The upper portion of the hip lies on the side, in the middle, and the navel in the centre place (*madhya sthala*).

The left upper arm is down wards and the fore arm is bent (upwards) along the (outer) line. On the left side she makes the beautiful gesture of touching the end of the branch. The right leg goes across the width (*prastha*) and touches the left oblique.

The right shank goes along the left triangle. The left leg is on the right side standing straight. The branch of the tree rests on the right triangle.

* *Padmagandha* This girl smells the lotus. Turned to the left, she is always beautiful. She stands more to the left side of the yantra, the head, the trunk and the legs are elegantly poised. The head is in the upper part and the chest in the third division.

The left upper arm is on the side lying along the forearm (bent upwards), she holds a fresh beautiful lotus in her left palm.

The right arm is going down straight and rests on the hip.

The right leg is slightly slanting and the lower part is receding backwards (touching the wall).

The left leg is straight like a rod along the side of the triangle. The beautiful bunch of hair is resting on the right shoulder. She enjoys the fragrance of the lotus and therefore is known as Padmagandha.

* *Darpana* She is a girl holding a mirror. Her left arm is beautifully raised above the head along the upper line of the left triangle, and the palm is placed on the hair towards the front.

Her looks are turned down towards the right side of the *madhya*-*rekha*. The lovely right arm goes downwards and rests on the middle part of the (right) triangle.

Holding a mirror she is beautiful and gives pleasure to the people. The two breasts are in front on the left side along the middle-line.

(The navel is on the *madhya- bindu*, Ms.I). The right leg goes down to the left corner; the left thigh goes down to the same triangle.

Then it slightly bends to the right side down to the base of the middle line. She should be made wearing a beautiful drapery around the hip.

This is the lovely maiden by the name of Darpana. The mirror can be placed in front of her face in various ways:

* *Vinyasa*   She is a girl having her mind fixed in meditation.This girl of beautiful limbs is turned to the right and her lovely face is seen in profile. The head is on the upper limit, the two arms are close to the beautiful shoulders (the body).

The left arm is along the left side of the triangle. The forearm is crossing in front along the horizontal middle-line.

The other arm has the same position and the palm is placed in *Nyasa-mudra*(*Karakacchapika-mudra*= small tortoise mudra). The left leg, starting from the *madhya-bindu* is straight like a rod.

From the side of the *madhya-bindu*, the right thigh goes down along the right triangle and the shin goes down to the end (the toes reach to the right triangle-line on the side).

With hands poised as if doing *japa-nyasa* (repeating and counting the names of the god), *Vinyasa* is lost in meditation. With lovely garments on her hips she most beautiful.

* *Ketakibharana*   She is wearing ketaki blossom.On the left side are head, chest, hip and arm.The breastsare across the centre upon the middle-line.

The right arm is raised along the right triangle line.The forearm starts from the uppermost side *bindu* (*chedabindu*) and goes on to the middle-line.

The palm is placed on the left side of her head. The hand holds a Ketaki leaf, this is the auspicious *Ketakibharana*.

The hip is heavily bulging out to the left. In the upper part above that the hand is placed with a flower.

The hip and the belly are wholly within the left side. The left leg of beautiful form goes to the lower part of thge triangle.

Down to the lowest right corner, where the foot is on the ground -line. Below, the right knee comes forward to the corner of the triangle. Below that, the beautiful right shank is crossing (behind the left leg) (chhanda padavat = Krsna's pose when playing flute).

Matrmurti   She is the image of a mother. Afterwards hear the description of the beautiful image of a mother.

The head is placed (standing) upon the middle-line, and so is the whole beautiful body. Hear the description of the limbs.

The left arm on the left side is near the left triangle, from the end of the oblique line (cheda rekha) the forearm lies on the horizontal middle-line.

Inside the left triangle is the figure of a child. From face to foot it is on the middle line(the bodt is nicely fat).

Hanging from the right shoulder, the right hand is placed on the thigh. Both feet are placed in an ordinary way. (The right and left leg are slightly turned to the right. They have to be smooth and both feet are placed in an ordinary way).

This image is in the beautiful likeness of a mother with a child.

Camara   She is holding a flywhisk. Now hear about another type, the camara, who is an attendant on the deities.

Both her feet are like those of the Matrmurti, in the same position, only the upper part (the head) is somewhat different.

The face is turned towards the right side, and the right arm is within the triangle, so is the forearm on her beautiful chest.

The lower part of the left arm is inside the left triangle. The forearm comes in front, holding the garment by which she is adorned.

In her left (should be right hand) hand is a fly-whisk, resting on her left (should be right shoulder) shoulder. This is the serene figure of *Camara*, who increases the joy of the gods.

Gunthana   She is a womanconceiling herself with a veil, always showing her back in three bends (Tribhanga). The head is straight in the middle of the (upper) horizontal division.

The hips are placed on the vertical middle-line and rest on the madhyabindu. The left arm is in front of the body, touching the lower lip.

The right arm is on that side near the upper line of the triangle. With the upper part and the head covered, that (girl) is Gunthana.

This young girl showing her full back, is standing firmly in a virile attitude (virasana). Below, the left foot is on a line of creepers.

The left thigh touches the right triangle, the left shin is on the the right side and touches the end of the ground-line.

She sometimes holds a drapery or flowers, or sometimes a fan. This supremely beautiful girl is Gunthana, loved by women.

* *Nartaki* The celestial lady is turning her body and looks towards the rightside. The head is above in the usual place (on the upper horizontal), and the arms are raised towards the sky.

Above, the hands are joined with interlocked fingers (Chanda Palli) and are lying on the middle vertical. The navel is on the madhya-bindu, she is attracting by her dance.

The beautiful hip is placed on the *bindu* of the right line (apex of the triangle). The right leg goes down to the left lower corner.

The left leg is crossing (chhanda) behind, along the middle line, and is placed on the ground. This Nartaki is the embodiment of dance.

* *Sukasarika* She is playing with a parrot or a maina. Her haid stands on the left side. The (left) arm is along the triangle and the left forearm is in front on the shapely breast.

The right (forearm) is a little raised up to the right triangle. In the hand she holds a parrot or maina, or other beautiful birds.

The navel is on the madhyabindu. Both legs are in a slant, the beautiful left shank is turned towards the wall.

By its side the right leg goes lengthwise towards the right. This girl is known under the name of Sukasarika.

* *Nupurapadika*   This girl is with ankle-bells. She has a

beautiful body; standing along the madhyarekha is drawn (or turned) towards the right. The left arm hangs down on the line of the left triangle.

The right hand is as described before (in previous image) and holds a beautiful flower bud. In the lower part, of the two legs the right one is bent.

The right knee there below touches the first horizontal. The position of the shank is obliquely set towards the left side.

The left hand is placed where there is a string of ankle-bells, her finger- tips arwe on the ankle- bells. The left leg is slanting down to the end of the middle-line.

* *Mardala*   She is a drummer. Her head is slightly bent, touching the left line (of the triangle). The chest is on the middle line, cut across by the left arm.

The shoulder part on the left side touches the line of the triangle. From there the beautiful arm is going down to the horizontal middle line. In the breadth of the middle line a divinelt beautiful mardala should be carved.

The right arm behind that (mardala) is up to the limit of the right triangle line, the sole of the left foot rests on the ground.

The right foot is at the same placealong the middle line. This is the extremely beautiful Mardala, intoxicated with her play.

With both hands joined (on one side) she gives joy by her rhythms. These are the sixteen maidens that dwell in a building made with art.

In the pages of the Bhadra and *Rekha* temples, they enrapture people everywhere. This delightful lot should be decked with various ornaments, with beautiful armlets, necklaces, earrings and bracelets.They should be adorned with all ornaments and with all auspicious signs (on the body). The *Naribandha* is always attractive, especially on the *sikhara*. In this way gavaksa and other parts should be decorated by the expert.

Having made the walls with all their distinctive features, all other works should be done in the same way.

SECTION-IV

Searching For The Deep Roots: Odisha in the Micro Histories

Sri Antaryami Sahu's *Neela Madhaba Kantilo* (1985), Sadanand Aggarwala's *History of Sonepur*, Satyabadi Baliarsinghs History of *Ranapur* (1988) Nabakishore Maharana's *History of Banki* (2001), Sri Kailash Chandra Panigrahi's *History of Nayagarh* (1982), Shri Rajendra Prasad Tripathy's *Dwitiya Konarka: History of the Sun Temple of Ghumusar* (1997), Sri Bimal Prasad Pattnayak's *History of Dharakota* and Dr. Dinanath Pathy's *Jagannath Temple of Dharakote* are some of the books the present author has encountered at the time of writing this book.These are the micro-histrories and during the last part of the 20th century, a new craze has developed in the state to investigate into the local histories and record them. The orthodox, colonial historians would call this impure history and reject such books as unscientific and raise controversies in the newspapers with regard to the courses formulated by theUGC.

These unacknowledged historians and some of the Ph.D. and M.phil scholars who have researched on regional history, have felt the need of documenting these regional histories since the mainstream authors have neglected their rich legacies(of their regions).

The major reason for neglecting the regional histories is the belief in colonial histriography, the idea of including facts according to the archaedogial evidences, copper grants, palm leaves etc. These are believed to be the only available methods of documenting authentic evidence according to the European standards that invade us through cultural imperialism-an inevitable consequence of our euphoria for globalization. Actually, the old obstinate logic of empiricism has been destroying our inner essences persistently and we fall prey to the labyrinthine maze of materiality. An empiricist would call it a recycling of the romantic values regarding culture and designate it as unscientific.But when the Europeans write their own history, they document their oral history and legends with a licence of neohistoricism.

William Bradford's (1589-1657) *History of Plymouth Plantation* is regarded as a classic abounding in scriptural, Christian references of the Calvinistic mode. The entire world acknowledges this Christian interpretation of history. Similarly, Voltaire, Gibbon and Thomas Hutchinson (1711-80) are now regarded as major authors of Enlightenment Histriography. Although the contemporary readers claim an amount of rationality in their works, the Christian interpretation of history is loaded with super-national events.

The histriographers of Orissa are so colonial in their attitude that they shirk back to record oral histories and legends of this state as a part of our history. Perhaps they can take up historical research from different angles and emerge as utilitarian historians, idealistic historians, romantic historians, social and economic historians and so on.

My purpose behind this diversion into the histriographical modes prevalent in the world is to incorporate the micro histories of the unacknowledged historians, who have written about the legends and oral histories of their regions basing on the chronology of the kings and events that are culled from mythology and supported by forgotten and otherwise lost evidences. However, they have made use of the palm-leaf accounts of the kings of Orissa who used to maintain their records of the family-tree in their libraries. The colonial historians did not make any endeavor to meet those kings. At times, the royal families did not allow the outsiders to enter into their private records.

I do not hesitate to include them as evidences because our history in India is accepted as *Pura Kalpa* and the *Puranas* are records of those ancient milieus. The departments of literature teach *Pura Kalpa* and *Puranas* as a special paper in the postgraduate departments of the Indian Universities. The era of adhering to the scientific/rationalistic treatment of history has already been elapsed with the emergence of the postmoden histriography around the second half of the twentieth century.

The History of Kantilo

I would, therefore, begin with a small book of history captioned *Neelamadhaba Kantilo* (1985) written by Shri Antaryami Sahu. The publisher of the book is Srimati Saraswati Debi and the book is available at Sri Sahu's residential address : Sri Antrayami Sahu, Vill/po : Kantilo, Puri-752078.

The book deals with the construction of the temple of Neelamadhaba and the history of Kantilo, basing on the evidences from different *puranas*. The deity of Neelamadhaba, which has later been stolen, brought to Puri, renamed as Jagannath and enthroned, has a Puranic antiquity and shri Antaryami Sahu's Puranic history traces the history of Neelamadhaba to the Hindu era called *Satya Yuga* taking evidences from *Kapila Samhita*, in which there is a particular reference to Brahmadri, the mountain abode of Neelamadhaba.

The temple of Nilamadhaba at Kantilo, however, was not there by that time. Sri Sahu states that the history of the temple can be traced tack to the period of the legendary king Indradyumna or to the period of Somavamsi Kings ruling in Boudh Kingdom between the 6th and 9th centuries. However, the Puranic story/history runs as follows :

There were two brothers named Nama and Kama born in a *Vratya* family and they meditated on *Shiva* till the lord was appeased. He blessed them with invincible divine powers. (Dear logic seekers! Do you disbelieve this as a Puranic fantasy? No! Come to me, and I will lead you to your required empirical inquisitive point- but I won't be responsible if you undergo any psychic devastation)

Thus, the brothers invaded the earth and the ocean and the Paradise and tortured the *Devatas(divine beings; but who are they in an industrial world? Please pause for a while and think. You are not allowed to act as superior bipeds because you have money and a logical mind)* everywhere. The Gods called for a conference to find out ways of solution and Lord Vishnu had to take an *avatar* (incarnation) transforming himself into a stone deity.Lord Vishnu positioned himself in the mountain called Brahmadri, that was situated in Kantilo forests. There was a fort called Jenavali, built by the Asuras (who were *Vratyas*). They named the deity as Neelamadhaba and worshipped him. Lord Brahma was the first divine character who had visited Jenavali fort to have a *darshan* of Lord Vishnu and since that day, the mountain region was called Brahmadri.

The legend narrates that the brothers Kama and Nama had invaded the southern countries and brought the Goddess Narayani to the jungle. The deity of Narayani is still worshipped near Pathara Chakada.

Years back, a frustrated mythical character named Parasurama had come to worship the goddess. Neelamadhaba had commanded him to continue the meditation in that dense forest and Parasuram spent some years in Ratnagiri hills singing the glory of Adya Sakti (primal energy) Bhattarika(the name of the goddess). This mythological event is being repeated as a ritual later, and thus, it lapses into history because of the continuation of the ritual,Even today, a symbolic Parasurama takes the flower garland of commandment (*Dhandamala*) from the temple of Nalamadhab and goes to Goddeses Bhattarika on the day of Mahastami (During Dussera) to invoke/invite her.

The legend further informs that during the same period of *Tretaya* epoch, Sri Rama, during his exodus into the jungle for fourteen years had passed through the Brahmadri forest hills. He worshipped the deities of Ramanatha, Simhanatha and Vaidyanatha on the banks of river Mahanadi and sojourned for some days at Brahmadri hills building a small hut of leaves. The Raghunatha Matha, a monastery situated at the eastern gate of the present temple is an evidence of that divine presence of the hoary past.

The history of Neelamadhaba is also associated with *Mahabharata*. When the Pandavas were banished into the forest, Arjuna had been frustrated and he hid himself in Manibhadra hills around Kantilo and Sri Krishna had come to the place to take his friend back. It was the month of *Chaitra* (March-April) and on the day of **Trayodasi** of the dark fortinight (the theirteenth day of the fortnight) Sri Krishna wanted to take a bath in the river. According to Hindu customs, the occasion is called *Varuni*, when people take a dip at the confluence of three rivers. The confluence of Ganga, Yamuna and Saraswati is prefered for this holy bath. But since the river Ganga was far away from the Brahmadri, Sri Krishna had to find an alternative spot. Arjuna found the *Triveni* (the confluence of three rivers) at the foot of Brahmadri hills. It was also a confluence of three local rivers - Mahanadi (as an alternative to Ganga), Chitrotpala (an alternative to Yamuna) and Kumarika (an alternative to Saraswati). However, Sri Krishna commanded Arjuna to invoke Ganga to the confluence. Arjuna arrowed the ground and with his magical power, the river Ganga sprouted tearing up the ground.

Another episode of *Mahabharata* is also related to the place by the legend makers. On one occasion, a mighty demon called Go-Simha threw Krishna and Balarama into the fire of

Yajna, kidnapped Satyabhama (Krishna's wife) and fled away. On his way, he was trying to enter into the fort of Jenavali when Arjuna fought with the demon, killed him and rescued Satyabhama. A nearby hill is named after Go-Simha.

These tales related to *Ramayana* and *Mahabharata* would appear as cock-and-bull stories to a generation of logic-seekers nurtured by the fake values of secularism that discards everything related to God. The believers of secularism, in the process of analysing all religions and religious belief-systems, finally find it convenient to do away with Gods/myths/values arguing for a value-neutrality as if it is an absolutely a no-error-zone. It is a pity that they are not able to identify that by rejecting all commitments to their inner space they tend to become an anatomical collage of a nose and two eyes and two hands and a genital etc.

Such people are so much infested with scientism and scientific evidences for building up a record of history that they would nullify such legends concerning the antiquity of Kantilo. But most of the Indian scholars in the past retrieved their past form the *Puranas*. The making of *Purana* is history-a history of achievements through value-judgements and characterization. This was never an act of fictionalization in the sense of falsehood. Indian writers believed in imaginative representation and the mysteries of imagination inevitably connected them to the cosmos. Since you live in a psychic desert and suffer from a terrible jealousy for fecundity, you can not, must not dare to declare our myths and legends as falsehood. Hell with your scientism and laboratories and the mode of understanding the world through eyes, noses, tongues, ears and skins. What about the sixth sense? Stupid people would not know. How can I explain them that the legends are also one-time record of history though the narrative representation is in the metaphoric mode. We, the tribals of Orissa, who have transformed our cave-like hearts into Cosmos, spit at all scientism, spit at the metropolises and the hybridized notions of cultural dementia they envision out of their deracinated cultural debris. You can't understand, like any other stupid, that the legends are culled from oral history. That is history, a functional history that has been kept enlivened in this country through its rituals. History is not a story here.

At this point, I would quote from B.Sheik Ali's book, *History: Its theory and Method, Second Edition, McMillan,* India, 1978. Mr Ali, in a chapter (13) captioned "Indian Histriography : Ancient and Medieval Period" writes :

"Ancient Indians did not build the historical mansions, but cut the quarries, brought the material, chiselled and softened it and conceived of a plot without proceeding further to finish the project. It was not beyond the reach of those who comprehended cosmic consciousness to narrate events happening around them in their contemporary period. Perhaps, they deliberately avoided doing these jobs, as it was too simple, and not challenging. Perhaps the psychology of the ancients may have something to do with the kind of priorities they fixed in which the ordinary events of this mundane world dealing with conflict, confusion, warfare, cheating, looting, change of fortune, rise and fall of dynasties and so on were pushed far below, causing a complete neglect of history Perhaps the intellectual leadership was aware that history is a Pandora's box whose opening might lead to unknown results." (p. 298-99)

Orissa being a *Vratya* state with tribal people, its history can hardly be periodized into neat western terms: Ancient, mediaeval and modern. The tribal people have their cultural continuity through an oral tradition as well as through a tradition of ritual practices that carry forward the ancient celebrations from their ancesters.

Thus, the story of the demons named Kama and Nama and that of Go-Simha can not be ignored by the socalled torch bearers of the scientific history, which would ultimately end up with a capitalistic assertion about the characterstics of a standard truth . They would throw some million dollars to prove that they are right and the Indians are wrong. Personally I do not subscribe to such colonial ideas and I connot dismiss Sri Antaryami Sahu's book "Neela Madhaba-Kantilo" as pure legend and fabrication. Legends are, after all, folk versions of the *Puranas*.

What is important to me is the presence of a place of divinity in Pre-*Tretaya* of Pre-*Ramayana* era, and the existence of a mytho-social milieu that belonged to the Savaras (Sauras) and the occasional visit of the political dignitories from North India like Rama and Arjuna etc. It seems that the hills of Brahmadri were filled with dense forests and the Northern Indian Kings of the Puranic period used the forest as a hide out, or, may be as a spot for banishing the defeated warriors. This Vratya land of the primitive tribes never cared for what happened in the wealthy areas of the Ganges valley.

History of Ranapur

Sri Satyabadi Baliarsingh's *Ranapur Itihasa* (The History of Ranapur. 1988) with a foreword by Prof. Manmath nath Das is a more authertic record, which traces the history of its kings chronologically and it corroborates some of the facts given in the history of Kantilo. According to Shri Baliarsingh, the first king of Ranapur was Viswa Vasava and he was coronated in 1727 B.C.

The great God Neelamadhaba appeared before him in a dream and commanded him to worship the stone called Chaka Sila (the rounded stone is still there) at Ranapur. His brother Viswa Vasu was also blessed to get an opportunity to worship the Lord at Sri Kshetra, Puri with king Indradyumna.

The Manuscripts No.3 of *Ranapura Rajavamsavali* informs that Viswa Vasava carried the Chaka Sila to Maninaga Parvata (the Maninaga Mountain), and worshipped the Lord with Goddess Durgamba. Oneday, the Goddess appeared before Viswa Vasaba and blessed him that She would be happy to see Viswa Vasaba coronated on the throne of Ranasura Pur since the throne was lying vacant after the death of the demon-king Rana Asura.

The Chaka Sila stone is still there on the Mani Naga Mountain with the Yantras of Vishnu, Shiva and Durga engraved on it. Thieves have attempted to steal the pearls and other precious stones from the Chaka sila which has been covered by a lid, but they had to retreat after hearing a horrific sound. These are twentieth century events in Orissa where thieves are layng their hands in the temple jewellery. But how shall I explain them the science of that horrific sound the thieves were driven by? If I explain that the sound was produced because of the science of Tantra, modern men with gross scientific orientation would call it an ancient conservative idea like black magic or something like that.

The state of Ranapur, during Viswa Vasaba's reign extended up to Boudh in the West, lake Chilka in the South, river Daya in the East and the state's Northern boarder was girded by river Mahanadi.

Viswa Vasaba had two sons according to the palm leaf records of *Ranapur Rajavamsabali* - Vikram Singh and Kalyan Bagadi. Sri Baliarsingh has traced the genealogy of the kings and their periods of regin from which the history of Orissa of the Harappan era can be traced.

Sl. No.	Name of the king	Years ruled	Period Events
1.	Viswa vasaba	35	1727 B.C. -1692 B.C.
2.	Vikram Singh	21	1692 B.C. -1671 B.C.
3.	Anant Singh	35	1671 B.C. -1636 B.C.
4.	Gopal Singh	20	1636 B.C. -1616 B.C.
5.	Gobind Sing	30	1616 B.C. -1586 B.C.
6.	Vasudeb Singh	35	1586 B.C. -1551 B.C.
7.	Narahari Singh	18	1551 B.C. -1533 B.C.
8.	Gouranga Singh	45	1533 B.C. -1488 B.C.
9.	Gopabandhu Singh	36	1488 B.C. -1452 B.C.
10.	Gourahari Singh	35	1452 B.C. -1417 B.C.
11.	Vishnu Singh	23	1417 B.C. -1394 B.C.
12.	Rama Chandra Singh	50	1394 B.C.-1344 B.C.
13.	Krishna Singh	47	1344 B.C. -1297 B.C.
14.	Damodar Sing	40	1297 B.C. -1257 B.C.
15.	Chandra Sekhar Singh	37	1257 B.C. -1220 B.C.
16.	Surapati Singh	41	1220 B.C. -1179 B.C.
17.	Dharanidhar Singh	35	1179 B.C. -1144 B.C.
18.	Sarangadhara Singh	15	1144 B.C. -1129 B.C.

19.	Sridhar Singh	32	1129 B.C. -1097 B.C.
20.	Damodara Singh	50	1097 B.C. -1047 B.C.
21.	Janardan Singh	13	1047 B.C. -1034 B.C.
22.	Gadadhar Sing	34	1034 B.C. -1000 B.C.
23.	Goutam Singh	56	1000 B.C. -944 B.C.
24.	Laxman Singh	11	944 B.C. -933 B.C.
25.	Gobind Singh	36	933 B.C. -897 B.C.
26.	Parasuram Singh	41	897 B.C. -856 B.C.
27.	Iswar Singh	25	856 B.C. 831 B.C.
28.	Bharat Singh	21	831 B.C. -810 B.C.
29.	Gopinath Singh	40	810 -770 B.C.
30.	Chandra Sekhar Singh	32	770 B.C. -738 B.C.
31.	Gangadhar Singh	27	738 B.C. -711 B.C.
32.	Adikanda Singh	18	711 B.C. 693 B.C.
33.	Kamapala Singh	28	693 B.C. -665 B.C.
34.	Vasaba Singh	44	665 B.C. -621 B.C.
35.	Nataba Singh	22	621 B.C. 599 B.C.
36.	Sanak singh	16	599 B.C. -583 B.C.
37.	Adikand Singh	32	583 B.C. -551 B.C.
38.	Dhanurjaya Singh	30	551 B.C. -521 B.C.
39.	Narahari Singh	21	521 B.C.-500 B.C.
40.	Shiva Singh	40	500 B.C. -460 B.C.
41.	Anatha Singh	21	460 B.C. -439 B.C.
42.	Banamali Singh	33	439 B.C. -406 B.C.
43.	Kapila Singh	25	406 B.C. -381 B.C.
44.	Narottam Singh	30	381 B.C. -351 B.C.
45.	Mohan Singh	35	351 B.C. -316 B.C.
46.	Sudarsan Singh	30	316 B.C. -286 B.C.
47.	Kshetribara Singh	35	286 B.C. -251 B.C.
48.	Chaturbhuja Singh	33	251 B.C. -218 B.C.
49.	Ghanasyam Singh	37	218 B.C. -181 B.C.
50.	Achyuta Siugh	52	181 B.C. -129 B.C.
51.	Murari Singh	40	129 B.C. -89 B.C.
52.	Makaradhwaja Singh	42	89 B.C. -47 B.C.
53.	Ananta Singh	54	47 B.C. - 07 A.D.
54.	Harihara Singh	55	07.A.D. - 62 A.D.
55.	Arjun Singh	40	62 A.D. - 102 A.D.

56.	Gopal Singh	41	102 A.D. -143 A.D.
57.	Dhaneswar Singh	25	14 A.D. -168 A.D.
58.	Niladri Singh	26	168 A.D. - 194 A.D.
59.	Patitapaban Singh	37	194 A.D. - 231 A.D.
60.	Ananga Singh	19	231 A.D. -2250 A.D.
61.	Lakshmana Singh	47	250 A.D. -297 A.D.

(1) The king of Kangoda Indra Burma came to Ranapur.
(2) Ashoka's invasior

62.	Bhagaban Singh	30	297 A.D. -327 A.D.
63.	Madhab Singh	25	327 A.D. -352 A.D.
64.	Meenaketan Singh	36	352 A.D. -388 A.D.
65.	Lakanath Singh	31	388 A.D. -419 A.D.
66.	Murari Singh	35	419 A.D. - 454 A.D.
67.	Karunakar Singh	33	454 A.D.- 487 A.D.
68.	Chakrapani Singh	50	487 A.D.-537 A.D.
69.	Satrughna Singh	30	537 A.D. -567 A.D.
70.	Purushottam Singh	48	567 A.D. -615 A.D.
71.	Kapila Singh	37	615 A.D.-652 A.D.

- Established Kapileswar pur village and built kapileswar temple.

| 72. | Suramani Singh | 50 | 652 A.D. -702 A.D. |

-Maharaja koshala kesari gifted him with two
horses and a long brass pipe.

73.	Daitari Singh	42	702 A.D. -744 A.D.
74.	Sadasib Singh	30	744 A.D. -774 A.D.
75.	Mukunda Singh	35	774 A.D. -809 A.D.
76.	Kruttibasa Singh	25	809 A.D. -834 A.D.
77.	Paramananda Singh	34	834 A.D. -868 A.D.
78.	Nilakantha Singh	40	868 A.D. -908 A.D.
79.	Kamal Singh	37	908 A.D. -945 A.D.
80.	Padmanabha Singh	45	945 A.D. -990 A.D.

-Maharajan Markata Kesari of Orissa awarded him with
jewellery and silk for his bravery.

| 81. | Achyuta Singh | 32 | 990 A.D. -1022 A.D. |

-Established Achyutpur village

| 82. | Gadabhar Singh | 49 | 1022 A.D. -1071 A.D. |

-Married in Dhelabhumi, to Ppuncess Prabhabati who was a trained warrer. She fought with a Muslim king of Bengal on her way to Ranapur.

Dhellbhum, Beerbhum, Singh bhoom, Sareikala, Kharswan and Tamralipta (Medini Pur) ware under the Orissa Kings.

83.	Bairagi Singh	30	1071A.D. -1101 A.D.
84.	Bankanidhi Singh (died in 1151)	27	1101A.D. -1128 A.D.
85.	Arjun Bhanja		Dates not available
86.	Pitambar Singh	55	

The Yavaraj got back his state from the king of Boudh.

87.	Baikunthanath Singh Anka (A great saivita king)		1183 A.D. 1237,1237
88.	Jagannatha Singh	52	

This king did not have Children. Went to Bankanidhi Deba of Siko village and prayed. Got 2 Children Rama Lautumaba (the ska of a goured made into a bag for the religious purpoes and mostly used by the ancient and midieaval Saints).

89	Skanda Singh	51	1289A.D.-1340 A.D.
90	Mardala Singh		1340A.D.-1390A.D.
91.	Kapardi Singh		1390A.D. -1442A.D.
92.	Arjun Singh		1442A.D. -1472A.D.
93.	Abimanyu Singh		1472A.D. -1494A.D.
94.	Uddhava Sing Narendra		

The kings of Ranapur used to maintain a cordial diplomatic relationship with the Maharjahs of Kangoda, Toshali and Koshala. The records show that the Maharajas of Kangoda (that constituted Orissa of those days) was Indra Burma and he had visited Ranapur during teh reign of Laxman Singh (250 - 297A.D) and the records show that Laxman Singh presented him with ivory (One full tusk). Bhanubardhan Deb, another Maharajan of Kangoda had donated two villages to meet the expenses of Lord Maninaga. A coppergrant 5 1/2" X 4" found from Ola Singh village (OHRJ vol.2.p.32) reads that the villages were Kumbhari and Sunakhala, situated at a distance of around 10-11 kms away from Ranapur. The names of the villages have been mentioned as Kumbharaka and Sunakhala. The expenses of the annual rituals of Durgamba and Maninaga were met from the revenue of these villages.

Pandit Suryanarayan Dash, in his book, *Naga Itihasa*

(History of the Naga dynasty) mentions about a rock edict that records that a village named "Urdhwa Shrunga" was donated to a brahmin of Maitriyaniya gotra by Maharaja Loka Bigraha of Toshali in 200 *Guptabda* (520 A.D.) to meet the expenses of *bali* (sacrifice of animal at Maninaga). It is presumed that the worship of Maninaga and Durgamba was considered important by the kings of other areas also and they were donated for the expenses of the temple.

Purushottam Deva (567-615 A.D.), the seventieth king of the estate had received a crown made of peacock feather from the grest Maharaja of Utkal, Jajati Kesari, and to commemorate the incident, he had established a village called Mayurajhulia (Mayura is a peacock and "Jhulia" is the oscilating feather in the crown). Kapila Singh (615-652 A.D.), the 71 st king of the dynasty had established a village called Kapileswar and a temple was built there naming the deity of Shiva as Kapileswar. The temple still exists there and *mantras* are still recited for the total wellbeing of the king of Ranapur.

A very interesting account of historical importance needs mention here as has been collected from the palm leaf records of *Rajavamsabali* (records of the dynasty) that pertains to the period of Gadadhar Singh (1022-1071 A.D.).

The episode refers to Gadadhar Sangh's marriage in Dhalbhumi (now in Bihar) which was in Orissa those days. Gadadhar married Princess Prabhabati Devi and was returning to Ranapur with the bride. On the bank of river Karima, Gadadhar heard that the Muslim army of the Nawab of Banga (Bengal) was setting out for an invasion of Orissa. Gadadhar felt the need of infoming this to the Maharajah of Utkal. He left his newly wed bride under the care of few military men and galloped to Cuttack. He met the Maharajah at Fort Barabati and helped him to prepare for a counter.

Prabhabati waited there on the bank of the river in a camp for her husband and when Godadhar did not return, she costumed herself as a Prince and went to the tribal people of Tamralipi (Modern Medinapur district of Bengal) to declare that the Prince of Orissa has come to attack the Muslim army.

Tamralipi was in Orissa in those days and even today lots of Odias are settled there.

Then tribal Odias were inspired to find the prince and they shouted the glory of the Prince of Utkal. The Muslim army of Bengal fled away. By that time the Maharajah of Utkal had reached Tamralipi to discover that some Prince of Utkal was fiighting them away. The Maharajah desired to know the identity of that prince and Prabhabati came to Gadadhar, put off her male garment and introduced herself as his newly-wed wife.

This episode of Prabhabati has been recorded by Pt. Neelakatha Das in a poem:

Dhalabhumi Jena jebeti Ranapura Kumare
Bari, Madhusajya bidhane hela kapisa kule
Sunile gauda katake saja pathana sena
Ajante pasiba Utkale karichhanti kalpana.etc.
(Qtd. in *Ranapur Itihasa*.p.8)

The queen of Utkal took her to her lap and threw a great reception party at Barabati Fort (Cuttack) on the eve of their marriage.

The History of Nayagarh

Nayagarh Itihasa (The history of Nayagarh) written by Sri Kailash Chandra Panigrahi informs that it had also a Baurani Thakurani (a tribal Goddess) which was a very fierce divine mother energy. But the history pertains to 13th century. The legends connected with this Goddess would help us in no way at this stage of this book that deals with the pre-vedic period in Utkal. Hence the details of the post-thirteen century records are not documented here

The History of Banki

But Nabakishore Maharana's *Banki Itihasa* (The History of Banki) dates back to the Puranic Period. Banki is famous for a Goddess named Charchika, who, too, does not figure in the

Dasa Mahabidya (the Ten potencies of the Goddess according to *Devi Bhagabata*). But it is difficult to classify Mother Charchika as a tribal Goddess since the records show that She was worshipped as the home Goddess in the Ashram of Ruchika Maharshi. Ruchika's grandson Parasurama had attained his Siddhi (highest spiritual attainment). Maharshi Ruchika had married Rishi

Rishi Viswamitra's sister was Satyavati and his son was Yamadagni. Maharshi Ruchika had specialized in Dhanur Veda (The Veda of the archers). He was the son of Maharshi Ourva (Maharshi Chyavan and his wife Sukanya's son) and his brother was that famous Ratnakar who transformed himself into Valmiki.

Goddess Charchika, as the Puranic legend says, has incarnated Herself from an apocalyptic vibration. When Goddess Durga killed two of the generals of the demon called Mahisha, the fire from her Ajna Chakra emitted this fiery vibration and a new feminine energy actuated. She was called Charchika.

Another source of Purana refers to Lord Shiva's marriage and the episode of his wife Parvati's suicide by jumping into fire when her father Daksha Prajapati insulted Shiva. Shiva had to carry her dead spouse on his shoulder and he began to articulate his psychic frenzy through a Tandava dance, when the body of his spouse was split into 84 pieces and fell scattered at diffrent places. The right hand of Sati fell at Banki and since then the place has been recognised as a seat of mother-energy. As a creative energy, she is treated at Banki like the cosmic nescience and the seed of the world. She is consciousness, energy, hunger, sleep, beauty, forgiveness, memory, compassion, contentment and error, all-in-one.

These legends about the incarnation of Charchika can also be found related to many other temples of India. One common feature in most of these legends is the conflict between the Devas and the Asuras, the conflict arising out of discord of desire, knowledge and emotion. The Asuras are just the embodiments of desire. They know only materiality and they fight to achieve it. The Devatas or the inhabitants of heaven have a glow of their own which is the lusture of knowledge.

This binary opposition does not stand for ever. The Asuras, at times, attain great power of knowledge, by continual meditation and the Devatas, at times, are found to have been lured by the lust of luxuries and weakness of showmanship. The Shakti or the Female power symbolised as multiple power variations incarnate for the coordination of diffused knowledge. What I am writing here is NEVER a theoretical abstraction, but a real and dominant principle of Nature, that repeats/has been repeated myriad times as a supreme evolvent. The Asuras and the Devatas are just archetypes that figure in the pages of the Puranas.

The Puranas were viewed with hatred and considered funny and incredible reading material by the Europeans during the 400 years of colonial rule and its hangover is still deposited in the minds of the scientists/champions of industrial advancement living in this century.

The "so called" intellectuals of Orissa still believe in the government's policies about " industrialisation", "globalization", "marketization" etc. It is a hysterical syndrome that affects the ordinary demons of democracy with a verb-form taking suffixes of "lization". These jargon creators of politics/bureaucracy and their conscious/ignorant believers are also "archetypes" of the Puranic demons. The mock fights and the funny televised shows in the parliament, conducted between the Ruling Party and The Opposition are episodes in a soap opera and the dominant theme of this show business is "lust for materiality".

The over emphacis on the "commerce" side of Civilization, consumerism and consequent marginalization of values during the last two decades of the twentieh century and its continuation in the 21st. century is a victory of the demonic forces or, at least, an invasion of the Asuras on the residual *devata* who could not escape the clutches of materiality .

The fight between the "haves" and "have-nots" is

triggered off from the basic "intolerance" and "jealousy" evolving the Demonic in the history of the bipeds repeatedly. The cultural historian of 2150 may, despite the self-manouevred Vedeo cassettes, C.Ds. and autobiographical fiction writing, discern a Puranic element in the fighting that takes place in the sky under the umbrella of Terrorism and other ego-demolition projects.

The future historians would decipher that *values* are just *"slogans"* and also commodities, instruments that can be deployed as game-weapons for the demonic star wars played RAW for defusion of menace; and indirectly displaying one's demonic force

The sculptures and the paintings of these goddesses are displayed in European/American night-clubs as nudes and the Goddess (! whether you belive Her or not) appears to them only as a wide-open vagina. These regurgitators of scientism and the defensive, diplomatical logic-mongers of International politics would never care to know that Mahalaxmi (Goddess of Materiality) has a fierce and destructive reverse side, and no megalomaniac rich man would be able to withstand the sight of the vagina only with a "fuck-her" attitude. In the 4th chapter of *Lakshmi Tantra*, Mahalaxmi identifies herself as follows in sloka No.40:

Mahalakshmi samakkshyata saham sar Vanga sundari
Mahashreeh sa Mahalkshmi schanda chandi cha chandika
Bhadrakali tatha Bhadra Kali Durga Maheswari
Triguna Bhagavatpatni tatha Bhagabati para.

[I am known as Mahalakshmi and I am beautiful from tip to toe. I am the embodiment of great wealth, peace and fame. I am the (violent) Chandi and Chandika. I am Bhadrakali, Bhadara, Kali, Durga and Maheswari, too. As the wife of Lord Vishnu I embody within myself the three facets of human nature: the spiritual, the functional and the dark/sinful. And yet, I transcend them all as I am the transcendental female energy.]

This inadequate, functional translation informs only that prosperity and destruction are the coexisting properties in Mahalkshmi and any act of human violation even at the psychic plane, would lead to the stiring up of the destructive energy of Chandika imbeded with in Mahalakshmi. Any flagrant act would, therefore bring in destruction. This has been proved to be obvious in the nightmares that the begining of the 21st. centurey has witnessed in the world.

Thus, there is nothing unscientific/disreputable in the study of of the *Puranas*. The physical sciences we study now may be totally discarded after some decades. A scientific knowledge that helps proliferation of materiality would, however, sprawl horizontally without any notion of height or depth.

Years back, during the colonial period, Max Mueller called the Indian *Upanishads* "the babblings of a child humanity" (p-9). Muller thought that the Sacred Books of the East contained much that was not only "unmeaning, artificial and silly, but even hideous and repellent (p.54) One may refer to Sri Aurobindos's *The Upanishads* (the page marks are from this book. Sri Aurobindo Ashram, Pondicerry, 1972) where in he "lashes out at European scholars for dubbing whatever they could not understand silly (R.Ramachandra *Indian Literary Criticism*.Reliance publishing house, New Delhi 1989, p.108).

Most of the Oriya painters and dancers who perform and sell themselves in European consumerist market do not represent Odia culture at all. European night-clubs exhibit the naked sculptures/ paintings of Indian Goddesses. As a by-product of such cultural consumerism, Orissan temples are continuously being looted. Haven't we inherited the legacy of the Puranic demons ?

The Puranic stories woven round the Goddess of Charchika are also allegories of a reality from which we are pathetically destantiated. Puranas are encyclopaediac histories in their range of subjects like rituals, cermonies, vows, modes of worship, notions about heaven and hell, codes of morality, sin, pilgrimages, reverence to Gurus and cults etc. They have great spiritual importance (I don't know how to rename it in an era of secularism and mafia economics) since they preach mono-theism, poly theism and pan-theism.

The micro history of Banki, published in 2001 is a contemporary record of monistic theism. But Sri Rajendra Prasad Tripathy's book captioned *Dwitiya Konarka* (the Second Sun Temple) records the history of Buguda, a place of antiquity in the Ganjam district. Sri Rajendra P. Tripathy traces the history of Buguda (Srikar Nagar) from the 1st century A.D. to 18th century A.D. that comprises of the Buddhist period (A cave called *Buddha Khole* still exists) and the time of the subsequent Sailodbhaba, Bhaumakara and Bhanja dynasties.

The History of Buguda

Buguda belongs to the ancient Madhya Kalinga of the Trikalinga (Three Kalingas) time. The place was in the Gummasar State, which was called later as Ghumusar. The historian records that Buddha Khole or the cave stands there as an ancient place of meditation since the 5th-6th century B.C., i.e. five hundred years after the hymns of Rigveda were compiled.

Padma Sri Satyanarayan Rajguru, the famous cultural historian of Orissa, has collected the copper grants and deposited them in the State museum. The copper grant informs that Madhab Burman of the Sailodbhaba dynasty (7th-8th century A.D.) reigned in Mukunda Garh which is still there renamed as Mukund pur.The history of the Sailodbhavas of Kangoda Mandala has been discussed already

By the 9th century the Somavamsi kings took over and by that time the Brahminical religion dominated and the Buddhist remnants were neglected. Later, this was included in Khinjili Mandala. However, during the Soma Vamsi rule, eight Shiva Temples were built around Buddhagiri hill : (1) Gangadhara Swamy (2) Jagadeeswara (3) Mukteswara (These three temples are built on the top of the hill) (4) Buddheswara (5) Siddheswar (These two temples are built near the water fall of the hill (6) Kubereswara (7) Lokanatheswara (a temple built of bricks and here the fountain water tastes sour) (8) Gupteswar (inside a dark cave). There is also an ancient Devi temple in which a primitive deity Sankulei is worshipped.

When the Soma Vamsi king Raja Kesari ruled over the place, the capital was at Purushottampur and it was the capital of Khinjili Mandala. The name Buguda itself provides evidence of a primitive, tribal culture. "Bu" in tribal language refers to food and "guda" is the place where food is available.

Srikar Bhanja (1789-1832) built a fort at Buguda and it had a cosy guest house during those days. He built the Viranchi Narayana Temple at Buguda. The temple is built of wood and it has 48 wooden poles modelled after the imaginary chariot of the Sun God. It has seven speeding herses made of stone and Lord Surya Narayana is worshipped there.

According to late Kavi Suryamani Chyau Pattnayak's *Bhanja Vamasabali* (palm leaf script) Hari saran Bhanja built this Sun Temple between 1701-1703. His successor, according to this palm-leaf script, was Srikar Bhanja and he remodelled the wooden Temple in 1822. Late Chintamoni Mahanty's *Gummasara Kavya* describes the temple as the **Second Konarka** and as a huge *Chitra Kavya* (a poem in pictures')

The Bhanja Kings ruled over Subarnapur and Boudh of Koshala region during the 8th century. Rana Bhanja was the king during 8th century and his son Satrubhanja-ii was killed by the Soma Vamsi king of Koshala (Janmejaya) in 857 A.D. Later, by 885 A.D. the Somavamsi kings designated themselves as *Kesaris* and invaded the Khinjili Mandala and built a fort at the foot of Malati Mountain, which demarcated the border of the Bhaumakara kings. This is ascertained from the Dharakote copper grant of 339 AD given by Subhankar Dev -iii. The copper grant mentions about the capital of the Bhauma kings which was called "Jaya kataka" situated at Purushottampur. Later, Jaya kataka was renamed as Jaugada. The Somavamsi Kesari kings invaded the Bhanja territories repeatedly. Sila Bhanja was the king of Khinjili Mandala during those days. Raja Kesari was the king of Malatigada and he annexed the kingdom of Jaugada around 9th century.

The queen of Malatigada (the capital city of the Kesari king Raja Kesari) expressed her desire to know about the war events. Raja Keshari showed her a huge stone lamp with a big wick burning at the top of the mountain of Malatigada (Malati Pahada) and told her that the king would be considered alive as long as the lamp burns. This huge stone lamp still exists in Malati Mountain. The lamp could contain 250 seers of castor oil. A cotton sari (9ft long and 3ft. wide) was used as its wick during the war.

The Bhanja kings knew the secret and turned the stone lamp upside down. The lamp was extinguished and the queens of Malatigada committed suicide by jumping into fire. The place was later called Rani Sarover (The pond for the queens). The Bhanja kings had destroyed Malatigada and the stone lamp still stands there turned upside down. The people call it "the inverted lamp of Malatigada".

Janmejaya-i, the SomaVamsi king (850-885) records in a copper grant in his 17th year of administration that the Kesava and Aditya Temples have been maintaned with full security. This shows that the SomaVamsi kings were Vaishnavites and also the worshippers of the Sun God. They had built some Sun temples at Malatigada which have been abandoned and destroyed in course of time.

the huge Sun temple of Malatigada was built by the SomaVamsi Kesari kings during the 9th century and the Konark temple was built later. The resemblance between the two temples proves theat the Konark Sun Temple was modelled after the Malatigada Temple. The Sun Temple of Buguda was built in between 1785-1789 AD.

Sri Kara Bhanja retrieved the image of Biranchi Narayana from the dilapidated Malatigada during an excavation and installed the image at Puranagada, Buguda in the wooden temple in 1822 (On the 10th day of the dark fortnight, *Bhadrapada* month) with proper rituals.

The records indicate that after some years, some worms appeared from the crevices of the image. The king was surprised since the image was treated with sandle paste, camphor and *gorachana* paste everyday. Then the king sat on meditation and Lord Biranchi Narayana appeared in his dream (this is neither a legend nor a Supenatural incedent, for your information) to convey that the *Poojakas* (Priests) did not wipe the water from the body properly and; hence the crevices in the image should be closed and the entire body of his image should be treated with water-proof paste so that water contents would not seep into his body. The king went to Monk Gobinda Das, proceeded to a villalge named Mathura, and brought some carpenters for the repair work. The sculptors closed the crevices by treating the image with a paste made of tamarind seeds mixed with herbal medicines.

According to the Sanskrit theserus *Amarakosha*, the word Biranchi refers to Lord Brahma. Lord Brahma is worshipped as Biranchi at Palia, a village situated at a distance of 12 kms. from Bhadrak. The image of Brahma has 4 heads and 4 gates have been constructed in the temple, with no *Parswa Devatas*. This seems to be a deviation in the history of Orissan Temple archetecture. Dr.Harekrishna Mahatab, in his *History of Orissa*, mentions that the temple of four-headed-Brahma (Biranchi) was built in the 9th century A.D. by the kings of Bhauma dynasty.

But Biranchi is treated as the Sun God at Buguda basing on one of the slokas referred Lord Surya. The sloka is very popular and most of the Hindu Brahmins offer their ovation to the Sun God everyday reciting :

Om namah savitre jagaddeka chakshuse
Jagat prasuti, sthiti, nasa hetave
Trayi mayaya trigunat ma dharine
Biranchi Narayana Sankaratmane namah.

The last line of the Sloka indicates that Surya, (the Sun God) Vishnu, Brahma and Siva are referred to by the word Biranchi (in South India He is Birinchi).

The mode of worship and the rituals of both the Biranchi temples are different. For example, the Biranchi (Brahma) at Palia is offered a fan and an umbrella made of flowers whereas the Biranchi of Buguda is offered a fan made of palm leaf and a sieve (*Chitki*) made of bamboo. cereals, coconuts, china roses and brinjals are offered to this Lord. The offerings at Buguda indicate that the Lord Biranchi (as Sun God) is treated as the Lord of the agricultural rituals (the Sun as *"sthiti"*, or, the continuation of the creation)

The history of Buguda, the reigning dynasties and its Biranchinarayan Temple provide a shift in our culture study of the state. The evidences of the Sun-worship at Konark, Palia, Buguda and the ancient Malatigada lead one to the belief-systems prevalent in the country of the Odias. The worship of the Sun God is a part of the Vaishnavite cult.

A Thread of Continuity

We have already mentioned about the history of Kantilo, its mythical framework, and historical timings (1700B.C.) collected from the microhistories (Ch-3) of this book. It is our responsibility now to juxtapose the findings with the mainstream findings of Indian histriographers. It seems interesting that the main stream historians have politicized Indian history and fictionalized archaeological findings to marginalize the Odisan context. Several political questions are now raised in the mind of this non-historian when he mingles mythologies with the microhistories maintained in the regional records of the kings. Who is this colonial historian to consider history on empirical evidences only? Indian historians are also mythographers and they never cared for empirical, logical accounts which would suit the Westerners. Now there is a vital question about the standards of argument maintained by the European Historians who are guided by their Christian biases only to the exclusion of the Indian as well as the Oriental views of life. To obey the guidelines of histriography given by the Europeans and Americans is to be forced by an academic mafiasm. The American histriographers have written history of the plantation workers and their ethnic taboos based on the legends and oral history, but they would call our legends fictional. I would show here some of the continuities of culture from 1700B.C. to the present day, basing on the history of Kantilo.

Let me repeat some of the historical facts about the history of Kantilo and Ranapur.The year 1700 B.C., when Viswa Vasaba was the king of Ranpur, is a period earlier to the time of Harappan culture. If the war of the Mahabharata is dated between 1500-1000 B.C., the time of Viswa Vasaba predates the war by two centuries. However, the milieu of *Rig Veda* can be found mirrored in Viswa Vasava's era.

About a millennium separates the Vedic era from the Harappan Age. The collection of the Hymns of Rig Veda was not completed before 1000 B.C. (though some of its myths originated in a far remote past). In the *Rig Veda* the bovine species, whether as buffalo or bull, lends its glamour to the evocation of the gods : Agni, Indra, Soma and Varuna - all of whom were invoked as bulls. The Saivite cult and the Sabara Culture of the Ranapur jungles, the worship of the tribal God Neelamadhaba, the Maninaga hills with Shiva and Durgamba images can be taken as parts of our national culture during the pre-Mahabharata era in a crude and underdeveloped primitive way, though. The bull is related to Shiva and also to the period of transition between the primitive fruit gatherers' society and the agricultural society. The bull is symbolic power in act, in manifestation.

Viswa Vasaba, as a king, was only an archer and Rudra-Agni, the wild archer had always saved him. The commandments of God given in the dreams is neither mythological nor an exaggerated blind belief. The Britishers wanted to deracinate our people from our own rich cultural heritages/power on administrative grounds and introduced concepts like science, reasoning and rationality etc to prove that this latter political religion and culture was an embodiment of progress and what they taught under the umbrella of occcidentalism was Enlightenment and Renaissance.

In other words, the belief of Viswa Vasaba in his intuitive dreams, and God's dream commandments would be thrown into the garbage of fantasy since no evidence is available as to whether Viswa Vasaba had really dreamt about worshipping

Maninaga Mahadeba and Durgamba. That is a subjective truth and no objective/ laboratory proof can be provided.

The person, who would ask such a question, would be distantiated from the dreamer Viswabasava by about three thousand eight hundred years across time.

Odisa has been invaded by alien cultures several times in the meanwhile. The brand of education introduced during the Imperial times has been accepted as scientific and modern and our ancient knowledge has been consigned to the burial ground by our so called educated folks during and after the colonial period for their own material benefits.

The younger generation is so cleanly cut off from these shaivite and Tantric roots of Orissa, that at this beginning of the 21st century, these events culled from the micro history of Ranapur would appear to them blasphemous and incredible at the first encounter.

The tragic part of our contemporary cultural belief-system is that we fail miserably to identify the tribal knowledge of Viswa Vasaba as a supra- scientific knowledge. If Viswabasu's dream commandments were not true, if the *Yantras* drawn on the Chakasila stone did not convey any truth, how could the facts come true and the evidences stand the test of time till today? How could the ritual worship of Maninaga (Mahadeva) and Durga (the primal mother force) attract the kings of Kangoda and Tosali who made occasional grants of villages to meet the expenses of the continuing rituals? The survival of the temples and the *Yantras* for 3800 years (From 1700 BC to 2100 AD) might evoke awe and wonder, but the efficacy and the authenticity of Viswa Vasaba's dreams actualising the presence of Shiva and Durga in 1700 B.C. cannot be consigned to the dustbin of fantasies. The advocates of the physical sciences can only venture to attempt such a stupid subversion.

The cultural belief has proved itself as a universal truth and it needs a thorugh discussion on two levels: (a) the relevance of Viswa Vasaba, the primitive Sabara king and his brother Viswa Vasu to the contemporary cultural milieu that precedes the civilization of Mahenjodaro by 200 years, or as a parallel civilization that runs along the Harappan stream and (b) the efficacy of the Saibite and Tantric culture of the Sabara kings of Ranapur in our post-modern era.

Maninaga of Ranapur (in (1700 B.C.) is directly related to the primordial phase of the *vratya* myth of creation and around seven hundred years before the collection of the hymns of *Rig Veda*, or the poetic codification of the powers like Agni, Varuna and Indra, who have later been considered as mythulal Gods. In his sacrificial role, however, Angni was equated to Rudra Brahman and both were related to the Savaras (Viswa Vasaba's tribe) as Supreme Archers. Agni was to play an analogous part, though transposed into the orbit of the sacrifice, to that of Rudra, the fierce archer. Agni himself is an archer. His arrows glow with heat (Rig Veda 4.4.1), but his office as a priest, he has no use for them. On the contrary, absorbed in sacred thought centered in his knowledge of the cosmic order (ruta) in its eternal truth, he concurred with the Father when the latter, benefaction in mind, offered up his seed in his daughter, Usas (RV 3.31.1). Then the Angirasas were born (cf R.V.3.31.3). This is the Vedic myth (?) of creation. I do not like to use the word 'myth' and to adjectify Veda. But we can juxtapose the myth of the tribals with those of the Vedic seers.

Agni is here treated as the primordial, paradigmatic flame arising as the sacred fire. Agni knows the cosmic order (ruta) for he is its first born in the earliest aeon (RV 10.5.7). In these cosmically and sacrificially ordered universe-to-be, Agni and the Father (Prajapati) are the cooperating powers. The Father (Prajapati) inseminating his daughter performs a cosmogenic rite to which the Angirasas and ultimately Man owe their position in an ordered world (please read the 8th *mandala* of *Rig Veda* to get the full story of the myth of creation).

By the time Agni and Rudra were recorded as powers in the Rig Veda, Viswa Vasaba's era was over. Rig Veda records the history of the universe around 1000 B.C. and the relation of Viswa Visava's dream, the worship of Shiva and Sakti in

Maninaga Mountain (which survives even today), the *Yantras* drawn on Chakasila stone, predates by 700 years. The records of Rig Veda are probably enriched by model kings/ archers like Viswa Vasaba and their worship of Mahadeva (Shiva) and Durga. The defination of Durga is given in *Atharva Seersha* and Mother Durga herself declares about her emergence in the primordial times. In Rig Veda (M.10.A.10.Mantra 1-9) there is a *Sookta* called *Ratri Suktam* which reads: "*Orvapra amartyanivato devyudvatah.Jyotisha badhate tamah*". This Devi (Durga) is eternal and She engulfs the entire creation, from the creepers on the ground to the upgoing trees. Not just this, She destroys the darkness of ignorance by her own glow of light/ knowledge).

In *Atharva Seersha* all the Gods come to the Devi and ask: "Oh Great Mother: Who are thou?" Durgamba answers:
1. *Aham brahma swaroopini.*
2. *Mattah prakruti purusha tmakam jagat. Soonyam cha soonyam cha.*
   [I am the *brahma*. From me has emerged the concepts of gender the mimetic forms of the Male and the Female. I am emptiness and the non-emptiness at the same time.]
3. *Ahamananda nanandau.* (I am the pleasure and the non-pleasure too)
   Ahamavijnana-abijnane. (I am the science and the non science too)
   Aham Brahma Abrahmani Vedityabe (I am the knowable Brahma and non-Brahma too)
   Aham panchabhootani Apanchabhootani. (I am the saturated compound of the five elements and I am also differentiated by the five elements.)
4. *Vedoham Avedoham* (I am the Veda and the Non-Veda, too.)
   Vidyaham avidyaham (I am knowledge and ignorance)
   Ajaham Anajaham (I am the born and also the unborn)
   Adhascha, urdhwacha, tiryak chaham (I am the upward, I am the downward, the obliqueword and also do I spread on to the sides)

5. *Aham* Rudrovirvasubhischarami (I flow and get conducted as/through the images of Rudra and the Vasus)

Seven hundred years before this hymn was written, Viswa Vasaba exprienced Her directly within his inner space. There is nothing to feel astonished about it. What Viswa Vasaba experienced in the remote jungles of Ranapur was condified later in Rig Veda, in the Ganges valley. The defination of Durga given by Durga Herself is not merely a fabrication of binary oppositions as an ordinary European intellectual would be able to analyse partnering with a megalomaniac scientist or a believer of secularism(Godless neutral zone). The propogators of institutionalised social religions would be able to build structures for God only to defile them in materialist pride. They are impelled by some demonic forces like cynicism and insistence on scientific verifiability. These stoopers would never know how Viswavasaba communicated with Neelamadhaba (the present Jagannath), Siva and Durga.

This pre-vedic Sabara (Saura tribe) must have been called as *Vratya* by the Ganges Valley dwellers. The Ganges Valley dwellers were outsiders/foreigners and they treated the Natives as the Others. Their education at Taxila (later to the Vedic period) was never indigenous and it was modelled on the Greek curriculum. But a king like Viswa Vasaba had internalized all our tribal knowledge with the blessings of Maninaga and Durga. He did not know the Vedic religion, but he was self sufficient in his own way. He did not feel the necessity of following the Vedic norms. He was born and brought up in the jungles of Utkal, not on the river banks of Ganges valley.

Viswa Vasaba's *chakasila* (the stone with etchings of a Yantra) is still there on the Maninaga Mountain and numerous attempts of thefts have been obstructed by the Goddess herself. How can a so called empiricist with a scientific bent of mind realise the truth behind such contemporary attempts of theft? The spiritual energy that exudes from this seat protects It self. The disbeliver may challenge the presence of the Goddess alongwith the efficacy of my statement and choose to get destroyed to make a stupid Western *scientific and rational/logical* experiment.There isa sense of adventure also in destroying oneself. This is a fashion with the socalled **liberal humanists** of the world. Committing suicide is a 'rich' cultural feature in societies that believe in global invasions of commercialism. I remember Hart Crane jumping into the sea because of his alchoholic/homosexual craze.

The power of Viswa vasaba's worship is an evidence of the practice of Shaktism in Orissa during the pre-Vedic and Vedic periods. The *Devi Purana* was composed much later, toward the end of the 7th or the beginning of the 8th century. The *Kalika Purana* was composed around the 11the century followed by the composition of *Yogini Tantra* in 16th century. The evidence of the traces of Tantrism can be descerned in the time of *Rig Veda* (1000 B.C.).

Cultural Roots Through Micro Histories

The study of the microhistories has helped us to locate the roots of Odia socio-political-spiritual conditions in and aorund the Harappancivilization in India. I am sure, the mainstream historians, if by chance care to read this book, would definitely feel excited to probe deeply into these histories and correct the dates/years which might vary according to different versions of readings from copper grants and palm leaf records available in different palace libraries of the kings. But we are not sure whether the second and third generation of the Royal families {after the merger of the princely states) have been able to preserve the palm leaf records. Some of the kings have donated their books to the colleges they have established and I know from my personal association that one of the sons of the late king of Badagada has donated some extant books to the central library of Bhanja Vihar, Bahampur University. Most of the extant books in Ravenshaw college library were destroyed during the Super cyclone of 1999.

However, with whatever residual records this researcher could retrieve from the uncared for debris, some interesting facts about the Kalingan people/culture could the discovered which need documentation here.

The history of the Kalingans as traced by the experts show that the people of Kalinga had migrated to this geographical location from three source areas: One from the northern part of India, the second from Gujarat and a third from the middle of the Western Ghats, from the Konkan area. They settled between the rivers Rushikulya and Godavari. A ghat road leading from Bhanjanagar (Ganjam) to Phulbani is called Kalinga Ghat. (A ghat or *ghati* is a mountain track or road-buses ply through Kalinga Ghat to Phulbani). The families of the Oda (Odia) Cultivators are called the *Kalinjis* in Ganjam. Because of these Oda cultivators' settlements, the place was later called Odisa/Udra Desa (the country of the Udras or Odias) Their settlements were not only limited to the coastal belt, it also spread to the tribal areas like Kalahandi, Koraput, Sambalpur and Patnagarh.The Pradhans living in those tribal areas were also cultivators and some of them might have grown up as Landlords in course of time. The most affluent landlords designated themselves as Rajahs.

This narrative of history, though speculative, seems viable. The entire Odra Desa was ruled by Savara (the name of a tribe) kings till 12th century A.D. This shows that the Savaras (now called Sauras) and the Nishadas were not treated as subalterns in those days. Rama, in Valmiki's Ramayana, had an intimate friend called Guhaka Savara. Sri Ramachandra, during his great exodus to the forests for 14 years, had befriended Sugriva. Late shri Ganesh Prasad Parija, a great mythologist and cultural historian of our times, in a feature captioned *Kalinga Desa -o- Kalinga Jati* (*The country called Kalinga and the Kalinga Folks*) published in the Sunday Daily *Dharitri,* dated. 3/11/1996 writes that the Lanjia Sabaras (the savara tribe with a tail like costumes made of barks) were studied by Valmiki and thus he imagined the character of Hanuman, Sugriva and the army of the monkeys deployed in the war against the Sri Lankan (Cylonese) king Ravana. Sugriva hid in Bali's house somewere in Phulbani jungles. The costumes and the physical behaviour of these people in the era of Ramayana was almost akin to those of the monkeys

River Rushikulya in Ganjam has originated from a mountain called Rushyamuka in the Eastern Ghats of Ganjam and there is a pond called Pampasar (A famous pond depicted in the Ramayana). It is the place where Ramachandra met a Sabari lady(a tribal lady) who fed the God with berries. She used to taste all the berries she plucked from the tree and offered Him only the sweet ones.(Please mark that there is a mother,a beloved and a devotee melanged together in the character of this tribal woman, who had been waiting for ten thousand years in the jungle for the arrival of Ramachandra)

A coppergrant found and read by Late Satyanarayan Rajguru informs that a village named Sampa near Pampasar was given to a Brahmin. Ramachandra met Hanuman on the bank of this pond in Ganjam and he was impressed by the kind of pure language he used for communication. Ramachandra could identify that Hanuman was well-versed in Vedic Sanskrit and he had studied the four Vedas. He informed Laxman that this person (Hanuman) could not have talked in flawless sentences if he was not a great scholar in Sanskrit grammar.

In this connection it may be reminded here that a study of the genomes of people and chimpanzees has yielded a deep insight into the origin of language, one of the most distinctive human attributes and a critical step in human evolution.The analysis indicates that language, on the evolutionary time scale, is a very recent development, having evolved only in the last 100,000 years or so. The finding supports a novel theory advanced by Dr. Richard Klein, an archaeologist at Stanford University, who argues that the emergence of behaviorally modern humans about 50 thousand years ago was set off by a major genetic change. The new study, by Dr.Svante Paabo and colleagues at the Max Planck Institute for Evolutionary Anthropology at Leipzig, Germany, is based on the discovery of the first human gene involved specifically in language.

As we talk about Hanuman speaking in unflawed grammatical sentences to Ramachandra,

A fresh study of Hanuman can be made in this light. This human gene is called FOXP2 and it is involved in the face and jaw-movements necessary for speech. The researchers said in a report in *Nature* "It is not the gene that made language possible", geneticist Wolfgang Enrad of the first human genes involved in speech and language, which are complex abilities.

But the gene seems to be very important as we re-evaluate the case of Hanuman.My question to the scientists, who boast of visible laboratory experiments: Is Hanuman only a figment of Valmiki's fantasy? Or, does it imbed any advanced genetic study in the characterization of Hanuman? Are all Indian seers only childish' as MaxMueller commented long ago about the Upanishads?

The research made in 2001 reveals that people who lack two normal copies of the gene have considerable difficulty in speaking. They not only make mistakes in grammar, but can not always articulate words clearly. Hanuman's clear and distinct articulation was deciphered by Sri Ram and he explained about this genetic evolution to his brother Lakshmana.

Dr. Paabo says the gene FOXP2 has remained largely unaltered during the evolution of the mammals, but suddenly, it started changing in humans after the hominid line had split off from the chimpanzee line of descent.The changes in the human gene affect the structure of the protein it specifies at two sites, Dr Paabo's team reports. One of them slightly alters the protein's shape: the other gives it a new role in the signalling circuitry of human cells.

The changes indicate that the gene has been under strong evolutionary pressure in humans. Also the human form of the gene, with its two changes, seems to have become universal in the human population, suggesting that it conferred some overwhelming benefit.

Dr. Paabo contends that humans must already have

possessed some rudimentary form of language before the FOXP2 gained its two mutations. By conferring the ability for rapid articulation, the improved gene may have swept through the population, providing the finishing touch to the acquisition of language. Dr. Paabo says," May be, this gene provided the last perfection of language, making it totally modern."(Collected from Nicholas Wade's report in *The Times of India, New Delhi Dated 17 August, 2002. P. 12*). This digression into the latest genetic explorations of linguistics provides us with new perspectives on the characterological dimensions of Hanuman. At the same time, this throws new light to our study of the tribal culture and the capacity of our tribal primates to interact with the developed Aryan species with greater linguistic ability.

A contemporary thesis by Ms. Rekha Devi captioned "Locational study of Tribal settlements" informs that most of the Lanjia sauras are found in Puttasing police station in Koraput district which is one of the most inaccessible part of the core area" (p.95). The mountain ranges of Ganjam and Koraput are contiguous and the culture of the tribals (Sauras) is almost synonymous. Perhaps they were treated as one region during the period of *The Ramayana*.

The present day Sauras living in Tumba area (Ganjam district) designate themselves as *Suddha Sauras* and *Bheema Sauras*. The *Suddha Sauras* living in a village called Madhuri, talked to us in pure Odia, but communicated amongst themselves in Saura dialect which is not intelligible to us.

A little away toward Tumba, there is a village called Haripur which is also a Saura settlement of 50 families. These Sauras have come down to this plain area from the mountain tops since they could get neither food nor water on the top of the mountain.

They report that the daughter-in-laws of that Saura village have come from 20 other Saura settlements. The village was established in 1994 when they came down from the mountains. They have dug a pond for themselves and live with lots of goats. Their staple food is *Kangu* (yellow mustard like seeds used as porridge). *Jana* (white seeds used as pop corn) and *Nigada* (a small *til* like seed used for porridge). The younger generation of these Sauras prefers to work as labourers in Madras and Kerala.

As one goes up the hill through Puriasahi to Anda Anda, two small settlements of Saura villages constituting of 18 families and 13 families respectively, can be found. The Saura women in Anda Anda do not put on any cloth on the breast and live in extreme poverty with no food to eat. But young Sauras (teen agers) are found dressed in Bermudas and tea-shirts bought from Tumba weekly fair. They call themselves as *Bhima Sabaras* or the descendants of Bhima, one of the five brothers of the Pandavas of the *Mahabharata*.

Near Tumba, there is a village called Bomkei where there is a big rock slab called *Bhuin Chancheda*. Two small water reservoirs are called *Bhima Kunda* and *Parasuranva Kunda*. The Saura tribals relate their history to the period of *Ramayana* and *Mahabharata*. The language of these Sauras sounds like Tamil. For example, the "curry" is called "tarangal" in their language and for going to the toilet, they would communicate as "asangada".

Sauras also live in Raikia area of Phulbani and Gunupur area of Koraput. They are almost naked peole.But the Sauras living at the foot Hill of Mahendragiri Mountain seem to be slightly civilized. The Christian missionaries come to these villages and convert them. Some of them also convert themselves as Hindus when the people of Viswa Hindu Parishad approach them. As a result of these conversions, the Sauras have given up their tribal culture and they undergo a process of heavy urbanisation.

A few years later, it would be difficult to trace any tribal culture in Kainpur area of Mahendragiri hills.

The Sauras have made a mark in painting. If you would go to a village called Jagannathpur in Chandragiri panchayat of Mohana block, you would definitely meet old Rupa Savara, a tribal painter. He has been painting since last four decades on the walls of the huts and on the places of worhip. The walls are given a background of maroon clay which acts as a canvas. Then he uses the powder of Kangu (mixture of yellow and brown) and rice (white) as the colours.

The Sauras still adopt the method of lifting a *Kania*, a bride for marriage. Young men lift the girls and later the parents institutionalize it by celebrating the marriage with a feast. Sometimes, the parents of the young man go and request the girl's parents. If they do not agree, the boy would lift the girl.

Valmiki has written how the language of the Sabaras was different from that of the description of the *Vratya* zone of India.Its culture is available to us as our ancient record. In the chapter, *Lanka Kanda*, Valmiki has not given any description of Ramachandra crossing the river Godavari. This means that Rama, Laxmana and Sita's tours during their exile terminated in Kalinga that extended upto river Godavari.

This leads to the conclusion that the characters like Bali, Sugriba and Hanumana belonged to the early Savara tribe who lived between Rushikulya and Godavari rivers. These Sabaras were never inferior to the Indus valley dwellers though the Aryans called them *Anaryas (non-aryans)*. But it is a paradox that the North Indian kings also married in the South India for having greater political control over the fringes of their empire.

The chapter *Shanti Parva* in *Mahabharata* informs that Duryodhana married Bhanumati, the daughter of the Savara king Chitrangada of Kalinga. The state called Kalinga and the stories about its origin can be found in the following three Puranas.

1. *Mahabharata: Adi Parva: Adhyaya* 104
2. *Vayu Puran Adhyaya* 99
3. *Harivamsa Adhyaya* 31

The ixth Skanda of *Bhagabata Mahapurana* (*Adhyaya* 23) corroborates the facts mentioned in the above *Puranas* and at the same time adds another new event. The event leads to Parasuram's oath to exterminate /destroy all the *Kshatriyas* from this land. He could be successful in his attempt of killing thousands of Kshatriyas. The Kshatriya women, who had been widowed came to this region to take shelter in the Ashramas (residential schools) run by the Rishis. Parasuram did not attack the Ashramas since those belonged to the Brahmins. Parasurama had visited the Savara inhabited areas of Kalinga in search of Kshyatriyas.

The history of Kantilo infoms about Parasuram's visit and stay in the dense forest of Brahmadri mountain at the behest of the tribal God called Neelamadhaba, who was later stolen and shifted to Puri to be worshipped as Lord Jagannath in a great temple. The Mahabharata (Shanti Parva) informs that Parasurama had established his Ashrama (residential school) in Mahendragiri.

There is a place called Bomakei near Tumba and it has Saura settlments. A large stone slab is named as *Bhuin Chancheda*. There are two small water reservoirs called *Bheema Kunda* and *Parasurama Kunda*. The names justify the once-upon-a-time presence of Bhima and Prasurama in this Saura belt. We do not know whether Brahmadri was in the Mountain range of Mahendragiri. But in the present geographical context, the distance between Mahendragiri and Brahmadri (Kantilo) would be around 100 kms on the mountain routes. Perhaps in Vyasa's time (the author of the Mahabharata) this Eastern Ghat mountain region was identified only by its forests and the North Indians used this area as a place for punishment and exile.

The language and the habits of the tribals provided a cultural contrast to the Aryans and the Sanskrit speakers, but the forest dwellers were not treated as subalterns by the kings of Aryavarta as they are treated today by the post independence politicians.

The *Mahabharata* also informs that Karna, the great archer had learnt *Dhanur Veda* (The Veda of the archers) from Parasurama staying in his Mahendragiri Ashram. Vyasa's *Vana Parva* of the *Mahabharata* mentions how the 5 Pandavas during their exile into the forest had been to Mahendragiri to pay a visit to Rama. Vyasa informs that the capital of Kalinga was Rajapur and the historians have proved that the present Rajamundry of Andhra Pradesh was the ancient Rajapur.

Rajamundry is situated on the bank of river Godavari. The place reappears in the 16th century history of Orissa, when the Suryavamsi king Prataprudra Deva ruled from Puri. Ramananda Pattnayak was in power at Rajamundray at that time and he propagated the philosophy of Vaishnavism in Puri.

At another point of history, in the post-*Mahabharata* period, the capital city of Kalinga was Danta Pur and Prof. Nabin Kumar Sahu, Late professer of history, has identified the place with modern Palur, situated on the bank of Lake Chilika.

Pargiter, in his book, *Ancient Indian Historical Tradition* consistently veers back to the Mahabharata to trace the origin of the Eastern states like the contemporary Manipur, Meghalaya, Arunachala Pradesh, Assam, West Bengal and Orissa. In those Puranic ages, the first four states mentioned above were called Anga: the contemporary Bengal was called Banga and modern Orissa was called Kalinga.

The *Mahabharata* mentions the name Kalinga at different places. The Ramayana has a few references to Kalinga, but the Brahminic literature (The Vedas etc) has totally ignored this state. The primitive men of Anga, Banga and Kalinga were hated because they flouted the Vedic norms and also the culture that prevailed on the river banks and the coast lines.

SECTION-IV

Folk Culture of Odissa

Any postulation on culture, today, is bound to be tagged with politics, especially with the democratic blasphemy, which vests power with "supplementary" delegate bodies that exist in the capitals. This game of decentering of sovereignty calls, paradoxically, for the existence of a capital, a centre of usurpation and of substitution. It leads to a cultural bipolarity and competition between the `dominant' and `subordinate' cultures. Bijoy Chandra Majumdar's drastic attacks on Bhanja literature during the colonial era, the subsequent tug-of-war between the two literary journals-*Bijuli* (1893) and *Indradhanu* (1894) as to the moral representation of Oriya literature through *Bhanja* poetry, publication of negative criticism about *Koti Brahmanda Sundari* in *Utkala Madhupa*, (1891) semioticize a literary-cultural politics on four levels:

a) Rejection of Indian notions of *rasa* in preference to British realism trickling down to us through the sub-ways of Bengal.

b) Attempt of the socalled modernists generated by Brahmo Religion (1870) that penetrated English education and Puritanic attitudes into Oriya cultural unconscious through back doors.

c) Such attacks are attempts to subvert a South Orissan writer of eminence and the tirades signify that Calcutta Presidency was superior to Madras Presidency. The Orissan culture at that time witnessed such cultural wars because the literatures under Calcutta Presidency assumed a self-complacent role that they could dominate and assert themselves on the poets of a subordinate culture like that of Ganjam.

d) The points of attack being *Brahmo Samaj* brand of morality and the victim, Bhanja, being a champion of soft-porno *kavyas*, (so goes the attack), the dominant cultural critics from Pyarimohan Acharya to Radhanath Ray extereorize the Oriya cultural attitude towards sex.

Bhanja belonged to a tribal kingdom in which description of a woman's body or aestheticization of a nude was never considered to be profane. Secondly, he represented the culture of a tantric belt and in Sakta cults the nude body of the mother-Goddesses has been described most dispassionately and with reverence.

This leads me to another statement given by Dr. Harekrishna Mahatab in his *History of Orissa* with regard to the sculptures of Kamasutra given in the Sun Temple of Konark. Dr. Mahatab is of the opinion that the Kamasutra images of Konark are disgraceful and harmful to the moral hygine of the Oriyas and they should be demolished. This politician turned historian's statement on Oriya temple culture opens up another angle of cultural domination/ superiority foisted on the illiterate artisans/ sculptors of Orissa.

Dr. Mahatab attempts to assert his own moral superiority and concern over our cultural notions of sex depicted through temple sculpture. His views on erotic sculpture seems also to have been influenced by the moral hypocrisy practised by the advocates of Brahmo Samaj, which emanated in West

Bengal and was circulated in Orissa as a dominant cultural manifestoe of modernity. The evangelists who were engaged in spreading the lights of a logical religion had also adopted the strategy of moral purity and during the colonial times, the notion of associating the erotic sculpture of the Sun Temple with the irrational primitivity of the Odias was a fashionable strategy to demolish the traditional pride the Odias enjoyed with regard to their arhetecture. The colonial rulers did not know that the erotic sculpture was a part of the Buddhist and Tantric mode of viewing art and religion. They also did not know that Odisa had produced theoreticians of temple archetecture and books had already been written long back justifying the necessity of erotic sclpture.

i) Folk literature

Initially our folk literature is connected with the oral tradition of telling stories. *Abolkara Kahani* provides the best example of our folk tales. Like all pilgrim stories of the medieval world, a B*rahmin pundit* sets out for pilgrimage and a stupid barbar follows him as an attendant. He asks peculiar questions about strange geographical entities and the *pundit* narrates the stories.

Folk legends offer another variation. The third, variation is offered by a collection of folk tales by late Prof. Kunjabehari Dash culled from oral tradition. However, the oral stories that I have heard from my granny during the 1940s are not available in this collection. They need to be collected and published. Chakradhara Mahapatra and Dr. Prasanna Kumar Mishra have also worked on folk tales and songs.

The second type of our folk literature can be discerned from the folk songs which offer ten varieties. (i) Ballads like *Kalijai* etc. (ii) Wailing songs as a daughter leaves her paternal home after marriage (iii) *Pala* songs in the performing art. (iv) Farmers' songs and the songs of the agricultural labourers (v) Folk proverbs (*dhaga-dhamali*) (vi) vow-songs (songs pertaining to *Oshakothi* and *Budhei-osha, Janhi-osha* etc.) (vii) Swing songs or *Raja-doli* songs related to fertility cult. (viii) Songs of the devotional beggars like *janu ghanta* and *chakulia panda* etc. (ix) *Mantra* songs (x) Tribal songs.

Under the rubric of contemporary 'folkloristics,' researchers have studied the (a) Oral traditions (b) folk customs (c) folk religions, (d) folk arts and crafts (e) folk rituals and (f) culinary culture.

This study makes an endeavour for a detailed description out of all such variations. However, the Oriya "folk linguistics" can be studied taking *Alchik* and *Kui* languages as specimen. These tribal languages are indigenously Orissan.

Some scholars from the *Anam* group of literary movement have made initial attempts to study the *'boli'* of Puri, (the folk slang language of the tribals of Puri,whom you see on the television on the car festival telecast carrying the image from the temple to the cars) which is connected with Jagannath temple. Others talk about jagannath culture.

ii. Folk Music

The earliest evidences of Orissan music can be deciphered from the rock edict of Kharavela. Paul Yule and Shri B.K. Rath have mentioned about the discovery of lithophones at Sana Kerajanga village which provide us with information about the primitive forms of Odia musical instruments. The 37th *Charya-geeti* (9-10th century) is an example of Odissi music of the *Udra-Magadhi* tradition. Besides, the *Dandi Ramanaya* and *Bhagavata* offer a folk musical style for the *Purana Pandas* (a worshipper class engaged in reading *Purana-that is also a style of singing*) of 16th century. The *Reeti* poets of 17-18th centuries- Deena Krishna, Upendra Bhanja and Abhimanyu and the 19th century Kavisurya Baladeva Ratha were great musicians and they had set their lyrics on cantos and music, which are exclusively Odissi in nature.

Odissi Prabandhagana offers the indigenous variations of a music which can now be treated as both classical and a part of our folk culture as well. These variations are (1) Odissi *dhrupadanga* (2) Odissi *Raganga* (3) Odissi *bhabanga* (4) Odissi *Natyanga* (5) *Chautisa* (6) *Chaupadi* (7) *Champu* (12) *Lakshyana Gita* (13) *Pallavi* and (14) Pure folk forms like *ghumar*.

A great Oriya music scholar, Pt. Raghunath Rath, a contemporary of Gajapati Dibya Singh Deb (1693-1720) and Upendra Bhanja had written a treatise on music, *Natya Manorama*, under the patronage of king Neelakantha, the king of Kerala.The patronage shows the ageold affiliation of Odissa with the South India. The book is reprinted by Orissa Sangeet Nataka Akademi, Bhubaneswar.

iii. The Tribal Songs

Orissa is the abode of sixty two varieties of primitive tribes and their music plays a major role in shaping the folk music of Orissa. These tribal ethnic groups range from nomads, hunters, food gatherers to peasant cultivators and labourers. Most of their songs are meant for recitation and are therefore lyrical. Their songs lend them the power to master over nature. But there is a variety in these tribal songs: songs for celebration of life, marriage songs, festival songs, funeral dirges, invocatory songs and riddle songs. A *push-parab (a festival of harvest in the month of December-January) song* says :

As the pumpkin creeper splits into
two leaves, its sorrow increases.
The folks pluck it out as spinach
Like that the sorrows of men
Begin with their childhood.

The love songs of the Kondhs are very intense and emotive. One can take a glance at the lines sung by a kondh male early in the morning after the 'night-long dance':

Why did you leave?
The dance is not yet over in the groves
The cock has not yet called the dawn in.
With what a magnificient dance you moved
The bangles in your wrist jingled
Like the falling hail stones in dark

What mist of illusion,
 Then devoured you
And you were lost?
You said, you loved me so much
 Like an anklet to the feet
And a ring to the ear
Why did you quit me?

The songs of the Mundas are more lilting, lyrical and poetic. They sing in *Sarhul* festival. Such songs, called *jadur*, vibrate with the subtelties of pain. A song addressed to a cuckoo would read like this:

Cuckoo!
You winged down on the *sal* flower
Cuckoo!
you descended down on the new leaves
Cuckoo!
you came for the rice and our *handia* liquor
Cuckoo!
You came for a chicken's leg bone
The rice and liquor exhausted
And you fled away
The leg bones were finished
And you fled away.

Dr. Sitakant Mahapatra translates a Munda song:

Dreaming of you in bed
I woke and took to the road.
Stumbling on the stone
On the village road I remembered
I remembered my caste, my gotra
And stood transfixed.

Love occupies a central position in the tribal life and the beloved is metaphorized as a 'distance fire fly' or a 'forest fowl' They have songs for the flowering trees, the Karama songs for *Karama* tree, the hunting songs and cow-shed songs for the worship of the cows.

One of the major characterisitcs of these songs and music is that there is no difference between the singer and the listener.

As the music starts, every one joins and the circumference of the communal dance widens. Then the children and the old men join. The tribal music, tribal songs and the tribal dance are inseparable.

As the primitive tradition of music comes down to the folk level, the same structural pattern is maintained. On the occasion of the swing festival and the *Budhei Osha*, the girls sing and dance, simultaneously. However, with the televisation of such rituals, the singers, dancers and the silent observers are seggregated.

iv. Folk Dances:

Every one in the world knows about Odissi dance, but since it has been classified as a "classical dance", we would not include it under the rubric of "folk dance". However, there is possiblity. The contemporary Odissi dance form is performed under three distinct *guru paramparas*, i.e., with three distinct notions of its origin and growth.

Kelucharan Mahapatra, originally a *pakhawaj* (a percussion instrument) player, believes in rhythmic narration and Pankaj Charan Das, hailing from a *Mahari* (*Devadasi*) family traces its origin to the temple tradition. But the most dynamic exponent, late Deba prasad Das deviated from the above two schools and included all our tribal and folk elements into his Odissi compositions. He has extricated Odissi from the *lasya* of Radha-Krishna -Jagannath cliche and has included *tandava* forms. Deba Prasad's Odissi compositions are comprised of all varieties of folk movements including *Mayurbhanj* Chhau and *Danda Nata*.

Danda Nata is the ancient most form of folk dance in which empty-space configurations are evidenced. This 4th century A.D. dance -dramatic form is connected with the Dravidian cult of Saivism and worship of the mother Goddess Kali, and at the same time it is related to the beginning of agriculture. Fertility cult dances like Chhau and Karama have also shaped the culture of Orissa.

v. Folk Performative Arts

Performative arts like *Ghoda Nata, Daskathia, Prahallad Nataka and Danda Nata* are connected with our folk religions and belief system. The fishermen community worship Goddess Basuli in the month of *Chaitra* (March-April) and this legendary worship is detailed in a folk religious treatise called *Kaivarta Geeta* (The Bhagabat *Geeta* of the Fishermen). Similarly, *Prahallad Nataka*, on one side is related the saivite and vaishnavite conflict and on the other, it is symbolic of the pole-worship (*Stambha puja*) of primitive culture. *Daskathia* deploys narrator- characters, which perform through role reversals and the technique of transformation, that are characteristic of our folk culture.

vi. Religions and systems of Belief:

The religious beliefs in a folk culture are in fact, folk beliefs. In other words, folk beliefs are replaced as folk-religion. These beliefs need not follow the path of logic, rationality and reasoning. This belief system originates in the secluded zone of archetypal consciousness and percolates into the folk culture because of their force and efficacy.

For example, the most controversial folk belief of Orissa is Meria sacrifice, a practice connected with the *Keduparab* of the Kondhs, in which human beings were sacrified for the propitiation of evil spirits and for the preservation of community life, agricultural prosperity or professional works like (fruit-gathering or hunting). The primitives believe in the continuation of life-cycle through re-birth and in the spiritual (essential) osmosis between the micro and macro forms of life. In a novel called *Dadi Budha* (The grand Old man), Gopinath Mahanty(late Jnanpeeth Awardee) gives a detailed account of the religious beliefs of the Paraja tribe. The *Paraja* tribals believe in *Duma* (a *preta* or ghost). The grand parents after death get reincarnated within the new borns of the family.

The famous novelist Shri Santanu K. Acharya told me recently that once he found a young boy in a dakbungalow situated in a dense jungle working as a watchman substitute. On being asked about ghosts and his fears, the ten years old boy replied that he played with the boy ghosts in the night. Sri Acharya has recorded such recent experiences in his book, *Karanjia Diary*. Karanjia is a small town in Mayurbhanj district. In Gopinath Mahanty's novel, a date-palm tree is worshipped as *"Dadi Budha"* (grand old man/ *preta/duma/* God) by cutting it and tying it up with red clothes and offering it with cock-sacrifices. Our tribals also worship sun, moon, earth, jungle, mountains, rocks, rivers and fountains, the entire nature. The red colour, associated with blood and the planet Mars is auspecious for them as it goes hand in glove with the *prithivi-tattwa* (the element of soil). The *desia kondha* of Phulbani give their young married daughters *tropendi dripedi* (red Sari) N.A. Watts in his book, *The half-clad Tribes of Eastern India* records, "Sacrificial rites among the Bondos relate chiefly to fecundity. At every religious festival seed grams are consecrated and reconsecrated in the blood and sacrficed animals to renforce their potency." (Watts 1970 p.79)

The Christian humanists with their torch of Enlightenment (I visualize this torch as a phallic symbol with a red plastic cover at its focal point) condemned the sacrificial rites practised by our tribals and the contemporary governments have introduced further enlightenment programmes through tribal development departments. I wonder as to how our pseudo-civilized bureaucats venture to foist their views on this great culture of the tribals, who invoke the entire cosmos to descend down their dark caves huts.

The priests of different tribal sects operate in different ways. The priest in *Desia Kandha* tribe is called *Tumba*, in *Paraja* tribe he is *Jani*, the *Juangs* have their *nagam*, the *Santali bui*, the *Bhuyans Dehuri* the *Mundas* have *Puhan* and the *Gonds-Jhankar*. In some other tribals sects the shaman is named differently: *Gurumai, Beju, Bejuni, Deonra, Rumukin and Kutagatali*.

Before the *puja* the tribals sanctify the place of worship with cowdung, the community leader takes a bath, puts on new clothes and fasts. The Gods and Goddesses are invoked with a yantra drawn with rice peste/ what stone powder and with vermilion sprinkled on it. The last item is sacrifice of blood and offering of wine. Since these worships are associated with Shamanistic rituals, most of the ignorant westerners and their Indian counterparts seem to despise them as barbarianism. Perhaps they do not know that Shamanism as an archaic.Such belief systems still continue in Nepal, Australia, America, Africa, Tibbet and in all oriental countries. Mircea Eliade in an essay captioned, *Shamanism and Comology*, writes, "The preeminetnly shamanic technique is the passage from one cosmic region to another, from earth to sky or from earth to the underworld. The Shaman knows the mystery of the break through plane. This communication among the cosmic zones is made possible by the very structure of the universe". (Eliade 17) The Tamang Shamans have a spontaneous vocation in which they are inflicted by spirits that possess them and drive them into solitude demanding him to become a Shaman. This unsolicited alterd state of consciousness that afflicts him is called crazy possesion.

Thus our Orissan primitive beliefs cannot be dispensed with as ignorance. These belief systems have also come down to the non-tribal folk. What today we call *dei-pindi* in brahmin and non-brahmin households is a transformed symbol of *Duma*, carried from the concept of a community God to a household god. The *Bhuyans* of the coastal districts who are no more recognised as tribals still continue the *Dharani Puja* (worship of the soil) which comes from the matru puja or the utpadika puja (fertility worship) of the tribals. The festivals of *Raja, Balijatra* and *Ashadha Parba* are modifications from the *Kedu Parab*. The presiding deity of the *Bhuyans* is *Thakurani Mai*, who is also known as *barha, kudra, dano, pacheria, hiseiwar* and *kohi*. Today, these goddesses are worshipped alsmost in every village as *Grama Devati*.

The tribal beliefs are reshaped as *Osha, Vrata* (Vows)

and *Upavasa* (fasting days like the eleventh day or the fourteen day of the lunar month) in our folk culture. The fasting ceremonies are inherited from Jainism. But the *Maha Yanis* and *Heena Yanis* of Buddhist sect have appropriated all the tribal goddesses worshipped in the form of stones. The concept of Tara and Ugratara as Goddesses are common to both the religions. However, the folk culture of the Oriyas has inherited *Oshas* like *Jagulai Panchami/ Mansa Panchami, Magha saptami, Kali puja, Ratanti Chaturdasi (tara puja), Rekha panchami* and *Dola puja* from the Buddhist culture. Orissa continues to be an important seat of Buddhism and I need not elaborate on that part of history.

The Saivites have given us Naga panchami, Ganesh Puja, *Bhairab puja, Kedar Brata,* and *Ananta Brata*. The Oriyas have inherited festivals like *Raja, Bali Trutiya, Durga Puja, Chaitra Mangalabara* (The Tuesday worship in the month of April), *Manabasa Gurubara* (Worship of Mahalaxmi on the Thursdays of the month of *Margaseersha*), *Gaja Laxmi Puja, Basanta Panchami, Khudurukuni* and *Sabitri Amabasya*.

There are other festivals and rituals the Oriyas have imbibed into their culture from the primitive tradition. a man marrying a fruit-laden mango tree, marriage between a banyan tree and a pepul tree, between a bull and a cow, and between dogs are rituals still practised in villages. I know a commerce graduate from Berhampur who complained that his businessman father ruined the fiscal status of their family arranging several marriages between bulls and cows.

There is nothing ridiculous about such practices. Our scientific temper, notions of logic, reasoning and rationality are getting blasted everyday by the post-modern standards of living. But the senior citizens of our culture still hold on to science and industrial progress. As they are basking under the umbrella of an outdated modernity, the real purpose of the Oshas, Vratas and *Pujas* have been lost. As the newly married daughter leaves the parental home, she bows down at the *Dei Pindi*.(usually this is placed in the corner meant for the worship of the home-goddess. This symbolic goddess is kept buried and when the Hindu joint family is divided, each of the married brothers take a part of that deity or soil or the symbolic entity and that is called the *dei pindi* in folk language: *dei* is the word for Devi (godess) and the word *pindi* denotes pedestal. Under the pressures of democracy and secularism such practices are now being discontinued. Migration to cities has also cut off the Odias from their traditional roots)The modern, educated daughters, however, donot know that the dei pindi is the revised shape of the *Duma*.

Even today, a Khandayat woman in the city, while describing a large-eyed girl would say, *"Duma duma akhi"* meaning the girl has eyes like a *"duma"*. The grammatical `qualifier' used here is a straight appropriation from Primitive Culture. The *Khandayat* lady has learnt the expression from her mother or granny, who used it long back to recreate the visual experience of a *preta* (dead soul) or duma. The verbal connotation, today, because of Christian influences on us, signifies a bit of deaestheticization of the eyes of the girl.

The girls in villages observe the swing festival (*Raja festival in the month of June-raja is the word for female eggs*) either for fun or for getting themselves televised, but most of them donot know that it is a continuation of the *Dharani puja* (The worship of the soil) of the Bhuyan tibals) and the puberty ritual of the Mother Earth. Biraja Thakurani of Jajpur is widely known through out the state, but very few of the contemporaries know that she is Bi-raja (the goddess without the fertile female eggs) or she is never under the spell of any internal cyclic order of her monthly periods. In the dense forests of Mayurbhanj, there is a larger- than- life size sleeping Devi dipped in water, and she is conceived as perenially undergoing the periodic cycle. The water can be tasted. It is like sulpher .Sacrificial ceremonies are held in Jagannath Temple on the day of *Mahastami* (Two days before Dussehra). Goats are sacrificed and fish is added to the *Prasad*. This non-vegetarian *prasad* is distributed among few. At this point, Jagannatha ceases to be Srikrishna and He changes into Dakhina Kalika, a fierce Godess, so that goats can be sacrificed in the temple precinct),Are these alibis for the continuation of anti humanistic practices? Are these practices of barbarianism? What then is the game of cricket? And the other games: space- games, war-games and political games? These acts of subverting our folk culture are game strategies adopted by the advocates of the dominant "high brow" culture living within the cocoons of modernity. All mythologies are discarded antiques for them and they continue to subvert all our cosmic visions. Fatuitously, though. I will quote a line from John Sturrock's essay on Roland Barthes-specially on Sturrock's interpretation of Barthes's *Mythologies*: "The bourgeoise is the villain of mythologies" (P 62).

Our decadent bourgeoise- professors, bureaucrats, engineers and doctors- to add to the list, cyberspace exponents and corporate executives- feel threatened by our folk culture. So, the Northern Indians have introduced "*Bol Bam*" practices and "*Rakhi culture*"in Orissa to expand the parameters of homosexuality and incest. The emerging capitalists could patronise them as a gesture of spiritual entrepreneurship. But they would fail to understand the sign systems of signification implicit in our folk culture and its connotative meaning/ symbolism. In the process, these dominating culture-tycoons have corrupted the youngsters of our society making them culturally castrated and sterile. They are all senior citizens of our society and they operate as great (pseudo) scholars.

Thus, it can be discerned that a peculiar casteist and regional politics operates before religious belief systems are introduced in the society. So far, we have discussed about our tribal religions only, and Jagannatha, as a God falls under the catwgory of tribal Gods. The tribal religions are emphasised because Orissa was never influenced by the Aryans who intruded into India through the Northwest Frontiers. These outsiders from Greece and Middle-east, after defeating the Indians entered upto Pataliputra and stopped there. Except occasional attacks like those of the Nandas and Ashoka, no one touched Orissa. The outsiders called themselves the Aryans and the defeated local people worked as their slaves. These slaves were called the *Sudras*.

Orissa was called by them a country of *Vratyas* and *Mlechhas* since the Odias flouted the Aryans' norms. However, the Odissi belief system has also been influenced by the Buddhists and the Jains. The vows (*Upavasa-a woman or a man takes a vow that he or she would fast or would not take certain food and practise some folk rituals*) and these rituals still prevalent in our folk culture still remind us of those influences. The primitive people of this land worshipped trees and poles, which, later on, entered into the Buddhist culture as the *Stupas*. The notions of temple sculpture, perhaps, emerged little later.

The trees and the poles were viewed as vertical intrusions into the void of the sky. This is a spatial negotiation defined the vertical stasis. Later, they understood it as an erected penis which also looked like a *stambha* (a pole). With this began the idea of phallus-worship, i.e. Saivism. The earth as the horizontal axis exuded a 'desire' to contain the vertical for fulfilling the wishes of the mother-creator, for balancing the cycles of creation, preservation and destruction. Perhaps the idea of creation in this symbolic spatiality generated the notion of eco-feminism, which was called the *Sakta cult*. Desire, in its multiple variations, was symbolized as different Goddesses. This was realised in the micro-cosmos, too.

To sum up the belief-system of the Saivite and Sakta systems, one had to muster up courage to encounter his own mysterious layer of the unconscious and the 'Not-I' (the Other) popping up from the buried level and entropying the conscious mind where the ego fragments play the games of reasoning, rationality and empiricism.

The Buddhists appropriated this symbolic language of the unconscious into their belief system later. Hence they had to stand at the opposite pole of the Aryan/ Brahminic belief system. The Jains came later and influenced our culture. However, the Brahminic religion was revived under the influence of Shankara's *Advaita Vedanta*. The marginalised brahmins of Orissa could realise that all knowledge comes through experience and reality, which included the exteriority as well as the interiority. It could be grasped in an experiential field even without delving into abstractions.

The notions of casteist power being reasserted, the believers of the transcastiest broadness felt that they were again marginalised. At this point, Orissa came under the cultural subjugation of the Muslims. With the revision of the land revenue system and the appointment of the *mansubedars*, a new power-heirarchy was created.

A set of cultivators were given farm lands and at the time of war, they were used as fighters. In course of time, they designated themselves as Zamindars (princes) and claimed themselves as *Kshyatriyas*. There were others who computed the revenue accounts and wrote administrative letters. They were called the *Karanas*.

Thus, two new unofficial castes were created. The former are the *Khandayats* and the latter, the *Karanas*. Now being nearer to power and earlier being marginalised by the Brahminic hegemony of culture, most of those new castes preferred to establish sexual and marital contacts with the Moghuls, for ascending the ladders of power.

At this interface of religious beliefs, Orissa came under the impact of Vaishnavism. Since most of the Orissan kings were South Indians, the worship of Mayon and Napinayi as the transfigured Krishna and Radha was prevalent in Orissa. Ramanuja came to Puri in the 12th century when Chola Ganga Deva (of the Chola dynasty_1078-1147 A.D.) ruled Orissa. Then came Madhavacharya, Vishnuswamy, Sridhara Swamy and Nimbarka. Sri Chaitanya arrived in 1509 A.D. Thus, the folk religious belief-system was influenced. A host of *Santh* poets (ascetic literateurs) wrote volumes of religious poetry. This was the time of the *Pancha Sakhas*: Jagannath Dasa, Balaram Dasa, Achyutananda, Sisu Ananta and Yasovanta Dasa.

The Vaishnavites allowed a casteless society and their spiritual euphoria was a leap from the springboard of Radha and Krishna's love. The followers were mostly the Khandayats and Karanas. The Young Widows of the social system that allowed child marriages were also there.

Hence the spiritual love of Radha and Krishna dwindled into physical experience. Whether the experience induced a transcendence is a matter of guesswork, but the Brahmins commented cynically: *"Barajati, tera gola: Vaishnava hele sabu gala"* which means that one loses all sense of caste and purity if one sits under the *vaishnavite* umbrella of spiritualism. It lapsed into tantric vaishnavism and these advocates of spiritual cultivation understood everything in terms of "tilling"(a metaphor for the sexual act) metaphors. But they continued to enjoy royal patronage and stayed glued to power and to the ideals of performative success.One can still notice, how these critics of Vaishnavism (mostly Brahmins) prefer to worship Radha and Krishna. Ramakant Rath's preference for writing the modern kavya *SriRadha is* an instance.

Perhaps, the worship of Krishna became a mask of civilisation and power. It is a tradition with the people in power to put on a mask of love (Srikrisna)for subjugating others.Most of the Zamindars of Odissa and their coercive tax-collectors used to put on basil tree beads to justify their option for love(and to hide the imbedded cruelty). The practice continues since the day Emperor Ashoka declared and continued great PR-work with regard to his transformation from Chandasoka to Dharmasoka. It started in Odissa, a place where rhetorics is politics and its people are easily bullied through the mask of suave externality. This primitive way of practicing cruelty has also been officialized in the post-capitalistic notions of humanism and their agencies of funding the THIRD WORLD. The cynics of Orissa call them as strategies to camouflage THIRD degree ulterioriy of motifs.

In the heydays of Vaishnavism the Britishers ruled over Orissa with their empiricism and the Renaissance brand of Enlightenment. The Brahmins could not come closer to them since they were afraid of losing their caste by touching them. The Khandayatas and the Karanas found a space here to manoeuvre their way into the corridors of power.

Earlier, they joined hands with the Moghul chieftains and Subedars for religious iconoclasm. Now, they could easily be inspired by English language and British empiricism that suited their obsession for the gross aspects of life. The transcendent entities such as God, Freedom and Immortality were outdated knowledge for them; dumped in brahminical, conservative, congested rooms of worship. So, most of them got themselves converted into Christianity to occupy key positions of power. Secondly, they endeavoured to avenge their earlier humiliations of getting derecognised as an official caste. They were neither Kshyatriyas nor Vaisyas. Sudra was too humble a caste to accommodate these highly placed individuals, who had developed superior ego to combat the inferiority complex that corroded their inner selves. So, they stood for a kind of negative value-system called "modernity" and "scientism" that equated material possessions with illusions of power, a surrogate superiority of caste. These comfort-seekers cut themselves off from their Odia roots and somersaulted into an unknown modernity. This was so shrewd an adventure that its externality bugiled the majority of our folks,and be they inhabitants of any platform of power, swindling stays imbedded to their core nature.Ask them why they sacrifice integrity and act like thieves--they would answer: "this is the trend!"

vii. Folk Arts and Crafts:

The history of Orissan arts and crafts can be traced back to the primitive days. Verrier Elwin in his *Tribal Art: the Adivasis* (1955) writes that the tribal people used to paint the mud walls of their huts with cowdung paste and then drew some pictures with whitestone powder. He is of the opinion that these primitives learnt it from the earliest Dramil (Dravidian) tribes who settled here. The *Savaras* used turmeric and other coloured pastes with colour. Certain leaves were also pasted and powdered to bring in the effect of green colour.

There are evidences about training centres for different crafts run by non-brahmin gurus managing Coaching Centres in Gurukul style. These *sudra- munis* had started residential schools for training pupils in palm-leaf engravings, wood engravings, stone work and *dhokra* art. The courses for these crafts varied from region to region.

Terracota horses were moulded in brown clay and then kilnfired. The Santals of Mayurbhanj knew the art of nurturing silk-worms and they trained pupils in weaving and *Tassar* painting. The gurus in the jungles of Kangoda taught the craft of weaving. They used tamarind gum to join two pieces of clothes. The origin of *pata* painting can be traced back to these areas. The tribal gurus of Koraput of Bastar (The South Kosala of those days) taught the craft of making toys and lacquer-boxes decorated with threads.

Kalinga was a repository of soap stones, sand stones and serpentine stones. Lots of *Pathuria* (stone carvers) Gurus taught courses in stone carving etc. The Gurus of the coastal districts knew the craft of making toys from the crab-shells. Mahendragiri hill dwellers taught courses in making toys out of horns of different wild animals. Besides these crafts, Orissa was also famous for alchemy and brass metal works. The *Kansaris* (brass- ware/bell- metal- ware workers) of Kalinga, Kangoda and Kosala opened worksops and training centres for the production of different untensils and for the commercialization of these Engineering Schools for craft.

A Tibbetan text *(Pag-Sam-Ion-Zang)* depicting the life story of Nagarjuna records that this great scholar-saint and the originator of the Madhyamika philosophy of Budhism, learnt the art of changing any metal into gold from a wine seller's woman of Madhya Desa (Maha Kosala).

In fact, Nagarjuna acquired this knowledge of alchemy from Nalendra (Nalanda). But he found that after some years the gold tranformed again into the original metal. Hence, on his way to Pu-lo-mo-lo-ki-li, (the Chinese pronounciation for Parimala giri or the present Hari Sankar, now in Bolangir district used invariably as a picnic spot) ., he learnt this tantric art of transforming the metals into gold from the wine seller woman of Mahakosala (Extending from Raipur to Koraput).

This is a story of the 1st.Century Orissa. Nagarjuna

stayed in Pu-lo-mo-lo-ki-li for about hundred and fifty years (Does it seem to be a cock- and-bull story to you? Then please read the above Tibbetan text published in translation in a famous Historical Journal:(Ref.cited)

After this small digression to the story of Nagarjuna, let us come back to our information about the Orissan Arts and Crafts. Evidences of the primitive Saura art like wall painting, geometrical configurations (triangles used for human figures) and *'jhoti'* are found in the existing concentrated areas of the tribes in Ganjam, Sambalpur, Sundargarh, Balangir and Koraput districts. The *'jhoti'* or the *'alpana'* paintings were done on the mud-walls either with cowdung back ground or with maroon soil that acted as the canvas for their paintings.

The practices have been handed down to the common folk from the tribals and even today, our ritual spaces are painted with such primitive figures. For example, the human figure would emerge (torso and groins) with two triangles. Similarly, the feet of Goddess Mahalaxmi would be painted on the floor with triangles. The style remains unaltered today since Orissa is resistant to modernity and the womenfolk learn it from their conservative mother-in-laws who had tribal connections till the 1950s.

I have seen regular traffic of the tribals coming from the highlands to the plainlands for selling honey, beads and birds even today. An open bodied man with thousands of live scorpions running on his body can be seen in Keonjhar district (Gonasika area) even in the 21st century. Thus, the practice of the saura and other primitive paintings still survive through interactions.

Thomas E. Donaldson has conducted a study of the Jain Art of Orissa. According to his study,"Jain monuments and images are scattered through out Orissa, but the largest concentration appear in the coastal districts of Balasore, Cuttack and Puri and in the hilly tracts of Keonjhar, Koraput and Mayurbhanj districts. The earliest surviving body of sculpture appears in the form of reliefs carved on the cave walls of Udayagiri and Khandagiri which date to the reign of king Kharavela,ie.,the first century B.C.

The reliefs of Cave-1(Ranigumpha) of Udayagiri embody the most extensive series of sculptured scenes to be found in any rock-cui examples of this period anywhere in India.They are divided into 9 compartments in two stories.

There are separate rooms for placing the Gods and doing the puja in Orissan South. The floors and walls of the houses would be painted everyday. The paintings would be done by rice paste on maroon back ground. The central and the North Orissan people and the Odias of the coastal districts have shunned these habits as conservative Southernism. Most of the Khandayatas do not have a plan for a room for placing the Gods in their houses. The Gods are kept in the bed rooms and drawing rooms. Rich people paint their mosaic/ marble floors permanently and they do not need regular painting. Such gestures of drifting may be termed as perverted modernity learnt from the Bangladeshi refugees who have settled through out Orissa in large areas. Others may term it as interculturalism.

However, the habits of painting the floors continue in the Orissan countryside. Most of our women folk paint their floors during Mahalaxmi pooja irrespective of their castes. According to the temple legend, Mahalamxi had been to the hut of an untouchable woman to bless her for her cleanliness. This could be detected by Balabhadra. As Mahalaxmi returned to the temple, Balabhadra asked his younger brother Jagannath to drive his wife out from the temple since she visited an untouchable's house. Mahalaxmi was driven out and the two brothers did not get anything to eat for some years.

The author of this oral legend appears to be a great reformer at this stage. The legend has been dramatised and filmised several times after 1947. But, with the popularisation of this story, the Odia women have retained the habit of our fertility cult paintings. Their simple line drawings record the figures of pregnant women, elephants, lotuses, child and men carrying posts, bullock and cow harnessed in ploughing work and a carlf standing by, stags, sun and moon. These standardised patterns of fertility symbols combinely present a figurative expression of agricultural prosperity and fecundity in all its variations/ manifestations.

The scenario of our folk arts and crafts offers a multicultural experience. One Mr. D.N. Rao, a lecturer in fine arts in B.K. College of Arts, Bhubaneswar, has experimented with Saura motifs extensively. The Sauras of Ganjam still testify our earliest modes of primitive painting, terracota, etching plates and printing technology. The *Navagunjara* or the collage of different parts of different beasts in one figure occupies a major space in D.N. Rao's ouevre. Rao also has followed the Saura pattern in his painting, captioned *Chamunda* with collaging of single pieces of mirror onto the canvas.

The Saura art is considered to be post modern. In Bhubaneswar Cultural Festival (1997) organised by Dr. Dinanath Pathy in which I collaborated, a winter camp of painters was organised in Saura settlements of Ganjam hills called the Saura country. The artists discovered that the Sauras are our ancient most graphic artists.

In West Nilgiri of Orissa one still finds clay vessels and animal figures like fish and snakes. Dr. Dinanath Pathy writes: "Orissa possesses in its psyche four thousand years of technological experience in all kinds of traditional arts from tool to ornament making, from temple building to metal casting, from town planning to painting, from crafting to weaving. This need not go waste because of nonuse in a derogative uneducative education system going hay wire under the burden of post-capitalist notions of consumerism". (Pathy.243)

The *chitrakaras* of Puri deploy folk motifs in their *Patachitras*. The earliest traces of mural paintings found in Khandagiri and Udayagiri hills date back to the 1st Century B.C. Sir John Marshall remarks, "Many of the buildings, both rock cut and sculptural show that the paintings were in yellow, Indian red and black colour on a lime base". (Qtd. in Pathy. p.16)

Evidences of tempera painting belonging to C. 4th-5th century are found at Sitabinji in the Keonjhar district.

Dengaposi and Sitabinji, the two neighbouring villages contain a number of natural rock shelters and Ravana Chhaya painting. A detailed study has been made by Mr. T.N. Ramachandran in an illuminating essay, capitioned, *"Find of Tempera painting in Sitabinji, District Keonjhar, Orissa in Artibus Asiae Vol. XIV. 1.1.* Institute of Fine Arts, New York University. (pp.5.25). The tempera painting represents a royal figure, seated on elephant with a goal in his hand, is preceded by a batch of footmen, one horseman and a dancing woman, and followed by an attendant woman. There is a line of painted writing below the scene which gives the name of the king-Maharaja Dishabhanja.

viii. Folk Rituals

This is a difficult area to concentrate. Before I write about the folk rituals of Orissa, our elderly scholars would ask me to define what a ritual is. Our scholars since renaissance are in the habit of understanding everything in terms of definitions only. Hence a small discussion on the theory of rituals would not be considered irrelevant.

Ritology is making serious inroads into the traditional preserves of cultural studies. Most of the ritologists of our times seem to be consociates of Victor Turner. Such scholars persist in probing the cultural core of the rituals, stripping it of its derisory religious connotations. But there are lots of mosconceptions about the term ritual.

Ritual is frequently defined by a number of commentators as a substitute for routine, habit, schedule or superstitious behavious. The psychoanalytic school conflates the term with symptoms of private pathology. In a 'prediscursive' society like Orissa, we have large scale, pluralistic practices. Human species living at Bhubaneswar or Rourkella belong to a 'hyperdiscursive' society. An elderly officer, business executive or a politician visiting a guest house with a young girl is a ritual. Diving at hotel Swosti or Oberoi is a ritual. Bragging about high connections is a ritual. As we are fast advancing toward a technocratic, wealthy society, the ritual becomes a cultural artifact if not a cultural peepshow in an anthropological circus.

I do not intend to sell Odia rituals either as artifacts or as anthropological wonders. To me our rituals are ensconced in the frame work of both private and institutional life; they are embedded in the socially conditioned, historically acquired and biologically constituted rhythms and metaphors of human agency. These rituals tend to sprout anywhere men gather in groups and cultivate them as dramas of the divine. Our Odia folk rituals have come down to us from two sources: primitive practices and Aryan codes.

The primitive rituals have come down to the *Kshyatriyas*, the Vaisyas and the Sudras where as the Aryan codes are followed by the Brahmins. However, Orissa being a Vratya country (those who flout vedic codes) certain rituals are common to all castes. For example, *raja samkranti* and *Budhei Osha* rituals are popular among the *Sudras*, while *Janmastami* and *Dola poornima* are Brahminical in nature.

The birth rituals, marriage rituals, survival rituals and death rituals vary from caste to caste. However, the Europeans have been successful in teaching us that these are "blind beliefs" and `superstitions'. Thus, they have been able to wipe our culture out through colonialism. Lurking around the edges of the anti-ritual arguments posed by the scholarly *gloseur* is a penumbera of doubt in the efficacy- or even in the existene of rituals in a post traditional, post-modern world. In some scientific circles rituals are overwhelmingly regarded as existing only in putatively diminished, debilitated or denatured forms, denuded of their presymbolic plenitude; they are regarded as innocuous, part of a bygone era-left overs perhaps from mythical cauldrons, 84 *narkas* (hells) or like the venom of the hidden snake of the garland of Pitei Savaruni (a *foldtale* witch). Such dombis, (low caste sorceresses emitting fire from the mouth in our 9-10th century *Charyapada* literature) are neither remembered as our earliest heroines nor as practitioners of our primitive rituals.

But our estrangement from these rituals is a discontinuity in the Odia cultural flow. It is difficult to revive them under the pressures of globalization of culture. The Sauras living in Anda Anda village are found putting on bermudas and teashirts bought from Tumba weekly market. However, we can still treat these rituals emancipating them from the strait-jacket of sacred/ symbolic versus practical/ profane/ instrumental categories.

The Odia folk rituals can be classified into four safe categories: (a) Birth rituals (b) marriage rituals (c) death rituals and (d) fertility rituals. These rituals also vary from caste to caste. The Brahmins call them *samskaras* which according to St. Gautama are 40 in number. But the principal birth rituals are 16 in number. Halayudha, the ancient Rishi enumerates only ten. Others have added two more.

i) *Garbhadhana* (also called *Chaturthikarma*) is the ceremony to be performed at the union of a married couple after the cessation of the menstrual flow of the wife in order to ensure conception.

ii) *Pumsavana* is the ritual observed in the third month from conception when the throbbing of the foetus is felt.

iii) *Simantonnayana*, according to *Smruti Tattva* of Raghunandana is the parting of the hair of a woman either in the fourth month or in the sixth month or the eighth month.

iv) *Soshyanti Homa* is an addition to Halayudha's ten birth rituals. (Hence the total number is 12). This ritual is observed when the labour pain of a woman is felt.

v) *Jatakarma*. This rite is performed when the child is born and the naval string is cut as under, with a view to ensuring his intelligence and longevity.

vi) *Namakarana*, according to Gobhila's *Gruhyasutra*, is performed either after 10/11 nights from birth, or after the expiry of 100 nights from birth or after the lapse of one year. It varies from home to home depending on other conveniencs/ inconveniences in the family.

vii) *Nishkramana* is a rite in which the child is taken out of home on the third day of the bright fortnight in the third month of the birth of the child. The rite is accompanied by some incantations.

viii) *Annaprasana,* according to *Gruhyasutra,* has to be performed either in the fifth month (in case of a male child) or in the seventh month (in case of a girl child). The child has to be adorned with ornaments and given cooked rice for the first time.

ix) *Chudakarana* is the ceremony of tonsure of the cutting of hair for the first time, which is performed in the first, third or fifth year from the birth o the child. An *audumbara kshyura* (a rajor made of copper) is recommended for the ritual. The hair is to be shaved in the premises of *Kuladevi* (the Goddess of the family) and the cut-off hair is to be placed in bull's dung and buried in the forest. Bhavadeva prescribes *Karnaveda* or the piercing of the ears of the child with this rite.

x) *Upanayana:* All the castes had to perform this ritual with small variations. Different periods had been prescribed for different castes.

(a) Brahmana: 8th year from conception in mother's womb.

(b) Kshyatriya: 11 years from conception

(c) Vaisya: 12 years from conception.

These days the *sudras* do not observer the *Upanayana* ceremany.

ix) *Samavartana* is alternatively called *snana* and *aplavana* in some of the *Gruhyasutras*. This rite had significance in ancient times when a student returned home after actually living for a prescribed period in the house of the perceptor. The boy performs a ceremonial ablution in the prescribed manner and feeds Brahmin.

xii) *Vivaha* is a liberal ritual which can be performed at anytime. The ritual commences with *Nandimukha Sraddha* performed by the father. The ceremony brings with the entrance into the compound, of the bride groom bathed with fragrant unguents.

Since I am referring only to the Brahminical texts, some contemporary advocates of casteist politics would argue that the birth rituals narrated above are elitist in nature. These rituals are also performed in the primitive communities with slight modification in our folk society.

Births in primitive as well as in folk culture are community events. The mother is kept confined to a room either for 21 days or for 30 days under warm condition. A large log of wood is burnt and he Bhagavata is read. Such a reading would enlighten the mother about the metaphysics of carrying the foetus in the womb and then delivering it. There are birth songs also in some primitive communities. (At this stage of my unfunded research, I am not able to collect those songs). On the twentyfirst day, usually, the mother is allowed to enter into the kitchen since the food that has to be cooked everyday has to be offered to the household deity. The household Goddess would not accept the food cooked by a woman who has given birth to a child recently.

On the fifth day of the birth, called *Panchuati*, the old women of the family and the community would collect five varieties of cereals (greegram, black gram, peanuts etc.) roast them on an earthen pot with sand (they would put some sand on our earthern pot and place it on the *Chuli*, the primitive (the elevated part of the oven on which the utensil would be kept) oven with three *inda-s*.The three *inda-s* represent the trinity of fire Gods. Everyday, the *inda-s* are to be plastered with red-clay as a purificatory ritual. The cereals are to be recasted dry with the hot sand. The roasted ceareals are to be offered to *Sathi Thakurani* "(the Goddess connected with the 6th day)" who emerges on the household of the new-born child for its protection. She is iconised as a symbolic betel nut in many families. Others put the grinder of the curry stone and wrap it with red, yellow or black clothes to worship it. The grinder that looks like a phallus takes the form of symbolic Siva and the curry stone turn into a symbolic vagina, the Sakti. The act of grinding is perhaps, a handy tribal image for the sexual act or the act of procreation. The twentyfirst day is celebrated as the "name giving" day, (*Ekoisa*: I make a literary translation to bring home the folk effect) for the new born. The same grinder and the curry-stone are used again as someone reads a chapter from *Bhagavata*. My grand mother, who was able to read *Puranas*, used to read when my younger brothers were born. In some other families the grandmothers used to name the children after the popular Gods. But those who did not worship a God named them according to the ays of the week on which they were born, e.g. *Mangalabaria* (Born on Tuesday), *Gurubaria/ Gurubari* (a female child born on a Thursday etc.) Naming a child after a day is a tradition carried over from the tribal rituals.

Our folk concept of life is full of ritualistic vibrations: never had it had an iota of cynicism. The Oriyas love life as their primitive forefathers loved nature. A blossoming flower whistles at them and invites them into the orbit of fragrance, which is life. This primitive tribal song defines life as follows:

Man's life is for two days
Let's, therefore laugh and play
Hey, my dear!
This life won't be available to us again!
When the earthen pot breaks
At the potter's place
It does not come again to him
Doesn't return.
Hey, my dear!
This life won't come back again.

Life for our folks has, very often, also been metaphorised as a tree. In the absence of love and affection it looks like an excoriated tree.

What I notice in the birth rituals is a fire place and some fire-burnt-offerings, the log of burning wood, the roasted cereals and the oven with three inda-s and the grind stone images. The fire is related to sun (Worship of sun is a major ritual in the primitive tribes), to cooking and purification and also to the womb that moulds a form out of liquid matter.

Death rituals are also communal. The members of the entire community praticipate in this consolatory process. Dead Children are buried and the adult bodies are burnt. The rituals of the funeral differ from caste to caste. Higher castes perform the ritual for twelve days and the lower castes minimize them. A continuously burning wick-lamp as a symbol of the dead soul occupies the central position in the funeral rites.

The rituals concerning marriage are most interesting in certain tribal communities. But the kinds of marriage that take place in different tribes can be classified into four categories.

i) The parents select a bride for the son. In *Munda* community the guardians take a decision and the sons and daughters are bound to obey. (ii) But in *Kolha* and *Juang* tribes the son would select the bride and communicate his intention to the parents, who in turn would mediate with the daughter's father. In *Sabara* and *Bonda* communities the son would himself propose with the help of his friends. *Koya, Oram, Kondh, Ganda, Bhuyan, Munda, Bhatara, Paraja* and *Santalas* believe in community marriages. (iii) However in Paraja, Kondh, Oram, Gadaba, Kolha, Juang and Kharia tribal communities there are instances of kidnapping (*Kania jhika, apara tipi* and *jika*). The Orams go to the village of the daughter with weapons and a mock-war takes place before the girl is taken away forcibly. But in *Kondh* communities, the girl is kidnapped from the community dance. The *Gadabas* kidnap a girl from the Uncle's family. This practice has been appropriated by nontribal communities also in South Orissa. (iv) Some other marriages can be termed as love marriages also. In such cases the pair would disappear from the community and get married. The *lithulia* of the Gadabas, *Manamani* of the Juangs, *Rajikhusi* of the Kolhas and *Dhara-pala* of the Bhuyans are instances of such love marriages.

In certain tribal communities like *Sabara, Oram* and *Bhatara,* instances of pre-puberty marriages are also observed. The girl is married to an arrow. The arrow would be tied to her hand. In all most all the tribal communities' widow-marriages are in vogue. However, the husbands have to pay money for that. Divorces are also allowed.

Such marriages include some interesting rituals. (a) The husband and wife feed each other from the meals served on their leaves (*Juang*) (b) The husband would stand on a yoke and the wife on a *ghorana* or a grinding stone (*kharia* tribe) (c) To put marks on the cheeks of the couple in burnt rice. (d) The groom would wash his head and the bride would drench her hair with that drained out water (*Koya* tribe) (e) To feed the couple with rice cooked by an unmarried girl (*Gadaba*) (f) The couple exchange their wine from each other's vessel (*Kolha*) (g) The wife puts vermilion in the parting of the hair of the husband and the husband does so (*Oram, Munda, Lodha* and *Santals*) (h) The husband lifts the wife and jumps over the three lines drawn (*Binjhal*) (i) The bridegroom inserts a ring into the bride's finger (*Gond*) (j) The groom and the bride would take two and half rounds around the *Poorna Kumbha* (the water filled ritual pot)on the marriage pedestal and then the *hatha-ganthi* (thread is tied up) (*Sabara*) (k) The bridegroom inserts a *khadu* (thick metal bracelet) on the wrist and the bride touches a hot pin on the bridegroom's chest (*Bonda*) (l) The bride and the bridegroom exchange crowns (*Bhatara*) (m) The bride and bridegroom eat from the same leaf (*Santal*).

These marriage rituals are fast changing under the pressures of modernisation and the migration of the tribals to industrial belts as labourers. However, these rituals have influenced our folk life immensely and most of the non-brahmin folk still perform some of these rituals.

ix. Folk Customs:

Customs in Oriya regional culture are called a *chara*. Folk customs are divided into three categories (a) *Desa-achara* or customs varying according to *desa* or country or geographical conditions. (b) *Kula-achara* or customs changing from family to family and (c) Customs changing from folks to folks or from community to community.

What we mean by Orissa is a mixture of three countries Kalinga, Kosala and Utkala, certain customs prevalent in Kalinga are not available in *Koshali* culture. For instance, the *Raja* Festival is observed in Utkala as a swing festival. The customs differ in South Orissa where they term it as *Vu-raja-swala utsav*. It is observed as the symbolic cyclic period of the mother earth. Since the mother earth is in her periods, no woman is allowed to cut vegetables, to grind anything on the stone grinder (a phallic symbol) and to put or pierce any iron equipment on the earth.

The *Nua Khai Parab* (the festival of cooking newly harvested rice) is still observed in Western Orissa as a community festival. But the North and South Orissan folk do not observe it as rigorously as the western Orissan people do. *Nuakhai* literally means to eat the rice of the first hervest. A particular day is fixed in the Western Orissa and the community celebrates it. The festival is also observed in the North and South as *Navanna*, but in a Brahminic order, either on the day of Dussehra or on some otherday that suits the astrological chart, of the worshipper Goddess Mahalaxmi is worshipped on that day. The cooked rice and the sweet porridge, after being offered to the Goddess is eaten in the family. The water for clearing the hand and washing the mouth is not thrown here and there. Generally, they wash their hands in a bucket and throw the water in river.

Savitri Amabasya in the month of May-June according to the alamanac is observed differently according to regional variations. This is a typical folk-custom, festival and ritual of Orissa and perhaps in no other state this is observed.

On this day, the family members of the daughter-in-law's home come with *puja* material for the worship. This establishes a link between the families tied up in marital bond. Coconuts, bananas, dates, jack fruits, mango, apples, guava, orange, promegranates, shaddoks, palm fruits and lemon etc are sent through a barbar. Besides, the parents of the married daughter also send a new *sari*, bangles, a casket of vermilion, a bottle of lack-dye, a mirror, a comb and a case of collyrium. All these materials symbolise auspeciousness for the married girl who wishes for the long life of her husband the parent's gifts symbolically suggest that she would use her vermilion and bangles as long as she is alive. To die before the husband's death is a '*soubhagya*' (good fortune) for the Oriya woman. Hence, she fasts for the entire day and after the *pooja*, she is given to eat the fruits. Besides, she wets green grams and get them sprouted the sprouted green grams are mixed with sugar, coconut powder, mango and jack fruits and are given to eat as a sacred ritualistic dish.

The custom with regard to the celebration of these vows and festivals vary from region to region. Hence they are called *Desachara*. But *Kaulachara* or the customs of the families also play an important role. In certain families the making of astrological charts are restricted. Families do not observe certain vows if there are not auspecious for the family. In some brahmin families *dussehra* is celebrated with symbolic sacrifices. A ridge gourd would be kept with four small sticks inserted into it. It would look like a goat. After the Puja, the gourd would be cut, representing the symbolic sacrific. But in some other families real animals would be sacrificed. This has nothing to do with the cry of the contemporary animal sympathisers. Most of them are human-haters, awefully rich and cruel and the sympathy for the animals is like putting on an animal mask.

The same *kaulachara* variations may be observed with regard to the *Sraddha* ceremony or the annual death ritual of the dead parents. In most of the Brahmin families of the South, the *Pinda patra* food (the banana leaf on which the food offerings are given) will be cooked with great austerity and with sacred intentions. But in most of the brahmin families of Puri, who claim to be of the highest order, fish is also cooked. This might also be a *tantric kaulachara*. However, I have asked them several times about the authenticity of this practice and instead of providing me with any *sastriya* answer, they have snobbed me out.

In some of the families, an arrow is kept on a winnowing fan and it is carried to seven homes by a woman from barbar's family. In some of the pre-puberty marriages of the tribals an arrow is tied up with the girl's hand. It is suspected that this *kaulachara* custom of using the symbol of an arrow in marriages has been appropriated from the tribal tradition. Similarly, the customs with regard to birth vary from family to family. A mother who has delivered a new born is kept away from the kitchen for thirteen days, twenty one days or thirty one days according to the individual family custom. In stead of reading Bhagabata the new born is dedicated to an untouchable family for its nurturing. The untouchables become its parents for all practical purposes. The child is also named 'Chamara', Hadi, Bauri etc. This saves the child from premature death.

Community customs (*lokachara*) identify the Oriya culture more distinctly than any other custom. The vermilion mark on the centre of the two eye-brows is the custom of the Oriyas. In some communities the women puts lots of vermilion on the parting of the hair. Another community custom is that the wife of the younger brother in a joint family would not even touch the tangents of the shadow of the elders brother of the husband. As a reverse, in Bengli films one finds them talking emotively and touching each other.

The Oriya food habits also lend an identity to its culture. Nowhere in India the typical Oriya food would be found. A food-lover Brahmin's sloka can be cited here:

Kharada barada loke beswaro vyanjaneswarah
Amala, Bimala Kantih Kanjika Panjikayushah.

In stead of explaining to sloka, I would only denote the items.

a) *Kharada* is *saga-kharada* in Oriya. Different spinaches are cooked differently.

b) *Beswara* is a mixed vegetable curry-boiled and spiced. Dr.E.Raja Rao in his essay, *Telugu diaspora in Orissa* mentions that this curry had been introduced in Jagannath temple by the Telugu kings who ruled Orissa and built the temple. They brought their own cooks and introduced *Beswara*. Oriya culinary culture has another variation. They put fish or boiled mutton into it to make a non-veg *mahura*.

c) *Kanji* : The residual water of the rice is seived and kept in a large pot for two/three days allowing it to get fermented. Then large pieces of brinjal, radish, pumpkin, papaya, yam, ladies finger, arum and the pith of the plantain tree are boiled in it. Turmeric would be added. At the end, mustard, garlic, chilli, coriander, ani-seed and asofoetida are fried popped in oil and put in it. However, there are different variations to this preparation. In Western Orissa, a feast without *Kanji* is incomplete.

d) *Amala/Ambila:* In South Orissan feasts and family *Pooja*-s including *Sraddha* ceremony, *ambila* constitutes a major food item. The vegetables mentioned for *kanji* are used also in *ambila*. But the fermented rice-water is not used. The vegetables are boiled in plain water, but tamarind and treacle would be added. At the end ani-sed, chilli etc would be fried popped with oil or ghee and added.

These food items can be preserved for some days without the use of a Frigidaire. In many of the South Orissan community feasts fish (mostly sea-fish which is cheaper) is fried and added to *Ambila*. They call it *Machha-ambila*. Another variation to *ambila* is *sakera* in which the quantity of tamarind would be reduced and the proportion of treacle would be more to sweeten the item. This curry would be dry after being boiled with no soup. The South Orissan folk add fried fish and boiled mutton to prepare and preserve non-veg *Sakera.* This dish seems to have originated from the community of fishermen of South Orissa/Andhra Pradesh. In ancient days when there was no frigidire for preserving food, this classical dish of Kalinga prepared with tamarind and treacle could be preserved for four/five days.

The north, western, southern and central Orissan folk use *saga* (spinach) and *pakhal* (watered rice). But *pakhal* is used also in Western and Southern regions of Orissa.

x. Folk Festivals:

Festivals signify a lot about a particular culture. The festivals of Orissa owe their origin to two sources- the tribal source, and the Vedic source. As a Vratya country, it was notorious for flouting the norms set by the intellectuals of the Ganges valley, the Aryans. The tribal people of this geographical unit always hated the Aryans as intruders into their native culture. Their language (Sanskrit), their socio-ethical codes, their ideas of heaven and hell appeared to them as immature and alien. The language and the culture of the Gonds was much anterior to those of the Aryans. This Dravidian group of people speaking a corrupted form of Tamil rejected Sanskrit.

However, the *Vratya Khanda* of *Atharva Veda* and the Vratya hymns have engaged the attention of many scholars in this region. *Vrata*, from which the term *Vratya* has been derived, is a vow taken by the individuals in this region to observe particular paraphernalia of worshipping a particular God who is not a part of the Vedic system. *Vrata* also means a group of non-aryan, non-brahminic group of people gathering in a festival for community worship followed by revelry and entertainment programs. The *Vratas* and the Oshas observed in Orissa are directly connected to the tribal communities and the Vedic people have mentioned about such festivities as *Gana Jajna* (Mass fire sacrifice). But actually there would be no fire and no sacrifice except staying without food for the day and observing certain codes of conduct related to the worship which is not Vedic. These *Vratas* and the *Oshas* are mostly observed by the female folk.Most of the festivals of Orissa are observed according to the indigenous *smriti sastras* written by diaspora Brahmins from Kanyakubja. These *Sastras* include Satananda's *Ratnamala* and *Satananda Samgraha* of eleventh century, *Krutya Kaumudi* of Brihaspati (14th century), Divyasingha Mohapatra's *Kala Deepa* (17th century) *Kala Nirnaya* of Raghunath Das (17th cent), Krishna Mishra's *Kala sarbaswam*, Gadadhara Acharya's *smriti* volumes (18th century), Upamanyu's *Panchapuja Vidhi* and anonymous/ authorless reprints of *Vrata Katha, Bibhinna Vrata Katha, Bibhinna Vrata Prakaranam* that describe the rules for observing festivals like *Ratha Jatra, Gundicha Jatra, Dola Jatra, Dadhi Jatra, Magha Saptami, Vajra Mahakali Puja, Lalita Saptami, Saptapurika Amavasya, Prathamastami, Rama Navami, Pravarana Sasthi, Savitri Vrata, Aparajita Dasami, Sri Panchami,*

Chhada Khai, Akshaya Trutiya, Kumara Purnima, Raja Samkranti etc.

The Vedic people do not observe/admit these *vratas*, but the Orissan folks do. Hence the Odias are Vratyas. Such a cultural gestalt can be referred back to our tribal roots. The people of Kalinga and Odra had a very advanced civilization much before the Aryan nomads came and settled in Indus Valley. They did not like the interference of these aliens in matters of culture. Kalinga was a flourishing kingdom much before the war of Mahabharata (1000-900B.C.) and our tribal kings did care little for the Indus Valley norms. Srutayudha was the king of Kalinga who joined the Kurukshetra war to fight for Duryodhana and he was slain by Bhima. The king of Udra Desa fought on the side of the Pandavas. Our historical studies inform us about king Sattabhu and Karakandu of Kalinga (9th and 8th. centuryB.C.) as friends of King Nemi and the Jain priest Parswanatha. Assaka Kalinga war was fought by Kaaling-II in 7th century B.C. King Brahmadutta fought a war in the 5th.cent B.C (Das Raicharan, P 4). The supremacy of Kalinga continued till fourth century B.C.till Mahapadma Nanda of Pataliputra defeated us. The *Puranas*, which are the only source of history, record 32 kings in Kalinga from the war of *Mahabharata* to the time of Mahapadma Nanda. But the colonial historians of Orissa did not admit these accounts given by the *Puranas*. They were trained by the imperialists who admitted only evidences and tried to prove that Christanity was the earliest record of history, and if there was anything earlier, it was the account of Meghasthenes. Under such wrong pressures the history of Orissa has been under mentioned and underemphacized. The Aryan Historians who knew nothing about Kalinga and Odra have totally bypassed Odisa and this has resulted in political- cultural marginalization. This author does not understand as to why the bright pages of this land's historical past be consigned to a dark corner because of an Imperial historian's sheer ignorance? It is like the UPA Ministry at the centre that has left Odisa unrepresented in a federal government. There is not a single minister from this state in 2004.The people of Odisa too doubt whether they actually belong to India, the land dominated by the Aryan Diaspora.

The people in the Suktimati valley (around c.1000B.C) had business transactions with the people of the 'naga country' or, the places where the kings of the Naga Dynasties ruled (South Indian countries). They refused to keep up links with the North. Such a tradition continued in this geographical region till the third century A.D., the time of the Guptas and the early Gangas, with whose invasions blew the wind of the Sanskrit culture. The festivals introduced after that in this Vratya land seem to have sprung from the *Prithvi Sukta* of *Atharva Veda* that imbeds as well as discusses the cultural plurality of this vast land. The *Papamochana Sukta* (the verse that is written for the expiation of sins) invokes around hundred deities for deliverance from distress. Innumerable *Gramadevatas* are invoked for treatment of diseases (a god or a goddess for the village who protects from diseases. The champions of science and, especially, the NRIs should note without a grin that even today epidemics are controlled by worshipping a goddess called Sitala. Small Pox and horpis joster are controlled by tantric puja. Hundreds of patients suffering from jaundice and rejected by the doctors of Bhubaneswar hospital go to the Baba of Barmunda, (unit VIII).This author has field-tested and witnessed this phenomenon in 2004 with extensive tours over the mountainous tracks and over the village sector for collecting data about this study.Each of the villages are found to have a godess called a Gramadevati (a village godess) with a peculiar name.

These few hundreds of Godesses and Gramadevis use to meet in huge gatherings called *Mela*. The gathering becomes a festival. The concept of *Mela* is gradually fading out since community life is getting destroyed and following the American pattern of individualism, Orissan joint-families have already been disintegrated. The selfish careerists and migrants to the metros consider such *melas* as wastage of social and fiscal energy . Gods/Godesses are irrelevant to them. But the *mela* was conceived as a *Vratya* parallel of a Vedic *jajna*. Those that could not avail of the opportunity of attending/participating in a jajna, did arrange such congregation of gods and goddesses. This is inherited from the tribal communities. Such *mela* festivals are mentioned with a prefix *"Maha"*(great) as they call it Maha Siva Ratri and Maha Vishuva Samkranti.

The *Kausika Sutra* of *Atharva Veda* and its *Parisista* (appendix) mention about a lot of *Maha* festivals.The common gathering and the common worship at a particular time sanctioned in the almanac

Folk festivals are mostly religious and connected with folk-rituals; customs and folk religious culture.Festivals indicate the communal mode of worship. All melas possess an element of worship and all communal worships have tended to assume the form of festivals. A festival in Odisa may include a *puja* or a *vrata.*A *Vrata* is an individual vow to worship for achieving some results, for fulfillment of small wishes like eradicating a particular skin disease, or for getting a male child. Some of the *Oshas/Vratas* (vows) take a communal form and like Khudurukuni osha, it takes the form of a festival. Similarly, a Ganesh Puja in the communal mode performed in the school also takes the form of a festival. It is a public festival at Jatni and Puri. Ganesh Puja Utsav includes big gatherings and entertainment programs. Thus, a festival encompasses ritualistic elements like *puja* and *vrata* along with song, drama, dance and other folk enactments. The participants are mostly from the agricultural class and from other productive sections of the society. These communal festivals are directly inherited from the tribal living styles. Yet these festivals depend on historical developments and embody revisions from time to time keeping in tune with the evolution of the societal norms and public taste.

It need not be reiterated here that the Oriya culture is an admixture of the Aryan, Dravidian and the proto Austroloid cultures. *Baudhayana* and *Dharmasutra* depicted the Kalingans of the 6th. Century B.C. as *Mlechhas* and Meghasthenes and

Pliny mentioned about the *suaris*(sauras) of *Oretes* (Odra) and mount *Maleus*(Malayagiri of Pallahara in Dhenkanal district) The ancient kingdoms of Vindhyatabi,Mahakantara, Kurala, Kosala and Atavika are traceable to tribal origins.Even the Bhanjas who were born of the peacock eggs were of tribal origin.

As a cultural entity, our belief-system admits certain Gods. But the Oriyas, perhaps, do not think God to be placed on a divine pedestal like it is done by the Aryans. The Oriya God that is politically central to their culture is Lord Jagannath. This God is not made of stone or metal. It is a God made of wood and his icons are renewed every 12 years during *Nava Kalevara* festival. The New Delhi politicians place themselves on a higher cultural pedestal considering themselves as Aryans with hazy notions of casteist/ regional superiority. A minister of culture seems to have abandoned his accomplishments in education (and, therefore in culture, too) and has preferred to join the power-game of politics to commodify our national culture in terms of "cultural grants" so that grants for investigation into our culture would be treated like ration for the prisoner. At one time, the Odias had to fight a great battle for beaming the car festival on television.

I was a live commentator for the car festival for four years in English language. My co-compeers who came from Delhi Doordarshan were found to be totally ignorant of the festival. Yet, they beamed it for India and abroad like tribal development educators, who themselves are Aryans. What I mean to suggest here is that because of our tribal contours, Oriya culture seems to them as something insignificant. Odias, as I wrote before, do not admit Gods as superior aliens of some extraterresrial world. They do not care much about power-games of culture.

Their main God Jagannath is embraced as a friend, as a relative who has come to him from a distant space. In fact, the Oriyas embrace a guest who has come from another village. Jagannath is also hugged. A devotee sings:

Asithili Kalia to darasana painre
Tote chhadi jibaku mo mana balu nahinre
[Aye, Kalia! (The Black one!=refers to Jagannatha) I had come for your *darshana(to pay my homage)*.And I don't feel like leaving you!]

This song of the devotee addressing the God as *tu* (as one would address a childhood friend) treats him most affectionately. In stead of falling at his feet, he hugs him with *sakha-bhava* (friendly emotion). Some traditional *Aryan* devotees might take such a culture with a pinch of salt. But as I understand, the *mudras* or getures of devotion, too, vary according to the variations of culture.

A culture in which the folks prefer to nurture the ethics of servility would prostrate. But the Oriyas with all their tribal humility and unassertive demeanour would never prefer to bow down for a small personal gain, be it audacity or a disqualification in the contemporary ground of corporate battles. To stand as upright as a *sal* tree in the inaccessible woods connotes some dignity, though it does not bring a short-spanned success.

As we talk about the big gatherings like melas (festivals), we may take the example of community feasts in the villages which also constitute a part of such festivals. These community feasts in the countryside of contemporary Orissa may be compared with the 'internal ecology' of man. The common reader is likely to be intrigued whether I am talking about 'culture' authentically, or I am politicising with my own personal prejudices with regard to acculturation of western 'buffet' feasts at the cost of our 'community' 'cultural' dinner The notion of a buffet, on the other hand, is a cultural contamination from the civilized cities and it has taken away the participatory pleasures of the folk culture. However, the phenomenon of hybridization can be described in three distinct ways:

a) ***Moving towards city culture:*** The contemporary man within the folk culture is inspired by the development programmes precipitated through media and he changes his traditional notions of culture. As a result he not only accepts his own estrangement from his native culture but the everyday realities pester him so intensely that an unknown fear haunts him all through and in his attempt to attain security and to carve out an identity for himself, he tries to win the affection of others and lean on them either politically, or economically to such an extent that his cultural existence is affected.

b) *Moving away from city and folk culture:* Certain folks, in their confusion, do not feel adequate either to belong to their native culture that has been corrupted, or to resist the existing norms. In this indecissiveness they feel safer to keep themselves apart from the rapid changes that occur in their culture. This leads them to isolation that ultimately disrupts their psychic stability. The disruption, in certain cases, creates a cultural schizophrenia.

c) *Moving against City Culture:* This is a strong tendency of resistance that can lead to hostility. These people accept and take for granted the hostility around them and they are determined to fight against them. Even the bus that plies through their route creates feelings of hostility against the city from which the bus started its journey. At times, the jeep of the bureaucrats entering into their village also generates an ambience of hostility. In the process, the friendly folks who join the bandwagon of modernity also seem repulsive to them.

The psychological symptoms narrated above with regard to cultural contamination affects the roots of Orissa. Terms like civilization and culture are used here synonymously basing on Edward B. Tylor's book on primitive culture (vol.1). Tylor writes, "Culture or civilization, taken in its wide ethnographic sense, is that complex whole which includes knowledge, belief, art, morals, law, custom and many other capabilities and habits acquired by man as a member of society. The condition of culture among the various societies of mankind, in so far as it is capable of being investigated on general principles, is a subject apt for the study of laws of human thought and action. On the one hand, the uniformity which so largely pervades civilization may be ascribed, in great measure, to the uniform action of uniform cause; while on the other hand, its various grades may be regarded as stages of development or evolution, the outcome of previous history, and about to do it, proper part in shaping the history of the fate (p.1-6)

Other writers who have differentiated between civilization and culture have offered some more interesting arguments. C.E.M. Joad, for example, talks about possesstion of technocratic materials as a symptom of civilization. In a modern society man's maniac pursuit for materiality lends him some identity and prestige. Joad explains that possessing a colour T.V. may be a civilized symptom, but to know its mechanisms and technical breed would justify the culture of the possessor. One may turn art into artifact and declare oneself as a member of modern civilization.

The "fried rice- chiken curry" syndrome may lend the neo-capitalist in the countryside a sense of modernity. An I.A. S.Officer, an industrialist publishing a book of poems may feel modern and feel flattered. A senior citizen in the city may eat `chicken pakoda' on a Monday (Lord Siva's day) and on beig asked as to why he flouted an Odia religious custom, he would reply that eating does not have any relation with spirituality in the modern sense. That is where modernity cuts one from his cultural-spiritual roots to end up in a den of final unrelatedness.A woman visiting a temple during her periods may declare herself modern. But such modernists are necessarily not cultured people. However, the people, who suffer from inferiority complex, very often regard emancipation from tradition as modernity.

Oriya festival donot carry any significance for them. They are neither the tribal Vratyas, nor are they admitted into the Aryan society. The local people call them "phoreners". But these "moderns" declare themselves as civilized bipeds. Is culture, then, an opposite of civilization?

This polarity between culture and civilization boils down to a dialectical relaionship between tradition and modernity which heavily affects the culture of festivals.. It is nothing less than a hiatus between theory and practice.

The cultural practices in contempoary Orissa offer most interesting examples. A young girl studying postgraduate courses in English literature is surprised to find her senior teachers talking about "blasphemous" subjects like astrology and planetary influences on ordinary mortals. Such a girl might deliver a somber lecture on platonic love and get indulged intensely in haterosexual activities. The body is so important to her that astrology, that imposes sexual discipline is rejected as 'Victorian' (pre modern, outdated). Her mother, aged about 40-45 in 2005/7 would be seen in the evenings blowing a conch shell in front of the hanging calender of Srikrishna or Hanuman. She might light the costliest incense sticks putting on a Benarasi Sari, but she might have been equipped with a "stay free" at that moment (running her periods). Our mela festivals may be of vratya origin, but they do not allow a woman in her periods to blow a conch shell before a god, or to conduct any spiritual activity in the *vratas* or the *oshas* (vows). The ancient man who formulated this law was extremely modern and perhaps, he was a futurist too. He knew why the woman folk should not enter into the kitchen (that is a spiritual space, too in the *Chhandogya Upanishad*) and engage themselves in spiritual activities during their periods. By flouting the norm under the influence of the Westerners, they gain nothing. Neither can they find themselves liberated nor modern. That would be a cultural stupidity whether they like that or not. That's a psychological issue, however, bringing them a compulsive pleasure by flouting the norms.

I have attempted to show how 'theory' and 'practice' interplay like tradition and modernity in our confused culture. Terry Eagleton has written a wonderful essay "Capitalism, modernism and postmodernism" on this subject. Let me quote:

"For if practice is defined in neo-Nietzchean style as spontaneous error, productive blindness and historical amnesia, then theory can of course be no more than a jaded reflection upon it ultimate impossibility." (p.390)

This English-*sloka* of Terry Eagleton need not be accepted unmeditatively though under the existing practices of our culture all quotations are applied in civilized discourses as unalterable truths. Eagleton's realization that hinging on theories would lead to no practical ends is itself a "sponataneous error" and a "productive blindness". The cultural practices in a highly materialistic society with `commodity-fetish' is also considered civilized, but such civilized possessions do not signify culture. The modern bike dashing off on the Paradeep road at midnight generates suspecions about waylaying or theft, not an idea about modern culture.

The analysts of Western culture have been emphacising "performative entreprises" as water-marks of success. This action oriented performance" takes various forms in our contemporary Oriya Culture. The third-raters of the 1960s and 1970s are now the most successful parents of the children studying in postgraduate classes. They have enticed the examiners with lots of money and political favour and bought "first class" for idiotic children, who, in turn, investigate into the possibility of finding a `short cut' to success through `possessing' a first-class by `any' means- as a symbol of performative authenticity. These actions come under cultural `practices' standing in opposition to fatuitous theories, theories that can be used only as instruments for deployment in performances.

Politicians of Orissa and some bureaucrates in power are driving the youth toward another cultural obfuscation- by naming some such actions as "positive" and others as "cynical". Such binary oppositions should be guarded against. The option for "affimative" action or "positive" action should not be a license for radical politics in which ministers and bureaucrats attempt to procure girls from ladies hostels of posh colleges of Orissa for exterorizing some of their repressed fantasies. But in verbal performance they would deliver a high order morality. This Nietzchean brand of deconstructive modernity has been commented upon by Egleton: "The Marxism of Louis Althusser comes close to this Nietzcheanism: practice is an imaginary affair which thrives upon the repression of truly theoretical understanding, theory a reflection upon the necessary fictionality of such action." (P.390-391)

The Marxists of different generations in post-colonial Orissa have tried to shape Oriya culture with another form of modernity. The Oriya modern culturist who endeavours to dominate the scene with their techno-scientific possessions, belong to the capitalist class. Since they achieve the power of money through insidious performative strategies, they are *sui generis* in nature. Their brand of modernity in culture, therefore, does not acknowledge a history and a tradition. Marxism, on the other hand, deployed the same scientific mode of interpreting society in terms of the 'haves' of the commodity culture and the 'have nots' who failed to succeed in the competitive game of acquisition. The capitalists believed in the concept of dehistoricization because it suited their status of the *sui generis*. They politicize theory and in the process, all essences. Their glamour-crazy children,too, reject everything "essential" since essences do not seem to them as escalators to lead them to a shopping mall, where they can buy fantasies with the stinking money of their parents.

As a result, a *Ganesh Puja* or *Dussehra* can be a commercial project for tent-house owners, light-gadget suppliers, practitioners of pop-archetecture and the subscription raisers on the road who encourage traffic police to imitate their strategy of raising subscription from the transporting bus owners. These Puja organisers in India may be sellers of a cultural commodity called Ganesh or Krishna, but are never cultured ones.

I am little intrigued to think whether such actions and violent performances of raising funds has already been officialized as culture since the politicians and bureaucrats are also involved in the process of criminalisation of Dussehra and Ganesh Puja where spiritual essence is marketed with a 'discount' to cheat the customers of culture with commercial games. But 'modernism' as a term at once expresses and mystifies a sense of one's particular conjecture about culture as being some how problematized by social crises and change. Probably, this has become a global phenonmenon.

Terry Eagleton writes "The modernist work-and all cultural artefacts are such is the one which knows that modernist (for which read also `political') experiment is finally impotent. The mutual parasitism of history and modernity is DeMan's own version of the post structuralist deadlock of Law and Desire, in which the revolutionary impulse grows heady and delirious on its meagre prison rations". (Eagleton, P.991)

As we are already in the first decade of a new a millenium, the notions of Jagannath culture shaping the Odissi festivals needs a brief reference. The idea of Jagannatha is postmodern in nature as far as it embodies the elements of the tribal culture. Even before the globalisation of *Rath Yatra*, the temple of Jagannath has been treated as an institution of Vishnu, Siva, Ganesha, Kali, Srikrishna, Budhism and Satyanarayana Peera (blending of the concepts of Narayana and Muslim Prophets). Besides this multigravitational force of a concept, this modern black hole of a temple never admitted any casteist differentiation. This symbolic God originated in primitive culture and even today, the Brahmins stay away from his ritualistic worship during *Anavasara*, a ritual before the car festival starts. As a syncretic culture of assimilations, acculturations and appropriations the cult of Jagannath cuts across all boundaries of sectarianism. It is just a symbol that communicates through symbols, all that it embodies under the package of Oriya culture. Oriya folks are therefore organisms in symbolic communication with each other. Therefore they have a culture. They are distinctly a symbol making and symbol using species. Neither the material culture (as Malinowski brings it out) nor the non material culture: habits, ideas and beliefs- can exist without a sign-system.

The sign system of our festivals is related to seasonal cycle. There are 11Summer Festivals, 5 monsoon festivals, 3 Autumn Festivals, 7 winter festivals and 4 spring festivals. They need a detailing:

xi. Summer festivals: Visuva Samkranti

In India the months and years are counted on the basis of lunar or solar movements. According to the solar system the month is counted from *Samkranti* to Samkranti and in lunar system it is counted from *Purnima* (Fullmoon) to Purnima. Visuva Samkranti is the first day of the month of Baisakh Samkranti. In northern India it is called Jala Samkramnti, in southern India Sakkar Pongal and in Orissa it is known as *Pana* Samkranti, named after *Pana*, the main drink offering (made of jaggery, meshed banana, cheese and other condiments like powdered pepper etc.) specially prepared for this occasion.

There are specific reasons as to why the Visuva Samkranti is considered as the first day of the solar year. It is only on two occasions i.e. Mesha Samkranti and Tula Samkranti that the Sun fully rests on the equator and on these two dates the length of days and nights remain equal. After Mesha Samkranti the Sun moves in the northern direction to our side as our country is situated to the north of the equator. It is, therefore, from this day of first movement of the Sun from Mesha Samkranti that the newyear is counted. All over the country this day is considered auspicious and is celebrated with social, cultural and religious performances.

In Bhabisya Purana, this festival has been mentioned as Jala Samkranti. According to tradition when Bhisma, the grand-father of Kuru and the Pandavas lay on the bed of arrows (Shara Sajya) he felt thirsty and there was no water nearby in the ravaged battle-field of Kurukshetra. Then Arjuna with his powerful bow thrusted an arrow deep into the ground and water immediately shot out in a stream to quench the thirst of the dying warrior. Out of contentment and compassion Bhisma conferred to Judhistira, "Those people who would offer cold water to thirsty people on this day would not only be free from all sins, but also the departed souls of their ancestors as well as the Gods in heaven would be pleased." This saying of the holy scripture is observed with great reverence and people all over the country offer sweet-water to thirsty people as a religious rite.

In Orissa, this festival is observed with great sanctity in various forms. On this day Chhatu (grinded corn powder), Pana (sweet water), umbrellas, fans (made out of palm-leaves or bamboo-strips) and Paduka (wooden slippers) are offered to Brahmins and the poor people. All these are remedies for the scorching Sun. Water as the vital source of life becomes more symbolical in another ritual of the festival. Above the Tulasi plant which is a must in every Hindu household of Orissa, a shed is prepared with branches of green leaves and a painted pitcher of smaller size filled with water is suspended with a rope hanger. Beneath it a small piece of straw is fixed to a hole in the pitcher through which water is drained drop on the Tulasi plant. This is called 'Basudhara' (the stream of the earth), Here, Tulasi plant symbolizes the human life and it is to be saved from the scorching sun by resting in the shed and taking enough water.

This festival is observed widely in some form or other, in the coastal areas and in some towns and villages of other areas a rigorous ritualistic observance is observed. Deeply connected with the mass religious culture of Orissa, a number of other festivals otherwise known as Jhamu Yatra, Hingula Yatra or Patua Yatra, Danda Yatra, Uda Yatra etc. which originated as ritualistic observance of Chaitra Parva culminate in the Visuba Samkranti and make a grand finale fo the whole celebration.(Collected from D.N.Pattnaik's Festivals of Orissa pp 19-20)

(Culled from D.N.Pattanayak's book *Festivals of Orissa*)

Hingula Yatra or Patua Yatra

Most of the festivals prevalent among the low-caste Hindus are either associated with the worship of Shakti or Shiva. It is believed to have grown out of the mass religious culture of the people under the spell of Tantrism in the remote past. One such festival is Hingula Yatra or Patua Yatra. There is a popular belief among the local people that on this day or

Visuba Samkranti Goddess Hingula appears and propitiation to Her removes all evil forces. She is worshipped in the village street on Her imaginary stride to the village. Offering to Her includes spitted new cloth, Pana (sweet-water), butter lamp and green mangoes.

In remote villages this festival is observed with much austerity. Those who observe fasting, especially women are called 'Osati' Prior to the day of worship the fasting worshippers (mostly men) move from village to village with the sacred pitcher symbolizing the Goddess. Their religious procession is always accompanied by singing and dancing. Thse worshippers are called Patua. The man who dances with the holy-pitcher on his head wears a black skirt, a red blouse and a long piece of black cloth tightly covering the head and having equal length on both sides to flow. While dancing, the Patua holds the ends of the cloth and moves them artistically with stretched arms in perfect harmony to the rhythmic pattern. Sometimes he dances on the stilts and performs difficult Yogasanas balancing on the head, the staff that holds the holy-pitcher (Ghata). A big brass bell played with a cane-stick provides various peculiar rhythms. Sometimes country drums are also played.

The head of the patuas is called Bada-Patua or Katha Patua. All the Patuas observe fasting on this day. In the afternoon they assemble near a tank or river where all the rituals take place. The priest performing the rites is always a non-brahmin known as 'Jadua' or Dehuri'. During the rituals men, women and children of the village congregate. The surrounding reverberates with auspicious 'Hulahuli' (a shrill sound made by wagging the tongue inside the mouth) and 'Hari Bol' cheers of men. Then, sharp iron hooks are pierced through the skins on the back of the Patuas. During this ceremony the morals of the Patuas are boosted through holy cheers of the onlookers and they themselves loudly continue singing in praise of Hingula or Mangala.

In some areas Jhamu Yatra is organized. Persons observing *Brata* or vow in honour of the deity walk on thorns and on the bed of live charcoal amidst holy cheers and loud drumming. Those who walk on fire are known as *Nian Patua* (Nian for fire) and those on thorns are called Kanta Patua (Kanta for thorn). Some worshippers stand on edged swords and are carried on open palanquins. They are called *Khanda Patua* (Khanda for sword). Some of them show some feats in deep water. They are called *Pani Patua* (Pani for water). Especially all these festivals are celebrated near a Shiva or Shakti Shrine. Therefore, scholars are of opinion that these rituals of inflicting injury to their persons by the devotees are related to the Tantra culture. By doing these they try to draw the kind attention of the God or Goddess whom they seek to propitiate.(Pattnaik pp. 21-22.)

Uda Parab

In some areas, especially in Mayurbhanj and Keonjhar districts of Orissa a flying-festival popularly known as Uda Parab' is observed. The participating devotees of this festival are called Bhokta or Bhata. As in similar other festivals almost all the devotees belong to the low-caste Hindus.

In a village field a long staff is fixed horizontally on a perpendicular pole. The Bhoktas, after having ceremontial bath and following other rituals in a nearby river, move dancing in a procession to this place accompanied by a cheering crowd and loud beating of drums. There a huge congregation enthusiastically awaits their arrival. Then, one by one, they are tied to the horizontal staff with a long cloth at the shoulders. Ankle-bells are fitted on their feet some devotees are not tied. They simply hold the staff in one hand and move hanging. With the help of a rope fixed to the perpendicular staff they are moved round and round by a person below. Profusely garlanded, the Bhokta flying at a height throws flowers from his garlands and green mangoes to the onlooking audience below, who collect them with great enthusiasm as precious possession. After this ceremony the Bhoktas go to the nearby temple and offer offering prayers to Shiva, Hingula, Mangala, retire.(Pattnaik p.22)

Baseli Puja or Chaiti Ghoda

In the month of Chaitra there is an exclusive festival for the bonafide fishermen community of Orissa who are popularly known as *Keuta (Kaivatra)*. This festival is held for a full month beginning from Chaitra Purnami (Full Moon of Chaitra in March) and ending with Baisakh Purnami (Full moon in April). During this festival Baseli, the horse-headed deity of the community is propitiated She is considered to be the tutelary deity of the community. She may be considered s a form of Mother Goddess who was earlier formless. Later she took various forms according to the conception and needs of the various communities living all over the country.

By 5th-6th century A.D., the worship of Shakti had gained tremendous prominence in Orissa. One of the four celebrated Peethas (Centres) of Buddhist Tantricism in India was located in Orissa. The Peethas had not only the support of a number of Sadhakas to go ahead with their spiritual pursuits but also gave an impetus to the people in general to appreciate the Tantirc practices. Rigorous religious practices involved in the Tantric way of worship became wide-spread.

It is believed that this festival originated during 10-11th centuries when Hindu Tantra and Buddha Tantra merged into one. Baseli is one of the various deities of Tantra culture which evolved during this period. The horse headed deity is seated on an earthen platform. She wears a blood-red cloth in her full feminine form. In temples and places of worship, She is propitiated on each Saturday and Tuesday through out the year. During the festival period where there are no such images; only the horse head made out of wood is worshipped. Peculiarly the worshipping takes place in a particular place of the horse and that is *Dhinkisala* (the place where paddy is husked). It is because, the subsidiary profession of the community is to prepare and sell flattened rice. (chuda).

Worship of Baseli or Basuli and the Dummy-horse dance are inexplicably connected with is rituals and celebrations. It is the most important festival of the fishermen community.

They observe it with great devotion and austerity. The details for the worship have been enunciated in *'Kaibarta Gupta Geeta'* by Achyutananda Das, a mystic Oriya poet of 15th century A.D.Various legends prevail about the birth of the community and their tutelary deity and this particular text records one. According to this Geeta, when the world was in a deluge Vishnu Bhagwan could not find a place to rest. So, He by His spiritual power reduced his form and rested on a floating Banyan leaf. As it was all the while dwindling on the stormy waves of the ocean He created a man out of the dirt of His ear-zone and asked him to hold the leaf still with the help of a row (*kandiara*). But, soon he fell into deep slumber. In the meantime a huge demoniac fish *Raghab* swallowed the man. Again the leaf began dwindling and God's sleep was disturbed. To His utter surprise He found the man missing. By intuition He could know everything and at once killed the *Raghaba* and got the man out. Then God transformed the banyan leaf in to a horse. He summoned *Biswakarma* and asked him to build a boat immediately. Then He said to the man' 'Hence-forward you and your community will be known as Kaibarta and you would be the king among them. Go to the country of Simhala and rule there happily. Make this horse your carrier and use his boat for trading. As you were swallowed and almost got killed by a fish, generation by generation you would kill the species and live on them." Baseli, became the name of the horse and God asked the man to worship him as his tutelary deity on the full-moon day of Chaitra. Since then the tradition is followed.

The Dasa king sailed to Simhala with the horse by boat. There he ruled for many years. The horse died at the age of one lakh years and out of his carcass came out a damsel as beautiful as Lakshmi She approached the king and lamented that no longer the name of Baseli would be associated with her. Taken by surprise the king was terrified. He then prayed Vishnu for His counsel. The God again directed, "This woman will be known hence-forward as Aswini Baseli whom you would propitiate for generations. Then only you can attain

Baikuntha". Since then, the woman became Goddess Baseli with a horse-head and continued to be venerated by the fishing community.

Another legend is associated with the worship of the horse-head and the horse-head deity. It is said that after the death of Baseli, the sacred horse. God distributed his limbs among fishermen, confectioners (Gudia), oil-merchants (Teli) and cobblers (Mochi). They continued to worship the limbs. Some time after an idea struck to them. All of them agreed to assemble the limbs and have the full form of the deity (horse) and worship him commonly. This was done. At one time the Kaibartas and the Gudias vied with each other. A communal riot ensured. Gudias being rich and powerful locked the deity in a house and deprived the Kaibartas from worship. The helpless Kaibartas simply prayed the deity with utmost devotion for His return. Moved by the prayers of the Kaivartas he crushed the wall with the force of his hoofs and escaped to their camp. Being enraged the Gudias chopped of his head and even then; the head lived to accept worship and offerings from the Kaibartas. It is, therefore, the Kaibartas who worship the horse-head separately.

Inexplicably connected with the festival is dummy-horse dance of the community. On the auspicious day of Chaitra Purnami, the Kaibartas worship a Bamboo with vermillion, sandle-paste, butter-lamp etc. Then the bamboo is split ceremonially into pieces out of which only twelve are taken out for preparation of the frame of the dummy-horse. The frame is dyed red with red clay and then covered with a Pata (indigenous silk cloth). Then a painted horse-head made out of wood is fixed to the frame. A garland of Mandara (Hibiscus) flowers is placed on the neck during worship. This particular garland is always intended for mother goddess. Thus the dummy-horse is worshipped till the eighth day of the dark fort-night after which it is taken out for dance. A man enters the cavity and hangs the frame on the shoulders and then dances to the rhythm of Dhol (country drum). Mahuri is the only wind-instrument played during the dance. Sungs are sung intermittently in votive dedication to the deity. Sometimes the dancer gets possessed and falls in to trance. Then somebody else replaces him. Two other characters *Chadhua-Chadhuani* or *Rauta-Rautani* also sing and dance. The male character dances with a long staff in his hand symbolizing the profession of fishermen's rowing of boats. The female character is played by a man. Both of them sing songs of love and daily household cares. Then a song combat ensues which lasts for the whole night. During this portion of the dance the dummy horse is ceremonially placed in the centre and the performance is held in front of it, people sitting all around.

There are regular amateur as well as professional groups for this dance. They perform on payment. Sometimes they move dancing from door to door and collect money. There are five to seven persons in all in a group including dancers and musicians. They continue to dance till Baisakh Purnami when they make a grand finale and then part for the next season.

Now a-days the votive dancers are not confined only to the kaivarta community. Since the dummy-horse dance is attached to mamy Shakti shrines of Orissa also, people of other communities have also taken interest to join the votive dancers.

The dummy-horse dance is mainly prevalent in the coastal districts of Cuttack and Puri. In Puri the dummy-horses are profusely decorated with flowers and the 'Tahia' (Archaic head-gear of florwer) presents a magnificent show during dance. When the festival ends the horse-head is taken out ceremonially from the frame and is preserved in a temple. Next year during the festival it is again brought out and repainted for worship and use during the dance.

Akshyaya Trutiya

This is exclusively an agricultural festival held on the third day of the Hindu year. On this day the farmer ceremonially starts sowing seeds in the field, especially paddy. Early in the morning, farmers in their respective homes arrange the materials for the ritual. After taking ablution in a river or tank they wear new cloths and carry the seeds in new baskets. In the field offerings are made of they sow sees ceremonially praying the Goddess for a rich bumper crop. In the evening feasts (strictly vegetarian) are arranged in respective homes. In western Orissa this festival is called *'Muthi Chhuan'* Eating of green-leaves (Shag) is forbidden for the day. It is observed by all farmers irrespective of caste and creed.

The famous Chandan Yatra of Lord Jagannath which is observed in various other shrines of Orissa starts from this day. Moreover, from this auspicious day the carpenters start building the cars (Ratha) of Lord Jagannath, Balavadra and Subhadra.

On this day women also worship 'Sasthi Debi' popularly called 'Sathi Duchhei'. The Goddess is said to be the guardian of children. She has also the power to bestow the women with children. Therefore, she is propitiated with great devotion.

Religious scriptures testify that Ganga, the sacred river of India landed on the Earth on this day from Heaven. She is the perennial source of water which is the need for agriculture. Therefore, is auspicious day was chosedn to start sowing seeds.

(From Pattnayak, 27)

Chandan Yatra

Chandan Yatra marks the conclusion of the cycle of religious festivals observed in the famous shrine of Lord Jagannath at Puri followed by similar other shrines of Orissa. The festival, starting from Akshyaya Trutia, lasts for twenty one days and is held in the month of Baisakh at the height of the summer heat when Chandan (sandle-paste) and water are essential to keep people cool. As the Hindu deities are modelled on the behaviour of human beings, they are also given the same treatment. During this festival they are taken out of the temples in procession fr perambulation in water on floats or boats. The richly decorated boats are called 'Chapa'. 'Chapa' is the Oriya equivalent of 'float'. In most of the Vishnu as well as Shiva temples the festival of the 'float' marks the conclusion of the prime annual festival and it is celebrated with much pomp and éclat. The belief probably is that the deity having concluded his ceremonial per ambulation with all attendant paraphernalia on land, must have hs aquatic sojourn before He returns to the sanctum of the temple to come out only for the next festival.

This festival is most elaborate in Puri and attracts thousands of poligrims from far and near. On all the twenty one days the entire road from the shrine of Lord Jagannath leading up to the Narendra Sarobar (a sacrd tank in Puri town) along with the houses on both sides is decorated. At some places, especially in front if Maths or at cross-roads big torants (arches) are erected where the idols take casual ! rest and receive offerings. The representative images of the deities installed in temple such as Madanmohan (representing Lord Jagannath), Laxmi and Saraswati are taken in a richly decorated palanquin by the sevakas accompanied by priests, musicians and dancers to the Nanrendra Sarobar at night. The tank is profusely lighted with thousands of spectators milling and josting all around in expectation of the arrival of the procession. The principal deities are also followed by different deities from different shrines of the town. After reaching Narendra Sarobar, the images are then placed on different well decorated boats and they are rowed for a long time by the Sevakas. During the rowing ceremony Devadasis (temple-dancers) dance and sing of the boat.

Generally, the colour chosen for the boats are red and white and they are so designed to look like hugs swans floating on water. The peculiarity of the ceremony is that Madanmohana with Laxmi and Saraswati rides on the white coloured raft where-as Ramakrishna with pancha Shivas rides the red one. All the deities on the boat take several rounds in the water which continue till early hours of the mornig and then retire to the respective shrines. The last day of the festival is called Bhaunri (Bhramari or circle) when special elaborate arrangements are made.

Most of the important festivals of Lord Jagannath at Puri are also followed in all other important shrines of Orissa. Following tradition of the Purin the images are taken out in procession on planquins to the nearby tanks and perambulated in water on boats. In all such temples it is obsereved only for the last three days. After the ceremony which usally takes place at mid-night, people enjoy performances of dance, drama and music specially arranged for his occasion.

At Bhubaneswar the Chandan festival of Lord Lingraj observed in Bindu Sarobar, a huge tank near the temple. Here, the float is moved to the Mandapa in the middle of the tank. The mandap is inlet-like structure which is more an elevated platform.

(Pattanayak-28-29)

Sital Shasthi

This particular festival strictly prevalent among the Bhrahmisn of Orissa I generally observed in Brahmin villages, popularly known as Sansans or in towns where Brahmins are more in number.

It is believed tht shiva or Hara became furious after Jagara amavasya and He was cooled down only by marriage with Parvati. So, this marriage festival of Shiva and Parvati is called Sital (cool) Shasthi and is held on the sixth day of the bright fortnight of the month of Jyestha.

Since the days of yore Orissa has been a seat of Shaivism. Only Bhubaneswar has about five hundred Shiva temples dating back from 6th-7th century A.D. In the early temples of Bharatswar and Parsurameswar there are elaborate scenes of Shiva's marriage with Parvati. It is, therefore, believed that this festival of Shiva's marriage is very ancient and is being carried down through centuries past.

In most Brahmin villages of Orissa there are temples of Shiva, parvati and Vishnu. During this festival the elderly Brahmins of the village act as the parents of the bride (Parvati) and the bridge-groom (Shiva) and all formalities of a Brahmin marriage are observed. In analogy with the society-marriages where somebody acts as a mediator, here, Vishni, the God

Himself takes the role. At first a proposal (written on palm-leaf) is sent from the bride's side to the bridge-groom's father through Sevak who also carries Mahaprasad (Food offering of Lord Jagannath), coconut, betelnut, and a piece of new cloth as prevalent in marriage customs. Whith him goes a procession of torch-bearers, drummers and pipers. Thereafter, on the fifth day (Panchami) at past mid-night parvati goes to the temple of Shiva in a procession where are marriage takes place with all vedic formalities. After the marriage is over a feast is arranged in which the Sevayats from both the sides participate.

The real festival takes place next day in the night when the marriage procession is taken out with pomp and grandeur. The images of Parvati and Vishnu are carried in a richly decorated palanquin (vimana) heading the procession. Shiva, seted on a bull follows them on a bullock cart. At cross-roads and important places the procession halts and there is lavish display of fire-works, dancing, drumming and various other kinds of merry-making.

Though this festival is held in the temples of Loknath at Puri, Lingraj at Bhubaneswar and in most of the important Brahmin villages, it is observed in a grand scale at Sambalpur where two groups of Brahmins exhibit rare enthusiasm to organize it with keen competitive spirit. During the procession lavishly decorated tableus are brought out. Traditional and local dance and music parties are engaged to move with the procession. Varieties of fire works are displayed. Each group tries its utmost to excel the other in every respect. The procession terminates at the respective temples and the festival ends.

On this day the town of Sambalpur wears a festival look. Thousands of people congregate from different parts of the district to witness the deities in procession. In the Puranas it has been said that one is expiated of all sins if he sees the Gods in procession. Therefore, there is a natural attraction for the common villagers to see the mounted deities in procession.(Pattanayak,30-31)

Savitri Brata(Vow)

The Amavasya (last day of the dark fort-night) in the month of Jyestha is known as Savitri Amavasya or Savitri Brata. This day is most auspicious for the married Hindu women with husbands alive. They observe it as a vow with great devotion and pray for the long life of their husbands.

The Brata has been named after Savitri. In Mahabharata and other puranas the romantic episode of Savitri-Satyaban has been elaborately narranted with ideogogical veneration. Savitri was the beautiful daughter of king Aswapati of Madra Desa. She was unparallel both in virtue and beauty. As a suitable groom couldn't be found out, her father gave her complete freedom to choose her own partner in life. With a band of veteran minister she traveled many countries and religious centres in search of a suitable partner, but couldn't find one of her choice. While returning desperately a handsome young man caught her eyes. He was engaged in cutting wood in a jungle. The young man was no other than Satyaban, a prince in exile who was living in the forest with his blind fater Dyumatsen. Savitri selected him as her life's partner. But Narada forecasted that he would die young. Then the king asked his dear daughter to select another. But, Savitri was firm in her determination and ultimately married him. She left the palace and lived with her husband and there in-laws in the forest. As a devoted wife and daughter in-law she took all pains to take care of them.

Gradually the ordanined time for the death of Satyaban drew near. One day while cutting wood in the jungle his head reeled and he got down from the tree and then expired on the lap of his beloved wife, Savitri. Then Yamraj, the death- God, appeared to take away the soul of Satyaban from his body. Savitri, deeply hurt pleaded to Yamraj not to be separated from her husband, if at all he would take away the soul of her husband she would also follow. Yamraj was taken aback at such a request and explained that it was Impossible. Instead he promised to grant three boons. Savitri cleverly asked for three boons and Yamraj, in haste, conceded to it. As a result, Savitri could regain the lost kingdom of her father-in-law by his first boon; could retrieve the sight of her in-laws by the second boon. The third boon was that she would be the mother of hundred sons. Savitri argued that the God of Death is a liar since he wanted to mke her a mother without a husband which was an impossibility. As a Sati, she can't take another husband. Yamraj, being outwitted and moved by the devotion of Savitri, returned the life of her husband. Satyaban came to life again and both of them lived happily thereafter.

In deep regards to Savitri all Odia Hindu women observe this festival by worshipping and propitiating her as a. Thus a character from the Upanishad is worshipped as a goddess. The festival is didactic in the sense it teaches the women to be virtuous, devotional and committed to their husbands like Savitri to make worldly life happy and peaceful. The younger generation of women who go for genital pleasures at a very young age would hardly find any reason to emulate Savitri, a character from the mythic era. A modern Savitri, probably a feminist, whould choose to stay a lesbian than to marry a husband from a family in which the parent-in-laws have gone blind and lost their kingdom, and a princely husband who lives by collecting dried wood from the jungle.

In the early morning the women take purificatory bath and wear-new cloths, new bangles and apply vermilion on the fore-head and the hair-parting line. Images of Savitri are never made. The grinding stone (sila-pua) is represented as Savitri and worshipped. Wet pulses and rice, mango, jackel fruit, lemon, banana and several other fruits are offered as Bhoga (offering). After observing fasting for the whole day they simply take the Bhoga. In the afternoon when all formalities of worship are over they bow low to their respective husbands and elderly people. (Pattanayak, 32-33)

Devasnana Purnima or Snana Yatra

This is exclusively a festival of Lord Jagannath and is said to be one of the oldest. According to Skanda Purana when Raja Indradyumna installed the wooden deities he arranged this bathing ceremony. This day is considered to be the brithday of Lord Jagannath. Held in the full-moon day of the month of Jyestha this festival is also simultaneously held in all other importants shrines of Orissa. However, the festival being most elaborate and important at Puri, it attracts thousands of visitors and piligrims from all over the country.

'Niladri Mohadaya', a religious text written in Orissa records the rituals of the festival. Shiharsa in his 'naisadhiya Charita' (XV. 89) also refers to this festival of Purusottama. This bathing ceremony has a speciality. As this festival does not find mention in the early religious texts, it is believed to be a tribal ceremony which later crept into the Hindu rites. Jagannath in its early from was being worshipped as Nilamadhaba by a Savara chief called Viswabasu. Till now it is the Daitas and Savaras (tribals) who have the exclusive right to conduct the festival. The tribals called Saoras (of southern Orissa) still perform a rite to bath their deities ceremonially on the last day of the month of Jyestha. For this they collect water from remote Jungles where it remains untouched even by the shadow of the animals. Most probably when Jagannath was a Savara God, this festival of the Savaras who tended Him was accepted by the Hindu.

On the previous day of Snana Yatra the images of Jagannath, Balabhadra and Subhadra along with the image of Sudarshana are ceremonially brought out from the sanctum in a procession to the Snana-vedi (Bathing pandal). This special pandal in the temple precinct of Puri is called Snana Mandap. It is at such a height that visitors standing outside the temple also gate a glimpse of the deities. After Mangla Alati, the Suaras and Mahasuaras go in a ceremonial peocession to fetch water from Suna Kua (Golden well) in one hundred and thirty, vessels of copper. All of them cover their mouths with a piece of cloth. Then all the vessels filled with water are preserved in the Bhoga Mandapa. The *Palla pandas* (a class of Brahmin priests) then purify the water with Haridra, Jaba, Bena roots, sandal paste, Aguru incence, flowers, and medicinal herbs.

On the fourteenth day (Chaturdashi) when the idols are taken out in procession, the whole process is called Pahandi or Pahandi vijay. Scholars have given different interpretations of the term ('Pahandi') Some opine that it hs been derived from the term 'Praspanda' meaning movement Some others are inclined to interpret it as a derivation from Pandya vijaya. For the festival the bathing pendal is well decorated with traditional paintings of trees and gardens. Flags and *toranas* (arches) are also put up. The images are profusely decorated with flowers. All kinds of perfumes such as Dhupa, Aguru etc. are then offered. As the 'Pahandi' of the deities takes place to the accompaniment of music and beating of various indigenous drums. Thousands of devotees jostle and crave for a look at the deities in procession.

The bathing festival takes place during the morning hours of the Purnima. The filled vessels are carried from Bhoga Mandap to the Snana Vedi by the Suaras in a long single-line procession. This ritual is called *'Jal-adhibasa'*. Prior to the bathing ceremony the images are covered with silken clothes and then smeared with red powder. Then water is poured, the rituals perfurmed and 'Pavamana' hymns chanted. After the bath the deities are so dressed that together they appear like the image of Ganesha. This is called Ganeshabesa. It is said that a staunch devotee of Lord Ganesha and himself a profound scholar visited Puri during Snana Yatra. He was amply rewarded by the king of Orissa for his scholarship. The king asked the scholar to accompany him to see Lord Jagannath which he refused under the pretext that he wouldn't worship any God other thatn Ganesha. Somehow he was persuaded and brought before the Snana vedi. To the utter surprise of all, Lord Jagannath appeared as Ganesha Since then during Snana Yatra when the sacred bath is performed, the deities are dressed like Ganesha. Various other legends are also told and reasons assigned explaining the Ganesha besa.

During the sacred bath the colours painted on the images generally fade. Seeing the wooden deities in discolour devotees may not have the appropriate devotional attitude and in fact may feel sinful repugnance. For this reason, the images are immediately dressed as Ganesha in which they rmain mostly covered.

After the Snana Yatra, the images are kept away from public view for fifteen days and during all these days the daily rites of the temple remain suspended. The images are kept on the Ratna vedi inside the temple. This period is called 'Anabasara' meaning improper time for worship. It has been said earlier that the images are discoloured as a result of the sacred bath. During these fifteen days the Daitas (descendants of Viswavasu, the Savara) repaint the images and make decorations. The period of colouring and decorating the images is divided into seven short periods, each of two days duration, and a short period of one day set apart to give finishing touches. Thus the period covers the whole fortnight. On the 16th day the images in their new forms after renovation become ready for the public view. The festival of the first appearance of the lord Jagannath to his devotees is called Netrotsaba or Nava Yaubana (new youth). According to popular belief the devotee washes away all his sins if he gets a vision of the Lord on this day. On this occasion, therefore, great rush of people occurs in the temple.

The *Shilpa Sastras* and Agamas testify that the images become suitable for worship only after the performance of the rite of 'Chakshyu Unmilana' (Opening of the eyes). During 'Anabasara', the Daitas offer to the deities' only fruits and water mixed with cheese. According to them during this time the deities don't keep well and therefore, take rest. Like human beings they are considered to have fallen all and are treated by the Raj Vaidya or the king's physician with specific medicines.

The temple-festivals which are held in a bigger ad elaborate scale in the important shrines of Puri and

Bhubaneswar are also held sumultaneoualy in all other small shrines of the respective deities, though in modest scales. Likewise the Snana Yatra is held in many other temples of Orissa.(Pattanayaka,34-36)

Raja Sankranti (Swing Festival)

Raja Sankranti or Mithuna Sankranti(indicating the puberty of the mother earth) is the first day of the month of Asara (June-July)in the solar calendar, which celebrates the beginning of the monsoon. It inaugurates and welcomes the agricultural year all over Orissa which marks, through biological symbolism, the moistening of the summer parched soil with the first shower of the monsoon, thus making it ready for sowing the seeds. To celebrate the advent of monsoon (and the puberty rites), the joyous festival is arranged for three days by the villagers. Though celebrated all over the state it is more enthusiastically observed in the districts of Cuttack, Puri and Balasore. The first day is called Pahili Raja (Prior Raja), second is Raja (Proper Raja) and third is Basi Raja (A kind of hang-over of Raja).

According to popular belief, the Mother Earth also runs her mestrual periods once in a year. So the womenfolk observe the menstrual festival for three days. The festive days are considered as the menstruating period of the Mother Earth. During the festival, all agriculture operations remain suspended. In traditional Hindu homes menstruating women used to stay away secluded and did not even touch the utensils of the kitchen. With the introduction of the working women and the concepts of secularism, and NRI-sm such scientific practices are discontinued as old-fashioned taboos. During the Raja festival all female beings are respected and placed on a cradle like swing as embodiments of the Mother Earth. They are given full rest for three days in Orissa.. Significantly, it is a festival of the unmarried girls, the potential mothers. They too observe the restrictions prescribed for menstruating women. On the very first day, they rise before dawn, do their coiffeur, anoint their bodies with turmeric paste and oil and then take the purificatory bath in a river or tank. Peculiarly, bathing for the rest two days is prohibited. They don't walk bare-foot, do not scratch the earth, do not grind, do not tear anything apart, do not cut vegetables and do not cook. During all the three consecutive days they are seen in the best of dresses and decorations, eating cakes and rich food at the houses of friends and relatives, spending long cheery hours, moving up and down on improved swings, and rending the village sky with their merry impromptu songs. The swings are of different varieties, such as Ram Doli, Charki Doli, Pata Doli, Dandi Doli etc. Songs specially meant for the festival speak of love, affection, respect, social behaviour and everything of social order that comes to the minds of the singers. Though anonymous and composed extempore, much of these songs, through seer beauty of diction and sentiment, have earned permanence and have gone to make the very substratum of Orissa's folk-poetry.

"While girls, thus, scatter beauty, grace and music all around, moving up and down on the swings during the festival, young men give themselves to strenuous games and good food, on the eve of the onset of the monsoons which will not give them even a mements respite for practically four months making them one with mud, slush and relentless showers, their spirits keep high with only the hopes of a good harvest." As all agricultural activities rmain suspended and a joyous atmosphere pervades, the young men of the village keep themselves busy in various types of country games, the most favourite being kabadi. Competitions are also held between different groups of villages. All nights 'Yatra' performances or 'Gotipua' dances are arranged in prosperous villages where they can afford the professional groups. Plays and other kinds of entertainment are also arranged by enthusiastic amateurs.

The special variety of cake prepared out of recipes like rice-powder, molasses, coconut, camphor, ghee etc. goes in the name of Poda Pitha (burnt cake). The size of the cake varies according to the number of family members. Cakes are also exchanged among relatives and friends. Young girls do not take rice during the three-day festival in the districtof Mayurbhanj and sustain only with this type of cake, fried-rice (mudi) and vegetable curry.(Pattanayaka 37-38)

Ratha Yatra

Ratha Yatra of the Car festival of Lord Jagannath at Puri is best known in the world as the biggest festival of its kind. It is observed on the Asadha Shukla Dwitiya i.e. on the second day of the bright fortnight of the month of Asadha (June-July). This annual festival at the first break of monsoon is the most ancient, most elaborate, biggest and the costliest festival of Lord Jagannath, who is believed to be the richest deity of the world. Millions of Hindus flock to the holy city of Puri to see the Gods in procession which is beliurd to expiate them from all sins.

The celebration of *Ratha Yatra* during the rainy season is significant. Scholars opine that the term 'Varsha' (year) has been literally derived from the term 'Varsa' (rain) and this prolific rainy season leads and represents all the seasons of the year. Rain appears to be the harbinger of hilarity and vitality to the human race and therefore, rainy season has been selected as the appropriate occasion for celebration of the festival.

In *'Satapatha Brahmana'*, the rainy season has been highly admired. In the said text an interesting legand has been narrated regarding the origin of Ratha. The Ratha or the car of the god was in heaven since ages past. It was never to be noticed on earth. Once there was a terrific battle between Indra, the king of the God and the demon Brutrasura. Seated on the chariot, when Indra violently flung the weapon of lightening (vajra) right to the chest of the demon, it broke to four pieces and the third piece was metamorphosed into a chariot (Ratha). Indra is also taken to be the God of rains and thunder. As the car is supposed to have been created out of his weapon, the car-festival at the beginning of the rainy season is mythically significant. Keeping aside the mythical account, historians and scholars propound various theories about how and when it came about, though the origin of this festival is still shrouded in mystry.

Ratha Yatra is also locally known as *'Gundicha Yatra'*. Gundicha was the mythical queen of Indradyumna who founded the great shrine and installed the deities. It is said that the images of Lord Jagannath, Balabhadra and Subhadra were first built by Biswakarma, the master-crafts man of the heaven who appeared as an old carpenter. The images were carved out of logs in a smaller shrine now known as Gundicha temple. They were then ceremonially brought in a procession and ceremonially installed in the main shrine. Since those days, the images make an annual sojourn to the Gundicha temple where they were originally given form and the car-festival is said to be that ancient.

Some scholars are of opinion that the *Ratha Yatra* originated as a festival of Buddhists which was later adopted by the Hindus. They claim that the present temple of Lord Jagannath stands on the site of Buddhist temple and contains the celebrated tooth f Buddha, which was kept there till the 4th century A.D. The Buddhists by their mass religious culture almost swayed back the cult of Brahmanism into oblivion. They used to hold a car-festival, once in every five years to propagate their religion. A huge image of Buddha, built out of log and in whose naval zone the tooth relic was placed, used to be taken out in procession on a Ratha or car. When Brahmanism was re-established through the ardent efforts of Sankaracharya, the Hindus accepted to an annual festival of Jagannath. Buddhism exercised deeper influene on Hindusim. The casteless society propagated by the religion was also adopted in the temple of Jagannath. Thus, Lord Jagannath is regarded as an incarnation of Buddha.

The Jains identify Lord Jagannath as a form of 'Jeena' and they claim that the Ratha Yatra is reminiscent of their ancient festival. History proves that Ashoka, the emperor of Magadha, after his eventful Kalinga war, carried away with him the 'Kalinga Jeena' or 'Adi Jagannath' as a war-trophy. This was later restored by Kharavela, the mighty emperor of Kalinga. The 'Kalinga Jeena' was brought in a car followed by a pompous parade of pageantry. This Ratha Yatra of the 'Jeena' was later adopted by the Hindus in the temple of Lord Jagannath.

In the festival each year three new cars are built for the three deities Balabhadra, Subhadra and Jagannath. For building of the new cars, the logs were hereditarily supplied by the Rajah of Daspalla (Now the Govt. of Orissa). The construction of the Rathas starts from 'Askhaya Trutiya' with a 'Vanajaga' ceremony. Each car has its own specifications.

The car of the Lord Jagannath is known as 'Nandighosa' supported on sixteen giant wheels, each seven feet in diameter; it stands forty five feet in height and is beautifully painted in yellow. *'Taladhwaja'* is the name of Balabhadra's car which stands forty four feet in height and stands on fourteen wheels. It is painted in blue. Subhadra's car is known as *'Darpadalana'*, *'Devidalana'* or simply *'Deviratha'* which stands forty three feet in height and is painted in dark red. The colours for the cars are significantly identical with the colour of robes worn by the deities. Lord Jagannath is *'Pitambara'* or robed in yellow, Balabhadra is *'Neelambara'* or robed in blue and Subhadra, a mother-goddess wears garments of blood-red (*Raktambari*).

When the Raths are ready they are brought to the simhadwara or the Lion's gate of the temple. On the beginning day of the festival, after the morning rituals are over in the temple, the deities are brought one by one from the temple to the chariots. All the deities are profusely decorated with crowns of flower (Tahia) and are brought by the Pandas on the twentytwo steps in a peculiar kind of swaying movement. The first deity to come out is Balabhadra, then Subhadra and lastly the Lord Jagannath. They are all installed on the respective chariots. The whole process of bringing out the deities from the temple and placing them on the chariots is known as 'Pahundi'.

The cars do not move immediately after the installation of the deities. The Rajah of Puri, who is popularly revered as the *'Chalanti Vishnu'* (Moving Vishnu) comes in a palanquin, pays his homage to the deities and then sweeps the platform of each of the cars in a golden broom. This process of the festival is known as *'Chhera Pahanra'*. After this part of the ritual, a large number of percussionists (drummers and gong players) play in unison and the sound rends into the air. Then the most auspicious moment comes, for the thousands of anxious pilgrims to pull the cars which they consider to be most sacred. With great enthusiasm they grab the huge ropes and begin to pull the cars. The cars grind forward slowly along the road till the journey ends at Gundicha temple. Balabhadra being the eldest in the family of the deities, His car is drawn first. Then follows the car of Subhadra as she is the youngest and loving sister of the Gods Lastly, but majestically moves the car of Lord Jagannath.

All the deities are then taken to the Gundicha temple where they stay for over a week. Then again they make their return trip to the main shrine. The return-festival is known as Bahuda Yatra, or the return-journey which falls on the tenth day of the month. All the cars are drawn again to the front of the main shrine and the deities with pure gold ornaments. This part of the ritual is known as *'Sunabesa'*.

An interesting ritual is observed on the return of the deities to the main shrine. Goddess Lakshmi, the spouse of Lord Jagannath has a separate shrine in the precints of the Jagannath temple. Mythologically she is the mother prosperity and the Goddess of wealth. But, as depicted in the ritual. She behaves like a common Oriya house-wife. As house-wives do not appear before their elder brother-in-laws, so also Laksmi never appears Lord Balabhadra. For this reason, Her image is never carried close to the image of Balabhadra. She acts as a devoted and ideal wife but at the same time gets touchy. Her sensitiveness is reflected on two occasions of the festival, the first occurs on the Hera Panchami (5th day of the festival) when she goes out to Gundicha temple where the other deities are resting and the later occasion is when the deities return to the temple.

Lakshmi gets hurt emotionally when she feels neglected by her husband (Lord Jagannath and Lakshmi are treated here anthropomorphically). When the Lord sets out for the summer tour in the cars with His elder brother and sister, leaving her alone in the temple. Being aggrieved She goes surreptitiously to Gudicha temple in a fighting and angry mood. In Her fatuitous anger, She breaks up one of the several wheels of Lord Jagannath's car and comes away to the temple as secretly as She had gone. The deva-dasies actualize the job representing Lakshmi in the festival her image is carried in a palanquin and the Devdasis execute the job on her behalf.

The next occasion comes when the deities return to the temple. To their surprise they find the main door of the temple bolted from inside. Laksmi does it to teach the lords a lesion.The Rajah of Puri, however, tries to patch up the differences between them. This part of the ritual is known as *'Lakshminarayana Bheta* (Meeting of Lakshmi and Narayana). At first an elephant is sent to fetch the goddess from the temple which she bluntly declines. On insistent appeal, She comes in a palanquin up to the door still nursing in mind the insult She was inflicted with. When Lord Jagannath appeals Her to open the door, She replies, "You are the Lord of the three worlds! Why do you come to me? Go back to your sister, for being left alone She may feel the pangs of separation" The Lord then says, "You know, my elder brother was also with me. How could you go as you were not supposed to show your face to the elder brother of your husband?" Then Jagannatha promises valuable gifts to Her which She refuses saying that being a woman from poor family (She is the daughter of the Ocean-God) She is unworthy of receiving costly gifts. In the end the insistent appeals of the Lord make Lakshmi open the door and all are allowed to come into the temple.

The song duel or the musical drama that takes place during the occasion is virtually sung by the Devadasis, on behalf of Lakshmi and the Daitas, (the non-Brahmin priests), represent Lord Jagannath. In the musical exchange of words, slokas in Sanskrit are also recited and the song-dialogue continues in the presence of those countless devotees.

On these two occasions the Gods and Goddesses are

brought down to the human level and they are made to behave like common human beings with same sentiments and sensitiveness.

Prior to the advent of foreign power, Orissa was ruled by the king of Puri who was revered as the divine representative by the Rajahs of feauditory States, who were under his command. Their number was fairly large and on the model of the famous shrine at Puri, all of them built Jagannath temples in their capitals where all the festivals related to the deity were observed. Though the car-festival at Puri attracts more people, similar festivals are held through out the state, though in modest scales. In the western part of the state viz. Sambalpur and Bolangir, the festival is also held in big villages. On this occasion the villagers wear new garments and auspiciously pull the car with great devotion. The festival is also held beyond the boundaries of Orissa where there are temples of Jagannath. A festival is now held in California, U.S.A by the converted Hindus.

(Pattanayaka, 39-43)

Nava Kalebara

Related to the car-festival, an important festival known as 'Naba Kalebara' is held once in every twelve to nineteen years according to the calculation of the year and date. On this occasion the wooden images of the deities are replaced by new ones. The principle adopted to fix the year of renewal is to find a year which has two full-moons in the month of Asadh (June-July). In every three years a lunar month is excluded from the circulation to keep a balance between the lunar and the solar years. This particular month, which is excluded from calculation is known as 'Adhimasa' or 'Mala masa' and is considered most inauspicious for any religious ceremony. But peculiarly enough this is considered most sacred for the renewal festival of the deities. Therefore, it is also called 'Purusottama Masa', as the other name of Lord Jagannath is Purusottama. During the last hundred years such festivals have been held only six times in 1863, 1893, 1931, 1950, 1969 and 1978.

For making the new images a number of rituals connected with it are observed. When the data is fixed for the festival the Gajapati Maharajah of Puri issues a proclamation to the Vidyapati, Daitas and Brahmins well-versed in the Vedas to go in search of the trees that would provide logs for making the images. Genearly this proclamation is issued on the 10th day of the full-moon of Chaitra (March-April). After the mid-day rituals of the Lord Jagannath, the Mahapatras receive 'Agnya mala', the garland as a token of permission from the Lord to go in search. Then the Mahapatras carry this garland along with four Daitapatis to the 'Anabasara pindi' (a platform inside the temple) where they are given new garments to wear. From there they go to the Jagannath Math, the place of starting. Accompanied by the Daitapatis, Deulakarana, Tudhan, Lenka and four carpenters they go to the temple of Mangala at Kakalpur which is about forty kilometers in the north. There they sleep in the temple to obtain permission of the Goddess in dream before proceeding in four batches to four directions in search of the trees.

There are strict injunctions for selection of the trees. The trees must be of Neemba. It should have four branches and must be in near vicinity of a buried ground or river. It shouldn't have cut marks. Snekes below the tree is an auspicious sign. Taking all these specifications into account the selection is made and the Daitapatis immediately place the garland on the trees. Then the area is cleaned. A platform is erected for Bana-yaga ceremony. Four Brahmins conduct the ritual. Then the Daitapatis sit in meditation for three days. After this the Vidyapati marks the tree with a golden axe and then the carpenters begin to cut the tree into huge logs. Theafter the holy logs are carried in four wheeled-cars newly the people. The sacred logs are taken into the temple compound through the northen gate and are placed in the Koili Baikuntha. On the day of Snana Purnima the logs are bathed along with the old deities.

Then the logs are carried to Darughara or the stack and eight Brahmins perform the ritual after which the carving of the images begins by a group of carpenters. During this period nobody is allowed to visit the place. After completion of the carving, the images are painted bright in their respective colours by the traditional chitrakars. The new images are then circumbulated for three times and brought to the Anabasarapindi for transfer of Brahma from the old deities into their new forms. The senior most among the Pai Mahapatras performs this rite at the dead hour of the night. He takes away the Brahmas from the naval zones and places them in the same position in the new forms. But, he does it blind-folded and with hands covered with cloths as he is not to see or feel the mysterious Brahma, which is not abstract concept, but a concrete object. During the last Navakalevara in 1994, a snake came out as the bramha and the insiders consider this as an auspicious sign. During the colonial times the British explorers came to witness Rath Yatra and described it as a show of the **Devils**. The Hindus of Puri did not dare to spit on the faces of those mean-minded missionaries. There was a severe famine in 1866 and lots of people were dying in hunger around Puri. The missionary men caught hold of one hungry Brahmin, gave his family some food and converted him into Christianity. Then the Missionaries publishized it informing how the Brahmins were convinced about the spiritual powerof Jesus Christ. They should know that the God called Jagannatha in Orissa is treated like a human being. The old images are carried and buried in the wells of *Koili Baikuntha*, a graveyard situated in the temple precincts. This act of ritualistic burial is done by the *Daitapatis* They are the descendants of the tribal King Viswabasu (chek up the cultural history of Odisa in 1700B.C.). They are the non-Brahmin servitors, appointed for suchpurposes. For this act they observe mourning for eleven days as is commonly done after the death of a man in a Hindu family.

xii. Monsoon Festivals

The festivals of Orissa are celebrated in tune with the changes that occur in the nature. Most of the monsoon festivals are held in the month of Sravana. The month Sravana is named after the season's accoustic effects. Sravana is also hearing. The ceaseless down pour of water on the roofs and on the leaves create *sravana* (accoustic) effects and this is also followed by the thunder sounds. The period in which the Sun stays in the cancer star sign is called Sravana. The period from the dark first day (*Pratipada*) to the full moon day that would fall after Simha Samkranti is called Chandra Sravana. Kalidas's *Katapaya* explains: "*Tarakatrayamite sarakrutya kesave gagana madhyvartini*". The Orissan astrologer, Samanta Chandrasekhar, also mentions about the arrow like position of Kesava, or *Sravana nakshatra* that occupies the space near *Uttarashasdha*.

The Odias celebrate six festivals during the monsoon season. These are (I) Manasa Panchami ii) Chitalagi or Chitou Amavasya, (iii) Gamha Purnima/Rakhi Poornima/Jhulana Poornima (iv) Khudurukuni OSHA (v) Ganesha Chaturthi and (vi) Janmastami.

Manasa Panchami is celebrated on the fifth day of the dark fotnight of the month of Sravana. Godess Manasa has a special energy that works like anti-venom therapy. The Puja starts in the courtyard of the house and later the ritual space is shifted to a tree under which eight cobra images are built in mud and worshipped. A classical book of rituals captioned *Kala Pradipah* in Sanskrit says *Devi sampoojyanatvacha na sarpa bhayamapuyat*. We may imagine the ecological condition of this mountaneous area in which the cobras/other snakes used to enter into the houses during the rains. The lines of the Pooja recital include the welcoming ceremony of a cobra, which is invoked to stay friendly with the family members.

Chitalagi Amavasya. The village women in Kalinga call it Chitou Amavasya. A steam cake made of rice paste is prepared at home and godess Kali is worshipped. The *sraddha* ceremoney of the ancestors is celebrated by offering this cake.

Others dig a hole in the field and bury a cake. Here the festival becomes an agricultural ritual. It is also related to the temple of Lord Jagannatha. A golden ornament called *Chita* is decorated on the forehead of Lord Jagannatha. It should be remembered that *chtraka, chitrabhanu* and *chita* are synonyms of a god called *Agni* (The Fire God). The agni that connects this life with the life beyond is called *chitagni*. The chitou cake is one sided and it is not turned on the pan while it s on fire. The turn would symbolize that the maker refuses to accept rebirth. The *atma* (soul which is also *agni)* should not be placed on fire again.

The various names given for the festival calledv Jhulana Poornima/Gamha Poornima/Rakhi Poornima shows that the rituals vary from region to region. In Kalinga an earthen mound of aound 15' to 20' height is constructed on the village -street on the day of Gamha Poornima. This earthen mound called Gamha creates an occasion for village sports. A little away from the earthen mound there would be T-shaped bamboo poles on which differents sweetmeats and gifts are hung. The young villagers would jump and pick their gifts. *Gamha* is related to the *amha (jivana* or life) of the *Go* (The cows). The day is the birthday of Lord Baladeva who is also the Lord of agriculture according to the Interpretators of the philosophy of Jagannatha. On that day Lord Jagannatha himserlf celebrates the day of emergence of this God of Agriculture by deputing his representative Sudarsana to the Gamha pedestal inside the temple. Lord Sudarsana is taken to the Markandeya Ashrama and the bulls are worshipped there. The ordinary farmers of Orissa give a clean bath to their bulls, annoint their horns with oil and turmeric paste and decorate their horns and the neck with seasonal flowers. The soil from the Gamha mound is cosidered sacred and the doors of the houses are pasted with that mud as it represents Lord Baladeva as the God of protection. The Odias believe that by worshipping the symbolic bull, they would please the starsign Leo (The lion) and the Lord Pasupati. Pasupati is Lord Siva and Baladeva is equivalent to Lord Siva. The concept of AnantaBasudeva in Bhubaneswar is related to the worship of

Baladeva of the Jagannatha temple. The other name for Lord Siva in Orissa is Kedareswar (The Lord of Kedar or the fields). Similarly *Go-Bramha* is *Gamha*.

In Cuttack and Balasore districts and in the entire Western Orissa people celebrate **Rakhi Purnima** (otherwise called Raksha Bandhan), a festival of sisters and brothers and in Puri people celebrate **Jhulana Purnima**, a festival of the temple related to Srikrishna. The seven days beginning with the *navami* (the ninth day) of the bright fortnight till the full moon day constitute the Jhulana festival. The festival again goes to the creation myth. The Creator divided himself into two parts-the left contained the female and the right side was designed as the male. We find the images of Srikrishna and his female nature/consort Radha as an embodiment of this half-male-half-female concept during the Jhulana festival.

Janmastami in the Jagannatha Temple of Puri is celebrated in a typical manner. After the evening aarati is finished, Lord Jagannatha, who represents both the genders, symbolically gets impregnated with a different mantra. The Jaya and Vijaya gate, shall be closed and then the Lord is offered *garva-udaka* (water for vthe uterus) with a special ritualistic karma. *Sitala bhoga* is offered tom the Lords. Two servitors would enact Devaki and Basudeva. Then Srikrishna will be born. The administrative authorities help the servitors for other rituaslistic services pertaining to mJanmastami.

The Kalingan homes have their own home-Gods and godesses and these rituals are dedicated to them. **Khudurukuni Osha** is a ritualistic festival of the merchant class women, who were once connected with commercial business on the ocean routes. The Kalingan merchants have settled in Burma, Java and Sumatra islands. Once upon a time, as the records of the ancient Greek historians show, the Kalingan weavers used to sell textile works in those far-off islands. Khudurukuni is connected with one such legend and a godess called Mangala is worshipped in folk style, specially, by the women folk who fast on the Sundays during the festival. Ganesh Chaturthi and Janmastami are common festivals in India.

xiii. Autumn Festivals

We may list three Major Autumn Festivals- Nua Khia, Dusserah and Kumar Purnima. Nua Khia is an agicultural rite in which the rice of the first harvested paddy is cooked either for the home godess or for the godess of the region. This is a majpor festival in the Western Orissa. But after the dismantling of the agricultural society and the dissolution of the nucclear families, the urban people gradually begin to do away with such ancient festivals that created a space for community gatherings. Everyone in the country knows Dusserah, but the Kumar Purnima that falls on the fifth day after Dussehra has regional variations. In Kalinga people put on new clothes and play games of dice or carXIIIds or any sort of gampling with occasional police raids. In Cuttack, the time of Dussehra brings tragic floods and if the weather is good people organize cultural shows.

xiv. Winter Festivals

The Odias celebrate seven winter festivals- viz.- Kartik Poornima, Deepavali, Prathamastami, Laxmi Puja, Samba Dasami, Makar Samkranti and Vasant Panchami. Kartik (October-November) is considered here as a holi month and one can see thousands of widows observing fasting and other rituals at the Jagannatha temple of Puri. The Mondays are observed as the special occasions for the worship of Lord Siva. Finally, the Poornima is also observed as an auspecious day for the end of *Panchaka* (the auspecious five days) on which none of the Oriyas take non-vegetarian food. The women folk get up very early in the morning and go to river ghats with toy boats made of the kernels of the banana trees and small flames burning within small earthen cup-like deepam. They celebrate the memory of the ancient sea-traders. The ritual is called Boita (boat) Vandana (prayer). It is not limited only to the family of the sea-faring merchant class but, the brahmin women also participate in the festival. Besides, the day is also devoted to the dead souls of the ancestors. A wick in an earthen lamp is burnt within a perforated earthen pot and it is hoisted either on a pole or on the top of a temple to propitiate the ancestral souls. Kartik Poornima in Cuttack is celebrated with a giant fair called Bali Jatra, a mega shopping –complex arranged for about a fortnight in which the folk arts and crafts are sold, and thousands of villagers from the neighbouring areas come to participate. This is also an occasion for the folk theatre troupes of the state to come to the Bali Jatra site and perform. One observes a Circus troupe performing occasionally. Prathamastami is the eighth day of the month of Margasirsha on which the mothers/senior ladies of the family bless the first –born. A special type of stew-cake is prepared at home.

One of the major fertility rituals of the winter is the **Manabasa Gurubara** or the **Laxmi Puja** connected to the newly harvested paddy. This agricultural ritual is very famous and the entire women folk, irrespective of the ancient/modern castes and creeds (richness is a modern caste and secularism is the modern creed) worship the godess Mahalakshmi, the Godess of wealth on the *gurubara* (the Thursdays) of the month. They recite one Purana called *Mahalaxmi Purana*. The Mahalaxmi Purana, written by Balaram Das, the Panchasakha poet of 18th century, is the highest circulated micro Purana of the world. No where is a piece of literature read so ardently and followed so vigorously in the entire world, if it is not rejected as a hyperbolic statement. The theme of the Purana preaches that Mahalaxmi makes herself physically present even in the house of an untouchable woman, if she prays her with a clean body and heart.

The tenth day of the month of Pousa (November – December) is celebrated as **Samba Dasami**, a day dedicated to the sun god. Samba is the son of Srikrishna who suffered from leprosy since he disregarded the sun god. The mothers for protecting their children from skin diseases celebrate this typical festival with special sweetmeats in the family.

Makara Samkranti is a south Indian festival and it is celebrated in the temple of Jagannatha on the Samkranti day of the month of January. The tribals who have Dravidian affiliations celebrate this festival since long. The Samkranti is an important day in the Orissan astrology. It celebrates the orbital movement of the sun whixh is divided into twelve months, named after the different rasis or the star signs. *Makara* (Capricorn) is one of them. The tribal people of Mayurbhanj, Keonjhar and Sundargarh celebrate this festival with great joy. However, the festival is typical to Kalingan part of Orissa (South Orissa) and it is a holy day on which a propitiatory family *jajna* is held to appease the ancestors. This is also a post-harvest fertility ritual in some other parts.

xv. Spring Festivals

Vasant Panchami is also called as the ***Sri Panchami*** on which Saraswati, the godess of learning is worshipped. The small children in the schools celebrate this occasion with great vigour. In modern colleges, in which one finds students from other communities and alien religions, this festival is observed without any religious bias.

Vasant Panchami may also be classified as a spring festival as Vasant is the spring season. The next important spring festival is ***Maha Siva Ratri***, a sleepless night devoted to Lord Siva by the devotees belonging not only to theSaivite cult, but also by the other Hindus. The Oriyas believe in the Puranic episode in which Lord Siva drinks the entire poison of his aquatic creation. Maha Siva Ratri is the comemorative night of that fatal event. The Hindus celebrate it as a ritualistic sign, which signifies the capacity of the metaphysical phallic god to interiorize the metaphorical poison. Our Puranas narrativize reality in an allegorical-metaphorical style. Fantasy is its dominant structure. The trouble with the empiricists is that they do not have a vision that can pierce through the surface.

Dola Purnima

The *Poornima* of the month of *Falguna* (The full moon day of the month of March) is called *Dola Poornima*, and elsewhere this festival is called *Holi*. This festival was originally called *Madana Utsava* (The Festival of the God called Cupid) and later, during the time of Srikrishna, this was called Holi. The etchings in the rock shelters of Vikramkhole and other rock shelters mention that in the early days (pre historic times) entertainment programmes (especially dances, song recitals and poem recitals) were held during this *Vasant Utsav*. This ancient festival is celebrated for five days in Orissa, even today in the capital city, Bhubaneswar and it is called *Panchu Dola* (*Dola* Festival for five-combined days). Different images of Lord Krishna would be brought in palanquins made of wood, by the devotees to a ground called *Melana* (congregation) *Padia* (ground) and a fair or a shopping complex in the ethnic style shall be arranged. In some places, earthn flames are used and electric bulbs are avoided during the night to bring the ethnic effect to the festivals. Fried nuts, candies and *chats* are sold in different joints and *keertan* is sung in loud voice by different troupes. The *mridangam* players from the villages beat the rhythms as if they have joined a competition. Some times the best troupe, percussionist and the best singer are awarded by the district administration.

Ashokastami

This festival is celebrated in the temple of Lingaraj at Bhubaneswar. This is the car festival of Lord Siva and this is celebrated with great enthusiasm at Bhubaneswar as if to compete with the car festival of Puri. The devotees celebrate the marriage ceremony of Lord Siva. The originators of this festival have assigned various Puranical logics and one such legendary episode is connected to the Ramayana. Rama could no kill Ravana since Goddess Kali protected him. Bibhisana,

Ravana's brother and a devotee of Rama advised him to worship Godess Kali and win her support. Rama took the God and the Godess in a car after he won the battle and rescued Sita. The pundits, with this whimsical legendary tale (may be a concocted tale spun out of their fertile puranic imagination) have started to celebrate this festival in the old Bhubaneswar area. A-soka is sans soka (grief) in Sanskrit language.

Rama Navami

The ninth day of the light fortnight of the month of Chaitra is celebrated as the Rama Navami in different parts of Orissa. In places like Asureswar in Cuttack and Daspalla in the Nayagarh district the festival is celebrated with pomp. In the district of Ganjam and Daspalla the Ram Leela is staged during the festival. Ramleela is a ritualistic theatre in certain parts of Orissa in Ganjam and the persons enacting the roles of Rama and Hanumana lead an austere life during this month long festival. It is strange to note that this year (2005) an artist from Digapahandi area enacting role of Hanuman in Ramleela performance of the local team violated the regimen pertaining to diet. As a consequence, he died on the night of the performance as he was jumping down from a tree in a drunken state. Ramleela is performed in Ganjam district as an Environmental theatre in which the performing space spills over to the ritualistic space as well as the to the surrounding landscape. The Hanuman actor used the long tree as his perching place and and jumped on to Ravana during the performance. He died on the spot.

xvi. Tribal Festivals

This state with 62 tribes occupies a major space in India in the tribal map and its common festivals need a mention as cultural symbols. This book contains chapters on tribal culture and their different traits have been recorded. But as we conclude the book with festivals, they need a separate space since all the festivals mentioned under this chapter are Aryan in nature. The primitive Oriyas was tribal people and they have resisted the process of Aryanization even in the 21st century. If a modern government in the centre neglects and marginalizes the case of the Oriyas, it is because the Oriyas are not Aryans and they still hate them. The Brahmins, for example, are seriously marginalized in the state to the extent that they are not mentioned and recommended for Central Academy Awards because of the strong tribal lobby formed by Sitakant Mahapatra, Pratibha Ray and others.

As far as the tribal festivals are concerned, we may name the **Karama Festival** widely prevalent in the tribal groups of Sundargarh, Mayurbhanj, Bolangir, Sambalpur, Dhenkanal and Keonjhar. The legends vary from the tribe to tribe, but generally young men and women cut branches of trees and plant in the ritual space plastered with cow dung. This plantation ritual is celebrated with offering the forest deity soaked and sproted grams. **Chaita Parav** or the spring festival is common among the Gadabas, Parajas and some other tribes of Koraput. The tribes called Bhuyans (Bhumij) of Sundargarh, Keonjhar and Mayurbhanj also celebrate this. This is a hunting ritual and it is celebrated with intoxicating drinks, singing and dancing with a common feast. The Koyas of the Malkangiri area celebrate the festival as **Bija Pandu.** They dance with bison-horns, cowries and peacock feathers. **Kedu Parab** was associated with Maria human sacrifice and the British government as an act of atrocity banned it. The western humanists, since the days of Enlightenment, considered our tribal people as a subhuman species, and interfered in their religious affairs when they failed to Christianize them. The religious subversion of the British peple, however, could not stop the practice and it continues even today as a tantric ritual with human sacrifice to enrich their fields for cultivation. The pole near which the sacrifice takes place is called the Yupa stambha, which is mentioned in *Gayatri Sahasranama* as the seat of this Aryan deity called Gayatri, a **hrim** energy of the Sun related to the process of creation. Gayatri is *yupa-stambha* *nivasini*. **Maghe Parab** is famous among the tribes called Ho, Oraon, Kisan and Kolho tribes. This is a festival cebrated for the propitiation of the evil gods and for getting the blessings for a good fortune.

Bibliography

Das Rajendra Prasad: "The study of *Silpa sastra* in pre and post independence Orissa in *The Continuity in the Flux*:" Orissa, vol.1. Dinanath Pathy and Ramesh P. Panigrahi Ed. Harman Publishing House. New Delhi.1999.

Eagleton Terry : "Capitalism, Modernism and postmodernism" in *Modern Criticism*. David Lodge Ed. Longman Group. UK Ltd. Harlow.1998.

Eliade Mercia : "Shamanism and Cosmology" in *Shamanism* in Shirley Nicholon Ed. The Theosophical Publishing House. Wheaton, III, USA.

Frankel Charles : "A Critique of Irrationalism" in *American Review. Vol.18 No.2 (Winter-1974)*

Gerini. G.E. : *Researches on ptolemy's Geography of Eastern Asia*. Oriental Book Reprint Corporation, New Delhi.1974.

Majumdar R.C. : *The Classical Accounts of India*. Calcutta, Firma KLM Pvt. Ltd. 1981.

Marshal John : "Qtd. in Traditional Painting of Orissa. Dinanath Pathy, WAA, Bhubaneswar, 1990.

Pathy Dinanath : "Designing : Changes and Challenges" in *The continuity in the Flux* : **Orissa, Vol. 1 D. Pathy and R.P. Panigrahi Ed. Harman Publishing House, New Delhi, 1999.**

Patra Benudhar : "Trade Routes and Trade in Ancient Orissa" in *Studies in History and Culture. vol.4 No.2, Sept.1996*, Berhampur University, Berhampur (p.9-21).

Rao Raja E. : "Telugu diaspora in Orissa" in *The Continuity in the Flux* : Orissa. Vol.1 Dinanath Pathy and Ramesh P. Panigrahi Ed. Harman Publishing House. New Delhi, 1999.

Rao Venkat D.: "The Stunting Lebensraum: Sudhir Kakar

and the subject of post-coloniality" *Journal of contemporary thought. Vol.1 No.1 1991.* Forum on Contemporary Theory. M.S. University Baroda.

Spivak Gayatri : "Can the subaltern speak ?" in *Marxism and the Interpretation of Culture.* Cary Nelson Ed. University of Illinois Press. Urbana. 1988.

Sturrock John : "Roland Barthes" in *Structuralism and Since* John Sturrock Ed. Oxford university Press. Oxford university press. Oxford. 1997.

Tylor. Edward B. : *Primitive Culture Vol.1,* Murray. London, 1891.

Watts. N.A. : *The Half-Clad Tribes of Eastern Orissa.* 1970.

Bibliography

Agarwal Vasudeva Saran. *Harsha charita : A study in culture*, Chowkhamba
Agarwal Sadanand : *History of Sonepur*, Varanasi, 1988
Apte, D.G. *Our Educational Heritage* P.9.
(qtd. Insufficienly in A.K. Mahanty's
"Educatin in Ancient Orissa", *Orissa Review*
Vol XLIV No. i. Aug. 1987 PP-63-99)
Abasyaka Sutra : P 219-220
Aiyengar. S.K. *Indian Historical Quarterly*
Vol XVI, 1940

Archeological Survey of Western India, Vol IV. P.10
Bailey, F.G. *Tribe, Caste and Nation*, Manchester Univ. Press, 1960

Banambar Acharya Ed.	*Bhanjamahodaya*, (Oriya) Ambika Press, Cuttack- 1946
Banarjee Rakhal Das. :	*History of Orissa Vol-I*, P. 60-61
Banarjee JN.	*Puranic and Tantrik Religion*, Univ. of Calcutta 1956
Barua B.M. :	"Kharavela"*IHQ, Vol, XIV*. P.46, 478
B.C. Law Tr/Ed. :	*Dathavamsa*. CH.III. IV (A work of the early 4th cent A.D.) Punjab Sanskrit series.
Beal, S.	*Life of Hiuen Tsang by the Shamana Kwui Li*, London, 1914
	Buddhist Records of the Western World, Vol-ii, Delhi, 1973
Bhattacharya, B. :	*An Introduction to Buddhist Esoterism*, Delhi,1980
:	*Sadhanamala*, Baroda, 1928
Borah, D.K. :	"Markets and Mercantile Communities under the Gangas of Orissa". *Journal of Historical Record. XIX (i): 1976.* PP 55-60

Behera, K.S.	:	"Trade and Patterns of Commerce in Orissa" U.U. *Historical Research Journal-II, 1991* PP-15
Beal. S.	:	*Travels of Fah-Hean and Sung-Yun.* Sushilgupta, London, 1964.
Baliarsingh Satyabadi	:	*Ranpura-ra Itihasa (The History of Ranpur)* published Satyabadi Baliarsingh, vill. Gada Banikilo, Via: Rajrajpur-752026, 1988
Bose, N.K.	:	*Tribal Life in India*, NBT, New Delhi, 1971
Chanda R.P.	:	*Memoirs of Archaeological Survey of India, No.44*
Chatterjee Suniti Kumar	:	*A.B. Memorial Lectures*
Chakravarti Syamalakanti	:	"Concepts of Yakshas and their Images", *Mystic India, vol-2, No. 18, (Dec 1996)*
Cunningham Alexandar	:	*Archeological survey Report Vol-XVI*
		Chyaupattnayaka Suramoni *Bhanja Vamsavali* (palm leaf script in Oriya)
Das Lochana	:	*Chaitanya Mangala, Madhyakhanda*
Durga Prasad Ed.	:	*Kamasutra*
Das B.	:	*The Bhaumakaras and their time*, Oriental Publishers and Distributors, New Delhi, 1978
Das R.P.	:	"The study of Silpa Sastra in pre and post independence Orissa" in *The continuity in the Flux, Orissa, vol-I*, Edtd. Dinanath Pathy and Ramesh P. Panigrahi, Harman publishing House, New Delhi, 1999
		Devi Bhagavata Venkateswara Press, 1982
Devi Rekha	:	*Locational study of Tribal settlements of Orissa*, Lark Books, Bhubaneswar, 1993.
Devi Pratibha	:	*Humanistic Education and the Upanishads*, Bharatiya Vidya Bhawan, Mumbai, 1998
Devid N. Lorenzen	:	Qtd in "Kapalikas and Kala0mukhas" *JKHRS, vol-II*.
Dwivedy Hazariprasad	:	*Hindi Sahityaka Adikal* (Hindi) Bihar Rashtrabhasa Parishad, Patna-1961
		Anguttara Nikaya(Pali Text-Society-I P. 213, IV pp-252-56.
Esslin, Martin	:	*The theatre of the Absurd*, Penguin Books Ltd. Harmondswooth, and Middlesex 1961 rpt. 1998
a)		*Epigraphia Indica, Vol vii* P. 60
b)		*E.I. vol. xii, xxviii (1905-06)*

c)	*E.I. vol ix, xxi, x (1909-10), No. 1113*
d)	*E.I. vol xxiii*
Eleade, Mercia	: "Shamanism and cosmology" in *Shamanism*. Shirley Nicholson Ed, *The Theosophical Publishing House*, Wheaton, III-USA.
Elwin, Verrier	: *The Religion of an Indian Tribe* OUP, London, 1955 *The Bonda Highlanders*
Foucault,M	: *The order of Things:An Archaeology of Human Sciences*, New York, 1973
F.E.Pargiter	: Qtd. In *Dyasties of Kali Age*. Pp. 53-54 Giacomo camuriAngelo Fossati and Yasodhar Mathpal *Deer in Rock Art of India and Europe*, Indira Gandhi National Centre for the Arts, New Delhi, 1993.
Ganguli D.K.	: *Historical Geography and Dynastic History of Orissa*.
Gerini G.E.	: *Researches on Ptolemy's Geography of Eastern Asia*, Oriental Book Depot, New.Delhi. 1974.
Hassan Ihab	: *The Postmodern Turn: Essays in Postmodern Theory and Culture*. Ohio State Univ. pres Ohio. 1987.
Houston Jean	: "Foreword": The Mind and soul of the Shaman" in Shirley Nicholson. Ed. *Shamanism*. The Theosophical Publishing House, Wheaton, Illinois, USA. 1987.
Hali Hadibandhu	: This historian from Bargarh, Bhubaneswar has provided me with the English translation of *Dasaratha Jataka*, an extant book that gives an alternate Buddhist version of *The Ramayana*, written in Orissa.

Indian History Congress (Proceedings), 199 Opcit, L.2. of Nasik cave Inscription.
I HQ Vol-I, pp-206-212

Jagannath Pathak Ed.	: *Harsha Charitam*. Chowkhamba, Varanasi, 1988
Jayaswal, K.N.P	: *Epigraphia Indica Vol. XX and XXXI* Govt. of India Publication, New Delhi P-85.
Jacobi, Herman	: *Sacred Books of the East Vol XIV (P-87)*
Jain K.C.	: *Mahavir and His Times P. 54*.
J.P. Singdeo	: "Cultural profile of South Kosala". Qtd in *Paschima Odisare Loka Samskruti* (Odia) of Mahendra K. Mishra friends Publishers, Cuttack, 1990 *Journal of Bihar and Orissa Research Society, Vol XVI (1930)*

Krishnamacharya V. Pt. Ed. :	*Laxmi Tantra*: *A Pancharatra Agama*. The Adyar Library and Research Centre, Chennai, 1959 rpt. 2000.
Krishna Mohan Sastri Ed. :	*Sahitya Darpana*, Chowkhamba Varanasi, 1988.
Kulke H. :	*The Cult of Jagannath and the Regional Tradition of Orissa*. Ed. Eschman, Kulke and Tripathy 1978.
Law, B.C. :	*Mountains of India* (1944)
Legge. J. (Tr) :	*A Record of Buddhist Kingdoms*, Oriental Publishers, Delhi 1972, *Matsya Purana*, 50,76
Levi, M. Sylvan :	*Translation of the Mahayana Sutralamkara,IHQ,Vol-ix, P-1*
Majumdar, R.C.(Ed.)	*History and Culture of the Indian People, Age of Imperial Unity(* Bombay,1968)
Mishra Sivasekhar :	*Bharatiya Samskrutire Aryetaramsa (Hindi)*, Dessertation, Lucknow Univ.
Mishra K.N. Oda	*"Samskrutira Chera-O-Fula: Oda, Odi, Odabadi", Akshyapada-20 Vi-2/3/4 (April-Dec-93) PP-55-59*.
Mitra Debala, *Indian Archeology* :	*A Review for the year, 1956-57*.
Mitra, R.L.	*The Antiquities of Orissa*, Calcutta, 1875
Mittal, A.C.	*Early History of Orissa*, Benaras, 1962
Mookerjee R.K. :	*Chandragupta Maurya and his Times*, Univ of Madras, 1952
Mohanty A.K :	Qtd. *Select inscriptions of India Vol VI*.
	"Education in Ancient India", *Orissa Review, Vol XLIV, NO.i Ang 1987 pp-63-69*.
Mann Gian Singh :	*Chanakya:His dictums on Religion, Moral Ethics, Social Conduct and Politics* Amar Prakasan, Delhi 1986.
Mandal Krishna Kumar :	"A note on the beginning of peasant mode of production in early India (C.600 B.C.-300 B.C.)". *Studies in History and Culture Vol 4, No.2, 1996, pp-1-9*.
Mazumdar R.C.	*History and Culture of Indian people Vol-II (qtd. In K.C. Panigrahi, History of Orissa, p-37)*
	The classical accounts of India, Firma KLM Pvt. Ltd., 1981
Mahapatra Kedarnath :	*Dhauli (Toshali) ra Itihasa* (Odia) published by the Author, Bhubaneswar, 1975.
Mohara Nabakishore :	*Banki Itiihasa* (The history of Banki) Guruji Prakasani, Jhanjirmangala, Cuttack, 2001.
Marshal John :	Qtd in traditional painting of Orissa, WAA, Bhubaneswar, 1990
Mahanty Chintamoni :	*Ghumusara Kavya*

Mishra Pramila, Ed.	:	*Gangavamsanucharita champu* (Oriya) Deptt. of culture, Bhubaneswar 1979.
Mahapatra, G.C.	:	*The stone age culture of Orissa1962*, qtd. In K.C. Panigrahi's *History of Orissa*, Kitab Mahal, Cuttack 1981.
Majumdar S.N. Sastri,		*M-Grindle's Ancient India as described by Ptolemy*, vol-ii-1 P.16, *Marcianus Periplous tes Exo Thalasses, Sec.39*.
Nehru Jawaharlal	:	*The Discovery of India*, J.NM. Fund: OUP, New Delhi, 1981 rpt-15th Edn.1985
	:	*Glimpses of World History*, J.N.M. Fund, OUP, New Delhi, 1934-35, rpt, 1982, rtp 1989.
Norris Christopher		*Derrida*, Fontana, London, 1987.
		O' Malley L.S.S. and Chakravarty M.M
		Bengal District Gazetter,1908- P-256
Patel C.B.	:	*The historical importance of Kalahandi*, Meera Publications, Bhubaneswar, 2001.
Padhi, Benimadhab	:	"Bharata Kahara" ? (Who does Bharat belong to ?), *Krusti-O-Drusti* (Oriya), Taratarini Pustakalay, Berhampur, 1988.
Pattnayak S.K.	:	"Routes in Ancient Orissa", *Journal of Orissan History XI*, 1991
Patra, Benudhar	:	"Trade Routes and Trade in Ancient Orissa", *Studies in History and culture*, Vol-4. No. 2. Berhampur University, Sept. 1996. PP. 21.
Panigrahi K.C.	:	*History of Orissa*, Kitab Mahal, Cuttack, 1981, Rpt 1995
Panda S.C, and Chopdar D.		Tribal Religious faith in Orissa: A case study of the Stambhesvari cult" in *Studies in Shaktism*. Ed. K.C. Mishra, T. Mishra and R.K. Mishra, Institute of Orissan culture, Bhubaneswar. 1995.
Pradhan B.C.	:	*Sakti worship in Orissa*, Sambalpur University, 1984.
Pattnayak S.	:	"Kodala Mandala-O-Stambhesvari" (Oriya) *Utkala Sahitya* Vol-XXVI No. 3 and 4. 1992. pp 7-15
Panigrahi Kailash Chandra	:	*Nayagada Itihasa* (Odia) (The History of Nayagarh) published by Bhagabata Sahu, Sunakhala, 1982.
Pathy Dinanath		"Designing: Changes and challenges" in *The Continuity in the Flux*, Ed. Dinanath Pathy and Ramesh Panigrahi, Harman Publishing House, New Delhi, 1999.
Pattnayak, D.N.	:	*Festivals of Orissa*, Department of Culture, Bhubaneswar.
Pathak Jagannath Ed.	:	*Harsha charitam*, Chowkhamba, 1988.

Pathak Sunit Kumar	:	Translation of *Pag-Sam-Lan-Zang*, *Indian Historical Quarterly*, vol-XXX No.1 (March, 1954)
Ptolemy, C	:	*Geographike Huphegesis, Vii, 1, 16-18.*
Rath, A.K.	:	"Krishnagiri and its Archaeological Remains", *Proceedings of the Annual Session of the Orissa History Congress*, 1979, Bhubaneswar.
	:	*Jainadharma-O-Samskruti* (Oriya). T.T. Bookstore, Berhampur, 1991.
Rajguru S.N.	:	*Inscriptions of Orissa, Vol-I*, Orissa State Museum, Bhubaneswar, 1950
	:	*Odisara Samskrutika Itihasa*, Sahitya Akademi, 1988.
Raychoudhury, H.C.	:	*Political History of Ancient India*, 5th edition.
Radhaswami Sivananda	:	*Mantras: Words of power.* Timeless books, Spokane-WA. USA, 1980 rpt. Sterling publishers, New Delhi, 1994
Rao, Raja E.	:	"Telugu Diaspora in Orissa" in *The continuity in the Flux, Orissa, vol-1*, Ed. D.Pathy and R.P. Panigrahi. Harman Publishing House, New Delhi, 1999.
Rao Venkat D.	:	"The stunting lebensraum: Sudhir Kakar and the subject of postcoloniality" *Journal of Contemporary Thoughts, vol-1, No. 1991*, Forum on contemporary theory, M.S. University, Baroda.
Ramachandra Ragini	:	*Indian Literary Criticism*, Reliance publishing House, New Delhi, 1989.
Sahu N.K.	:	*History of Orissa vol-1*, Utkal University, Bhubaneswar.
Sahu Antaryami	:	*Nila Madhav of Kantilo* (Oriya) Pub. Smt. Sarasvati Devi, Kantilo-752026, Sri Printers, Khandapara garh.
Senacharya Jeena	:	*Harivamsa Purana*-17-1-38
Singh Deo, J.P.	:	"A Bird's Eye view of Anthropological and Archaeological Traces in Western Orissa", *Confluence*, vol-1-Ed. Dr. P.M. Nayak and Prof. S. Muduli. Sambalpur, 1998
Surcar, D.C.	:	*Geography of Ancient and Mediaeval India*
Sastri, P.S.	:	Some Buddhist Thinkers of Andhra", *IHQ, Vol XXXII, No. 2 and 3, Jun-Sept, 1956 (Buddha 25th centenary issue)*
Sastri R.S. Ed.	:	*Artha Sastra* of Kautilya, Govt. Branch Press, Mysore, 1924.
Shrigondekar G.K. Ed.	:	*Mana Solasa* of Someswara Deva, Baroda, 1930.
Shanin Teoder Ed.	:	*Peasants and peasant societies*.Penguin, Harmondsworth,1971
Sheik Ali, B. B	:	*History:Its theory and Method*, 2nd Edn. Mc Millan, 1978.

Srivastav. B.	:	*Iconography of Sakti, Varanasi, 1978.*
Sharma P.K.	;	*Shakticult in Ancient India,* Varanasi 1974.
Spivak Gayatri	:	"Can the Subaltern speak?" in *Marxism and the Interpretation of Culture,* Ed. Cary Nelson, Univ. of Illinois Press, Urbana, 1988.
Sturrock, John	:	"Roland Barthes" in *Structuralism and Since* Ed. John Sturrock, OUP, Oxford, 1997.
Sahu Bhagaban (Padmasree	:	"A Brief Sketch of Ranapa Dance"(Oriya) in *Souvenir, Bhagaban Sabu Memorial committee,* Ed. Bighneswar sahu, Badakusasthali, Sept, 2002, pp-50-51.
Suri Bhavadeva	:	*Parsvanatha charita,* Ed Hargovinda and Pt. Bachara Dasa. Pp 269-270. *Slokas:* 155.
Toynbee, Arnold J.	:	*Mankind and Mother earth,* Granada Publishing Ltd. London 1978.
Tucci Tr.	:	"*Vigraha Vyavartani* of Nagarjuna" *GOS. Vol-XLIX, verse NO. xiii* *JBORS, vol-XIV, p-282.*
Tripathy Rajendra Prasad	:	*Dvitiya Konarka: Ghumusar Suryamandira Itihasa* (The second Konark: the History of the Sun Temple of Ghumsar), Published by Smt. Surama Tripathy, Aurobindo Nagar, Buguda (Ganjam), 1997.
Tylor, Edward B.	:	*Primitive culture, vol-I,* Murray, London, 1891.
Tripathy, Gobinda Chandra		"*Odisare Prak Brahmilipi Khodita Girigumpha Bikramkhole*" Bikaram khole Caves: Pre-Brahmin engravings in Orissa (Oriya*) Dharitri, Annual Issue, vol-XXX,* 2003 pp-40-42. *Vayu Purana:* 45, 47, 48, 126, 99, 38 *Vishnu Purana:* 24, 62
Watters, T	:	*On Yuang Chwang's Travels in India, Vol II* London 1914, pp-196-198
Watts, N.A.	:	*The Half-Clad Tribes of Eastern Orissa,* 1970.

Black Eagle Books

www.blackeaglebooks.org
info@blackeaglebooks.org

Black Eagle Books, an independent publisher, was founded as a nonprofit organization in April, 2019. It is our mission to connect and engage the Indian diaspora and the world at large with the best of works of world literature published on a collaborative platform, with special emphasis on foregrounding Contemporary Classics and New Writing.

www.ingramcontent.com/pod-product-compliance
Lightning Source LLC
Chambersburg PA
CBHW020513080526
44583CB00013B/579